The Transformation of Europe's Armed Forces

As a result of new strategic threats, Europe's land forces are currently undergoing a historic transformation which may reflect wider processes of European integration. Europe's mass, mainly conscript armies are being replaced by smaller, more capable, professionalised militaries concentrated into new operational headquarters and rapid reaction brigades, able to plan, command, and execute global military interventions. At the same time, these headquarters and brigades are co-operating with each other across national borders at a level which would have been inconceivable in the twentieth century. As a result, a transnational military network is appearing in Europe, the forces in which are converging on common forms of military expertise. This is a groundbreaking study of the military dimensions of European integration, which have been largely ignored until now. The book will appeal to scholars across the social sciences interested in the progress of the European project, and the nature of the military today.

Anthony King is Professor of Sociology at the University of Exeter. He has written extensively on social theory, football and the armed forces. Since 2003 he has been conducting intensive research on the armed forces, observing military training, exercises and operations as a result of which he has developed close relations with the armed forces at the highest levels. He has co-written parts of Britain's new stabilisation doctrine and has recently worked for NATO's Regional Command South Headquarters in Kandahar, Afghanistan. On the basis of this work, he has contributed to public debates about security and defence policy, appearing on the BBC and writing for *The Guardian*, *Prospect* and the Royal United Services Institute publications. In September 2010, he gave the Chatham House Annual Defence Lecture, 'Military Command in the Next Decade'.

The Transformation of Europe's Armed Forces

From the Rhine to Afghanistan

Anthony King

CAMBRIDGE UNIVERSITY PRESS

CAMBRIDGE UNIVERSITY PRESS
Cambridge, New York, Melbourne, Madrid, Cape Town, Singapore,
São Paulo, Delhi, Dubai, Tokyo, Mexico City

Cambridge University Press
The Edinburgh Building, Cambridge CB2 8RU, UK

Published in the United States of America by Cambridge University Press,
New York

www.cambridge.org
Information on this title: www.cambridge.org/9780521760942

First published 2011

Printed in the United Kingdom at the University Press, Cambridge

A catalogue record for this publication is available from the British Library

Library of Congress Cataloging in Publication data
King, Anthony, 1967–
The transformation of Europe's armed forces : from the Rhine to
Afghanistan / Anthony King.
  p. cm.
Includes bibliographical references.
ISBN 978-0-521-76094-2
1. European Union countries – Armed Forces. 2. European Union
countries – Military relations. 3. European Union countries – Military
policy. 4. Strategic culture – European Union countries. 5. Combined
operations (Military science) I. Title.
UA646.K47 2011
355.0094–dc22
2010030519

ISBN 978-0-521-76094-2 Hardback

Contents

Figures

Abbreviations

ACCHAN	Allied Command Channel (NATO, Northwood)
ACE	Allied Command Europe (NATO, Mons)
ACLANT	Allied Command Atlantic (NATO, Norfolk, Virginia)
ACO	Allied Command Operations (NATO, Mons)
ACT	Allied Command Transformation (NATO, Norfolk, Virginia)
ADZ	Afghan Development Zone
AFCENT	Armed Forces Central Europe (NATO, Brunssum)
AFNORTH	Armed Forces Northern Europe (NATO, Kolsas)
AFSOUTH	Armed Forces Southern Europe (NATO, Naples)
AJP	Allied Joint Publication (NATO doctrine)
ANT	actor network theory
ARRC	Allied Rapid Reaction Corps (NATO, Rheindalen); originally Allied Command Europe Rapid Reaction Corps
C^4I	command, control, communication, computers and interoperability
CAOC	Combined Air Operations Centre
Centag	Army Group Central (NATO, Heidelberg)
CFSP	Common Foreign and Security Policy
CIFS	close in fire support (team)
CIMIC	civil–military co-operation
CO	Commanding officer
COG	centre of gravity
Conops	concept of operations
CSG	Command Support Group
DCOS	Deputy Chief of Staff
DSACEUR	Deputy Supreme Allied Commander Europe (NATO)
EBAO/EBO	effects-based approach to operations/effects-based operations
ESDP	European Security and Defence Policy
EUFOR	EU FORCE (Bosnia)

FM 100-5	Field Manual 100-5 *Operations* (US doctrine)
FOFA	follow-on forces attack
FOO	Forward Observation Officer
FST	fire support team
GOC	General Officer Commanding
GOP	Guidelines for Operational Planning
HRF HQ	Higher Readiness Force Headquarters (the Rapid Reaction Corps)
IDF	Israeli Defence Force
IED	improvised explosive device
IFOR	(NATO) Intervention Force (Bosnia), to implement Dayton
ISAF	International Security Assistance Force (successive rotations of the headquarters are designated by Roman numerals)
ISR	intelligence, surveillance and reconnaissance technology
ISTAR	intelligence, surveillance, target acquisition, reconnaissance
JFCB	Joint Force Command Headquarters Brunssum (NATO)
JFCN	Joint Force Command Headquarters Naples (NATO)
JFHQ/JHL	Joint Force Headquarters Lisbon (NATO)
JIB	Joint Influence Branch
JRDF	Joint Rapid Deployment Force
JRRF	Joint Rapid Reaction Force
JWP	Joint Warfare Publication
KFOR	Kosovo Force (NATO)
LCC	Land Component Command/Commander
LOT	liaison and observation team
NGO	non-governmental organisation
Northag	Army Group North (Rheindalen)
NRF	NATO Response Force
OPP	operational planning process
PGMs	precision-guided munitions
PJHQ	Permanent Joint Headquarters
REME	Royal Electrical and Mechanical Engineers
RMA	'revolution in military affairs'
SACEUR	Supreme Allied Commander Europe
SACLANT	Supreme Allied Commander Atlantic
SAS	22 Special Air Service Regiment

SBS	Special Boat Service
SFOR	Stabilisation Force (NATO, Bosnia)
SHAPE	Supreme Headquarters Allied Powers Europe
SOF	Special Operations Forces
TACP	Tactical Air Control Party
TLAM	Tomahawk Land Attack Missiles
TRADOC	Training and Doctrine Center (US Army)
UAV	unmanned aerial vehicle (a drone)
UNPROFOR	United Nations Protection Force
WMD	weapons of mass destruction

Preface

I was born too late to remember where I was on the day JFK was killed in Dealey Plaza. Of course, there are other random more or less historic moments which remain unforgettable: the shooting of John Lennon; the Argentine invasion of the Falklands; Thatcher's resignation; the start of the Gulf War; Eric Cantona's kung-fu kick; Princess Diana's death. Yet none remotely approaches the intensity of 11 September 2001. I was working in my office at Exeter and, since it was a warm, late summer afternoon, I rang a friend to ask whether he wanted to come out climbing on Dartmoor that evening. He was incredulous that I had not heard the news, 'It's all going off; you need to get yourself to a television set now.' I checked the Internet and was startled by the images of the Twin Towers. Later that evening I did go out to Dartmoor, bouldering on the harsh granite of Saddle Tor. The evening was limpid with long views over the moor to the west and out east over the shining sea; sky larks sang above. There I met some other friends who were also out climbing. 'It is a beautiful evening,' I said as we talked in the car park. 'Except if you are in New York,' replied one of the climbers. In that tranquillity, the turmoil in Manhattan was quite unimaginable. It was inconceivable to think that 3,000 people had just died in a deliberate attack.

This book is ultimately a response to that day, now nearly nine years ago. In 2001, I had just finished a project on European football and was about to start writing a book on social theory. Yet it was clearly necessary that as a sociologist, I had to make some sense of that September day and how it would impact on our lives as Europeans. Although personal memory is a dangerously mutable archive, I believe I made a resolution soon after 9/11 that my next project would be on war. As the so-called 'War on Terror' unfolded with attacks on Afghanistan, it soon became clear which route this research should follow. I had long been interested in military history but, as first Britain and then other European forces committed themselves to Afghanistan, a clear fusion of past and future research horizons appeared. One of the questions which the 9/11 attacks raised was how Europe's armed forces would transform in the face of new strategic imperatives. However, for at least a year, between the start of the project in October 2003 and the summer of 2004, I had no clear concept of what it was I wanted to say about Europe's armed forces or the wars they were fighting. At this time, the European Security and Defence Policy (ESDP) was beginning to be activated and I planned merely to look at the military dimension of this policy, an area on which I presumed not much was being done. A little research proved otherwise. However, during that first year, as I spent days and nights freezing with Royal Marines sergeants as they trained young officers on Woodbury Common, Salisbury Plain and Sennybridge, a more coherent research concept crystallised. By the summer of 2004, it became apparent that Europe's armed forces, and especially their reaction forces, were undergoing a revolution which was compatible with globalising changes which had been noted widely across a diversity of institutions by sociologists, including sport. The dynamic of localisation and globalisation or concentration and transnationalisation was evident among the armed forces, as it was in the commercial and industrial sectors. It has taken me nearly five years to produce a piece of work which tries to support that research thesis.

The research findings are self-evidently my responsibility and many with whom I talked will not agree with my analysis. However, the armed forces were overwhelmingly supportive and helpful throughout the project and I am deeply grateful to them and, particularly, to all the individuals who assisted in this project. It is impossible to name them all. However, there are a number of military personnel who were particularly important to the research in terms of the insights or access they provided: Colonel Bill Aldridge, Sergeant Peter Baldwin, Brigadier Eric Bonnemaison, Sergeant Andy Bridson, Brigadier Ed Butler, Sergeant John Byrne, Lieutenant Colonel Peter Cameron, Major Richard Cantrill, Major Alex Case, Colour Sergeant Kevin Cheeseman, General de Division Gael Flichy, Lieutenant Colonel Stephen Gent, Brigadier Tim Gregson, Lieutenant Colonel Carl Harris, Major Chris Haw, Sergeant Robbie Hawkens, Brigadier Carl Hewitt, Lieutenant Colonel Matt Holmes, Lieutenant Colonel Justin Holt, Colonel Richard Iron, Major Alex Janzen, Lieutenant Colonel Jörg Keller, General de Corps Yves Kermabon, Colonel David King, Lieutenant Colonel Richard King, Major Peter Little, Major-General W-D. Löser, Brian Lovatt, Major Duncan Manning, Sergeant Peter McGinlay, Colonel Ewen McLay, Brigadier Richard Nugee, Lieutenant Colonel Joe O'Sullivan, Major General Nick Parker, Major Richard Parvin, Brigadier Nick Pounds, General de Corps Jean-François Py, General Egon Ramms, General Sir John Reith, General Sir David Richards, Major General Andrew Ritchie, Lieutenant Colonel Johnny Rollins, Brigadier John Rose, Colonel Eric

Roussel, Colonel Jed Salzano, Major John Shirras, Lieutenant General Richard Shirref, Sergeant Martin Small, General Lance Smith, Lieutenant Colonel Stuart Tootal, Air Marshall Peter Walker, Major Phil White and Rear Admiral Witthauer. A number of scholars helped me: Heiko Biehl, Sven Biscop, Christopher Coker, Randall Collins, Paul Cornish, Stuart Croft, Christopher Dandeker, Theo Farrell, Anthony Forster, Richard Gowan, Ulrich vom Hagen, Paul Higate, Anand Menon, Delphine Resteigne, Martin Shaw, Joseph Soeters, Terry Terriff, Maren Tomforde and Claude Weber. I am particularly grateful to Andy Dorman, Tim Edmunds and the recently deceased and much missed Liz Kingdom for reading drafts of this manuscript. Their assistance and support which went well beyond mere commentary was invaluable. The research for this book could not have been conducted without the support of the British Academy (NATO Transformation and the New Networks of European Military Expertise, January 2007–December 2007, The Transformation of Europe's Armed Forces, January 2005– December 2005) and the ESRC (Europe's Rapid Reaction Forces: an institutional and interactional sociology, RES-000-22-1461, September 2005–December 2006).

ANTHONY KING
27 September 2010

Part I

Strategic context

1 Towards a sociology of military transformation

Afghanistan

On 18 August 2008, a company of French paratroopers, recently deployed to Afghanistan by President Sarkozy, were patrolling in the Sorobi district some 40 miles east of Kabul when they were caught in an ambush by insurgent forces. The ambush developed into a running battle which lasted 36 hours and was eventually terminated after US air strikes. Ten French soldiers were killed and a further twenty-one were wounded in the ambush and the fighting which followed.[1] Disturbingly, four of those killed seemed to have been captured and executed. It was the single worst loss of French forces for twenty-five years, and the greatest loss of life for NATO forces in Afghanistan caused by enemy action since 2005. On 21 August, the soldiers, all awarded the Légion d'Honneur, were buried in France with full military honours. It was of immense significance that the funeral service was not only attended by (a visibly shaken) President Nicolas Sarkozy and other senior ministers, but took place at Les Invalides in Paris, the site of Napoleon's tomb. In this way, the paratroopers' deaths were linked with a grand tradition of national sacrifice and honour. After the ceremony, Sarkozy affirmed France's commitment to Afghanistan: 'We don't have the right to lose over there, we cannot renounce our values.'[2] A month later, *Paris Match* published an interview with the insurgents responsible for the attack.[3] They were pictured on the front cover of the famous magazine wearing the combat smocks, helmets and watches of some of the paratroopers whom they had killed.[4] Their leader,

---

[1] It later transpired that the Italians had made an agreement with local insurgents, paying them not to attack coalition forces. The French were unaware of this arrangement.

[2] www.highbeam.com/doc/1P2–17064886.html.

[3] Although described as Taliban, the fighters were probably from Gulbaddin Hekmatyar's Hezb-i-Islami, an Islamicist mujahiddin group which had been involved in fighting since the Soviet invasion.

[4] The photograph of the Taliban fighter on the front cover has intriguing parallels with the famous picture of the saluting black French soldier which Roland Barthes famously analysed in *Mythologies* (1972). It is unclear whether the editors of the magazine were deliberately drawing upon this historical connotation when they published the image.

3

Commander Farouki, claimed they were tipped off about the French mission in their area and were able to prepare an ambush with 140 highly trained insurgents. Although he denied the rumours of torture, he boasted that 'If night hadn't fallen we'd have killed every one of the soldiers.'[5] The publication of the photograph caused outrage in France; Sarkozy described the Taliban as 'barbaric' and 'medieval'. Others, including the mothers of one of the deceased, demanded the withdrawal of troops, while opinion polls suggested that two-thirds of the population were against the deployment.

On 11 March 2004, while promoting his proposed reforms of the Bundeswehr and attempting to sustain popular support for Germany's involvement in Afghanistan, Peter Struck, the German Defence Minister, famously declared that 'Germany is also defended in the Hindu Kush.' The death of the French paratroopers in 2008 demonstrates the potentially fatal implications of Struck's aphorism for Europe's armed forces more widely; nearly 500 European soldiers had been killed in Afghanistan by the beginning of 2010. Those deaths might be taken as a signifier of a fundamental strategic re-orientation in Europe. Within fifteen years of the end of the Cold War, Europe's military focus has switched from the Rhine to the Hindu Kush. Yet this re-orientation is not merely geographical, it also represents a transformation of strategic culture. The fact that the paratroopers killed in Sarobi were French illustrated this shift very clearly. Since its withdrawal from NATO's integrated military command in 1966, France had always been the European nation least committed to NATO and it had few, if any direct, strategic interests in engaging in Afghanistan. Yet here in August 2008 the most US- and NATO-sceptical nation suffered the single greatest loss inflicted by enemy forces on any European country. France, and by extension Europe, has now committed itself to a globalised counter-insurgency in Afghanistan alongside US allies. The move to the Hindu Kush demonstrates an increasing interdependence of European states in an unstable global order and, in the security sphere, their increasing, though contentious, allegiance to the United States.

The re-orientation to the Hindu Kush represents a rupture not just in where Europe's armed forces operate, but also how they are increasingly trying to conduct their campaigns. Although it threatened nuclear oblivion, the Cold War, as a competition between recognised state militaries fighting for territorial sovereignty, was a conventional conflict. In Afghanistan, Europe's forces are engaged in a quite different venture. They are seeking to re-build a fragmented state while confronting

---

[5] http://news.bbc.co.uk/2/hi/europe/7598816.stm.

irregular, insurgent forces. It is not merely that the opponents which Europe's forces face are unconventional. The very way in which European forces are prosecuting this campaign is profoundly different from twentieth-century approaches. The mass divisions of the Cold War are absent; European forces under NATO are actively avoiding any repetition of the heavy Soviet approach of the 1980s (Grau 1998). Instead, relatively small numbers of Western troops, co-operating with each other ever more closely, utilising digital communications, precision-guided munitions delivered from the air, new surveillance assets, including unmanned aerial vehicles, are trying to pacify hostile groups while facilitating the stabilisation of the country. Indeed, the move to the Hindu Kush might be seen as a revision of the European way in warfare. In the twenty-first century, mass armies dedicated to national territorial defence against the forces of other states are being replaced by smaller, professionalised forces which are increasingly engaged in global stabilisation missions. This move to the Hindu Kush, geographically and conceptually, is central to any account of contemporary European military transformation.

The research

Since the end of the Cold War, there has been extensive research into the issue of European security and defence. Given the speed and scale of the changes, this intense academic interest is only to be expected. Scholars have accordingly analysed the changing nature of warfare: they have examined national, EU and NATO security and defence policy[6] and they have explored the institutional transformation of the armed forces themselves at national, EU and NATO levels.[7] Seth Jones' recent work (2007) on the development of EU security co-operation is one of the more prominent recent contributions to this literature. There, he claims that his study 'offers a comprehensive approach' (Jones 2007: 5); it analyses all the relevant data. The present study sets itself more modest objectives. It aims to examine how Europe's armed forces are re-organising themselves and revising established practices in the face of alternative missions. However,

[6] For example, Biscop 2005; Buzan et al. 1990; Cornish and Edwards 2001; Gnesotto 2004; Howorth 1995, 2000, 2001, 2007; Howorth and Menon 1997; Kupchan 2000; Menon 2000, 2009; Missiroli 2003; Shepherd 2000, 2003; Smith 2004; Tonra 2001; Webber et al. 2002.

[7] Arquilla and Ronfeldt 1997; Bellamy 1996; Böene 2003; Booth et al. 2001; Burk 2003a, 2003b; Dandeker 1994, 2003; Demchak 2003; Dorman et al. 2002; Farrell 2008; Forster 2006; Kaplan 2004; Moskos et al. 2000; Risse-Kappen 1997; Schmidt 2001; Sloan 2003; Terriff et al. 2004a, 2004b; Thies 2003, 2007; Yost 2000a, 2000b.

it does not claim to provide a definitive analysis of all European military transformation today. A complete analysis of European military transformation would require the investigation of the armed forces of all EU and non-EU European nations. Consequently, current changes involve over a million European service personnel and a vast array of institutions. The armed forces of each nation consist of headquarters, divisions, fleets, air wings, training establishments and logistic bases. The EU and NATO also have their own structures and assets, each of which is undergoing interesting and important formation or re-formation. A comprehensive analysis would need to conduct research on a large sample of this military population and establish the interconnections between all these armed forces and the institutions which they comprise. No attempt at such universality is attempted here. It would be impossible to analyse the transformation of all these institutions in all these different countries in a single study. Indeed, it is questionable whether genuine comprehensiveness is possible or even desirable in this (or any other) area.

For heuristic purposes, a much narrower perspective is taken here. Since it is concerned not with defence policy, but specifically with armed forces, this study seeks to examine European developments at the 'operational' and 'tactical' levels. The operational level refers to the planning of campaigns; in short, it refers to what happens in major military headquarters, especially those which are designated for command at the corps level (60,000 troops). The tactical level refers to the activities conducted by European forces in theatre as they engage with local populations, friendly or otherwise. In this study, the tactical level is located at the level of the brigade (approximately 4,000 troops) and the battalion (600 troops). The book is not, therefore, primarily concerned with how governments, the North Atlantic Council, the European Council or the diverse ministries of defence decide upon defence policy and strategy. That is a crucial and deeply interesting topic which other international relations and security studies scholars have investigated at length (Kaplan 2004; Michta 2006; Sloan 2003; Sperling 1999; Yost 2000a, 2000b). Rather, this study is interested in how Europe's forces currently conceptualise, plan, command and train for military operations, especially in Afghanistan. These changes are of potentially historic importance. They seem to imply the supersession of the mass army by smaller, professional forces, not entirely dissimilar to the small mercenary armies which were evident in Europe in the seventeenth and eighteenth centuries, before the first levée en masse in France in 1793 (Luttwak 1995).[8]

[8] This book does not examine the rise of private military companies (Avant 2005; Singer 2003; Smith 2004), although their importance to military transformation is recognised. It

Critically, as the Cologne Declaration emphasised, Europe's forces are being turned into deployable reaction forces, capable of rapid intervention in regions of ethnic and religious conflict and state failure. Accordingly, this study focuses on Europe's reaction forces at the operational and tactical levels; it investigates selected military headquarters and intervention brigades. There are, however, inherent problems with such an approach. Rapid reaction forces are unusual and distinctive formations in Europe today. They are privileged in terms of personnel, resourcing and training. Indeed, the appearance of rapid reaction forces in Europe has led to under-investment in other forces. In some cases, the emergence of a two-tier military is observable in Europe; focused investment in reaction forces has led to under-investment in regular troops. The development of rapid reaction forces can in no way be taken as indicative of all aspects of military transformation in Europe today. Those differences are recognised, but this study does not pretend to analyse what has happened to less deployable forces. Their experiences are not unimportant and others (e.g., Forster *et al.* 1999) have begun to analyse their predicament in Central and Eastern Europe. There is no implication intended here that European military transformation is defined only by the emergence of rapid reaction forces. However, precisely because rapid reaction forces have been prioritised in defence policy, they are necessarily at the forefront of military transformation. No story of military innovation today can ignore these forces. Consequently, they have been selected as the focus of this study.

The book, then, examines European rapid reaction forces at the operational and tactical levels; it is interested in headquarters and in brigades trained for and tasked with global intervention. Even then a further delimitation has been required. In order to achieve the necessary depth of interpretation, the book primarily focuses on changes within Britain, France and Germany (although, as will become clear, NATO is critical to current changes). The contribution of Italy, Spain and the smaller European nations is not disparaged; the Dutch, Swedish and Danish militaries are particularly interesting in the way they have reformed themselves. Deeply significant changes, which are consonant with those in Britain, France and Germany, can be identified. However, Britain, France and Germany are the major military powers of Europe which are necessarily at the forefront of current developments. The transformation

is simply impossible to analyse their appearance and potential impact on Europe's military in the context of this study. In addition, with the exception of Britain, their impact is currently relatively small on European military operations. The Bundeswehr has out-sourced uniform production and some other peripheral services, but in both Germany and France the armed forces have remained overwhelmingly the preserve of the state.

of their armed forces are likely to be the most significant for Europe and, indeed, reforms in these major countries are driving adaptations in the other smaller European nations. This book focuses on the appearance of new corps level 'operational' headquarters in Britain, France and Germany (and NATO), which plan and command current operations especially in Afghanistan and the Balkans. These headquarters constitute a critical organisational transformation, which also provides the institutional framework for further developments especially at the tactical level. At the tactical level, this book examines the appearance of selected reaction brigades, which have featured prominently in recent operations, in Britain, France and Germany.

There is one further qualification. This book is concerned almost exclusively with ground forces: with armies (and marines). There are reasons for focusing almost exclusively on land forces. Although naval and air forces remain important on operations today and they are themselves undergoing interesting and important adaptations, their performance is not decisive to the outcome of current missions. Europe's land forces, especially the identified rapid reaction brigades which spearhead Europe's military endeavours, will play the critical role. Air and naval forces provide vital support for these deployed brigades, but it is the brigades themselves which will finally determine whether Europe's current military operations are successful. Since the outcome of the campaign in Afghanistan is likely to define European military posture in the second and third decades of this century, their strategic importance recommends them as the primary object of investigation. They are at the heart of European military transformation.

The research into these distinctive military institutions involved three techniques: archival work on primary sources, principally military 'doctrine' (the formal published statements of military concepts, practices and procedure); interviews; and fieldwork observation. Military doctrine, as a written description of existing practice, has always been important to the armed forces. However, in the last decades, there has been a notable expansion of doctrine-writing and publication. As the armed forces have sought to transform themselves in the light of the new mission, it has been increasingly important for them to agree upon and articulate new procedures in order to maintain organisational unity and to justify governmental investment in them. At the same time, as national forces have had to work with each other ever more closely, doctrine has been a means of trying to co-ordinate and unify military reform between allies. Doctrine is, therefore, a major element of military reform in itself and constitutes a lucrative source for investigating European transformations.

Nevertheless, although doctrine is a useful source, alone it is inadequate. It is often easy to misinterpret what doctrine means in practice, especially as a civilian observer. Moreover, there is an inevitable gap between published doctrine and stated practice. The application of doctrine always differs from the formal statement of practice. Consequently, it is necessary to triangulate doctrine with other methods of collection. To this end, the research described here used a series of interviews with members of the armed forces and periods of fieldwork observation and visits. The research involved formal interviews or focus groups with 234 officers up to the rank of four-star general, although the views and experiences of many more military personnel including privates and marines were also recorded. The interviews were open-ended, allowing interviewees to explain their perspective on military transformation and the central reforms that the organisation of which they were part or which they commanded were enacting. Typically, interviews were conducted as part of a longer research visit, which involved observation of training, exercises or operations. This included visits to selected British, French, German, NATO and EU staff colleges,[9] operational headquarters[10] and rapid reaction brigades.[11] In all, I spent 135 days at these institutions.

Although the original plan was to research all three militaries equally, the reality proved different. I gained excellent access to EU and NATO HQs, but entry to the French and German militaries was not easy. Questions of national security, confidentiality and, potentially in some cases, institutional defensiveness arose. I was consequently able to do fieldwork at French and German staff colleges, but not their operational headquarters and brigades. I was limited to visits and interviews with personnel in these headquarters and brigades. In Britain, by contrast, I was given open access to military formations, watching troops and headquarters training, on exercise and on operations in Basra and Kabul. The result was that while the material from Germany and France was adequate, it was not as dense or extensive as the British material. Consequently, it was necessary for the British studies to predominate, using France and Germany as avowedly supporting cases. The

[9] Collège interarmées de défense, the Joint Services Command and Staff College, Führungsakademie, NATO School.
[10] The Allied Rapid Reaction Corps both in Rheindalen and, as ISAF IX, in Kabul, the Permanent Joint Headquarters, the Multinational Brigade (South East) Iraq in Basra, Centre de planification et de conduite des opérations, Einsatzführungskommando, Allied Command Operations, Allied Command Transformation, Joint Forces Command Brunssum, EUFOR Headquarters, Sarajevo and the EU Military Staff Brussels.
[11] 3 Commando Brigade, 16 Air Assault Brigade, 9 brigade légère blindée de marine, Division Spezielle Operationen.

distinctiveness of the British case is always recognised in the study, but the French and German studies are used to show that, while national differences remain, the general trajectory of institutional change in Europe is similar. All three militaries are converging on a broadly shared organisational model, while common concepts and practices are being instituted so that operational headquarters and rapid reaction brigades can co-operate with each other. NATO plays an important role in the research, providing an institutional framework which has mediated and co-ordinated changes within each nation.

There has been extensive discussion about the decline of the mass army in the late twentieth century, a reduction which has been described as down-sizing (Dandeker 1994; Haltiner 1998; Kelleher 1978; Manigart 2003: 331; Martin 1977; Shaw 1991; Van Doorn 1968). This book claims that the armed forces today are not so much shrinking as concentrating. They are, indeed, smaller than they have been for decades but, in some ways, they are more capable than their mass army forebears. The professional expertise of the forces across both combat and support roles is being intensified. It is here that rapid reaction forces are particularly important. They are the forces that have been at the forefront of this process of concentration. Defence resources, which have declined in general, have been focused on these emergent forces so that, while the armed forces as a whole have contracted, these privileged formations have expanded in size, capability and strategic significance.

In their study of the 'postmodern military', Charles Moskos et al. (2000: 2) claimed that one of the defining features of the armed forces today is the development of multinational and international forces. The process of 'multinationalisation' is central to this book. Europe's armed forces are co-operating with each other ever more closely, and at an ever lower tactical level, than would have been conceivable during the Cold War. Moskos uses the terms multinational or international to describe these emergent cross-border interactions. In this book, I have preferred to use the term 'transnational' rather than multinational. Military forces are not merging across borders to create supranational military formations, least of all a European army. Nation-states maintain their authority over their forces; indeed, in many cases, they have re-asserted their sovereignty over their troops. However, rapid reaction forces in each county, as concentrated nodes of national military capability, are interacting with each other more closely across borders which continue to exist. A thickening *transnational* military network is appearing in Europe between these condensations of national power. The interactions between national forces are sanctioned by the state, but they have transcended the level of intercourse which might be termed international. National borders have become porous and interactions between rapid reaction forces occur, especially in-theatre, independently of specific state direction (once states have sanctioned their participation). Rapid reaction forces are actively seeking to learn and develop together in a mutually supporting network. A transnational network is identifiable. The nation remains a critical political framework for the armed forces even though these forces are increasingly incorporated into a dense and complex web of relations which exceed national borders. Indeed, the problems of access which I encountered in France and Germany were evidence of this transnationalisation. Europe's militaries are converging on common organisational models and shared forms of practice, but national borders, sovereignty and differences remain. These borders are precisely those which I encountered as I embarked on the research, preventing the possibility of dense fieldwork research in France and Germany which the British military were willing to grant to a British national.

The fundamental dynamic of European military transformation today described here involves a simultaneous process of concentration and transnationalisation. It seems likely that in the coming decade this trajectory will continue and, indeed, deepen so that by 2020 Europe's armed forces will be even smaller than they are now, but they will also be more professional and capable, having developed deeper co-operative links with each other. However, caution needs to be exercised here. The process of concentration and transnationalisation has engendered huge frictions at the domestic levels within the armed forces and internationally between European militaries. This friction cannot be ignored. Moreover, as I will discuss in the final chapter of the book, the future of the armed forces is uncertain and the processes of transnationalisation and concentration are reversible. While it seems inconceivable that Europe could return to the mass armies of the twentieth century, the current path of reform could be broken by a number of historical contingencies and specifically by defeat in Afghanistan. The military could suffer a major retrenchment in budget, status and mission leading to a reversal, especially of the process of transnationalisation and a move away from highly resourced rapid reaction forces. While this book cannot predict precisely what will happen in Afghanistan, it does seek to explain the current trajectory of change and suggests that the pattern of reform which is now underway is likely to continue into the next decade.

The research focus

In 1957, Samuel Huntington published *The Soldier and The State* (Huntington 1957); this was followed three years later by Morris Janowitz's *Professional Soldier* ([1960] 1981), which explored many of the same themes. Huntington and Janowitz sought to define the nature of the military professional in Western democracies and, above all, in the United States, in order to analyse the relationship between the armed forces and civil society. They came to differing, but not radically incompatible, conclusions about the military profession. While Janowitz maintained that the post-Second World War officer corps were under increasing civil control and were themselves becoming more civilianised technical managers through closer links 'with a variety of civilian enterprises and organizations' ([1960] 1981: 372), Huntington, by contrast, insisted that the officer corps should remain a specialist status group whose very professionalism and discipline would ensure 'objective civilian control' (1957: 83). Indeed, controversially, Huntington regarded the armed forces as offering potential redemption from the Babylonian decadence of civil society: 'The greatest service they can render is to remain true to themselves, to serve with silence and courage in the military way. If they abjure the military spirit, they destroy themselves first and their nation ultimately' (1957: 466). The work of Janowitz and Huntington has rightly remained an enduring reference point for the analysis of the armed forces. However, their interest in civil–military relations is not the focal point of this work. This book is not primarily interested in analysing the relations between the armed forces and state, even though it is recognised that, especially in an era of military privatisation, it is a critical question. Nor does it not seek to provide a comparative framework for analysis, as Huntington's does. The strategic and institutional context in which European military transformation takes place is discussed and the new forms of strategic and budgetary pressure, which are demanding change, are identified, but this book aims primarily to map the specific organisational geography of a changing military. It describes the fundamental features of Europe's new military itself in order to identify the realities of military development today. It is possible that other scholars may be able to trace similar processes which are occurring in differentiated ways around the globe on the basis of the analysis presented here, but this work does not aspire to provide any such generalising framework.

In this way, this work is also distinct from some existing scholarship on military transformation, although it draws upon it. Thus, for instance, Barry Posen (1984) Stephen Rosen (1991) and Deborah Avant (1994) have sought to develop more general theories of military innovation by investigating specific examples. These remain interesting and important contributions and, especially in the case of Rosen's work, there are evident theoretical connections with the argument forwarded here. For instance, closely reflecting my interpretative position, Rosen understands military development in terms of the situated interactions of numerous participants in a politico-military complex over time. However, contemporary developments in Europe are not used here as a basis for forwarding a general theory of military change. The aim is to provide a historically specific interpretation of European military innovation through the analysis of the practices, interrelations and hierarchies of the armed forces today. This book seeks to identify an emergent military order in Europe, delineating innovations in expertise in decisive headquarters and rapid reaction brigades. By identifying the central features of Europe's transformed military, it may be possible to contribute to wider debates about the processes of European integration.

In this way, although the interest in civil–military relations is missing, the approach advocated here may be seen to have some affinities with the work of Huntington and Janowitz fifty years ago. Huntington provided an historical and sociological analysis of the culture of the professional officer corps in the United States and Western Europe from the late eighteenth century to the 1950s. Janowitz similarly explored the changing culture of the US officer corps in the twentieth century as its warrior ethos softened into a more technocratic spirit. Both scholars explored the armed forces as a 'form of life' (Wittgenstein 1976), seeking to show the ways in which the corporate identity and shared interests of the officer corps influenced both their interactions with government and civilian society and also the military's own institutional development. Both scholars were interested in how this form of life changed in the course of history. In the last decade, scholars have intensified their interest in this kind of deep sociological investigation. They, too, have become interested in the armed forces as a form of life which must be understood in its own terms. Ben-Shalom et al.'s recent work is a good example of this hermeneutic trend (2005). They have shown how members of the Israeli Defence Force (IDF) are able to engender 'swift trust' among themselves through adherence to common professional practices (2005: 73). The culture of the IDF does not prioritise affective bonds of comradeship but technical military drills. In this move to the exploration of military lifeworlds themselves, social scientists reflect a much wider move away from structural or systemic approaches to interactive or 'practical' analysis (Bourdieu 1977), which is itself a product of the so-called 'linguistic turn' of the late 1960s.

The 'practical' or interpretive perspective adopted here does not imply that military organisations as large institutions should be ignored or that European military transformation can be comprehended merely by reference to opinions or actions of individual soldiers.[12] On the contrary, in

---

[12] To this end, it is notable that the work on military transformation in strategic studies is deeply pertinent to military sociology. The work of Stephen Biddle represents a model of this approach where he has analysed the actual operational performance of US forces in

order to understand the practical competences of European staff officers and soldiers, the wider organisation of the armed forces has to be recognised. It is imperative to understand the broad organisational transformation of the armed forces, situating it in its proper historical context; current changes are, for instance, part of a long-term shift away from mass, conscript forces to specialised, professional militaries. However, although the organisational level will remain vital to the study in contextualising specific forms of military expertise, it is a mistake to reify military organisations into asocial systems, despite their evident power. Military transformation involves the revision of collective practices at a number of decisive points in the armed forces by commanders, staff officers and soldiers. At critical points since 1990, the armed forces have been forced or have sought to perform new missions. These new tasks, the very definition of which has been the result of intense political contestation, have forced the members of the armed forces to co-operate with new military groups in other organisations with whom they had no or little interaction the past. In order to co-ordinate these new institutional relations, new definitions, procedures and practices have been established collectively. As a result of many minor revisions, a new military regime is beginning to crystallise in Europe. Yet the grand reformation of the armed forces has, in fact, involved a multitude of small, situated changes in professional self-definition, expertise and interrelations in a diversity of locations. Military organisations are hierarchical, but they should not be understood as pre-ordained, static or monolithic structures. They are a complex chain of recurrently enacted social interactions. Through repeated practices, a multitude of military personnel, many unknown to each other, have together transformed the headquarters and brigades of which they are part; typically in directions of which even the most senior commander is not fully aware. In short, military transformation has involved the germination of new lifeworlds across a multiplicity of military sub-organisations.

Bruno Latour's actor network theory (ANT) is useful in comprehending institutional transformation in this way. ANT seeks to understand institutions and social processes not in isolation but as manifestations of wide social networks consisting of actors utilising actants; a diversity of participants and things all comprise the network in which any particular activity has its meaning and even possibility. Latour in no way denies the

order to illustrate the likely and most desirable trajectory of change. Other commentators such as Robert Scales and Williamson Murray (2003) and Dan Macgregor (1997) have also been similarly detailed in their analysis of contemporary military. This study takes its cue from this concern with the actual performance of military headquarters and formations as they prepare for new military operations.

manifest potency of large organisations, but he understands their existence and reproduction in terms of the dense interaction of the multiplicity of agents both inside and outside who are essential to them: 'For
ANT, if you stop making and remaking groups, you stop having groups.
No reservoir of forces flowing from "social forces" will help you' (Latour
2005: 35). For Latour, the groups, organisations and institutions which
constitute social reality are neither pre-formed nor pre-existent: sociologists cannot appeal to objective background forces that compel individuals
to act in prescribed ways. For Latour, there is only a front-stage in social
life – the recurrent interplay between interdependent and mutually
susceptible actors using actants in a vast self-generating and self-
referential social configuration. This book is avowedly influenced by this
kind of approach to sociology where social reality is seen as the complex
achievement of recurrently interacting participants united, sometimes
only temporarily, around collective projects. It aims to investigate the
way in which operational headquarters and rapid reaction brigades in
Europe are re-organising themselves in order to conduct new missions.
In order to explain that process of transformation, it is important to
recognise external strategic pressures which are always mediated by existing institutional practices and interests. It is these which are the focus of
interest here.

The book is divided into three parts. In Part I, the context in which
contemporary European military transformation is taking place is
described. The 'new wars' in which Europe is increasingly engaged in
the Balkans, Africa and especially Afghanistan and declining defence
budgets are identified as the critical drivers of military transformation.
These pressures are forcing the armed forces to re-organise themselves
and to develop alternative forms of expertise. This part concludes by
arguing that, despite the development of the EU, NATO will remain the
critical institutional framework for European military development. In
Part II, the emergence of 'operational' headquarters is analysed. A new
transnational network of headquarters, as concentrations of national
resourcing and expertise, organised and trained to conduct global stabilisation missions, is identified in Europe, differing profoundly from
the hierarchies of the Cold War. The appearance of new planning concepts and practices within this network and the convergence of these
headquarters on a common form of expertise is examined. Finally, in
Part III, Europe's rapid reaction brigades themselves are investigated.
These forces represent the national concentration of combat power.
They have benefited from governmental patronage, but their increased
prominence is a result of their distinctive ethos and enhanced cohesiveness. In Part III particularly, Britain's rapid reaction forces provide the

prime material, supported by interview and documentary material from France and Germany. In this way, the debates about post-Cold War security pressures and the relative merits and demerits of the EU or NATO constitute the conceptual and historical framework in which a deep reading of specifically military reform in the three chosen countries is conducted. The book focuses on NATO, Britain, France and Germany in order to provide a hopefully useful insight into those armed forces, but the analysis of those militaries within a three-part structure is intended as a general framework into which the forces of other European countries might be inserted. It is hoped that further work might be carried out on operational headquarters and rapid reaction brigades in other European countries.

The armed forces as a dimension of European integration

Many scholars, including Michael Roberts, Michael Howard, Charles Tilly, Martin van Creveld and Charles Mann, have all recognised an intimate connection between the armed forces and the formation of the early modern state. For these scholars, the armed forces are not simply an important public institution. The appearance of standing armies (and navies) in Europe from the sixteenth century represented a profound social and political transformation. Indeed, for Foucault and Elias, the appearance of an army with its drills and barracks represented one of the most profound expressions of the new disciplined culture of modernity. The armed forces may be one of the decisive institutions of modern society. Minimally, the development of the modern army has provided a fertile focus for the sociological investigation of much wider social processes: the constitution of modernity itself. European nation-states and the EU itself are undergoing a profound transformation and the analysis of this process has become central to the social sciences. Perhaps the analysis of Europe's armed forces today might continue to provide these sociological insights into wider processes of European development – and state transformation – today. It might be possible to contribute to these discussions through this analysis of one distinctive aspect of European transformation.

In their important work on European integration, Milward (1992) and Moravcsik (1998, 2001) claim that the most convincing theories of European state transformation remain resolutely based on the empirical analysis of particular institutions. Through close engagement with decisive political institutions, they illuminate the complex intergovernmental dynamics of European integration. Whether their arguments about intergovernmentalism are correct or not, Milward's and Moravcsik's approach

may offer a more fruitful starting point to the analysis of current development of the European state than the abstract and idealising theory which
has often dominated debates (see Bogaards and Crepaz, 2002;
Chryssochoou 1998; Lijphart 1979, 1984; Pinder 1995; Siedentop
2001; Teunissen 1999). Indeed, many sociologists have adopted precisely
this empirical approach in order to elucidate the reality of the EU. In his
recent work on mobile European professionals ('Eurostars'), Adrian
Favell (2008) has sought to analyse individuals who are the often
self-conscious vanguard of European integration. These individuals
have freed themselves from local and national connections, traversing
the EU fluidly to take up the new opportunities for professional employment, especially in cosmopolitan cities like London, Amsterdam or
Brussels. It is unlikely that the transcendence of national affiliations
which he describes is borne out in most professions, and it is certainly
absent in the military. However, Favell usefully grounds the question of
European integration in the activities of living Europeans. The armed
forces constitute a very different field to Favell's Eurostars, but perhaps by
adopting a similarly ethnographic perspective it may be possible to provide the kind of insights which Favell seeks to deliver in his work. In this
way, it may be possible to supplement the work of Milward and Moravcsik
with the analysis of other spheres of state activity.

It may be possible to make this connection to debates about European
integration by means of literature on organisational sociology. The military is clearly a distinctive social organisation, but the dual dynamic of
concentration and transnationalisation described here might be related to
wider processes of organisational reform today. Globalisation theorists
(Castells 1998; Dicken 1998; Held and McGrew 2000; Robertson 1992;
Sassen 1991) have argued that a compatible double movement is evident
in other spheres of human activity in Europe and other parts of the world.
Globalisation is characterised by simultaneous processes of localisation
and global expansion. Private and public sector organisations have re-
focused themselves around their core areas of expertise, retracting into
condensed centres in selected locales. At the same time, they have sought
to create alliances with associated organisations on a regional and sometimes global scale. The fundamental thesis of this book is that the armed
forces of Europe are undergoing a compatible but differentiated process of
'glocalisation'. They are concentrating at decisive locales from which
they are extending out increasingly deep institutional relations to produce
a new military order of multiple, interdependent nodes and interconnected transnational networks. The emergent military order in Europe
is complex, but this complexity is not due to the fact that the process of
reform is unfinished. It seems unlikely that even in its mature

manifestation, Europe's armed forces will have the simple international, vertical structure of the armed forces of the twentieth century. The organisational future of Europe's armed forces would seem to be fundamentally complex, just as analysts have emphasised with regard to European integration more widely. Europe is entering an era of 'neo-medievalism' with overlapping institutions, sovereignties and powers. As the armed forces are increasingly interdependent, an intricate mesh of horizontal alliances, relations and associations is appearing that is extremely challenging for scholars and military practitioners to conceptualise accurately. This book cannot claim to depict that web of transnational interdependencies in its entirety. However, by taking one small slice of Europe's armed forces – a selection of operational headquarters which plan and command today's multinational missions and the rapid reaction brigades that conduct them – the book attempts to describe these processes of concentration and transnationalisation and to depict what a multipolar, 'globalised' military is beginning to look like more generally. It is hoped that the detailed investigation of this admittedly select sample will illustrate wider processes of European integration. Certainly, the general pattern of military transformation in Europe will be differentiated within each nation; this is even more true of transformation in the civilian sector. However, by focusing on a small but decisive selection of military organisations it is hoped that this book will contribute to the formation of an empirically rich analytical framework which may be generally applicable to the question of contemporary military transformation. Today's transnational military network is, of course, quite different to the military order which characterised Europe in the Cold War, when NATO's armoured divisions were drawn up along the Rhine, just as the EU represents a radical adaptation of the institutions originally created under the Treaty of Rome in 1957.

Although naturally of primary interest to scholars interested in war and the armed forces, this analysis of European military transformation is, therefore, intended to be a focused and empirically specific contribution to debates about European integration more widely; it examines one sphere of European activity in detail in order to illuminate much more general processes. The military sphere is certainly to be differentiated from the civilian spheres, where processes of integration are also occurring. It is vital that this account of military transformation is faithful to the distinctive reality of military reformation. Nevertheless, with great care, it may be possible to note commensurate processes in both civilian and military spheres and to trace the existence of similar dynamics occurring in both areas of European activity. The description of how European armed forces are currently re-organising themselves to fight global insurgencies may usefully illustrate what it means to be a European more widely. The organisation of European forces for new operations may actually parallel the way Europeans conduct themselves in a diversity of other activities. It is possible that the dynamics of concentration and transnationalisation which are at the heart of this study may have much wider applicability to the process of European integration. Perhaps, private and public institutions in Europe much more widely are also being re-configured along the trajectory of concentration and transnationalisation evident in the military. It may be possible that banks, hospitals, universities, professional sports might be going through a compatible, but, of course, differentiated and distinctive, process of transformation. Perhaps the future of Europe more widely will be a complex transnational reality of concentrated but interdependent national nodes in a mesh of relations across borders within and without the EU. Although the issue is not explored here, it is possible that those ten French paratroopers killed on 18 August 2008 over 3,000 miles east of Paris might represent and be the victims of this new transnational order.

2   Europe's new military

Europe's new wars

Since the 1990s, scholars have begun to analyse the appearance of new kinds of conflict and its implications for the armed forces.[1] Among the more prominent of these contributions was Mary Kaldor's concept of 'new wars' (1999) which, she claimed, had 'to be understood in the context of the process known as globalization' (1999: 3). The subversion of state authority through new global economic flows has differentially advantaged and disadvantaged certain groups, precipitating friction, hostility and ultimately conflict. Decisively, 'new wars arise in the context of the erosion of the autonomy of the state and in some extreme cases the disintegration of the state' (Kaldor 1999: 4). The concept of identity politics is central to Kaldor's concept of the new war, and she distinguishes between the identities around which modern conflict was organised and the new identities which fuel postmodern war. 'Earlier identities were linked either to a notion of state interest or to some forward-looking project – ideas about how society should be organized' (1999: 6). Modern wars were fought between state armed forces on the basis of national identity and affiliation. The population was mobilised by a unifying state. By contrast, 'the process of globalization, it can be argued, has begun to break-up these vertically organized cultures' (1999: 71). In the light of this fragmentation, 'identity politics' involve 'movements which mobilize around ethnic, racial or religious identity for the purpose of claiming state power' (1999: 76). Novel social groups have emerged which have sought to seize hold of the remaining assets of the state

[1] Adam and Ben-Ari 2006; Arquilla and Ronfeldt 1997; Booth et al. 2001; Burk 2003b; Caforio 2003; Coker 2001, 2002a, 2002b, 2007; Connaughton 2000, 2001a, 2001b; Croft 2006a, 2006b; Croft et al. 2001; Dandeker 1994, 2003; Dorman et al. 2002; Farrell 2008; Farrell and Terriff 2002; Glasius and Kaldor 2006; Goldman and Eliason 2003; Gray 1997, 2002, 2006; Hirst 2001; Kaldor 1982, 1999; Kaldor et al. 1998; Latham 2002; Moskos et al. 2000; Shaw 1988, 1991, 2005; Strachan 1999; Terriff 2004a, 2004b, 2007; Toffler and Toffler 1995; Van Creveld 1991, 2006.

(administrative powers, including the police, prisons, justice systems and, decisively, the armed forces) and to monopolise resources such as land, minerals, industry or people. In this fight for resources, new social groups have found it increasingly effective to mobilise themselves around new ethnic and religious identities.

There has been extensive debate about Kaldor's concept of the new war. While most scholars are broadly in agreement that these new conflicts are a product of globalisation and that belligerents have increasingly mobilised around recently invented ethnic and religious identities, there have been some important qualifications of the original thesis. Kalyvas (2001, 2006) has, for instance, objected to Kaldor's claim that there is anything really new about her 'new wars'. Putatively, new wars have been little different from the civil wars which punctuated the modern period. Indeed, Kalyvas demonstrates the way in which civil wars in the twentieth century bore an overwhelming similarity to current conflicts in their brutality, opportunism and geography of mobilisation; while Münkler sees little difference between new wars and the religious wars of the early modern period (Münkler 2005: 9). Bowen (1996) has also emphasised the external causes of these wars, particularly Western influence, which Kaldor potentially underplays. Others like Berdal (2003), Keen (Berdal and Keen 1997) or Gagnon (2006) emphasise the opportunistic economic or political agendas behind much contemporary conflict. As a result of these interventions, there has been a tendency to move away from the concept of the new war to a more nuanced understanding of 'complex emergencies' in recent literature (Duffield 2001; Keen 2008). This conceptual development seems to be sustainable, but there is very broad agreement among all these scholars that global forces have precipitated the conflicts which are evident in Sierra Leone, the Great Lakes Region, Darfur, the Balkans and Afghanistan. In the Balkans, the central communist state ruled by Tito until 1980 began to fissure as new political groups, mobilising on an ethnic basis, emerged to struggle against each other for political sovereignty and territory (Gagnon 2006; Glenny 1992; Woodward 1995). Similarly, the Afghan state collapsed in the late 1970s, precipitating thirty years of war between regionally-based groups united on ethnic grounds (Goodson 2001; Roy 1986). European militaries have been increasingly engaged in these complex struggles.

European nations have recognised the transformation of the strategic situation which confronted them following the Cold War and have sought to redefine their armed forces in the light of these changes. They have realised that interstate war has given way – perhaps, according to Colin Gray (2006), temporarily – to complex ethnic conflicts, precipitated by globalisation. Accordingly, in Britain, France and Germany defence policy and military doctrine has similarly identified regional instability, ethnic and religious conflict, failed states, terrorism and crime as the central defence and security threats of the early twenty-first century. Introducing New Labour's *Strategic Defence Review* in 1998, George Robertson, the then Minister of Defence, declared that: 'The Review is radical, reflecting a changing world, in which the confrontation of the Cold War has been replaced by a complex mixture of uncertainty and instability' (1998a: 1). The *Review* itself affirmed the shift in strategic context:

> The strategic environment we face today is very different to that of the previous fifty years. The risks and challenges we face are not simply those of the Cold War minus the threat from the Warsaw Pact ... Instability inside Europe as in Bosnia, and now Kosovo, threatens our security. Instability elsewhere – for example in Africa – may not always appear to threaten us directly. But it can do indirectly. (Directorate of Defence Policy 1998a: 5)

The *Review* identified hostile regimes, but also prioritised organised crime and terrorism as major threats. German defence policy statements from the late 1990s accorded closely with the findings of the *Review*. Peter Struck's *Outline of the Bundeswehr Concept*, issued on 9 August 2004, demonstrated this transformation:

> The security situation has changed fundamentally. In the foreseeable future German will no longer be threatened by conventional armed forces. Its security is being defended in Afghanistan as well as wherever else threats to our country arise, as is the case with international terrorism. Dangers must be countered where they originate, for they may impair security even over long distances unless action is taken. (Bundesministerium der Verteidigung 2004: 2)

Struck's point was confirmed by his successor, Franz-Josef Jung, who affirmed that terrorism, weapons of mass destruction (WMD) and 'the aftermath of intrastate and regional conflict, de-stabilisation, and the internal disintegration of states as well as its frequent by-product – the privatisation of force' were the key threats which faced Germany (Bundesministerium der Verteidigung 2006: 5, 14–15). Nicolas Sarkozy's 2008 *Livre Blanc* begins grandly:

> Globalisation is profoundly changing the fundamentals of the international system. The global distribution of power is modifying to the benefit of Asia. States are competing strategically with newly powerful actors. The typology of threats and risks necessitates a redefinition of the conditions of national and international security. The role and place of military instruments has been modified. Complexity and uncertainty constitute the major characteristics of this new environment. (*Livre Blanc* 2008: 13)

Interestingly, the document evidences the new concerns of France (and other European states) with China, but non-state actors, including organised criminal networks, insurgents and terrorists, remain central to France's definition of the strategic context and to its re-structuring of the armed forces (*Livre Blanc* 2008: 24–8). In stark contrast to the twentieth century when France's foreign policy interests were focused primarily on Africa, the *Livre Blanc* defines Asia and particularly the 'Axis of Crisis' (between the Middle East and Afghanistan) as the 'centre of gravity' in the coming decade. Instability, insurgency and terrorism, prosecuted especially by ethnic and religious groups and exacerbated by environmental crises, are regarded as central threats.

Germany, France and Britain have re-defined the strategic context individually, but they have also done so collectively as part of NATO and the EU. For instance, following the London Conference, NATO issued a New Strategic Concept in 1991. With the 'threat of full-scale attack ... removed', NATO forces had to re-invent a role for themselves. Although the Balkans crisis was only beginning to emerge and there was, as yet, very little evidence that Islamic fundamentalism would become a major threat, the Strategic Concept presciently identified that while 'the threat of full-scale attack ... has been removed', the risks were 'now multifaceted' and included 'the adverse consequence of instability ... ethnic rivalries and territorial disputes' and the proliferation of 'weapons of mass destruction' (NATO 1991). By the time of the ratification of the 1999 Strategic Concept, NATO explicitly recognised that it 'must take account of the global context of Alliance security interests' (NATO 1999: 24). Although 'large-scale conventional aggression' (1999: 20) was not impossible in this globalised context, the 1999 Strategic Concept identified the proliferation of nuclear, biological and chemical weapons and the emergence of non-state actors as the core threats (1999: 22). 'Alliance security interests can be affected by other risks of a wider nature, including acts of terrorism, sabotage and organised crime and by the disruption of the flows of resources' (1999: 24). Whatever the lengthy debates about out-of-area deployments in the mid-1990s, NATO recognised that it now operated in a 'global context'. This represented a revolution in strategic affairs (Freedman 1998).

A similar process of strategic re-orientation has been evident in the EU. In 2003 EU member states ratified the EU's Strategic Concept. There is a typically softer tone in EU documents, but the identified threats are almost identical:

The post Cold War environment is one of increasingly open borders in which the internal and external aspects of security are indissolubly linked. Flows of trade and investment, the development of technology and the spread of democracy have brought freedom and prosperity to many people. Others have perceived global-isation as a cause of frustration and injustice. These developments have also increased the scope for non-state groups to play a part in international affairs. And they have increased European dependence – and so vulnerability – on an interconnected infrastructure in transport, energy, information and other fields. (European Security Strategy 2003: 2)

Within this globalising environment, the EU identified terrorism, the proliferation of WMDs, regional conflicts, state failure and organised crime as the critical security threats (2003: 3–5). Like NATO, the EU does not explicitly identify ethnic or religious conflicts as a prime concern, but since it cites the examples of Kashmir, the Great Lakes Region and the Middle East, it is clear that the EU regards ethnic and religious frictions as a central element of the globalising process. In December 2008, a revised *European Security Strategy*, 'Providing Security in a Changing World', was presented to the European Council.[2] The new document was intended to highlight the changing threats which Europe now faces, assess the imple-mentation of the original document and describe measures that needed to be taken to improve European security co-operation. Although the docu-ment has been described as 'thorough', its production was hurried and politically problematic. Instead of a clear list of security priorities (upon which agreement could not be reached), the document described a diver-sity of plausible threats, but nowhere did it clearly identify the policy implications of these new threats for the EU. Consequently, although potentially important, it is likely to re-affirm the original European Security Strategy with its emphasis on failed states, regional conflict and crime. European military reform has been substantially predicated on these strategic statements of defence policy. They represent the institu-tional understandings of European states, NATO and the EU which have demanded and justified contemporary military transformation. Europe's armed forces have been consciously reformed in order to address these new threats identified as critical.

The fact that Europe's armed forces are being reformed for new mis-sions, precipitated by globalisation, cannot be seriously disputed. Nor can the existence of new forms of threat be usefully denied. Globalisation has released a wave of instability in critical regions like the Balkans and Afghanistan which it is difficult for European states to ignore. In addition, the belligerents that have emerged in these groups have posed a manifest security threat to European citizens. However, neither claim should encourage the belief that the decision to re-organise Europe's armed

---

[2] For an assessment of the European Security Strategy see Biscop and Anderson 2008.

forces along narrow expeditionary lines is in any way self-evident. Even in the face of these serious security and defence threats, it was not inevitable that European states should decide to prioritise regional instability as a prime defence threat or choose to reform and deploy their troops on these missions. Alternative options were potentially open to European states: they could potentially have prioritised internal homeland security above deployment; they could have prioritised the development of training teams whose aim was to build up local militaries as proxy forces for the West. Moreover, the concept of intervention could itself have been different, less reliant on the fairly conventional use of military force than it has in fact been; diplomacy and economic incentives might have been used more effectively.

Although now strategically vital (because Europe is committed to it), it was not inevitable or a necessary that Europe should have become involved in Afghanistan. It was not logically demanded by the new definition of Western security. On the contrary, the Afghan campaign became obligatory only in the light of Europe's political commitments and interdependencies; it was precipitated by institutional dynamics not strategic logic. In response to the 9/11 attacks, NATO countries invoked Article 5 of the Washington Treaty in solidarity with the United States, and even France, the European country most hostile to the United States, affirmed its support. On a visit to Washington after the attacks, Jacques Chirac, the then French president, declared: 'We bring you the total solidarity of France and the French people. It is solidarity of the heart. We are completely determined to fight by your side this new type of evil.'[3] Initially, the United States had only limited need for European support. Soon after the attacks of 9/11, Al Qaeda networks in Afghanistan were identified as the source of training, funding and planning for the terrorist cells that perpetrated the assault. Their close connection with the Taliban was well documented and, having failed to surrender Al Qaeda leaders, including Osama bin Laden, the United States initiated a UN-mandated assault on the Taliban and Al Qaeda, resulting in the rapid elimination of the Taliban regime. After the fall of the Taliban in November 2001, the United States continued to pursue Taliban and Al Qaeda fighters, finally terminating Operation Enduring Freedom as an autonomous coalition operation (but not as a NATO operation) only in October 2006. At this point, European forces were drawn into the struggle in Afghanistan.

At first, Europe Special Forces troops, including British and German troops, contributed to Operation Enduring Freedom from 2001. At the

[3] http://articles.latimes.com/2001/sep/19/news/mn-47340.

same time, it became clear that a stabilisation operation was needed to implement political reforms in the light of the collapse of the Taliban regime. Accordingly, an International Security Assistance Force headquarters (ISAF) was established in Kabul in December 2001 to command the stabilisation efforts being conducted initially in Kabul by mainly European forces and in the north by a German Provincial Reconstruction Team. Britain and Turkey provided the initial staff for that headquarters. From that time, Europe's forces have become increasingly committed to Afghanistan as the mission has expanded. European countries have contributed to the ISAF not because Afghanistan is objectively the most serious strategic threat that Europe faces, but because European nations have been drawn into the campaign in order to sustain their alliance with the United States which affords them significant military, security and political benefits. Indeed, as surveys of European publics have demonstrated, the mission is not obviously in the direct national interest (or interpreted as such). Moreover, it is expensive and dangerous.

This co-operative pressure on European nations became particularly obvious after 2003 with the invasion of Iraq. The decision to invade Iraq eroded much of the genuine solidarity which many Europeans felt for the United States after the 2001 attacks. A significant number of European nations were opposed to or reluctant to involve themselves in Iraq. However, having professed their support for the United States, it became very difficult for European leaders to fail to deliver any tangible assets to either theatre. Accordingly, although Afghanistan was not ideal, it was infinitely preferable as a theatre of operations for major powers like France, Germany or Spain. Following the war in Kosovo, the United States was sceptical about the utility of NATO, but since it was difficult for most European countries to commit to Afghanistan either politically or militarily outside a NATO framework, the United States finally had to compromise on its preference for a coalition of the willing. NATO became involved in the mission, in the first instance, providing crucial command and communication support for the German–Netherlands Corps which assumed command of ISAF III in August 2003. NATO has provided the command structure for the mission since that time. However, even with NATO involvement, it is clear that European nations have committed to Afghanistan primarily in order to sustain relations with the United States. In 2007, as British and Dutch forces sustained significant casualties in the south, Germany was pressurised to contribute more troops to Afghanistan and authorise their use in the south. It has yet to bow to this pressure. Nevertheless, one of the fundamental justifications of Scharping's and Struck's Bundeswehr reforms was to sustain Germany's international alliances (Bundnis), which required greater inter-operability on the part of the German armed forces (Bundesministerium der Verteidigung 2004: 7, 18; Leersch 2003; Scharping 2000: 12). Although the German government might be averse to combat operations, it has not risked being incapable of contributing to its international alliances. It seems possible that German troops will have to be deployed south under pressure from President Obama. Similarly, Nicolas Sarkozy's fateful decision to deploy a paratroop battalion to the region was substantially a result of his wider strategy of re-integrating France into NATO; he recognised that this organisation offered concrete security and defence benefits. Indeed, the *Livre Blanc* explicitly identifies continued access to collective security goods provided by international alliances as a fundamental principle of contemporary national policy (*Livre Blanc* 2008: 37, 113–24). The British have been highly susceptible to these co-operative pressures. As a result of their failure to 'surge' with their American allies in Iraq in 2007 and their precipitate withdrawal from Basra, the British military lost credibility with the United States. In an attempt to regain favour with (and, therefore, sustain special access to) the US military, Britain had increased its troop numbers to 9,500 by the end of 2009. In each case, European states and their armed forces have deemed it necessary to sustain their access to the security goods which the United States offers its partners by committing to Afghanistan.

Europe's commitment to global stabilisation missions and the subsequent re-orientation of its armed forces should be understood as a product of the growing importance of collective security goods for states, which were once able to guarantee their own security and pursue their foreign policies more autonomously. For European nations, Afghanistan became a means of showing solidarity with the United States after the 9/11 attacks. Of course, European states have not just committed themselves to expeditionary stabilisation missions to show solidarity with the United States. Crucially, European states have recognised their own growing interdependence and have deployed to the Balkans, Africa and Afghanistan in order to sustain and develop joint security partnerships. They contributed to these missions in order to guarantee their access to collective security goods. The European commitment to Afghanistan – and the wider move to expeditionary forces ready for stabilisation missions – aims to sustain crucial international alliances. Indeed, the strategic re-orientations which are evident in national, EU and NATO policy have been performative statements actively affirming security alliances and the benefits which accrue from them.

However contingent or self-referential in origin, Europe's entry into Afghanistan is likely to be decisive in the transformation of Europe's armed forces. In 2006, while he was acting as Commander ISAF, General Richards recognised the seriousness of the NATO mission: 'We can't afford to lose this. And we will dig deeper if we have to. If NATO doesn't succeed in the south, it might as well pack up as an international military alliance.'[4] His sentiments were reflected throughout Europe: 'If we fail in Afghanistan with or without heavy losses, then that will produce a big discussion. Then it will be a decisive point for the Bundeswehr in the future. If the mission fails, it will trigger a discussion in EU and world-wide.'[5] Against all predictions in the 1990s, the Hindu Kush is becoming the crucible of European military transformation. The armed forces are being forced to adapt to a highly particularistic kind of conflict. In particular, although equipment is still being procured with the prospect of interstate war in mind, the expectations and expertise of Europe's armed forces are increasingly being moulded through adversarial encounters with ethnic militants in Afghanistan. Europe's military is being marked by current operations in Afghanistan whether such an influence is desired or not. Whether Europe becomes involved in an interstate conflict in the future or not, the way it fights such a conflict will be substantially – at least in the initial phases – influenced by current engagement in new wars, above all in Afghanistan. In order to sustain international alliances especially with the United States, European forces are now engaged in a complex, geographically dispersed stabilisation operation which involves intense fighting against insurgent forces. The real pressures, which this mission is placing on Europe's forces and the need to co-operate with the United States and with each other, are demanding military transformation – and convergence. Europe's militaries are being forced to develop new concepts, doctrines and practices in the light of a highly motivated, intelligent and adaptable enemy and in an attempt to stabilise an entire country.

Defence budgets

The new strategic context is crucial in understanding military innovation, but there is a second condition that has fundamentally contoured the trajectory of military transformation in Europe: defence budgets. Finances have constituted a major limiting condition for Europe's armed forces. In the first half of the 1990s, the 'Peace Dividend' resulted in a significant reduction in defence budgets across Western Europe. For instance, the United Kingdom's annual defence budget decreased from £33.5 billion in 1986 to £23.5 billion in 2000 (in 2000 prices); a reduction from 5.3 per cent of GDP in 1986 to 2.4 per cent of GDP in 2000

---

[4] General Richards, personal interview, 11 July 2006.
[5] Colonel, Einsatzführungskommando, October 2006.

(Alexander and Garden 2001: 512). Germany's defence budget declined from 3.2 per cent to 1.4 per cent of GDP between 1975 and 2004 (Sinjen and Varwick 2006: 97; Thomas 2000: 25). In contrast to other public services, German defence spending shrank significantly (Sattler 2006: 279, 281) and remained one of the lowest in Europe despite the size of the Bundeswehr (Sinjen and Varwick 2006: 96). France's defence budget similarly declined from 3.9 to 2.7 per cent in the same period. By 2000, Europe was spending on average 1.7 per cent of its GDP annually on defence in contrast to 3 per cent in the United States (Shepherd 2003: 49).

The situation has changed somewhat since the attacks on 9/11. However, defence budgets have increased in Britain, France and Germany only marginally, and not significantly, in relation to GDP. Between 2006 and 2010, Germany's defence budget increased from €27.9 billion, to €30.1 billion, and between 2006 and 2007, France's defence budget increased from €35.4 billion to €36.1 billion (IISS 2007: 116, 110, 148, 2010: 124; Sattler 2006: 280). In Britain, the 2007 *Comprehensive Spending Review* announced that the defence budget would rise to £34 billion in 2008–9, £35.3 billion in 2009–10 and £36.9 billion in 2010–11 (Cornish and Dorman 2009: 258; HM Treasury 2007: 231;[6] IISS 2010: 158). Sarkozy's *Livre Blanc* represents an important departure for France. In it, Sarkozy has pledged €377 million for the armed forces from 2012 until 2020, with €200 million assigned to equipment; just over €47 million a year.[7] Interestingly, Sarkozy has called for a 'massive' investment in intelligence. This will involve re-structuring defence institutions as well as the development of tactical surveillance assets. These are important changes. Nevertheless, not only are these increases relatively small, starting from a low starting point, but they are also fragile. For instance, in December 2008, following the collapse of the financial system, British defence spending was the first public sector to be targeted for cuts by the government despite the *Comprehensive Spending Review*'s commitment to 1.5% increases in defence spending up to 2010–11 (HM Treasury 2007: 231). The Royal Navy's aircraft carriers, the RAF's new Typhoon fighter and the Army's Future Rapid Effects System vehicle have all been delayed by two years at least. Indeed, in 2008 and 2009, substantially as a result of the recession, French defence spending declined from €36 billion in 2007 to €30 billion in 2008 and €32 billion in 2009 (IISS 2010: 119). Even though the German defence budget has not yet been reduced,

[6] www.hm-treasury.gov.uk/d/pbr_csr07_annexd8_143.pd.
[7] http://tempsreel.nouvelobs.com/actualites/social/%2020080617.OBS8774/armee__nicolas_sarkozy_confirme_une_baisse_des_effectif.html.

there is significant doubt whether the projected increase in the German defence budget will survive political pressures. Even if it does, it is questionable whether such a small increment on an already meagre defence budget will be sufficient to implement the very ambitious programme of reform outlined by Peter Struck in 2004. Several significant commentators have maintained that funds will be insufficient and note that no increased budget has been secured (Sattler 2006: 279):

A real rise in the defence budget requires a successful reform of the social service system, continuing economic growth, the decline of unemployment and the consolidation of the public spending budget . . . Since there is no possibility of these scenarios in the foreseeable future, a responsible defence policy should be ready to bridge the coming years by muddling through. (2006: 288)

Sattler concludes:

The responsible use of soldiers and Alliance partners demands an honest consideration of all aspects of the procurement plan in relation to current adaptation goals, a subsequent prioritisation in relation to the deployable posture of an intervention army and a cancelling of all prestige procurement plans which do not match current needs . . . On its 60th Birthday (2015), the Bundeswehr does not want good wishes but the presents its 50th Birthday (2005) demanded.[8] (2006: 288)

Franz-Josef Jung's 2006 *White Paper* does not suggest there is much optimism in this area (Bundesministerium der Verteidigung 2006). The *White Paper* notes that defence spending is some €3 billion below 1991 levels, but insists that 'there is no margin for any further reductions in spending' (2006: 62). Yet the document sounds a note of caution: 'The ever present dichotomy between the requirements of defence policy and the financial needs of other national tasks will continue into the future' (2006: 10). It is unclear whether, especially following the current financial

---

[8] One of the most important features of European defence spending is its relative decline in relation to the United States, to whom its military transformation is institutionally tied through NATO. European NATO military expenditure declined steadily between 1996 and 2007 from 2.16% of GDP to 1.73% (IISS 2007: 98, 2010: 106); non-NATO European military expenditure shows a similar decline from 1.75% of GDP to 1.19% (IISS 2007: 102, 2010: 110) Thus, by the early 2000s European NATO nations spent $150 billion annually on defence in contrast to the $380 billion spent by the United States in 2003. While the US figure rose to $450 billion by 2007, the combined budgets of European NATO and non-NATO EU countries have continued to decline (Binnendijk and Kugler 2002: 122). There is an increasing divergence between Europe and the United States, which has increased following the 9/11 attacks despite the new global deployments being demanded of European armed forces. The armed forces are fully aware of these pressures which budgetary constraints place upon them. British, German and French generals have stressed the problems of financial constraints in reforming their forces and adapting to new operations.

crisis, the Bundeswehr will be able to defend its projected budget in the face of the demands of other public services.

The problem is not merely that current budgets may be insufficient, but that they are declining in real terms all the time. In their interesting analysis of defence budgets, Alexander and Garden have described the predicament facing European militaries as 'the arithmetic of defence policy': 'it is increasingly apparent that, looking over the next two decades, the traditional national approaches to defence problems are not going to provide adequately for Europe's defence and wider security needs' (2001: 509). The problem is not simply that defence budgets have tended to decline in relative terms as a percentage of GDP due to political pressures, but that in absolute terms these budgets are also shrinking. The problem here is the dramatic inflation within the military sector. While personnel and running costs have generally matched the rate of inflation, 'each generation of combat aircraft has been significantly more expensive in real terms than the one it replaced' (2001: 517, 516). Focusing on the United Kingdom, Alexander and Garden note that: 'If all goes well, the UK will have sustained growth of around 3% GDP. If it manages to keep defence spending level in real terms, its share of GDP will have declined to 1.3% by 2020.' Defence programmers in this situation will have to reduce the size of forces and the number of platforms so radically that on this model the United Kingdom will have negligible military capability. The problem is that the inflationary situation will affect all European nations: 'Our European allies will be following a similar path towards having no useful military capability – indeed, many are a long way down this path already' (2001: 521).

The budgetary problems which confront Europe's armed forces are compounded by the inefficiency of the military industrial base. The defence industry has been a sensitive area of national sovereignty. States have never wanted to be dependent on others for the production of their military capabilities. Moreover, especially in the twentieth century, military production has become a major form of employment for the workforce. Richard Overy (2006) has emphasised the significance of war production in reviving the US economy after the Depression in the 1930s. Similarly, in Europe, defence industries have been fragmented into discrete national markets. During most of the twentieth century, defence nationalisation was a sustainable policy. The infrastructure required to build even sophisticated modern military equipment could be lodged at the moderate level of national production units. Towards the end of the twentieth century and especially after the Cold War, such a model of industrial production has become unviable in Europe. As a result of technological advances in micro-electronics and computing, the capital and infrastructure required to develop and manu-facture new military equipment exceeds the traditional national industrial base. Moreover, in the light of the reduction in defence budgets, the national market is no longer generally sufficient to sustain the develop-ment of a major project. Consequently, European nations have increas-ingly sought to commit themselves to transnational procurement programmes. For instance, in order to suppress costs, Britain, France, Italy, Germany and Turkey jointly committed themselves to the develop-ment of a strategic transport aeroplane, the A400M. As Alexander and Garden described (2001), co-operative procurement projects are a rational response to economic problems, but they create their own prob-lems. They require co-ordination and co-operation. For instance, Germany unilaterally reduced its order of A400Ms from seventy-five to sixty-five, threatening to increase the unit costs for all partners. At the same time in the 1990s, partly encouraged by the Commission, there has been a trend towards transnational mergers of the European defence base (Bitzinger 2003). Major national companies have merged with compatible entities in other countries. The appearance of British Aerospace Systems and, most famously, the European Aeronautic Defence and Space Company are examples of this trend. Nevertheless, while the development of a transnational industrial base and procurement agreements have been significant developments, Europe still falls a long way short of the United States in terms of efficiency. Despite the development of transnational industrial production, Europe's defence base is still contoured by national interests and agendas. Unlike the United States, Europe does not enjoy an economy of scale, and the enduring fragmentation of the defence indus-trial base ensures that European defence budgets buy less for their money than their US counterparts. European armed forces are doubly disadvan-taged economically. The long-term decline in defence budgets, especially in relation to GDP, and the inflation of costs have led to the reduction in force sizes across Europe. 'Down-sizing' is the inevitable result of relative reductions in defence spending and inflation.

Concentration

From the 1970s, sociologists began to record the decline of the mass army, emphasising the process of fairly dramatic reduction which has occurred since the end of the Cold War (Haltiner 1998; Kelleher 1978; Martin 1977; Van Doorn 1968). Martin Shaw's concept of the 'post-military society' (1991) is an exploration of the social and political implications of this retraction of the armed forces. In his work on the rise of a 'new military', Christopher Dandeker (1994: 645–7, 1998) has similarly emphasised the gradual appearance of smaller ('down-sized'), more agile and professional forces in the last decades of the twentieth century; he, too, describes a process of concentration (see also Manigart 2003: 331). Similarly, Kaldor *et al.* (1998) have discussed the disappearance of mass armies. Although its has provoked criticism (Booth *et al.* 2001), Moskos' postmodern military might also be read as a contribution to the end of the mass army thesis, where smaller forces have replaced the large conscript armies of the twentieth century. This study regards this long-term historical process as fundamental. However, it does not primarily see the numerical diminution of the armed forces merely in terms of reduction or decline.

Today's armed forces are significantly smaller than their forebears in the Cold War; indeed, in most European countries they are the smallest they have been for over a century, and even longer in the case of Britain. However, despite the economic constraints the armed forces should not be understood merely as in numeric decline. They are qualitatively different from the European forces of the twentieth century. As they have become professionalised, they have specialised. Indeed, as they have moved to a professional model, resources have focused on particular forces within the military; investment has been directed to selected forces which have actually increased in size and capability. The concept of downsizing is not wrong – forces are shrinking – but it may not capture the full dynamic of contemporary military transformation. Although national forces have decreased in absolute size, there are some interesting trends within Europe's armed forces which need to be recognised and which, in fact, contrast almost directly with the general trajectory of decline. Selected elements of the armed forces have benefited from increased investment, strategic priority and, above all, professionalisation (in the sense of the institution of full-term career soldiers and an increase in expertise). These forces are more capable than their Cold War forebears and, accordingly, it may be more accurate to describe the dynamics of military transformation not as one of reduction – of down-sizing – but of concentration: a condensation of military power rather than its mere diminution.

The process of concentration is observable in all three of Europe's major military powers. Britain is unusual in Europe in that it abolished conscription in 1963, nearly forty years before most other European countries. Consequently, for most of the Cold War, Britain's forces were relatively small in comparison with their European partners which were able to field much larger (mainly conscript) armies. It might be argued that Britain had already begun to concentrate itself in the 1960s as it began to professionalise. Even if that is the case, the process of concentration has been accelerated in the post-Cold War period. Since 1990, Britain's military capability has been significantly reduced; the number of service personnel dropped from 346,000 to 212,450 between 1977 and 2000, regiments and battalions declined from 114 to 76, frigates and destroyers from 50 to 31 and RAF squadrons from 38 to 22 (Alexander and Garden 2001: 515). Since 2001, Britain's armed forces have been reduced still further to approximately 180,000 personnel. On land, while it retains a NATO corps headquarters (the Allied Rapid Reaction Corps Headquarters, ARRC), Britain no longer possesses an organic corps formation (of 60,000) as it did during the Cold War: the British Army on the Rhine based on 1 Corps has been dismantled. In its place, Britain currently possesses two deployable divisions (of approximately 15,000 troops each), 3 and 1 Division, and eight deployable brigades: three light (3 Commando Brigade, 16 Air Assault Brigade and 19 Brigade), three medium (12, 4 and 1 Mechanised Brigades) and two heavy (20 and 7 Armoured Brigades). Britain's armed forces today are smaller than their Cold War professional forebears, but they demonstrate some improved capabilities especially in terms of their relative sizes. Indeed, in areas of mobility, strike and Intelligence, Surveillance, Target Acquisition, Reconnaissance (ISTAR) assets, they have capacities which were absent in the past. More specifically, there has been an active attempt to exploit existing and new capabilities by uniting the best forces from across the services. Following the Conservative Government's White Paper on defence, *Options for Change*, in 1991, a Joint Rapid Deployment Force (JRDF) was formed in April 1996. The JRDF brought together specialist units from the three services to create a unified formation which was capable of rapid global deployment. In the late 1990s, the importance of the JRDF was affirmed and extended by New Labour's 1998 *Strategic Defence Review* (McInnes 1998). The JRDF was converted into a Joint Rapid Reaction Force (JRRF) which had a more permanent and established institutional footing with units more closely integrated with one another. The JRRF has only ever been used for Operation Palliser in Sierra Leone in 1999. However, the elements, especially elite ground troops, which make up the force have been consistently favoured in terms of investment and operations since that time. Britain has focused its resources on this force so that the concept of a 'two-tier' army has now been discussed referring to units within the JRRF and those outside it.[9]

---

[9] For a longer discussion of this process of concentration, see Chapter 8.

Even with an all volunteer professional force of long-standing, the appearance of an elite core is observable.[10]

Despite its early professionalisation, the example of the United Kingdom is not unusual in Europe. France's armed forces had declined from 573,000 military and civilian personnel in 1996 to 440,000 in 2002. By 2007 this figure had declined further to 354,000.[11] However, once the gendarmerie at 96,000 and civilian administrators at 47,000 are excluded from this figure, France's armed forces similarly consist of 211,000 personnel, with an army of 136,000, in contrast to over 300,000 thirty years ago, and they have been fundamentally reformed. The poor performance of French forces in the Gulf in 1991 shocked France. France could deploy only 14,000 soldiers to form the Daguet Division, even though their army at a strength of 280,000 was more than double the size of the British Army who deployed 40,000 troops. Moreover, these troops were of little operational value since they were improperly trained and equipped to integrate with US forces (Bratton 2002: 92; McKenna 1997: 133). The performance of French troops in the Gulf led to the publication of the 1994 *Livre Blanc* which outlined military reform (Bratton 2002: 92). In 1996, Jacques Chirac announced that the French military would be converted to an all-volunteer force with the abolition of military service by 2002 and initiated the Military Planning Act (Johnsen *et al.* 1999: 63; McKenna 1997: 136). More recently, in 2005, the French established a new Corps Headquarters, based on the old French 1 Corps in Lille, to command these deployable forces. They have organised their land forces into eight independent combined brigades. Like the British, the French retained heavy capabilities in the form of two armoured and two mechanised brigades, but their forces structure has shifted towards lighter forces which consist of two light armoured brigades, including the amphibious 9 brigade légère blindée de marine, one mountain brigade and two airborne brigades (including Foreign Legion battalions). Significantly, the marine

---

[10] A similar process is observable among British headquarters. During the Cold War, operations were commanded by three separate military headquarters, Land, Fleet and Strike. However, the Permanent Joint Headquarters (PJHQ) established in 1994 now plans and commands British operations worldwide; it has jurisdiction over all operationally deployed British forces. The old independent service commands, Land, Strike and Fleet, remain but they are principally tasked to generate the forces which PJHQ then commands on operations. Britain's all-volunteer force is certainly smaller than its Cold War predecessor and is under huge financial pressure. However, it is not accurate to understand current processes merely as decline and reduction. Some elements of Britain's armed forces are more potent than ever; they are recipients of major investment. PJHQ and the JRRF would be prime examples here; they represent the concentration of resourcing and professional expertise.

[11] Official French military presentation, Joint Services Command and Staff College, 2006.

and mountain troops and the Foreign Legion were the only professional formation throughout the post-Second World War period and conducted overseas operations in Algeria, Chad and the Ivory Coast. During this period, they were peripheral to France's force structure. They have now become its core element. The armed forces will be reduced in total to approximately 225,000 in the next six to seven years. The Army will lose 17 per cent of its personnel, the air force 24 per cent and the navy 11 per cent, reducing the forces to 131,000, 50,000 and 44,000, respectively. Significantly, the reductions will be focused on logistics and support units, which currently represent 60% of the armed forces, rather than on operationally deployable forces: 'My concept of the armed forces assures national security not the management of territory.' Sarkozy's *Livre Blanc* is an active attempt to augment the capabilities of France's armed forces while shedding superfluous numbers. Investment will be focused on the remaining, rationalised forces. France's armed forces are not simply shrinking; they are changing in structure and capability. French forces are beginning to concentrate themselves into professional and specialised units which are more expert and capable than their mass, conscript forebears.

During the Cold War, the Bundeswehr was 500,000 strong, but this figure declined dramatically in the 1990s. After the implementation of the Scharping reforms in 2001, the Bundeswehr shrank from 338,000 in the 1990s to 277,000 by the early 2000s (Longhurst 2000: 36–7; Meiers 2001: 17; Scharping 2000; Shepherd 2000: 22). Following Struck's Defence Policy Guidelines in 2003, the Bundeswehr was reduced yet further to 252,000 in 2010. The decline is particularly marked in Germany because during the Cold War the National People's Army of the Democratic Republic of Germany consisted of some 300,000 personnel, making the total number of German military personnel during the Cold War some 800,000. Today, the re-unified Germany has a military force which is a little more than a quarter of that which the divided Germany contributed to NATO and the Warsaw Pact in the Cold War. Peter Struck's reforms aim to restructure the Bundeswehr so that it consists of a smaller but more professional core. The prime force will be a specialist 35,000 rapid reaction force, augmented by a 70,000 stabilisation or reinforcement force and a tertiary 135,000 support force (Leersch 2003). Germany's rapid reaction force involves the development of innovative new formations. Although the Bundeswehr provides commanders and officers for the German–Netherlands Corps and for Eurocorps, the German field army no longer operates at corps level as it did during the Cold War. German forces are organised into five divisions. While five mechanised divisions form the backbone of the future Germany Army, a specialist operations division (Division Spezielle Operationen) has been created consisting of two Airborne Brigades 26 and 31 and, particularly notably, the Kommando Spezialkräfte (Special Forces Command) was established on 1 April 1996. The Ministry of Defence has been explicit that it is following a strategy of concentration. In order to offset budgetary cuts, the *White Paper* of 2006 declared that: 'A multitude of measures are helping to reduce operating expenditure. They essentially include further personnel cutbacks, the new stationing concept, material and equipment planning, and continued stripping-out of bureaucracy ... The Bundeswehr will consistently concentrate on its core tasks' (Bundesministerium der Verteidigung 2006: 62).

Of the major European powers, only Germany still retains national service (Wehrdienst) for historic and political reasons which seem to deny the process of concentration. Germany still seems to be wedded to a mass, participatory model of the armed forces rather than a profession-alised, specialist military. In fact, there has been extensive debate about the issue of conscription since the 1990s. In October 1998, Gerhard Schröder commissioned two independent reviews of the German armed forces by Richard von Weizsäcker and Inspector General Hans-Peter von Kirchbach, respectively (Sarotte 2001: 34). The Weizsäcker report was extremely critical of German military capabilities, arguing that the Bundeswehr was 'too big, ill-composed and increasingly out of step with the times' (Maull 2000; Meiers 2001; Sarotte 2001: 36). Weizsäcker saw no future for the current structure, though he regarded conscription in some form as a continuing necessity. Von Kirchbach's report was more conciliatory and, in the end, Scharping adopted von Kirchbach's report almost totally. However, the number of conscripts has been reduced in the German armed forces and normal military service has been reduced to 9 months with an option to extend to 23 months, but they are still significantly short of an all-professional force. There is little sign that national service will be abolished. German generals are publicly unani-mous that its retention is essential. Peter Struck, while acting as Defence Minister, was adamant about its retention; his successor Franz-Josef Jung has confirmed its status. The military and political consensus is that conscription ensures a close connection between civil society and the armed forces; conscription maintains political oversight and sustains moderation by ensuring that the Bundeswehr is populated by individuals from the entire spectrum of German society. The fear is that without this civil–military connection, extremists will infiltrate the Bundeswehr. The fear of a radicalised Bundeswehr is understandable given the history of Germany and there is no prospect of establishing an all-volunteer Bundeswehr in the coming decade. Indeed, Peter Struck advanced some plausible reasons for the retention of conscription. Conscription, he emphasised, remains a major source of recruitment for the Bundeswehr, as a proportion of national service personnel become full career professionals. As Struck appositely noted in a barbed observation, that while all-volunteer forces like Britain have to recruit soldiers from across the world, who have little connection to Britain, the Bundeswehr has been able to sustain its numbers from the domiciled citizens of Germany.

Continued national service distinguishes Germany from its European allies, but its retention does not fundamentally deny the thesis of concentration. With a projected force of 252,000 out of a population of over 80 million, the Bundeswehr cannot realistically be described as a mass formation. Moreover, the process of concentration has, in effect, been institutionalised by the retention of conscription. There are volunteer national service personnel in interventionist brigades like Airborne Brigade 26 but, proportionately, national service personnel are assigned duties in the augmentation or stabilisation forces. Although national service is costly for the Bundeswehr and may have reduced investment in capabilities and expertise, it has institutionalised the development of a two-tier military. In Germany, an interventionist core, consisting of professional soldiers and long-term national service volunteers, has crystallised over the last decade, supplemented and supported by a periphery consisting of a professional cadre and national service personnel. The retention of conscription has formalised the process of concentration in Germany giving it a legal, institutional basis.

Indeed, investment patterns in the Bundeswehr affirm the creation of a core and periphery. While new formations like the Division Spezielle Operationen are privileged in the level of resourcing they receive, there are serious shortfalls in financing which only accentuate both the problems of budget and the process of concentration. Struck's reforms create a three-tier military. Although some strategic explanation of this division has been made, the underlying rationale is financial. The Bundeswehr has insufficient funds to provide the same level of investment to all its forces. Indeed, even within the same divisions there are discrepancies in investment which are the result of financial constraint rather than operational utility. For instance, two of the parachute battalions in the Division Spezielle Operationen are resourced for reaction, while the other two in Brigade 31 are only stabilisation forces. Ideally, both would be capable of intervention and resourced for that level of mission. However, the funding is lacking to maintain all the battalions at that level of training. The intervention forces in the Bundeswehr represent a deliberate attempt to concentrate defence resourcing in a small number of favoured units at a time of fiscal constraint.

In the face of defence budgets which are declining in relative and absolute terms it is possible to identify a developmental trajectory for Europe's armed forces. In the face of new strategic demands and reduced defence budgets, Europe's armed forces have drastically reduced in size since 1990; on average they are approximately a half to two-thirds of their size during the Cold War. However, they have not merely shrunk or down-sized. Mere reduction misrepresents the details of current defence dynamics. The armed forces as a whole are smaller and significant elements in them are less capable and less well resourced than in the Cold War. However, certain favoured elements, namely, specialist, light, interventionist forces, have grown in relative and often absolute size and enjoy a higher level of investment than in the Cold War. In his analysis of the rise of special operations forces (SOF), Rune Henriksen has usefully elucidated the wider logic of concentration: 'With limited budget, political will and manpower, Western militaries are being forced to make sure every individual who is willing to fight is not just an able individual, but a very capable one. This is in part the reason for the relative doctrinal surge of SOF in postmodern militaries' (Henriksen 2007: 214). In Britain, France and Germany, it is possible to trace the concentration of military capability within each army. Overseas commitments to the Balkans and, above all, Afghanistan, has propelled this logic of concentration yet further. Only highly trained, expert forces seem to be appropriate for new missions. In particular, the most specialised and professional elements of Europe's forces are increasingly involved in the Afghan operation. In the cases of Britain, France and Germany, their elite forces (especially paratroopers) have dominated the deployment and suffered the majority of casualties; the deaths of the French paratroops in August 2008 should not be seen as a tragic contingency. It was a manifestation of this process of concentration in which particular kinds of troops, favoured by defence policy, have taken a prominent position in current operations.

It does not seem to be coincidental that the decline of the mass army began to be noticed in the 1970s at precisely the time that the mass industrial workforce was dissipating (Amin 1995; Harrison 1994: 194ff; Hutton 1996; Jürgens 1989; Jürgens et al. 1986: 265; Lane 1988; Murray 1990; Piore and Sabel 1984; Smith 1997: 321; Vallas 1999; Wood 1989). From the 1970s, economic globalisation fragmented established markets and created new competitive pressures, compelling Fordist industries in Europe and America to reform themselves. In the 1990s, the armed forces have faced consonant strategic pressures as a result of globalisation; new competitors have appeared while budgets have been reduced. In the face of related global pressures, military and industrial institutions began to reform themselves. The current concentration of Europe's armed forces into smaller but more professional cores accords similarly with developments in production. Just as the mass workforce has been replaced by a specialist core, so the mass military is being superseded by an all-volunteer, professional elite. As in industry, the appearance of this new military core has involved the creation of new kinds of military organisation – new headquarters and new brigades – new kinds of soldiers and different concepts of operation. The purpose of this book is to try and provide some insight into selected aspects of these important historical transformations.

Transnationalisation

At NATO's Lisbon Conference in 1952, the Long Term Defence Plan called for ninety-six ready and reserve divisions, with a standing force of thirty divisions in the central area. Only eleven ready and three reserve divisions actually existed before 1952 and they were poorly equipped and trained (Duffield 1995: 30). By 1952, the situation had improved modestly: twenty-five ready divisions were stationed in Germany, though this had fallen to eighteen divisions by 1956. During the 1950s, NATO's conventional force structure fluctuated dramatically, but after 1960 its conventional force posture remained stable. NATO forces fielded between twenty-six and twenty-eight divisions in Europe for the rest of the Cold War; almost half a million men were at arms. However, once the reserve divisions were activated, NATO had over 1.5 million troops at its disposal. NATO's land forces, consisting primarily of heavy armoured and mechanised forces, were organised in a NATO 'layer-cake' (Figure 2.1) along the West German border. More or less independent national corps, each of about four divisions or 60,000 troops, were assigned their own areas of responsibility with clear lines of demarcation between them. Logistics and support were provided autonomously by each nation. Within their areas, the corps operated autonomously under NATO's Main Defence Plans. In the 1980s, some attempt was made to unlock the rigid structure of the NATO force posture to facilitate movement across corps lines and to create rapid reaction forces capable of deploying for intervention or reinforcement. However, overwhelmingly the corps borders remained. NATO was an international organisation. Nations co-operated with each other for a common goal, but there was minimal interaction between nations below government level.

This 'strategic' – or military – geography (Faringdon 1986) has undergone fundamental revision since the end of the Cold War. In the mid-1990s, a wave of multinational formations came into being, such as the German–Netherlands Corps, Multinational Division Centre (Germany,

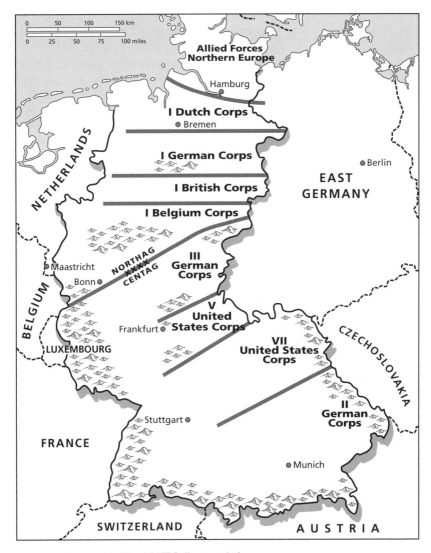

Figure 2.1 The NATO 'layer-cake'

Belgium, Holland and the United Kingdom), Eurofor (the Rapid Deployment Force) (France, Italy, Portugal and Spain) and Euromarfor (European Maritime Force) (France, Italy, Portugal and Spain) which fundamentally altered the character of the NATO alliance (Cameron 1999: 75; Edwards 2000: 8). One of the most significant of these was the Franco-German brigade which was founded in 1987 and subsequently became Eurocorps when Spanish and Benelux elements were incorporated into the formation in 1992 (van Ham 1999: 6). Multinationalisation was an understandable response to the immediate post-Cold War context. Multinational formations offered nations a means of sustaining their military capability in the face of often drastic budgetary reductions. At the same time, national militaries and NATO itself supported the formation of these multinational formations because they maintained the Alliance at a time when there was significant scepticism about it. Whatever their operational usefulness, these formations affirmed the commitment to the Alliance and made it difficult for governments to dissolve them. While it is potentially possible for any member to disband independent national forces, it is much more difficult to withdraw from multinational commitments.

These multinational formations have not been irrelevant to the transformation of Europe's forces. However, increasingly a process of transnationalisation – of cross-national co-operation and interaction – has occurred in theatre. Here under the pressure of new missions, which have to be conducted with minimal resources and personnel, transnational accommodations have been demanded by operational need. Accordingly, in contrast to the clearly defined national corps areas in the Cold War, the Balkans demanded a different approach from Western forces, especially since nations lacked the capability and will to take on the operations unilaterally. Consequently, small national contingents, typically of company or battle group size, were assigned contiguous areas of operation under a multinational command structure. Battalions and even companies began to operate together. This first occurred under the United Nations Protection Force (UNPROFOR) in Bosnia and was formalised under NATO in December 1995 with the Intervention Force (IFOR) and its eventual conversion into the Stabilisation Forces (SFOR). In many cases, the development of these transnational relations was quite informal and unplanned. Indeed, General Sir Michael Rose, Commander of UNPROFOR in 1994, colourfully records the way in which shared social events encouraged increased co-operation:

Some evenings I would dine with Soubirou [Brigadier General André, French commander, Sector Sarajevo]. After dinner he would call on his officers one by one to sing legionnaire songs, which are very slow, with a sadness all of their own. One evening he invited a colonel to declaim Victor Hugo's 'Waterloo'. By the end, everyone including the British, had tears in their eyes at the image of wavering lines of soldiers vanishing into the smoke and fire of battle. (Rose 1999: 40)

These novel transnational relations began to be institutionalised as stabilised command structures developed in Bosnia. Thus, by 2000 Britain, France,

Germany and Italy had taken command of regional multinational task forces in Bosnia, built around a national battle group but including significant forces from other nations. A similar arrangement was developed in Kosovo. National forces began to co-operate with each other at ever lower levels during these stabilisation operations within and across the multinational areas. Moreover, and distinctively, national forces came under the tactical command of other nations. A company or battalion from one Western nation was often commanded by a brigade or battle group commander from another NATO country. Thus, when EUFOR took over Bosnia in 2004, only 7,000 of the original 60,000 NATO force still remained in theatre. These forces were organised into four multinational task forces: North-west, North-east, Central and South. In the North-west, the British-led task force was structured around a British battle group (and included a significant Dutch contingent) until its withdrawal in March 2006. In the other areas, there were composite task forces with rotating commands.

Current operations in Afghanistan demonstrate transnational linkages at their most developed. Since the assumption of command by NATO in 2006, Afghanistan has been administered by four regional commands, East (United States), North, West and South. The Germans command a Regional Command North, based at Mazar-e-Sharif, of some 4,500 troops with augmentations from other countries. The Spanish and Italians have created a joint Regional Command West with rotating command positions. Beneath the Italian or Spanish commander, these countries have provided more or less an equal contingent of troops for Nimroz, Farah and Herat. The British, Dutch and Canadian Regional Command South was established in April 2006. A rotating Dutch, Canadian and British two-star general now commands three national task forces which have increased to approximately brigade size. In Regional Command South, major tactical operations at battalion and brigade size are being conducted under a multinational command structure. The contrast to the Cold War is stark, where, in line with NATO doctrine, command remained exclusively national up to corps level of 60,000 troops.[12] In the current era it is possible for companies of 100 soldiers or less to be commanded by an officer from another nationality.

Indeed, in Afghanistan transnational co-operation has not merely involved a willingness to be commanded by another nation or to work

---

[12] The Korean War provides a deeply interesting comparison to current operations in Afghanistan as European battalions and two British brigades fought under US command in a manner which has evident parallels with Afghanistan. However, in contrast to the current 'transnational' arrangements, at that time European governments were willing to relinquish control of their troops to other nations. This is particularly evidenced in April 1951 when Britain lost an entire battalion because of a misunderstanding between the

on a multinational staff. Distinctively, troops in the field are operating together on high-intensity missions. Indeed, these dense transnational relations have become essential among European NATO forces, which have struggled to deploy sufficient troops. In 2006, while he commanded ISAF, General Richards, for instance, emphasised the innovativeness of these new transnational arrangements:

> In the south, this is the 'new NATO'. How deeply it is transforming is demonstrated by Operation Turtle. We moved the best part of a Portuguese company in 7 C-130s from Kabul to Farah. We got support troops patrolling there; in fact one has been killed. The omens are good therefore.
>   The Italians, for instance, had provided two companies and a Special Forces Task Force. (General David Richards[13])

His description of Operation Turtle is more widely corroborated. In 2008, 16 Air Assault Brigade deployed to Helmand province for a second tour. On its previous deployment, due principally to undermanning, the Brigade had failed to contribute to an important NATO operation to defeat a Taliban assault on Kandahar in August 2006. The British Helmand Task Force was focused on its national objectives. However, during the 2008 deployment, it assigned one of its battalions (3rd Battalion the Parachute Regiment) to the Regional South Command to act as the theatre response force. Partly as a result of this assignment, the Helmand Task Force was able to draw on a transnational force of Canadians, Danish, Australian and US forces to conduct possibly the most important operation which British forces have commanded in Afghanistan: Operation Oqab Tsuka in September 2008 to deliver a new turbine to the Kajaki dam.[14] Similarly, in December 2008, a major British operation, involving the seizure of insurgent strongholds, was similarly conducted with Danish tanks and Estonian troops.[15]

Conclusion

Europe's armed forces are in a vexatious predicament. At a time when they are smaller than they have been for nearly 200 years, they are being

British brigade commander and his US divisional commander. The armed forces co-operate ever more closely with each other today, but the state's sovereignty over them is also increasingly closely controlled.

[13] Personal interview, 16 July 2008.
[14] www.mod.uk/defenceinternet/defencenews/militaryoperations/kajakidamtroops returntobase.htm.
[15] www.mod.uk/DefenceInternet/DefenceNews/MilitaryOperations/InPicturesOpRed DaggerStrikesInHelmand.htm.

deployed globally on increasingly demanding stabilisation missions. In order to address these dual pressures, European states have effectively adopted a strategy which is evident in industry. States are concentrating their military power into a selected core of specialised professional forces. At the same time, in order to conduct current operations, European militaries have been forced to co-operate with each other ever more closely. European forces are now developing transnational relations at ever lower levels which would have been inconceivable during the Cold War. There is no prospect of a European army, however, in which nationality becomes irrelevant as member states commit forces to a supra-national command structure answering to the EU. Significantly, it is precisely the national military cores which are engaging in the most operations and which are therefore forming the most transnational link-ages. The military geography of Europe is changing. In the Cold War, the NATO alliances could be described as an international structure. National military forces, assigned a particular area of responsibility, had little horizontal interaction with other forces. National forces were co-ordinated above the level of national corps only. The conversion of political grand strategy into military strategy required international con-sent, but operational issues of how exactly each corps was to fight were under the jurisdiction of the nations. Today, a new transnational network is appearing in Europe between the concentrations of military power. The network paradoxically transcends national boundaries while simulta-neously affirming the link between the armed forces and the state. By examining Europe's new headquarters and reaction brigades sufficiently closely it may be possible to define this emergent transnational military network more precisely.

3 The capacity for autonomous action?

Military reformation is, predictably, taking place primarily within the framework of European nation-states. States have directed and funded military reforms and sanctioned increased transnational interaction between their forces on operations. However, although European states remain substantially autonomous in the realm of defence policy, military reforms within each nation have not occurred in isolation. On the contrary, European military transformation has been facilitated by wider institutional frameworks which transcend the state. In particular, national military development has occurred within existing international structures and, above all, NATO and the EU. States have not autonomously developed their own military reform strategies. On the contrary, they have interacted through NATO and the EU and sought actively to converge with each other on the basis of cues from other member states and alliance partners. Britain and France have conducted a number of autonomous missions since the end of the Cold War but, for the most part, European nations have conducted operations as part of a coalition. In order to gain an accurate perspective on European military development, the relative importance of NATO and the EU for European military development must be ascertained. It is necessary to establish where the key international influence for military reform lies and which of these international organisations has been primary in encouraging European militaries to converge on a similar expeditionary form for global stabilisation missions. There are only two institutions which are relevant in this sphere: NATO and the EU.

For the European Union

For some commentators, there is little doubt which organisation is becoming the prime reference point for European military development. In his recent book, Seth Jones explicitly seeks to challenge 'the deep scepticism about the extent of European security cooperation' (2007: 5). For him, institutionalised European security co-operation represents

46

the future. Jones has been deeply impressed by the St Malo agreement of 4 December 1998, when Tony Blair and Jacques Chirac took what appeared to be an historic step for European military development at the Breton port. There, Blair and Chirac announced their commitment to co-operative military action as a 'significant step forward'. As a result of the St Malo announcement, the European Security and Defence Policy (ESDP) was developed as a specific programme within the Common Foreign and Security Policy (CFSP) at the Cologne Summit in 1999, setting ambitious goals for Europe: 'the Union must have the capacity for autonomous action, backed up by credible military forces, the means to decide to use them and a readiness to do so, in order to respond to international crises' (European Council, 3–4 June 1999). Jones has taken this declaration as evidence of the creation of a European defence community sixty years after initial efforts to create one foundered.

According to Jones, the origins of European security co-operation lie in 'the structural shifts in both the international and European systems' (Jones 2007: 8). As a result of the end of the bipolar Cold War, EU states have been able to project power abroad and to increase their autonomy from the United States; indeed, they have felt compelled to develop an independent security and defence capacity (2007: 9). At the same time, while the United States does not, of course, pose a military threat to Europe, its unipolarity does encourage EU states to aggregate power. Consequently, for Jones, the future of European security – but, more relevant here, defence – co-operation lies not in NATO but in the EU. Citing a speech in which Gerhard Schröder claimed that 'it [NATO] is no longer the primary venue where transatlantic partners discuss and coordinate strategies', Jones claims that European states are increasingly looking to the EU as their primary security institution (2007: 55). Indeed, Jones is finally condemnatory about NATO:

NATO still exists – and may continue to exist – as a transatlantic defence organisation, even though it increasingly resembles Oscar Wilde's Dorian Gray. It appears youthful and robust as it grows older, but is becoming ever more infirm. The North Atlantic Treaty will likely remain in force, NATO may even continue to issue upbeat communiqués and conduct joint training exercises, and the Brussels bureaucracy may keep NATO's webpage updated – so long as NATO isn't actually asked to do that much else. (2007: 56)

By contrast, Jones claims to have identified the origins not just of some sharing of security concerns and roles, but of genuine military co-operation. Jones cites the Headline Goal (the Helsinki proposal for a 60,000-strong rapid reaction force), EU battle groups (the 2004 proposal for small, 1,500-strong reaction forces) and Europe's missions to

Macedonia, Congo and Bosnia as evidence of growing military co-operation.

A number of European commentators have shared Jones' analysis of European defence development. In his work on the changing international order, Robert Cooper has been a strong advocate for the EU as a governance model: 'The logic of European integration is that Europe should, sooner or later, develop common foreign policy and a common security policy and, probably, a common defence' (Cooper 2004: 171). Mark Leonard shares Jones' perspective on Europe and, following Michael O'Hanlon (1997), argues that 'by diverting just 10 per cent of their defence budgets to buy specific types of equipment – such as long-range transport planes and ships, unmanned aerial vehicles and precision guided missiles – within a decade, they could deploy 200,000 high-quality professional soldiers anywhere in the world' (Leonard 2005: 67–8). Sven Biscop (2005, 2009) and Jolyon Howorth (2007) similarly advocate that European security strategy represents a positive global commitment.[1]

Euroscepticism

Jones' enthusiastic and well-informed Euro-advocacy is a useful contribution, especially to American security debates which have tended to dismiss the validity and even legitimacy of EU efforts at autonomy. However, it is hugely questionable whether Jones' optimistic assessment can be sustained. It is very doubtful whether the EU really is, or will be, the prime institutional framework in which military development will take place in the coming decade. Many commentators assess the prospects of European military transformation quite differently to Jones. James Sheehan has argued that EU states today have little genuine interest in military activity. Sheehan shares Jones' assessment of the strategic situation. Europe has been favoured by the post-Second World War international order in which the United States has guaranteed Western Europe its security. Precisely because of this favourable strategic situation, they have become unwilling to invest in their own militaries. For instance, the European rapid reaction force proposed at Helsinki requires computers, precision-guided munitions, lift and logistics which are likely to cost more than $50 billion but 'there is little evidence that most Europeans are

---

[1] More recently, Fotios Moustakis and Petros Violakis (2008) have outlined measures, especially in terms of military training, which would be required to fulfil the goals of the ESDP. They, like Jones, presume that these goals are both achievable and actively sought by European states. However, they identify 'structural' problems which have increasingly impeded EU developments.

willing to spend that kind of money' (Sheehan 2008: 217). Other commentators have affirmed the point. Gompert *et al.* (1999) have underscored the fragility of Europe's military power. While European nations have significant military power in global terms and Britain and France have small but relatively capable expeditionary forces, Europe lags far behind the United States in terms of critical military capabilities. European Union nations lack strategic air and maritime lift, intelligence, surveillance, target acquisition, reconnaissance (ISTAR), digital communications, precision-guided munitions and logistics support to conduct autonomous military operations today and the gap between them and the United States is increasing every year: 'Why European states share over 50 divisions that cannot be projected is harder to understand than why they have a handful that can' (Gompert *et al.* 1999: 10–11). Although Gompert *et al.* proposed a series of reforms to address the shortfalls, there is little evidence to suggest that Europe is, independently, significantly more capable than it was a decade ago when the study was published.

It is not merely that European nations are reluctant to invest in their armed forces. For Sheehan, the problem is more fundamental. The EU is not, and has no intention of becoming, a military power:

Because the European Union does not claim Carl Schmitt's 'monstrous capacity', the power of life and death, it does not need citizens who are prepared to kill and die. It needs only consumers and producers, who recognise that the community serves their interests and advances their individual well-being. And as consumers and producers, most European have usually been rather satisfied with the Union's accomplishments. (Sheehan 2008: 220)

The EU has been successful as an economic project which has required significant sovereignty-sharing in particular areas, but there is no prospect of a European unitary state with its own military force able to prosecute unified foreign policy goals: 'Viewed from the perspective of twentieth-century European history, we can understand why the European Union is not a superpower and why it is not likely to become one in the foreseeable future … As a result, the European Union may become a superstate – a super civilian state – but not a superpower' (Sheehan 2008: 220–1). Despite the Cologne Declaration's nominal intention of creating an 'autonomous capacity for action', European states have demonstrated only limited political will to create an effective EU defence capability. In this vein, Julian Lindley-French has expressed deep scepticism about whether the CFSP and the ESDP could be anything more than a latter-day Treaty of Locarno, tying states to mutual military support but ultimately proving empty (Lindley-French 2002: 790). Lindley-French points to fundamental flaws in the ESDP: 'the fanfares that marked the

Anglo-French relaunch of European defence at the St Malo summit in December 1998 have given way to growing belief that the ESDP is a sideshow for the British who are still, by and large, committed to their special relations with US and NATO' (2002: 792–3). However, France is in a similarly ambivalent position, 'unsure whether to place emphasis on a more nationally based security solution, a European solution or, indeed, a transnational solution' (2002: 793). Germany meanwhile 'thinks the enemy has gone away' and is reluctant to use military power at all (2002: 794). Lindley-French is critical of some aspects of US foreign policy and military doctrine, but Europe can realistically criticise the United States only if it invests in its military capabilities and demonstrates a will to act which was so manifestly lacking in the Balkans: 'What is needed is a new concert for Europe.' Yet, Lindley-French is pessimistic about the prospects of such unity. There seems to be a lack of political will to create an autonomous EU defence capability.

It might be argued that these expressions of scepticism are premature, written too early, before the ESDP has had time to develop. However, nearly a decade after the Helsinki Headline Goal, there is no prospect of Europe developing its own 60,000-strong rapid reaction force. This is not to deny that there have been some significant institutional developments. In February 2004, following a mini-summit, France, Germany and Britain proposed a 'battle group' concept. Instead of the Headline Goal of 60,000 troops restricted to Petersberg tasks, the three premiers sought to create a strategic concept which would be better adapted to the post-9/11 context. They emphasised that Europe needed a more responsive and flexible military, capable of deploying on a number of concurrent operations.[2] The proposed battle groups (based on battalions) would consist of about 1,500 troops including supporting elements and would be ready for deployment within fifteen days. The aim was to create two to three high readiness battle groups by 2005 and up to nine by 2007; and, indeed, a roster of EU battle groups has been established (Schmitt 2004: 98; Terriff 2004a: 150–76). The EU battle groups have been a useful performative statement of EU intent and evident training benefits have accrued from them. These units selected for EU battle group status have conducted exercises, which have improved their reactivity, while their rotation has encouraged some limited convergence of military

---

[2] General Klaus Naumann, the former Deputy SACEUR, has claimed that Europe should not be satisfied merely with 'clearing up work' (Aufraumenarbeit). For him, Europe must develop its defence capabilities so that it is a credible military actor in global politics. For Naumann, the EU needs to transcend merely Petersberg tasks, and the EU battle group concept seems to be a way of responding to Naumann's concepts. See Naumann (2000: 48).

expertise in Europe (Jacoby and Jones 2008: 316–17) . However, as yet no EU battle group has been deployed as such. Indeed, in a recent assessment of the ESDP, Anand Menon (2009) provides a sobering view of current developments. While he recognises that the ESDP is relatively new and the EU has conducted twenty-two missions under this policy, he identifies fundamental political, institutional and resourcing weaknesses at the heart of the ESDP. As Richard Gowan (2009)[3] has confirmed, the EU has not invested sufficiently in its armed forces, nor does it seem willing to employ it.

All these scholars identify the same underlying problem with the ESDP. There seems to be a fundamental lack of political willingness to commit to European operations. The EU has failed to generate the forces for its Headline Goal, a European rapid reaction force, and even the battle group project has been compromised by the reluctance of member states to contribute to it. As Britain's commitments to Iraq and, especially, to Afghanistan have become more burdensome, its initial participation in the ESDP has waned. Despite its advocacy of the battle group concept, Britain has not contributed to this development; its forces are already overcommitted. Although Germany remains formally committed to the ESDP, its willingness to contribute to the battle group programme is conditional. For instance, the EU mission to the Democratic Republic of Congo in 2006 posed significant problems for Germany. The mission was eventually scheduled for September to November 2006, when the German Fallschirmjägerbataillon (Parachute Battalion) 26/3 was on EU battle group stand-by duty. Operationally, the battalion could have deployed without excessive difficulty and, formally, it should have deployed. However, the German government was reluctant to release the battalion; the deployment did not seem to be in the national interest, it would incur costs and there was an element of risk involved (Menon 2009). Germany has appeared 'hostile to any European Union involvement in African interventions for a long time' (Bagayoko 2005: 100). Consequently, Berlin initially refused to deploy the battalion, insisting on support from other European nations. Eventually, France agreed to support the mission, providing most of the troops and the in-theatre commander, while Germany set up an 'operational' headquarters to co-ordinate the political–military interface with the EU: 'After a lot of fuss, Potsdam [Einsatzführungskommando] was stood up as a multinational Operational Headquarters (OHQ) quite smoothly. A German operational commander will work with a French force commander. They sorted out

---

[3] See www.europeanvoice.com/article/2009/02/europe-retreats/63883.aspx.

the force. It was a battle group size but it came from different places.' 'The Germans felt they had to deliver something',[4] but only a company from Germany's EU battle group (Bataillon 26/3) eventually deployed. In 2007, Angela Merkel announced that Germany was attracted by the possibility of an independent EU defence policy and this seemed to be a potentially important moment for the ESDP. Germany seemed to have revised its position following the success of the Congo mission. However, it subsequently refused to send troops on the EU mission to Chad in 2008. It seems likely that Merkel's sudden advocacy for EU action was a political ploy. She was not genuinely committing Germany to autonomous EU military action, but rather her appeal to the EU was designed to deflect the pressure which had been exerted on her government and the Bundeswehr for their refusal to deploy into the south of Afghanistan. Indeed, describing fundamental tensions between the commitment to the EU battle groups and to the NATO Response Force (NRF) (see Chapter 6), Esther Barbé and Elisabeth Johansson-Nogues have emphasised that Merkel 'favours a further expansion of the civilian facet of NATO's crisis management' (2008: 300)

France, of course, remains the nation most committed to the EU; the *Livre Blanc* (2008) has re-affirmed this commitment under the significant title of 'The European Ambition' (2008: 81). Yet France's own strategic orientation must be recognised before taking its advocacy of the ESDP as evidence of genuine European commitment to its own defence. France has long-standing strategic interests in Africa and has used the EU as a means of supporting its existing strategic goals in that theatre. In line with long-standing Gaullist traditions, France has also used the EU to assert its autonomy from the United States and NATO. The EU's first operation to the Congo,[5] Operation Artemis, demonstrates both of these features very clearly. In June 2003, the EU responded to a UN appeal for humanitarian assistance in the Democratic Republic of Congo. Under the ESDP, a force of 1,800 troops, of which 80 per cent were French (Loisel 2004: 85), were deployed to stabilise security conditions and assist in improving the humanitarian situation in Bunia, the capital of the Ituri region in Congo where the problems were most serious (Loisel 2004: 71–3; Missiroli 2003). The EU force was tasked with re-imposing peace in an area

---

[4] EU diplomat, personal interview, 12 May 2006.
[5] Since its formal ratification at the European Council meeting at Nice, the ESDP has been invoked for a number of military interventions, including a military peace support operation to the former Yugoslav Republic of Macedonia from March 2003, crisis management in the Democratic Republic of Congo from June until September 2003, EUFOR in Bosnia from 2004 to the present, the Lebanon in 2006, the Congo in 2006 and Chad in 2008.

which threatened the political stability of the entire region. The mission was successful, although the EU forces were engaged in some significant hostilities; the Swedish Special Forces element which deployed had to extract themselves from an ambush, for instance.[6] However, there are a number of caveats which need to be recognised before the operation can be interpreted as evidence of Europe's will and capacity for genuinely autonomous action. The operation was extremely small in terms of size (under 2,000) and duration (four months). It is also questionable whether the operation can be interpreted as evidence of a properly European concert. As commentators have noted, Artemis was a political reaction to the crisis over Iraq; France 'wanted to dispel criticism of pacifism laid against it because of Iraq' (Loisel 2004: 73). The operation was conceived by the French government with the support of Javier Solana's office in Brussels, keen to show that the ESDP was not a 'paper tiger' (2004: 81). Re-affirming European unity and demonstrating to the United States that Europe could still operate independently on the global stage, it did not demonstrate a 'distinctive and coherent European approach to African conflicts' (Bagayoko 2005: 104; Loisel 2004: 91).

The deployment to Chad and the Central African Republic from January 2008 to February 2009 may have been a significant development for the EU, but it seemed to demonstrate the same weaknesses as the previous operations: excepting France, there is a lack of general commitment to autonomous EU action. This force is the largest and most multinational the EU has deployed to Africa, consisting of 3,700 troops from fourteen countries. It was tasked to conduct humanitarian and stabilisation operations for a year against the disturbances precipitated by the war in Darfur. The French element was once again central to the mission. Although the operational commander was an Irish three-star general, the operational headquarters was located at Mont Valérien near Paris and the force commander was French Brigadier General Philippe Ganascia. Once again, the vast majority of the deployed forces were French, with small multinational contributions principally from Austria, Sweden and Ireland (all neutral, non-NATO states). Of course, the mission itself has relied upon the already well-established French military infrastructure in Chad, although the Irish operational commander in Mont Valérien exerted an unexpected level of control over the operation. Reports from the mission

[6] Reports from the EU mission to Congo in 2006 were similarly positive: 'I am positively struck by the strength of the commitment: by the sense that they had to do something. They fought getting this thing through with massive controversy. To deliver German troops to Africa: that is very significant' (EU diplomat, personal interview, 12 May 2006).

indicate that the EU force conducted a robust mission which involved casualties and some combat activity.[7] However, the operation illustrated the enduring unwillingness or inability of the EU to engage in autonomous missions; the troop numbers were 1,000 below the stated mandate as EU member states failed to contribute the requisite number. Moreover, the mission was delayed by nearly five months by political discussions in the EU after the initial UN mandate on 25 September 2007, and was further obstructed by fighting in the Central African Republic as it was about to deploy.

On 2 December 2004, the EU took control of the security of Bosnia, creating EUFOR and designating the mission as Operation Althea. Operation Althea is the largest ever mission and might be interpreted as a sign of the ESDP's maturation. The mission has continued to be successful and, in March 2007, the EU's presence was reduced to 2,500 troops. Although a multinational battalion has remained in Sarajevo for contingencies, standing forces have been replaced by a network of liaison and observation teams (LOTs), which currently live in dedicated houses throughout Bosnia interacting with locals and providing situational awareness for the EU. The LOT system is intended to provide the EU with early warning of any tensions. Over the horizon, forces provided by the EU and NATO are on stand-by to be re-inserted into Bosnia if ethnic tensions re-appear.

EUFOR has played an important role in Bosnia which the EU has understandably emphasised. In contrast to NATO, the EU has been able to work cross-departmentally in Bosnia to much greater effect. The EU institutions in Sarajevo describe the evolution of an 'EU family' – the unity of civil and military agencies – and it seems to have been able to co-ordinate the instruments of power more effectively than NATO's Intervention Force (IFOR) or Stabilisation Force (SFOR). Yet, it is important to be realistic not only about the current functions performed by EUFOR but also its likely implications for the future of European intervention. EUFOR is currently operating in a militarily benign environment, as General Leakey, the first commander of EUFOR, emphasised when he identified civil crime as the critical focus. Operation Althea may not demonstrate the EU's superiority over NATO, but rather the fact that it is easier to co-ordinate different agencies when the environment is benign and the military component consists of 2,500 rather than 60,000 troops.

The ESDP represents a very interesting development and the operations it has performed have not been insignificant. However, it is

---

[7] British major, French liaison officer, personal interview, November 2008.

important to be realistic about these operations. They have generally been small-scale, relatively benign militarily and strategically peripheral and, in Africa, dominated by the French. EUFOR is the one exception to this. In addition to any humanitarian considerations, the stability of Bosnia is of strategic importance to Europe and the EU. EUFOR may create the conditions in Bosnia for eventual EU membership. Yet even here care needs to be exercised. Although the initial NATO intervention into Bosnia was large and carried great risks, by 2004 the situation was fundamentally different. EUFOR and the wider ESDP has not yet proved itself capable of anything but the most minor and benign operations. Significantly, despite the apparent popularity of the ESDP, there is limited support for EU operations themselves among European voters: 'they have the maintenance of peace and stability inside Europe in mind. This, however, is exactly what the ESDP, with its focus on global crisis management, is not intended for' (Brummer 2007: 194).

The end of NATO?

Consonant with his Euro-advocacy, Jones dismisses NATO as the appropriate and relevant institutional framework for European development. Jones is far from alone in his denigration of NATO. There is a great deal of scepticism about and criticism of NATO among the Alliance's policy-makers and senior military personnel. As one British general emphasised: 'NATO is a convenient form of alliance . . . However is it up for anything genuinely difficult? It is all we've got. We have got to keep it.'[8] Yet academics need to be careful in interpreting this pessimism as evidence of genuine institutional decline. In response to recent Cassandras about the future of NATO after Iraq, Thies has usefully contextualised the current NATO 'crisis', assumed to be NATO's 'worst ever'. Thies appositely notes that mere 'vitriol and pettiness are unreliable indicators of the Alliance's health' (2007: 34). Indeed, politicians, some of whom engage in this vitriol, have every interest in exaggerating the extent of the crisis in order to demonstrate their political acumen by resolving it. Despite the certitude that NATO is currently on the verge of collapse, it was similarly about to collapse in every year throughout the 1980s except for 1984 and 1985 (Thies 2007: 36). In order to know whether NATO is in actual crisis or not, it would be necessary to have some criteria defining what a crisis is. Here commentators are, according to Thies, lacking. Signally, for all their mutual calumnies, no member of NATO has ever withdrawn from the

---

[8] British two-star general, personal interview, 29 March 2006.

organisation. France withdrew only from NATO military structures in 1966, not from the organisation altogether. Under the concept of a 'Transatlantic Renovation', the *Livre Blanc* states France's intention to re-integrate with selected military structures. The *Livre Blanc* is critical of NATO, but recognises that 'it is in the interests of France and its partners that it [the Alliance] should be maintained and adapted' (*Livre Blanc* 2008: 102). For France, the best way to achieve that goal – and to influence the United States – is to create a 'credible' European military within NATO (2008: 102). It is important to recognise that France's re-integration into NATO's military structure is not an act of political convenience which may be quickly reversed. It represents a long-term strategic re-orientation. Menon (2000) has traced this ambivalent relationship back to the 1980s. One of the most interesting and important manifestations of this re-orientation was President Chirac's proposal to President Clinton in 1994 that France was willing to re-integrate into NATO on the basis that a European commander was appointed to Armed Forces Southern Europe Headquarters at Naples. That proposal was rejected since Armed Forces Southern Europe commanded the US Sixth Fleet in the Mediterranean, but it marked a reformation of French security policy which has matured in Sarkozy's *Livre Blanc*. In addition to France's rapprochement, eleven new members have joined NATO since the end of the Cold War and it is possible that others in the Balkans will follow in the coming decade. Thies concludes that NATO is a 'permanent alliance between liberal democratic states' (2007: 42). Consequently, against current hyperbole, Thies maintains that 'it is precisely because NATO members agree on so many things that they can afford to engage in public spats over one or a few points of disagreement. What has appeared to many as a source of weakness is better understood as a source of strength' (2007: 43). Assumptions of the death of NATO are premature, according to Thies. Thies' position is supported by the overwhelming evidence about the relative organisational strengths of NATO in comparison with the ESDP. Financial data is not always the best evidence of the political strength of an organisation, but it is as a minimum a useful indicator of the likely robustness of an institution. A strongly supported institution is usually one which is well endowed financially. NATO's finances in comparison with the ESDP's are instructive here. NATO's budget in 2007 exceeded $1.5 billion.[9] The ESDP's budget was, by contrast, €100 million ($1.28 million) in 2007: approximately 15 per cent of NATO's budget.

---

[9] The United States, Germany and Britain contribute the most at 29 per cent, 23 per cent and 13 per cent of the NATO budget, respectively.

As Jones emphasises, the EU has made very considerable progress in its recent history. Five headquarters have been designated as possible EU operational headquarters for ESDP missions: Northwood, Mont Valérien, Potsdam, Larissa and Rome. This is a significant development. However, none of these headquarters is an independent, standing institution. A small nucleus of staff from within existing national headquarters has been assigned – or double-hatted – for EU operations on a more or less *ad hoc* basis to be augmented by a multinational element. Only the European Union Military Staff (EUMS) in Brussels has 200 permanent staff (IISS 2007: 95). The comparison with NATO is stark. NATO currently consists of eleven standing strategic or operational headquarters and a further six higher readiness land headquarters, of which sixteen are located in Europe. NATO is going through major restructuring which will reduce the complement at some of the operational headquarters but, in 2008, NATO employed 9,000 military staff. In addition to its European headquarters, NATO re-designated Allied Command Atlantic, based in Norfolk, Virginia as Allied Command Transformation (ACT) in 2003. The role of ACT is to precipitate European military transformation by connecting with current US processes. ACT was described as 'leading at the strategic command level the transformation of NATO's military structure, forces, capabilities and doctrine. It is enhancing training, particularly of commanders and staffs, conducting experiments to assess new concepts, and promoting interoperability throughout the Alliance' (NATO 2009).[10] The Supreme Allied Commander ACT is double-hatted with the US Joint Forces Command, which is dedicated to the transformation of US forces. Moreover, the majority of ACT's staff is European and the rest of ACT's commands are in Europe. ACT has been assigned command of the Joint Warfare Centre in Stavanger, Norway, which stages exercises for operational level headquarters, and for the NRF, a Joint Force Training Centre at Bydgoszcz, Poland which provides tactical training for component commands and the Lessons Learned Centre in Poland. It also organises a number of other smaller schools including the NATO School at Oberammergau, Germany. ACT and its training centres in Europe have a total staff of approximately a further 3,000.

Not only is the ESDP far smaller, but the EU has in reality been dependent upon NATO for some of its operations. This dependence is recognised by the Berlin Plus agreement of 1996 which allowed European operations to use NATO assets. Under this agreement, EU FORCE

---

[10] See www.nato.int/summit2009/summit-guide.

(EUFOR) has taken responsibility for security issues in Bosnia, but a NATO HQ remains, providing the communications infrastructure for EUFOR. Indeed, this subordination to NATO is affirmed by the latter's command authority. Although nominally answering to the EUMS in Brussels, the EUFOR command structure actually emphasises its political and military linkage to NATO and the United States. The EUFOR commander is subordinated to the Deputy Supreme Allied Commander Europe (DSACEUR), and, whatever the stated role of the EUMS, the higher headquarters for EUFOR is provided by a small EU planning cell of twenty-nine officers in Supreme Headquarters Allied Powers Europe (SHAPE) who operate under the DSACEUR's guidance. As noted by General Reith (DSACEUR 2004–7): 'I command the EU Cell here mainly for Bosnia. It consists of twenty-nine people but it draws on the full SHAPE staff of 1,200.'[11] In 2007, EUFOR's Chief of Staff (a British brigadier) confirmed the point: 'I take my guidance from John Reith, DSACEUR, through the EU Staff Group [in Mons].' EUFOR's chain of command becomes quickly entangled in and dependent upon NATO.

NATO operations demonstrate its priority over the EU still further. The EU has deployed some 1,500 troops to the Congo twice and 3,700 to Chad. It has had 2,500 troops in Bosnia. By contrast, under NATO, European countries are prepared to deploy more troops on missions of higher risk. Denmark formally withdrew from the ESDP at an early stage, while re-affirming its active commitment to NATO. It has deployed some of its best trained and equipped forces to fight alongside the British in Helmand. There, under NATO, they have been involved in heavy fighting and have taken a large number of casualties. Similarly, the Netherlands, traditionally Atlanticist, has prioritised NATO above the EU and in 2006 took over responsibility for Oruzgan. In order to cement their links to the United States, Central and Eastern European states have also prioritised NATO missions in Afghanistan and Iraq. In Afghanistan, Polish, Estonian, Czech and Romanian forces have been involved in heavy fighting as part of NATO. Although Germany seems to be committed at least politically to the ESDP, it has prioritised NATO deployments to Kosovo and Afghanistan.

Consequently, in addition to the 1,000 NATO troops who remain in Bosnia, NATO has 16,000 troops in Kosovo, most of whom are European. The mission in Kosovo is certainly not high tempo but, especially with the unrest which followed the declaration of Kosovan independence, robust peacekeeping has been necessary. There is the potential for significant civil and ethnic unrest as the riots in March 2004 and

---

[11] General Reith, personal interview, 25 July 2007.

February 2008 demonstrated. Decisively, NATO assumed responsibility for Afghanistan in 2006, and its commitment to Afghanistan is likely to intensify until at least the end of 2011. With the withdrawal of US troops from Iraq and Obama's 'surge' in Afghanistan, NATO, under strong US leadership, is becoming an increasingly important and potent institution in that region. Short-touring the incumbent ISAF commander, General McKiernan, General Dan McChrystal has been explicitly appointed by General Petraeus, the new commander of Central Command, to provide a more focused approach to the campaign. With this new political and military emphasis, it is undoubtedly the case that in Afghanistan the United States plays the critical role, providing over 80,000 troops, most of the air assets and much of the enabling communications and logistics infrastructure. However, until 2009 European forces comprised a third of ISAF forces with nearly 20,000 soldiers, and they have been involved in dangerous missions, as mounting casualties demonstrate. It is undoubtedly the most serious active mission which NATO has conducted or with which European nations, under NATO, have ever been involved. Although it may be inconvenient for EU advocates, the European military commitment to Afghanistan promotes NATO as the prime institutional framework in which European military transformation will take place and, indeed, will be driven.

Clearly, there are fundamental flaws in NATO military structures, which will be discussed later, but it would require a peculiar perspective to suggest on the present evidence that NATO is a failing entity which is about to collapse and be replaced by a confident and consensual ESDP. All the evidence points the other way. This may not be convenient either politically or conceptually. It might be politically preferable for many that Europe had its own autonomous military capability. Certainly, such a reality would make European military transformation easier to analyse as an aspect of European integration; military transformation could be mapped on to the wider processes of specifically EU integration without the inconvenience of considering the transatlantic dimension. However, the fact remains that today and for the foreseeable future, European defence is overlaid by the US and European military development will take place under the aegis of NATO heavily influenced by the United States. European military transformation – and European defence integration – will necessarily take a distinctive course in comparison with other aspects of integration. However, just because European military development is almost certain to take place under US influence, this does not mean that a distinctive European military capability will not develop. On the contrary, France's decision to re-integrate into NATO seems to suggest that it now recognises that the most effective way forward for Europe's armed forces is not to pursue an artificial and weak autonomous European project, but rather to develop European capacities – which may in decades become autonomous – within NATO.

The problem with the EU may not be that it simply lacks military capabilities or political will. The EU is compromised by a fundamental organisational problem. Although NATO is an international alliance in which all members are nominally equal, Alliance unity is substantially aided by the fact that NATO is US-dominated. The advantage of this is not merely that the United States has prodigious military capacities, though they are not insignificant. The overwhelming dominance of the United States has organisational advantages at the military level. NATO is effectively a 'framework-nation' alliance. The central force is the United States and all the other nations orient themselves around this single centre of gravity. Organisational sociologists have demonstrated the advantages of this kind of arrangement where many smaller institutions unite around one major partner over the integration of peer groups. Although the dominance of the United States is problematic politically, as political debates over the Balkans and Iraq have demonstrated, it is more efficient for smaller military forces in the Alliance to unify around one dominant military model than to negotiate compatibility between military peers. The problem with the EU is not only differences in strategic vision, but also the lack of a dominant framework nation. An EU 3, consisting of Britain, France and Germany, has emerged but, as events since the Iraq invasion have demonstrated, it is not always united. The French military may have been influenced by Britain in the last decade, but the British military in no way assumes the position of primacy in Europe which the United States enjoys in NATO. Britain cannot offer the kinds of security benefits that the United States has been able to deliver. Britain has limited influence even over smaller nations within Europe outside the EU 3. Similarly, France, with a military potential comparable to the British, has failed to attain the leadership over the EU which it would like to exercise, while Germany has no desire to take any leading role in defence. The EU is a genuinely multinational venture and suffers from the inefficiencies of an alliance of peer groups. There is no single dominant power around which the smaller nations can, or are willing to, orient themselves. The mere fact of the relative size of the United States in comparison with all the other Alliance partners recommends NATO as the prime organ for military transformation.

Conclusion

It is possible that Seth Jones is correct and that the future of European military transformation does indeed lie in Europe. Given the aggressive unilateralism of the United States and the global diasporas now living in Europe, many maintain the desirability of a credible European military capable of conducting operations around the world. Yet on the basis of the evidence which Jones cites and an analysis of current EU operations, his optimism is unjustified. Europe's armed forces are indeed undergoing profound transformations as this book is intended to demonstrate. However, the fundamental institutional framework for these changes is not the EU. On the contrary, in every instance, NATO and therefore the United States, takes precedence. Since 1949, Europe's national militaries have been structured and developed within the NATO framework. Despite dramatic changes to NATO structures and operations, the priority of NATO remains the case today. This does not mean that the EU or the ESDP is irrelevant. As Paul Hirst (2001) has noted, multiple institutions can exist claiming different kinds of sovereignties over different areas. The ESDP has established itself as a significant element within the EU project. At a military level, it will continue to conduct small missions to areas in which NATO has no interest. The round of ESDP missions and EU battle group certifications are likely to have some effect on the European military forces, playing a small role in unifying them around increasingly convergent professional standards. However, on current evidence NATO is the prime institution for commanding European military operations, the development of European forces and in the dissemination of shared military expertise. Even the most ardent advocates of European military integration are finally aware of this and eloquently recognise the blunt facts which have prioritised NATO: 'If something is very high intensity and risky, there is only one country that can do it: the US. That is why most commanders like working with NATO – it is the biggest risk insurance policy.'[12]

Because the NATO alliance includes the United States, it offers European armed forces collective benefits which are completely absent from the ESDP. The size and potency of US military forces reduces the operational risks on Europe's armed forces. Brutally, by operating within NATO, it is less likely that European troops will be killed; that is the palpable benefit of working within NATO. By contrast, the ESDP offers no such comfort. It is precisely the fear of taking casualties that prevents the ESDP from developing beyond benign missions. The ESDP seems to expose EU countries to risk without having the capabilities to assure them. France and Britain are willing to take risks as independent nations, but there seem to be few circumstances in which, operating as part of an

---

[12] EU/ESDP official, personal interview, 12 May 2006.

EU force, Britain and France would be empowered to do things that they could not do alone or in which co-operation with EU forces would reduce their risk. John Reith, DSACEUR from 2004 to 2007 and strategic commander of all EUFOR deployments, was very clear about the valid but limited military competence of the EU:

> The EU has no real appetite for combat; it is not structured for it. The EU is better at dealing with the next level down: beyond the combat phase providing assistance in order to accelerate reconstruction. The EU can come in with military capabilities to provide a safe and secure environment. It can guarantee security with police missions. We need the rule of law. We need to train the police. In Bosnia, its judicial and penal system needed reform. The advantage of the EU is that you also have the political and economic power of the EU. Linking with police and law and order and the military: the BiH (Bosnia-Herzogevina) operation is probably the best example of this co-ordinated approach.[13]

Of course, it is possible that the ESDP will develop into a genuine military alliance capable of significant military interventions; unexpected historical ruptures occur. Yet the current strategic context would suggest otherwise. The EU offers European states few defence benefits that they do not enjoy independently. Britain and France can act unilaterally more effectively. Indeed, apart from EUFOR, all EU operations have effectively been conducted under a French framework-nation format. The future of EU missions is likely to continue under this French-led form. In terms of European military transformation, this is a crucial point for it means that in the foreseeable future the framework and, indeed, the catalyst of development will remain NATO and the United States. The processes of concentration and transnationalisation which are currently occurring should be situated primarily within a NATO framework and the influence of the Transnational Alliance on the dynamics of military transformation has to be recognised.

[13] General Sir John Reith, personal interview, 25 July 2007.

Part II

Operational transformation

4   The operational network

Introduction

The importance of competent headquarters and coherent planning to military success is demonstrated most clearly by the numerous historical occasions when command has failed. Notoriously, during the Franco-Prussian War, although the forces were broadly matched in terms of weaponry and numbers, the French Army suffered a series of catastrophic defeats culminating in Sedan on 1 September 1870. While the Prussian Army was co-ordinated by a potent and capable staff system, which disseminated clear and actionable orders to its corps, the French headquarters, under the now calumniated General MacMahon, was paralysed. Only hours before the final collapse, MacMahon sent out orders – unopened by at least one of his corps – which recommended that his forces should rest on the following day, even though the Prussian Army was at that very time encircling Sedan (Howard 2000: 206). The fractured corps of the French Army were quickly surrounded and destroyed. The Franco-Prussian War demonstrated the critical requirement of military forces: effective headquarters able to plan and command operations.

One of the most decisive changes to the armed forces in Europe since the end of the Cold War has occurred at the level of headquarters. In contrast to the Cold War, military headquarters and their commanders must now deploy and sustain forces, often at short notice, on complex global emergencies. They differ profoundly from military command during the Cold War, although, as we shall see, important operational continuities exist. In Europe today, hidden away in a diversity of anonymous sites, new 'operational' headquarters are appearing, implementing new planning and command techniques. This analysis of operational transformation accordingly examines the organisational reformation of European operational headquarters since 2000, and examines the emergence of new forms of expertise – operational art – in these changing institutions. The investigation begins by identifying the emergence of a new network of operational headquarters that are critical to European military activity, and then in Chapter 6 explores the expertise that is appearing in these institutions. National operational headquarters[1] are an element of European military transformation that are impossible to ignore. However, although France and Britain have continued to conduct autonomous military missions, the most important operations in the current era – and, indeed, the only operations which the Bundeswehr conducts – are multinational ventures, especially with NATO. Consequently, the decisive headquarters are, therefore, NATO. NATO operational headquarters have played a crucial role in Bosnia, Kosovo and Afghanistan and in the development of the NATO Response Force (NRF). Accordingly, this chapter traces the evolution of NATO operational headquarters in Europe. To identify the significance and novelty of these new operational headquarters, it is necessary to have an understanding of the Cold War command structures that these headquarters have superseded.

NATO military headquarters in the Cold War

Following the signing of the Washington Treaty in 1949, NATO eventually took command of a vast area extending from the Arctic Ocean in the north to the Azores and the Mediterranean in the south, from Norfolk, Virginia in the west to the Black Sea in the east. This theatre was subdivided between the three main NATO commands. Allied Command Europe (ACE, Mons, Belgium), assumed control of mainly land operations in north-western Europe, though it also commanded operations in the important Mediterranean theatre. Allied Command Atlantic (ACLANT, Norfolk, Virginia) controlled naval operations in the Atlantic and Allied Command Channel (ACCHAN) (Northwood, London) assumed control of naval and air operations in the English Channel, North Sea and Arctic Ocean. Below the main NATO commands, a cascading hierarchy of main subordinate, principal or sub-principal subordinate commands were established to control air, maritime and land forces within designated sub-areas. In all, sixty-five NATO commands had been established by the end of the Cold War.

It is unnecessary to describe all sixty-five main subordinate and principal subordinate commands in NATO during the Cold War. In terms of contemporary European operational developments, the decisive commands in the Cold War were located in Europe under ACE. During the Cold War, Western Europe was divided into three subordinate areas of

---

[1] The Permanent Joint Headquarters in Britain, Centre de planification et de conduite des opérations in France and Einsatzführungskommando in Germany.

operation: Armed Forces Northern, Central and Southern Europe, respectively, based at Kolsas (Norway), Brunssum (Netherlands) and Naples (Italy). Of the three headquarters, Armed Forces Central Europe (AFCENT, Brunssum) was the most important main subordinate command for the territorial defence of Western Europe during the Cold War. It controlled the 'central front' in Europe – and remains particularly significant to this day. Brunssum was predominantly a land headquarters, though it did have some air assets under its command. It provides a useful focal point for understanding the dynamics of transformation at the operational level in Europe.

AFCENT was originally based in Fontainebleau but, after the departure of France from the NATO military structures in 1966, it was moved to Brunssum. AFCENT was always the most European NATO command, responsible for the bulk of indigenous land forces in Europe. Subordinate to AFCENT were two principal subordinate commands: Army Group North (Northag, Rheindalen) and Army Group Central (Centag, Heidelberg).[2] Northag and Centag were responsible for the organisation of the familiar NATO 'layer-cake' in West Germany, commanding the national corps beneath them. Thus, Northag commanded the Dutch 1 Corps, the German III Corps, the British 1 Corps and the Belgian 1 Corps which were all assigned areas in northern Germany behind the Elbe; Centag commanded the US V and VII Corps and the German II and III Corps. In all, Brunssum commanded eight corps of which six were European.

In this way, AFCENT usefully illustrates the distinctive institutional structure of European NATO command during the Cold War. ACE commanded the whole of Europe. Under ACE, AFCENT commanded the 'central front', a geographic area of responsibility which ran from the North Sea coast down to the Swiss border, while its Army Groups, North and Central, covered two discretely bounded sub-areas within Germany. Northag commanded all land forces north of Bonn; Centag commanded the forces in central and southern Germany. There was little horizontal co-ordination between these commands. Indeed, there was for the most part no multinational co-operation at the tactical level; the corps were independent of one another, assigned to their own discrete geographic areas. Consequently, although AFCENT commanded all the forces assigned to it, its operational direction of these forces was limited. AFCENT ensured that Northag and Centag enacted NATO's Main Defence Plan, but did not actively seek to co-ordinate forces itself.

---

[2] Brunssum also commanded two other PSCs, Allied Air Forces Central Europe consisting of 2nd Allied Tactical Air Force and 4th Allied Tactical Air Force.

Indeed, until almost the end of the Cold War, neither Northag nor Centag had genuine authority over how the national corps assigned to them conducted their specific defences. Although AFCENT was co-located with Britain's Tactical Air Command, there was limited ability to conduct joint air and land operations. AFCENT and its subordinate army groups conducted land operations, while the air force was tasked with strategic attack and defensive missions. AFCENT ensured coherence between NATO strategy and national corps tactics, but did not actively intervene with its assigned forces. Accordingly, NATO might be described as an international organisation, unified strategically but dividing military responsibilities discretely between nations on a geographic basis. In this way, it accorded with a number of other international organisations which were created in the decades immediately after the Second World War. Most obviously, and perhaps significantly, the European Economic Community ratified at the Treaty of Rome in 1957 had a similar structure; it facilitated greater economic co-operation between the six member states while leaving regulatory independence untouched.

After 9/11: the new NATO

There was significant revision of NATO headquarters following the Kosovo War in 1999, with whose conduct the United States was deeply unhappy. Following the Washington Summit in 1999, the 50th anniversary of the Alliance, major command reforms were implemented which reduced the number of NATO headquarters from sixty-five to twenty. However, the Prague summit in 2002, self-referentially defined as the 'transformation' summit and specifically responding to the new strategic situation created by the 9/11 attacks, was a decisive moment for NATO operational innovation. At the strategic level, ACLANT was re-established as Allied Command Transformation (ACT) and tasked with overseeing the digitalisation of the European NATO forces and the re-conceptualisation of operations. ACT and its subordinate commands have sought to play an important role in NATO transformation. However, the operationally decisive changes implemented following Prague related to the other strategic command, Allied Command Europe (ACE). ACE was re-designated as Allied Command Operations (ACO) and became the sole strategic command for NATO with global operational responsibilities for all NATO's deployed forces, maritime, air and land.[3]

---

[3] NATO's third strategic command Allied Command Channel (ACCHAN) (Northwood, London), which assumed control of naval and air operations in the North Sea and Arctic Ocean, was reduced to a regional command after Washington, becoming a maritime component command, following Prague.

The centralisation of strategic command authority – and military assets – into ACO was accompanied by changes among subordinate commands, with new commands explicitly designated as 'operational level' headquarters appearing for the first time.[4] AFCENT was reconstituted as Joint Force Command Headquarters Brunssum (JFCB); Armed Force Southern Europe (AFSOUTH, Naples) converted into Joint Force Command Headquarters Naples (JFCN). The somewhat surprising development was the decision to reconstitute the old Joint Subordinate Regional Command South East (originally under Allied Command Atlantic) into the operational level Joint Force Headquarters Lisbon (JFHQL). JFHQL was not a fully joint command but a small predominantly maritime headquarters, which explains the title headquarters rather than command.[5]

The definition of JFCB, JFCN and JFHQL as operational level headquarters represented an important change. Unlike their forebears, Armed Forces North and Armed Forces South, which merely controlled subordinate commands, JFCB and JFCN were now being actively tasked to co-ordinate forces in real time and space on operations. They were to plan and command global intervention operations, rather than merely ensuring the downward implementation of NATO's strategic defence plan. Some active military creativity was expected of them; they were to design and implement campaigns. To this end, while Naples and Brunssum (as Armed Forces South and North) had previously been land and maritime-centric headquarters, both now became joint headquarters. JFCB assumed operational command of Afghanistan, while JFCN continued to act as the operational headquarters for Kosovo; Bosnia being handed over to the EU in 2004.[6]

---

[4] After the Washington summit, a selection of main subordinate commands, including Brunssum, were re-designated as regional commands. The Prague summit re-designated or disbanded all these regional commands.
[5] Given NATO's operations in the Balkans and Afghanistan and the establishment of the NRF, there was a military argument for the creation of a third operational headquarters around which NRF cycles could turn. However, Lisbon's conversion into a joint operational command was a substantially political decision rather than a military one. It sustained relations between the United States and Portugal, especially since, without this command, Portugal would have been the only established NATO country without a NATO command on its territory.
[6] Below these commands, some 1999 joint sub-regional commands have been retained or converted into component commands. Thus, Brunssum and Naples were each assigned a maritime, air and land component command at the tactical level. Thus, for instance, Brunssum was assigned Heidelberg (the old Central Army Group headquarters), Ramstein and Northwood as its component, land, air and maritime commands. Naples was assigned components located in Madrid (land), Naples (maritime) and Izmir (air).

The Prague reforms represented a further concentration of command authority. As a consequence of the Prague reforms, NATO commands were reduced from twenty to eleven: two strategic commands [Allied Command Transformation (ACT) and Allied Command Operations ACO)], three operational commands (JFCB, JFCN and JFHQL) and six tactical commands (Heidelberg, Ramstein, Northwood, Madrid, Izmir and Naples). In terms of conducting operations, however, NATO consists of ten commands, since ACT has no responsibility for deployed active forces; it is dedicated to the internal reformation of Europe's forces.[7] Since the end of the Cold War, a blunt fact has appeared about NATO command structures. There are far fewer headquarters, less than a sixth of the number during the Cold War; ten versus sixty-five. Moreover, although fewer in number, these commands now co-ordinate all NATO air, land and maritime forces. Indeed, like ACO (Mons), the operational commands at Brunssum and Naples are similarly unconstrained by geography. JFCB is an important example of the transformation of a European headquarters. The once land-centric Armed Forces Central headquarters with delimited geographic responsibility for northern Germany now commands joint operations in Afghanistan, as well as in any other area NATO might deploy. For all the politicisation of NATO's reforms, there has been a very significant rationalisation of operational command structures so that authority has been centralised in fewer commands. NATO command structures (Figure 4.1) have undergone a simultaneous process of contraction and expansion; command authority has been condensed in fewer headquarters which now have global responsibility (Figure 4.1).

This process of condensation is evident in other spheres. In her important work on global cities, Sassen (1991) has analysed the dynamics of organisational transformation in a globalising era. Focusing on corporate headquarters in the financial services industry in Tokyo, London and New York, she has identified a common pattern of adaptation: 'The fundamental dynamic posited here is that the more globalised the economy becomes, the higher the agglomeration of central functions in relatively few sites, that is, the global cities' (1991: 5). She has described a paradoxical process of centralisation at the level of management and simultaneous de-centralisation or 'dispersal' of production. In the face of the global competition, the old vertically integrated structure of corporations has been revised in order to exploit the potential of the global

---

[7] Below the air component commands, six former joint subordinate regional commands have been re-designated as Combined Air Operations Centres (CAOCs) or Deputy CAOCs. These centres are important in co-ordinating air traffic, but they are not designated as commands.

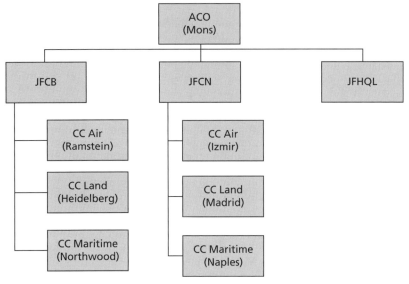

CC: component command

Figure 4.1 NATO command structure 2004–8

labour market (1991: 31). Sassen notes an important self-perpetuating dynamic: dispersal necessitates more sophisticated, centralised management able to co-ordinate complex networks of production, but centralised management itself depends upon new technologies 'which make possible long distance management and servicing and instantaneous money transfers' (1991: 19). In turn, these technologies themselves 'require complex physical facilities, which are highly immobile' (1991: 19). In order to co-ordinate their supplier, production and distribution networks, global corporations have invested heavily in communications infrastructure and personnel. It is logical to focus this investment in fewer, larger locations. Consequently, the management of multinationals has been centralised and clustered into single urban locations, while the sites of production and distribution are being dispersed globally to maximise the local opportunities. In this way, multinationals are best able to cope with the exigencies of the global economy: 'the spatial dispersion of economic activities and the reorganisation of the financial industry are two processes that have contributed to new forms of centralisation' (1991: 19).

The centralisation of strategic command in joint headquarters both within nations and NATO might be seen as a military manifestation of this process. Where ACE used to command from the apex of an organisational pyramid directing subordinate commands vertically in well-defined

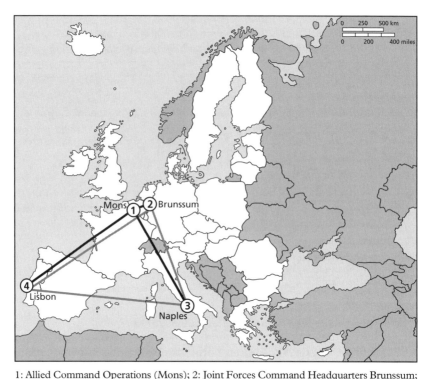

1: Allied Command Operations (Mons); 2: Joint Forces Command Headquarters Brunssum; 3: Joint Forces Command Headquarters Naples; 4: Joint Forces Headquarters Lisbon.
   Command relations from ACO indicated in bold lines. Co-operative relations between the three operational commands suggested by thinner lines.

Figure 4.2 The location of NATO strategic and operational headquarters in Europe post-Prague

geographical regions, ACO and the headquarters below it designated as operational commands now deploy a diversity of forces across a global operating space. Command authority – and NATO resources – have been invested in these headquarters. There has been a contraction in the number of headquarters, with a simultaneous rise in their areas of responsibility. Command authority has been condensed into fewer, more potent sites.

The reality of NATO Europe: the example of Joint Force Command Brunssum

The 2004 NATO command structure represents a centralisation of Europe's command structures; it has been a significant institutional process. It appears to be coherent. It is neatly organised into strategic, operational and tactical levels and each command appears to have a clear role. ACO gives strategic direction and tasks its subordinate operational commands with missions, primarily Afghanistan, Kosovo and the NRF. JFCB has taken responsibility for the operational command of Afghanistan, while JFHQL controls Kosovo. Those commands co-ordinate the in-theatre campaigns to ensure continuity and unity of effort. The structure appears to be a rational response to strategic contingencies. Responsibility for the NRF rotates on a yearly basis around the three operational commands.

In fact, the current structure of NATO is hugely problematic. In particular, it is very doubtful whether the European commands designated as 'operational' in the new structure – Brunssum, Naples and Lisbon – contribute significantly to the Alliance at all in military terms. Throughout the Cold War, various commands were sustained, which provided little military benefit but which encouraged the allegiance of the state favoured by the positioning of a command on its territory; the Lisbon Headquarters and the Baltic Approaches headquarters were two of the most obvious examples of this political expediency. Yet even in the current rationalised structure, the operational commands at Brunssum, Naples and Lisbon owe their existence more to politics than to operational effectiveness. They play a political role of sustaining the Alliance by providing posts for officers and buttressing the local economy. Their military role is unclear; it is not obvious that they provide the operational command and guidance for which they are designated.

JFCB is the starkest example of their superfluity because, of all the operational headquarters, it would appear to be the most effective. It is the operational headquarters for NATO operations in Afghanistan and claims with some evidence to be the most professional, resourced and organised operational command in Europe. It is certainly superior to the JFHQL, which is widely disparaged, and it is probably more effective than JFCN. Yet even within the organisation its role is unclear to many of its own officers. This internal doubt is corroborated by widespread scepticism in NATO about the function of JFCB. For instance, the British-led Allied Rapid Reaction Corps (ARRC), which formed the core of the International Security Assistance Force (ISAF IX) Headquarters in Afghanistan between April 2006 and February 2007, were dismissive of JFCB. The ARRC wrote its own operational plan for its command of ISAF which it then sent up to JFCB for endorsement only. Although the subordinate command in theory, JFCB was dependent upon the ARRC. This problem became acute in-theatre. Throughout their period as ISAF Headquarters, ARRC staff would ask JFCB for information critical to the mission, but which they did not have the resources in-theatre to access. One staff officer noted the operational acuity of ARRC's requests: 'They were asking questions about things we hadn't even thought of, never mind the answers to them.' These difficulties were compounded by relations between the commander of ARRC and ISAF IX, General Richards, and the commander of JFCB, General Back. There were immediate status problems in that both were four-star generals, although Richards, who was significantly more operationally experienced than Back, was formally subordinate to him. General Richards, Commander ISAF, was respectful to General Back, although he was widely regarded as ineffective and indecisive. As a result, Richards tended to rely more on General James Jones [the Supreme Allied Commander Europe (SACEUR)] or US Central Command for direction and assistance. The problem with JFCB is institutional, however. Richards' successors, generals MacNeill, Mackiernan and McChrystal, have similarly been in closer communication with their American superiors at CENTCOM and Supreme Allied Command Europe.

Moreover, although JFCB has provided some supporting staff work for ACO in relation to Afghanistan, the in-theatre ISAF Headquarters in Kabul have found JFCB to be irrelevant or a hindrance to what they do. ARRC officers found JFCB's regular demands for information or directives intrusive and unhelpful. Although JFCB has belatedly written the campaign plan for Afghanistan, it has yet to be endorsed. JFCB is not the only operational command that has been disparaged. Following his experiences as part of the NRF, one British officer observed: 'NATO [operational] headquarters are just not that good. Even Naples would probably crack under pressure'.[8] Perhaps most suggestively, in 2007, a review of NATO command structures proposed a staff reduction at JFCB (and JFCN) of half from 1,200 to 590 personnel and its marginalisation in NATO command structures; the review recommended a closer connection between ACO at Mons and the tactical commands, side-stepping JFCB. The review implies that NATO as a whole does not believe that JFCB is contributing sufficiently to NATO missions and to ISAF in particular.

There are further problems with JFCB as a multinational headquarters. All multinational forces are compromised by national agendas and this problem is an enduring feature of NATO. In Brunssum, the problems of national agendas have been identified by senior officers as a fundamental weakness of the organisation. In particular, national interests infiltrate the

---

[8] British brigadier, personal interview, 2 June 2006.

functioning of the headquarters, especially at flag officer level where they exercise most influence. It was apparent that it was very difficult for the chief of staff to maintain any unity of effort within the headquarters, as the commanders' intent was re-interpreted (or even ignored) by colleagues promoting a national line. Moreover, flag officers admitted that they would interact with the commander quite independently of the chief of staff. In certain cases, there was evidence of a direct status battle between the chief of staff and a fellow flag officer. It is unlikely that such actions would be tolerated in national headquarters. They persist at Brunssum because the commander and chief of staff have no sanction or incentive at their disposal. Staff attached to the headquarters are promoted by their national militaries and, consequently, the headquarters could not demand their allegiance. At JFCB, an order or directive is at best a request; this breaks a fundamental rule of military organisation: there is *de facto* no unity of command.

There are further problems. Many senior members of the organisation spoke extensively of the lack of competence in the headquarters. Officers working in JFCB have divided the organisation into 'swimmers and non-swimmers':[9] competent and incompetent staff officers. Although some senior officers rejected this concept, it was a widely held view, and even those who rejected the distinction recognised that staff within the head-quarters had different levels of ability. Staff at JFCB put different esti-mates on the proportion of swimmers to non-swimmers. However, there seemed to be consensus that between 60 per cent and 80 per cent of the staff at Brunssum were ineffective. All staff officers stressed the need for greater staff competence and suggested various training mechanisms which might improve performance. However, it is questionable whether any improvement will be possible. The ineffectiveness of JFCB is well known within the Alliance, and consequently nations, except for Germany for whom it is the only 'operational' command, avoid sending their best officers to the headquarters. This does not mean that all staff officers at JFCB are weak – there are many highly competent individuals. However, the average standard is very low and there are some very poor staff officers with inadequate English, undermining the effectiveness of the organisation as a whole.

---

[9] The origins of this term are interesting. In the 1980s, Sandhurst trained a number of officers from African countries, whose performance was often sub-optimal. However, sensitive to the issue of race, the training staff would distinguish them from British cadets not by reference to their African origins, but to the fact that they were almost invariably unable to swim. They became known as 'non-swimmers', which usefully alluded not only to their aquatic deficiencies but also their general military incompetence. The word has been introduced into NATO by British officers and at JFCB has been applied in a quite new way.

The Prague reforms represented an attempt to rationalise NATO command structures and there is a clear logic to the creation of a three-tier command hierarchy. Moreover, the centralisation of command authority in fewer, more potent centres accords with organisational concentration widely observable in the commercial sector. However, although nominally a rationalisation, the current structure of NATO commands is misleading. ACO plays a crucial role at the strategic level, but at the operational level JFCB, JFCN and JFHQL make only a limited contribution, despite their formal status. Decisively, while they provide useful staff support for ACO, they cannot really be described as commanding current missions at the operational level: they do not design and implement in-theatre campaigns. The redundancy of NATO's operational headquarters should not obscure the fact that Brunssum, Naples and Lisbon have had some residual impact on European military transformation. In particular, they provide posts for a coagulating group of professional European staffs officers who rotate around these headquarters, in-theatre NATO headquarters and their own national forces. Officers from different European nations are working together more often than during the Cold War, and are forming a series of transnational professional links between each other as they work together recurrently in these different headquarters. Nevertheless, these benefits fall well short of the role which is nominally given to these headquarters. They are not agents of European military transformation at the operational level nor, indeed, ultimately, operational headquarters at all. They do not decide how best to deploy tactical forces to achieve strategic goals: the definition of operational art according to current military doctrine.

Higher Readiness Forces (Land) Headquarters: the concentration of operational competence

The superfluity of much of Europe's new operational network is perhaps surprising. However, their ineffectiveness does not mean that NATO headquarters based in Europe are irrelevant to European military transformation or that NATO is a hollow alliance. On the contrary, there are crucial developments which have taken place under NATO within Europe at the level of headquarters which are central to military transformation. They are obscured from view, however, because the truly significant innovations have been lodged at a lower, less conspicuous level than those formally designated as operational headquarters. Their significance for contemporary European military transformation can be easily overlooked. The decisive transformation at the operational level is not found at the Joint Forces Command level, but rather among the so-called NATO

Higher Readiness Forces (Land) Headquarters (HRF HQ): the Allied Rapid Reaction Corps (ARRC, Rheindalen: British), Eurocorps (Strasbourg: French, German, Spanish and Benelux), the Rapid Deployable German–Netherlands Corps (Münster), the NATO Rapid Deployable Corps–Italy (Milan), the NATO Rapid Deployable Corps–Spain (Valencia), the NATO Rapid Deployable Corps–Turkey (Istanbul), the NATO Deployable Corps–Greece (Thessaloniki) and, although not declared to NATO, the French rapid reaction corps–the Corps de réaction rapide–France, Lille) (Figure 4.3). These are corps

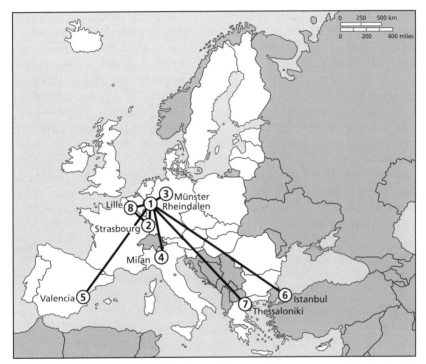

1: Allied Rapid Reaction Corps (Rheindalen); 2: Eurocorps (Strasbourg); 3: Rapid Deployable German–Netherlands Corps (Münster); 4: NATO Rapid Deployable Corps–Italy (Milan); 5: NATO Rapid Deployable Corps–Spain (Valencia); 6: NATO Rapid Deployable Corps–Turkey (Istanbul); 7: NATO Deployable Corps–Greece (Thessaloniki); 8: Corps de réaction rapide–France (Lille).

Some network links between the headquarters indicated (demonstrated at Land Component Conference, ARRC, November 2008).

Figure 4.3 The rapid reaction corps/higher readiness forces headquarters

level commands which are formally designed to act as deployed land
component commands in a theatre of operations; they are, according to
NATO doctrine, tactical level headquarters.

Following the London Declaration in 1990, NATO re-oriented its
strategic focus and instituted some important military innovations. One
of the most interesting, and potentially historically significant, innovations
was the creation of two corps level land headquarters organised for intervention operations, the Allied Command Europe Rapid Reaction Corps
and Eurocorps. In 1992, NATO established a new British-framework
headquarters based on the British 1 Corps at Rheindalen, the Allied
Command Europe Rapid Reaction Corps, which was renamed the
Allied Rapid Reaction Corps (ARRC) after the Prague reforms.[10] For
the British Army, the establishment of this headquarters was a major
political achievement, since it defended Britain's 1 Corps from threatened
de-activation as part of the post-Cold War peace dividend. The creation of
the ARRC could also be seen as a US reward for Britain's contribution in
the Gulf where they performed an important role despite their relatively
poor equipment. The Bundeswehr and Bonn were unhappy about the fact
that ARRC was a British framework nation headquarters. There is some
indication that the German officer corps felt slighted by the creation of this
new headquarters and, of course, the NATO funding which it attracted,
especially since the headquarters was in Germany.

ARRC benefited from being the first HRF HQ and from the fact that it
was based on an already highly experienced British corps headquarters. It
has subsequently gone on to become the most important corps level
headquarters in Europe:

The peers are nipping at it [ARRC] but that is out of envy. The ARRC: it is the best
joined up and trained headquarters to have commanded Afghanistan by a mile.
They did great work and came through lots of things. I saw this because I was
training them in the Joint Warfare Centre.[11]

British officers no doubt have every interest in promoting the ARRC. The
headquarters provided the in-theatre land command for the IFOR operation in Bosnia from December 1995, and then commanded ground forces
in Kosovo in 1999; in both cases it commanded the initial interventions.
Decisively, its proven ability to command intervention operations led to its
appointment as ISAF IX in 2006, at a crucial stage in the mission when
NATO was taking over full command of the country. General Richards was
explicit about why the ARRC was selected for this mission:

[10] Allied Command Europe became Allied Command Operations and was dropped from
     ARRC's title. The acronym for the ARRC was retained.
[11] British general, personal interview, 29 March 2006.

We have combat operations on the ground. Bosnia and Kosovo were essentially peacekeeping operations involving complex counter-insurgency operations. But this mission is at its most demanding – and it has been given to NATO. This is where NATO transformation will happen as long as nations commit to it. And ARRC is the only headquarters that can do it . . . Other HQs could not do it. At the operational command level they still have their 'L' plates on. The UK should be proud of the ARRC. It is visionary. It is at the forefront. Will that pre-eminence last forever? No.[12]

The Afghanistan mission is the most significant that the ARRC has conducted and will be discussed at length in Chapter 7. However, the Kosovo intervention, when ARRC spearheaded NATO's land intervention, usefully demonstrated the potency of the ARRC. That deployment led to the famous conflict between Lieutenant General Mike Jackson, Commander ARRC, and General Wesley Clark, SACEUR (the commander of Allied Command Europe, ACE). Jackson famously refused to wrest control of Pristina airport from Russian paratroopers at the order of General Clark with the retort, 'Sir, I am not going to start World War III for you' (Jackson 2008: 336). General Clark has since cited the incident as an example of the culture of mission command in the British forces. 'In the British System, a field commander is supported. Period. That is the rule' (Clark 2001: 396). Clark interpreted Jackson's independence as evidence of the distinctiveness of British command culture; in the British forces, complete authority is devolved to the commander on the ground. This may not have been irrelevant. However, an alternative explanation of Jackson's intransigence seems plausible. Lieutenant General Mike Jackson, Commander ARRC, entered Kosovo and began to conduct a successful stabilisation campaign all but independently of General Wesley Clark, SACEUR, Jackson's nominal commander. Embarrassingly, Jackson received his operational plan for the campaign from General Clark after he had already established himself in-theatre. The late delivery of the plan undermined the legitimacy and relevance of any subsequent orders from SACEUR almost totally. Indeed, many stories now circulate among staff officers who served in Kosovo about the late arrival of his operational plan. Jackson reputedly used Wesley's operational plan as a door-stop in his command post, having informed Clark that he had received it but had no intention of reading it. In his own memoir, Jackson is candid in his assessment of Clark, of whom he (and many of his American and British fellow officers) were critical; he was regarded as interfering and seemed to want all-out war with the Serbs (Jackson 2008: 292–5). This general mistrust of Clark

---

[12] General Richards, personal interview, 11 July 2006.

seems to have encouraged Jackson to challenge his superior. However, it seems likely that Jackson was able to refuse his superior's order at Pristina airfield only because he was also so supremely confident of his head-quarters' competence. It was already in *de facto* control of the operation. Indeed, Jackson notes that his staff was openly critical of Clark: 'the feeling among my staff was that Clark was shooting from the hip' (2008: 321). It is noticeable that as Chief of the General Staff between 2004 and 2006, General Jackson, no longer supported by the ARRC headquarters, dem-onstrated a more conciliatory approach to his military and political supe-riors: he consented to the Iraq War, even though he had personal doubts about its wisdom and legality (2008: 391–9, 402).

The ARRC's success as a headquarters has transcended the generalship of its individual commanders. Its potency rests on wider and more endur-ing institutional factors. The fact that ARRC is a British headquarters may be significant. Despite the British Army's traditionally poor staff work and lack of operational ability,[13] in the post-Second World War era the British officer corps became far more competent. The professionalisation of the Army in 1962 is likely to have had some effect here, but other factors seem to have contributed to this improvement. Northern Ireland seems to have been critical here. As a result of the Army's role in a complex politicised insurgency campaign from 1969, the British Army was forced to reform itself. In particular, after the initial disasters of internment and Bloody Sunday, the British Army developed a mature approach to the campaign. The importance of planning, tempo and flexibility were imposed upon commanders and staff officers by a very sophisticated opponent. The result is that the British armed forces and British officer corps is among the most experienced and militarily competent in Europe. European allies often complain (correctly) of the arrogance of British officers, but they also acknowledge the high levels of competence found among British headquarters.

Britishness is one plausible explanation as to why ARRC might have become NATO's prime higher readiness force headquarters. However, there may be a simpler but more fundamental reason why the ARRC has attained its prominence. Roger Palin, a retired four-star RAF general, highlighted a critical point: 'The rapid progress in these areas [operational concepts, intelligence requirements, force packages, national logistics,

---

[13] General Erwin Rommel famously noted this failing in British commanders during his African campaign: 'Prejudice against innovation is a typical characteristic of an Officer Corps which has grown up in a well-tried and proven system ... A military doctrine has been worked out to the last detail and it was now regarded as the summit of all military wisdom. The only military thinking which was acceptable was that which followed stand-ardised rules.' (Basil Liddell Hart 1987: 203–4).

command, control and communications and exercise schedules] is due largely to the framework nation concept, which allowed the leading nation to take the initiative in developing the appropriate plans but within an alliance framework' (Palin 1995: 56). In order to develop a unified organisational culture, framework nation headquarters seem to be advantaged. Unlike binational, multinational or composite headquarters, they seem to benefit from the presence of a core of officers from one nation in the key positions. These officers already share a language, common professional practices and, in some cases, are known to each other. Headquarters are able to unite around this core staff; staff from other nations automatically have a single common professional and organisational reference point to inform their interactions even if they occur independently of framework nation staff. This unification is very difficult for multinational or binational headquarters. As JFCB demonstrates, once there is no majority nation to which individuals from other nations relate, it is very difficult to limit political fragmentation or to instil organisational unity.

The benefits of building a staff around a national core has been widely noted in the sociological and management literature. In the last thirty years, transnational corporations have operated globally, creating headquarters and subsidiaries in many countries away from the home territory and seeking to exploit temporary fluctuations in the global economy. They now operate in an environment in which there are rapid economic flows. This has encouraged some sociologists to claim that corporations have become placeless (Appadurai 1996). They transcend any notion of territoriality and the locales they inhabit are just fetishes conveniently constructed as marketing devices. In fact, empirical analysis of corporations today shows that indigenous national culture is central to corporate success. The most successful globalised corporations structure themselves into a dense core of national expertise around which professionals from other countries unite in the organisation. Successful Japanese, American and German corporations in a variety of sectors demonstrate the same point (Dicken 1998). However global their operations become, the organisation retains a unifying national culture in its headquarters. Multinational operations may be conducted by foreign professionals employed in their own countries but the headquarters, increasingly concentrated in a global city, remains national (Sassen 1991).

The ARRC seems to confirm the validity of this organisational principle. Certainly, General Richards was explicit that the strength of the ARRC lay in its national unity: 'The power of my own group is that it is a framework nation headquarters and has trained together.'[14] Indeed,

[14] Personal interview, 16 July 2006.

from 2008, the national principle was accentuated. Following a review of defence expenditure, the MOD decided to return the ARRC from Rheindalen and relocate it in Innsworth, Gloucester.[15] The move has reduced the expense of sustaining the ARRC, but is also increasing the linkage between the ARRC, and the investment made in it, and Britain's armed forces. The ARRC remains internationalised, but has come under increased British rather than NATO jurisdiction. In this way, the ARRC represent the concentration of national command competence into single headquarters within NATO. The operational level seems to be prosecuted most effectively by headquarters dominated by a single national culture.

Significantly, the enduring importance, and perhaps even increased validity, of the national principle can be best seen by comparing the ARRC as a framework nation headquarters with Eurocorps, the other rapid reaction corps to be created in the early 1990s. Eurocorps was developed from the Franco-German brigade, which was founded in 1987; was established as NATO's second rapid reaction corps in 1992 when Spanish and Benelux elements were incorporated into the formation (Cameron 1999: 75; van Ham 1999: 6). Eurocorps, as one of the two original rapid reaction corps, undoubtedly remains one of the most important multinational experiments comprising five nations. However, its operational performance, especially in contrast to ARRC, illustrates the shortcomings of multinationality. Roger Palin has noted that 'Euro-Corps suffers from a number of deficiencies, not the least of which is the paucity of organic corps troops'; 'A second deficiency, not unique to Euro-Corps, is the lack of air-lift capacity' (Palin 1995: 63–4). Significantly, Palin notes a fundamental political problem which affects this headquarters: 'To what extent the corps is expected to be a usable military instrument, in the short term, as opposed to a political symbol of an emerging European defence identity, and hence an investment for the long term, is debatable' (1995: 64). Crucially, like JFCB, Eurocorps is compromised by its multinational constitution. Thus, in assessing the Afghan deployment, senior officers, including the ISAF IV Commander, General Py, have stressed the weakness of the organisation. Eurocorps was structurally compromised by the fact that forces deferred to their national commands, constantly undermining the commander's attempt to sustain united planning goals. As noted by General Py:

There were thirty-six nations in Eurocorps and, consequently, you couldn't do what you wanted as commander. There were national caveats . . . In this situation, the commander cannot make decisions. He doesn't know what the reaction will be

---

[15] This move has been designated Operation Horrocks.

in national capitals. For instance, I wanted to lower the security state in Kabul to authorise soldiers to go downtown. However, I had to unofficially consult nations before I could make the decision. This is very difficult to manage and you are never sure whether troops will obey. It puts great restriction on the flexibility and autonomy of commander. It reduces the manoeuvrability of the commander by a great coefficient.[16]

It might be argued that this was primarily a result of co-ordinating not merely the five constituent nations of Eurocorps but the thirty-six ISAF contributors, as General Py emphasises. Certainly, the sheer number of nations which General Py had to co-ordinate added to the friction of his command. However, there is good reason to believe that, in fact, the Eurocorps' difficulties in Kabul were related to the standing constitution of that headquarters itself. As one British brigadier, seconded to the headquarters as a provincial reconstruction team director, noted, 'When I went out there, I thought I would find international accord and good relations. Not at all. They distrusted and hated each other and, as the stranger, I became the recipient of complaints about each nation. And these undermined the unity of the staff effort and impacted on the mission.' He summarised the situation lyrically: 'The Germans and the French would criticise each other. The French were considered impulsive; the Germans too cautious. Both disliked the Belgians and everyone hated the Spanish.' Decisively, the core staff – not their augmentees – in this headquarters could not work together. The British brigadier claimed that Eurocorps' planning practices were weak and, while individuals were competent, much of the documentation was underdeveloped. Because there was no unified national organisational culture, the headquarters was fragmented and could never develop effective military procedures.

Significantly, many of the tensions and frictions observable in Eurocorps have been replicated in the binational German–Netherlands Corps. In a volume, perhaps ironically entitled, *True Love*, Rene Moelker and Joseph Soeters have examined solidarity in 1 German–Netherlands Corps headquarters. They began their research from the hypothesis that 'the more military personnel from both nations work and live together, the more they will like each other' (Moelker and Soeters 2003: 17). Their research reveals interesting differences in perceptions between the Dutch and German soldiers. The Germans saw the Dutch as more independent, less formal and more comradely. By contrast, the Dutch saw the Germans as hierarchical, dependent upon the orders of superiors and stiff; the favourable attitude of the Germans to the Dutch was not reciprocated (2003: 39–40). The German–Netherlands Corps consisted of an equal

---

[16] General Py, Commander ISAF IV, personal interview, 14 December 2005.

representation of German and Dutch personnel in the formation, sharing decisive command and staff positions. The density of national associations within the respective group has impeded cross-group interactions, while the corporate identity of each group has tended to encourage rivalry and distrust. It has been more difficult to unify the German–Netherlands Corps. These differences in military culture and the lack of trust between the groups were some of the precipitating factors in the problems at Camp Warehouse, Kabul in 2003. During this deployment to Afghanistan, there were intense conflicts between the Dutch and German elements within the deployed formation.

The early research conducted by Klein *et al.* (2003) focused overwhelmingly on what Dutch and German personnel in 1 German–Netherlands Corps thought of each other; ultimately, on whether soldiers liked one another. In fact, professional trust may not require personal affection (MacCoun *et al.* 2006). Trust is not necessarily an index of friendship, but rather more bluntly a product of military competence and mutual professional respect. Accordingly, Ulrich vom Hagen has more recently asked German and Dutch personnel not what they personally think of each other (away from the professional military context). Instead, he has focused on what staff in this headquarters do together. Vom Hagen specifies many of the tensions identified more generally in the initial surveys. He records how Dutch officers criticise the headquarters: 'Overall I find command and control dogmatic [within HQ 1 GNC], bureaucratic and timid, not at all what I had experienced in other UK and multinational formations. Mission command is not generally practiced' (vom Hagen 2006: 23). There were further confusions: 'We have German, Dutch and NATO procedures working here. They sometimes simply don't match' (2006: 26). In practice, successive Dutch and German commanders have instituted their own national procedures. However, following a round of NATO certification, exercises and deployment to Afghanistan, 'the introduction of NATO SOPs [Standard Operating Procedures] is viewed as positive' (2006: 27). Vom Hagen concludes: 'Though there seems not to be much space for emotional sameness between the members of different military cultures, there is a lot of common ground when it comes to pursuing a commonly shared idea on the basis of collective professional standards' (2006: 33). Gradually, through the adoption of common practices – staff drills – a higher level of unity is being achieved than in the past, but the headquarters has been handicapped by its binational constitution.

The experiences of Eurocorps and the German–Netherlands Corps suggest that the framework nation rapid reaction corps in Spain, Italy, Greece and Turkey offer potentially more coherent command structures

for European forces. Although all of these headquarters include significant international elements in order to tie them into the Alliance, five out
of seven of them, including the ARRC, are framework nation headquarters with the core staff provided by the home nation. Describing
NATO's land component headquarters, a British commander has
emphasised precisely this point: 'While the multinational element remains
important, the national command link is likely to strengthen, which is
understandable given the increasing number of HRFs [Higher Readiness
Force Headquarters].'[17] The British general is careful not to disparage
multinationality, but he envisages it occurring in a context where the framework nation principle and the connection between the lead nation, their
armed forces and these commands are strengthened. Higher Readiness
Force Headquarters (HRF HQ) (rapid reaction corps from now on)
represent national condensations of operational authority and expertise.

Six other rapid reaction corps headquarters have been established since
the 1990s. One of the most interesting and potentially important examples
of this re-nationalisation of commands is France's new rapid reaction
corps at Lille. Although France initiated the development of Eurocorps,
they seem to have become disillusioned with it since ISAF IV, as General
Py's comments suggest. Accordingly, in 2005, a new Corps de réaction
rapide–France began to be established; to be activated in 2007. There
were clear strategic and economic reasons for the creation of the Corps
de réaction rapide–France. Its inauguration coincided with the professionalisation of French forces and the new strategic emphasis on global
deployments rather than territorial defence. The Corps de réaction
rapide–France represents a significant step forward from the 1 Corps on
which it was based. While 1 Corps was dedicated to the territorial defence
of northern France, the new Corps de réaction rapide–France's area of
responsibility is quite different:

There is no geographic pre-emption. It is completely open. It could be Afghanistan.
The French Rapid Reaction Corps, unlike Eurocorps, could be deployed to
Kosovo or Africa. Take the NRF in July as an example. We acted as Nation 1 at
the end of this year and Multinational Force in 2008. We are on standby for NRF
11. For that, we are engaged fully as a corps with a 60,000 person force as an initial
entry force. But we could be engaged using a smaller part of our HQ.[18]

The new headquarters is tasked to command national, EU and NATO
missions. However, despite France's traditional preference for national
autonomy, the Corps de réaction rapide–France underwent a NATO

---

[17] British two-star general, personal interview, 29 March 2006.
[18] Commander Commander Corps de réaction rapide–France, personal interview, 4 May
2007.

certification process in 2006 and 2007; it is able to act as a NATO HRF HQ (a rapid reaction corps), although it is not exclusively declared as such; the French wish to retain national authority over the command. Nevertheless, the creation of a NATO certificated national headquarters represents one of the most profound alterations in French strategic policy since 1966 when France withdrew from the integrated military structure:

> The French Rapid Reaction Corps is in the hands of the French government for national missions. But it can also lead in coalition operations either for the EU or NATO. It has three possible directions. It is very flexible. It is also very expensive. But it is possible to use it in national and coalition missions.[19]

Interestingly, because the Corps de réaction rapide–France is a national headquarters, not a NATO one like ARRC, it may eventually display greater coherence than ARRC. Certainly, visiting British officers have noted that the national autonomy of the headquarters is an advantage in comparison with ARRC. It has a close connection to the Quai d'Orsay and is not compromised by internal political agendas. Headquarters like the ARRC and the new Corps de réaction rapide–France represent an important development in Europe. They constitute national concentrations of military expertise and resourcing. Importantly, as national centres of excellence (augmented by international attachments), they have contributed decisively to NATO campaigns in the last decade in the Balkans and Afghanistan.

Given their contribution, there is increasing dissonance between the official status of the HRF HQ and their actual capabilities, which has been widely noted by the officers within them. Officially, the rapid reaction corps are tasked to provide the land component command for major operations which would be commanded by the operational commands, such as JFCB; they are only tactical commands. In reality, these corps headquarters transcend their official designations. Consequently, there is currently a struggle between the rapid reaction corps and the established command structure for status and authority. Significantly, the commanders of the rapid reaction corps headquarters reject this designation of themselves as merely tactical headquarters of lower status and authority than JFCB, JFCN and JFHQL:

> When you look at evolution of NATO, it is confused about the level of command. SHAPE [Supreme Headquarters Allied Powers Europe, Mons] is a strategic command. But with the Joint Forces Commands and then Component Commands: this is a useless structure ... For example when I was commander

[19] Commander Corps de réaction rapide–France, personal interview, 4 May 2007.

of ISAF, the operational commander was Brunssum. However, in fact, the commander of ISAF was an operational commander. In that environment, I had relations with the country, relations to the UN Secretary General, to NGOs and so on. I needed political advisers in order to manage this environment and to conduct psychological ops. If you consider different levels of command: strategic, operation and tactical levels. This is not quite right in NATO at the moment. I was operating at operational level. My DCOS Ops [Deputy Commander Operations[20]] concerned himself with tactical level. The operational level has expanded. The operational level can be at the brigade level. A brigade commander may have operational responsibility for a country. NATO is still in the past. However, the HRF concept is very good ... We should stick to HRF [Higher Readiness Force] Corps HQ and do operational command from there. We should give that commander the capabilities to assume responsibility.[21]

Another French commander emphasised the potency of the rapid reaction corps:

We have an air force cell to coordinate air assets and a Navy LO [liaison officer]. We are able to take on a maritime component or a land component. We have to be flexible. If you look at NATO, KFOR was a tactical command, JFC Naples was the operational command and SHAPE was the strategic command. But this is not true. KFOR involved a lot of operational things. JFC Naples had some political and joint issues but I had to deal with many operational issues. Similarly, JFC Brunssum can't deal with many issues concerning Afghanistan. When I was COM [Commander] KFOR, Naples asked for a list of key players in Kosovo whom they could call. I refused. The locals would have thought it was strange to have someone from Naples calling. I said I would call them – I knew them – Naples could not call them.[22]

The same point was confirmed by British officers:

In my humble view, the process of NATO transformation is not going far enough or fast enough. That is a political issue with a small 'p' but potent all the same. The powerhouses of the new structure are without doubt the HRF HQs. Some are certainly better than others but, in general, they have framework nations, money, infrastructure, training and deployability. They also attract the best of the framework nations' commanders and staffs. And yet, if I may over-egg it a little bit, NATO subordinates these lions to standing component command and joint command 'donkey' HQs that pale in comparison. They do not attract the first rate commanders who will eventually lead their nations' armed forces. They don't have the assets, infrastructure, money, training, quality of staff or deployability. And they fundamentally lack understanding of the operational level of command in the way that the HRFs must.[23]

[20] The DCOS operations co-ordinates the J2 (intelligence), J3 (operations) and J5 (plans) branches.
[21] General Py, personal interview, 14 December 2005.
[22] Commander Commander Corps de réaction rapide–France, personal interview, 4 May 2007.
[23] British brigadier, personal communication. 9 January 2008.

Although General Richards implied that perhaps not all of Europe's HRF HQs were of the same capability, he had absolutely no doubt that ARRC as ISAF IX was an operational headquarters and that this was the decisive level on missions today: 'The operational level is what separates the men from the boys. It is too daunting for most HQs but unless you are working at this level, you are pissing in the wind.'[24]

The rapid reaction corps provide Europe's real operational level command and they demonstrate some important organisational characteristics. While Eurocorps and the German–Netherlands Corps have been organised as multinational formations, the six other commands are framework nation headquarters. This national core seems both vital to operational competence and is increasingly being reinforced; these headquarters are, in contrast to the weak NATO operational headquarters, centres of national operational excellence. As such, they cannot really be reduced to tactical level commands which are concerned with purely military activity in the face of the enemy according to traditional definitions of the tactical level. In most cases, they are far more competent, knowledgeable and capable than their supposed operational commands, JFCB or JFHQL. They have engaged, or are engaging, in a range of activities, including political ones, where they are co-ordinating military operations simultaneously with political engagement strategies exceeding any established notion of the tactical. In reality, they then interact directly with ACO from whom they take direction; the formally designated operational commands are superfluous intermediaries which are typically regarded as hindrances to the in-theatre commands. As *de facto* operational commands the rapid reaction corps are fundamental to European military capacity and development. They usefully illustrate the likely organisational form which European military transformation is taking at the operational level. It is notable that while the ESDP's concept of a European Headline Goal has failed to materialise, and Europe may not possess a 60,000-strong rapid reaction force ready to deploy, in the shape of these rapid reaction corps, it does in fact possess the capability to plan and command major intervention operations – with the support of the United States. Indeed, as Bosnia and Kosovo have shown, the ARRC has already performed this role. Equally significantly, in Afghanistan, rapid reaction corps have consistently provided the staff and commander for subsequent rotations of ISAF: the Turkish, German–Netherlands, Eurocorps and Italian Corps have all acted in this role. Europe has manifest operational skill lodged in these military centres.

---

[24] General Richards, personal interview, 11 July 2006.

The NATO Response Force

In addition to reforming the NATO command structure, the Prague summit announced the creation of the NATO Response Force (NRF) (Binnendijk and Kugler 2002: 126–7; Clarke and Cornish 2002: 787). The NRF consists of joint air, maritime and ground forces deployable within five to thirty days to international trouble spots, and able to remain operational for up to three months if required. It is based on a brigade of three to five mobile ground battalions with logistic, air (three to five fighter squadrons) and naval (seven to fifteen vessels) support to create a force of about 21,000 in total (Binnendijk and Kugler 2002: 127). The NRF is specifically aimed at developing Europe's armed forces. Of these 21,000 personnel, only 300, located in the planning and headquarters cells, are American, and, operationally, it is commanded by a senior European general under the authority of the American SACEUR. Significantly, the European general commands a genuine transnational force, comprising battalions, aircraft and ships from contributing European Alliance members.

The NRF has played a number of useful roles, including a disaster relief operation to Pakistan in 2005, but it falls well short of a genuine intervention force despite the rhetoric around it. Nations are unwilling to bear the financial and political costs which such a commitment would entail. The NRF is not a credible intervention force, despite its recent certification. Indeed, in September 2008, there were suggestions that the NRF should be abandoned precisely because nations could not generate forces for the rotation cycle: NATO 'lacks the money, the troops and the equipment' (Dempsey 2007).[25] However, this does not mean that the NRF has been totally ineffectual. On the contrary, it has played an important role in catalysing developments at the operational level.

An NRF rotation system has now been established within NATO working on a six-monthly cycle. Forces assigned to the NRF undergo a six-month training and exercise programme in order to bring them up to NRF standards, followed by a stand-by period when they are nominally ready and available for rapid deployment should the North Atlantic Council call upon the NRF. The first NRF cycle, identified as NRF 1, started in 2003 and by 2009, NRF 13 had been reached. Operational command of the NRF has circulated on a six-monthly cycle between JFCB, JFCN and JFHQL, and they have accrued some benefit from the process. However, the NRF has had its most obvious benefit below the level of the operational commands, especially among European rapid

---

[25] http://www.iht.com/articles/2007/09/20/europe/force.php.

reaction corps which have provided the land component command (LCC) for the NRF. As the NRF concept has developed, the LCC of the NRF has circulated around the rapid reaction corps.[26] The impact of the NRF on these commands can be demonstrated by examining the rapid reaction corps' own assessments of their time as the nominated LCC: the NRF 6 cycle is a useful initial example here.

In January 2006, ARRC was scheduled to provide the LCC for NRF 6. However, the commitment to the NRF clashed with the selection of the ARRC as ISAF IX HQ: ARRC was to deploy to Afghanistan in April 2006. In the light of the rancour caused by the Iraq War within the Alliance, Britain felt impelled to honour its commitment to the NRF. Consequently, the UK Ministry of Defence proposed that 3 Division act as the NRF 6 LCC. This was a novel proposal since doctrinally LCCs are situated at the corps level. However, the solution was accepted and in 2006, 3 Division performed the role of the nominated NRF LCC.[27] In the event, 3 Division proved to be very capable of fulfilling the role as LCC. Indeed, the period as NRF component commands had major benefits for the Division of which senior officers were well aware:

The NRF was an opportunity and we used it. It showed us how to integrate and we were able to test this through Exercise Allied Warrior which was the culmination for 2005; we got a full Field Training Exercise out of it. We improved and increased our standard operating procedures dramatically. Every one of them was very useful and those SOPs are a reference now; they show we have got our act together. It allowed us to practise the integration of 101 Brigade (logistics brigade) into the [3 UK] Division. We were able to [be] certified as CT5 [Collective Training Level 5, i.e. battalion manoeuvres). For 19 Brigade, it was the same. The whole force is now at UK HR [Higher Readiness] standard. It was cracking. I am not positive about NATO. But internally, it is a mechanism to parasite off. We squeezed the money from MOD. It was a gold mine for us. Basically Land [HQ] were not that happy about it but they could not refuse: we had to get NATO certification.[28]

3 Division's chief of staff was effusive about the beneficial effects of the NRF and his statement is instructive. Even for a well-trained, professional force like the British Army, the NRF cycle has been very useful. It enabled

---

[26] NATO Rapid Deployable Corps–Italy commanded NRF 3 from July to December 2004; German–Netherlands Corps, NRF 4 from January to July 2005; NATO Rapid Deployable Corps–Spain, NRF 5 from July 2005 to January 2006; UK 3 Division, NRF 6 from January to July 2006; Eurocorps, NRF 7 from July 2006 to January 2007; NATO Rapid Deployable Corps–Turkey, NRF 8 from January to July 2007; NATO Rapid Deployable Corps–Italy, NRF 9 from July 2007 to January 2008. The cycle of NRF commands has been organised out to NRF 13 in 2010.
[27] General Shirref, personal interview, 29 March 2006.
[28] Brigadier, personal interview, 2 June 2006.

3 Division to develop its staff systems and to test out new procedures. The NRF presented 3 Division with an ideal opportunity to conduct training which would not be possible under national constraints. The British brigadier also illustrates a very important process which has been initiated by the NRF. On the basis of Britain's NATO commitments, 3 Division was able to force the Ministry of Defence to fund an exercise for which there were formally no national resources and to which Land Command was itself opposed. In Britain divisional level exercises have become extremely rare.

3 Division's period as NRF 6's LCC was unusual because it was not one of NATO's rapid reaction corps headquarters. However, the processes identified by the chief of staff and commander are replicated among the established rapid reaction corps. In other countries, the same process of increased investment and new training opportunities during NRF cycles has been evident. This is demonstrated particularly clearly by the example of the NATO Rapid Deployable Corps–Italy (based in Milan), Italy's rapid reaction corps. The Rapid Deployable Corps–Italy acted as ISAF HQ VIII from August 2005 to May 2006. On its return from that deployment, it reconstituted itself and prepared for its NRF stand-by period from January to July 2007. The period of training for the NRF involved five events culminating in Exercise Steadfast Jackpot. At the end of 2007, in their assessment of their period as NRF LCC,[29] the Rapid Deployable Corps–Italy dismissed the notion that the NRF could be a serious deployable force. There were decisive shortcomings in the concept. For any operation, NATO issues a Combined Joint Statement of Requirement (CJSOR) which requests the necessary forces from Alliance members. During Rapid Deployable Corps–Italy's period as NRF 9, critical CJSORs were missing. For instance, the exercises revealed a serious lack in communications and information systems. During Exercise Steadfast Jackpot, for instance, three days were lost because the email system collapsed. In any real operation, shortcomings of this scale would be potentially fatal. Accordingly, Rapid Deployable Corps–Italy questioned the fundamental credibility of the NRF concept. In the event of a genuine operation, the Italian officers questioned whether nations would actually be willing to contribute forces and, even if they did, whether they would be fundamentally compromised by the imposition of caveats. Certain critical capabilities were also lacking. Despite these criticisms, the Rapid Deployable Corps–Italy made some interesting observations

---

[29] ARRC Land Component Command 'Arcade Nelson' conference held at Rheindalen on 26–27 November 2007. The conference was itself evidence of the transnational operational network with representatives from all the rapid reaction corps present.

about the NRF. The headquarters found that the staff were able to improve their common procedures significantly during this process. The Rapid Deployable Corps–Italy recognised that the NRF had enabled the headquarters to attract national investment out of a reluctant defence ministry. Like 3 Division, Rapid Deployable Corps–Italy emphasised the localised benefits of the NRF process even if the NRF was itself, in their words, 'incredible' (i.e., without credibility).

Other European rapid reaction corps recorded the beneficial training opportunities provided by the NRF. In a recent certification process of one of the other rapid reaction corps,[30] various lessons were identified during an exercise. The rapid reaction corps and its staff was very familiar with conventional war fighting, but it recognised that it was less adept at the complex stabilisation and counter-insurgency missions which it was actually rather more likely to conduct. Related to this misunderstanding of the nature of the environment in which it now operated, the headquarters was organised sub-optimally. The headquarters had been organised on a staff-led basis, which prioritised accurate process over the commander's intuition. In the current era of complex operations, the staff-led systems proved to be too cumbersome and commanders, especially since they are interacting dynamically with a diversity of agents, need to have the freedom to steer and direct the planning. Consequently, the NRF process advanced a commander-led system to this rapid reaction corps headquarters. Other more serious problems were highlighted. Some of the personnel, schooled in interstate warfare, were simply not of the quality required for the tempo of current operations. Closely related to this, the staff struggled to produce timely and clear orders during the exercise for the subordinate brigade; in particular, they noted the inadequate use of graphics to illustrate the orders. The headquarters explicitly drew across from accepted NATO planning doctrine to assess their own performance and, using the NATO criteria, identified weaknesses. The rapid reaction corps' report on itself was deeply self-critical.

The experiences of these three headquarters illustrate one of the most important elements of the NRF process: it has tested the staff processes of the rapid reaction corps and ranked them against each other. The NRF process has demanded that headquarters improve its staff expertise and prioritised common NATO procedures as the basis for development. It has been a forum for operational convergence, disseminating common procedures across the rapid reaction corps network, and has actively encouraged interaction and mutual comparison. On the basis of their

---

[30] The source wished the headquarters to remain anonymous.

commitment to the NRF, the rapid reaction corps have been consistently able to demand additional investment promoting them above other formations. The NRF has played into the process of concentration. The recurrent process of testing has also affirmed the framework nation principle: successful rapid reaction corps have been those with a strong national core of staff. Indeed, this national principle has been self-consciously advocated by members of this group. In response to Rapid Deployable Corps–Italy's presentation at the ARRC Land Component Command Conference in November 2007, the ARRC's chief of staff similarly advocated that the LCC for the NRF should always be conducted by a framework nation headquarters in order to reduce some of the frictions which the Rapid Deployable Corps–Italy experienced. In particular, he identified the German–Netherlands Corps as a headquarters which should take on the framework nation principle. With its training and exercise opportunities, the NRF has played an important role in crystallising a new operational network.

The NRF process is having a tangible effect on European military transformation, but its consequences are potentially surprising. Europe is not creating a genuinely deployable reaction force as General Jones declared back in 2003, nor is it improving the capacity of designated operational headquarters in Brunssum, Naples and Lisbon to provide command for such a force. Rather, the NRF is promoting Europe's rapid reaction corps. While JFCB, JFCN and JFHQL act as supporting enablers, these headquarters have actually enacted the NRF in practice. The NRF has actively presented them with an opportunity to develop themselves through exercises and two small missions. The NRF has effectively become a circulating international good which has stimulated localised national military development. It has provided the rapid reaction corps with an excellent opportunity to improve and develop themselves.

The transnational network

Rapid reaction corps are emerging at the national level, but, simultaneously, they are demonstrating the other key feature of contemporary military transformation: deepening cross-border, transnational relations are developing between them. The rapid reaction corps have become a self-referential status group which shares knowledge, expertise and training opportunities. As the newest member of this HRF group, the Corps de réaction rapide–France, demonstrates this process of transnationalisation with particular clarity. From its inception, the Corps de réaction rapide–France chose to undergo the NATO certification process. This decision accorded with the subsequent decision outlined in the *Livre Blanc* to renovate the transatlantic Alliance, although the Corps de réaction rapide–France's certification process preceded this formal change of policy by four years. As the Commander Corps de réaction rapide–France emphasised: 'It is impossible to have certification from anyone else.'[31] He described specific operational and organisational benefits which have encouraged the French Army to choose to certify its Corps de réaction rapide with NATO. Crucially, the Corps de réaction rapide–France's NATO validation process was specifically designed to access the network of operational competence which is appearing under NATO's aegis: 'We did not get the certification just for itself. Certification creates the possibility to train with other HQs and to command operations.'[32]

The statement by the Commander Corps de réaction rapide–France is very important. He recognised that future military competence relied on being part of an emergent rapid reaction corps community. NATO explicitly provides a forum for French forces to develop ever closer relations with other European headquarters and to co-operate more closely with them. In this the Commander Corps de réaction rapide–France represents the view of the wider French military:

Following the example of European partners, France is convinced – from lessons of recent conflicts – that it is necessary to talk the same language: of reactivity, projection and interoperability at the higher level. A unique standard for collectively facing the recent evolutions in the strategic environment, which is the goal of the HRF, has become the doctrinal reference point of operational land command. (Tarin 2005: 27)

Pointedly listing all the other rapid reaction corps, the French Army noted in 2005 that: 'Only France is not yet represented by its contribution to Corps Headquarters in Europe' (Tarin 2005: 27). As Colonel Dexter, head of the G5 planning branch, noted, 'France cannot be absent from the club of great powers equipped with certified HRF commands' (2005: 27). The Corps de réaction rapide–France is actively seeking to situate itself within this privileged group of commands in order to benefit from exchanges with others and to gain status and influence. Sassen has observed a similar process in the financial services industry. There she notes that not only have headquarters located themselves in major cities, but also they have tended to cluster together to form 'milieus of innovation'; staff, in the informal setting of bars and restaurants near their offices, often exchange ideas. The rapid reaction corps might perhaps also be described as a compatible military 'milieu of innovation' in Europe and

---

[31] Personal interview, 4 May 2007.   [32] Personal interview, 4 May 2007.

the Corps de réaction rapide–France has deliberately situated itself in this milieu in order to share and develop expertise with others. It is noticeable that there is a cluster of headquarters, all within convenient travelling distance of each other in northern Europe; ACO (Mons), Corps de réaction rapide–France (Lille), the German–Netherlands Corps (Münster), ARRC (Rheindalen), Eurocorps (Strasbourg) and Brunssum. The Corps de réaction rapide–France is situated at the heart of this milieu. Moreover, only under NATO could the Corps de réaction rapide–France hope to command operations. France now recognises that national military effectiveness depends upon closer co-operative links with NATO members. It would be impossible for a single nation to create a rapid reaction corps without drawing on the operational expertise that already exists in other European rapid reaction corps. Ironically, in order to sustain their military effectiveness, French forces are increasingly finding that they must integrate with other NATO headquarters to share knowledge and expertise. NATO has effectively become a vital forum in which these headquarters are able to interact with each other; it provides an institutional framework for the interaction of national centres of excellence.

The process by which this integration has taken place for the Corps de réaction rapide–France is interesting. Significantly, the Corps de réaction rapide–France has based itself closely on the ARRC, not on the partly French Eurocorps:

When I was with ARRC, I was commander of the rear headquarters when they were doing KFOR. There were twenty French officers there – in 1996 – 'spying' on us. They were thinking of creating their own rapid reaction corps. And the French Rapid Reaction Corps HQ is close to ARRC; it was the model. It was the only one.[33]

Affirming the connections between the Corps de réaction rapide–France and ARRC, General Richards visited Lille before leaving the ARRC in 2007, and the Corps de réaction rapide–France has given the important staff position of Assistant Chief of Staff Operations[34] to a British brigadier. The current incumbent had previously worked in the ARRC and his expertise was used to ensure that the procedures which the Corps de réaction rapide–France is currently trying to develop are

[33] British three-star general, personal interview, 29 March 2007.
[34] Joint military headquarters (like the HRF HQs) are organised into nine branches; J (Joint) 1 (personnel), J2 (intelligence), J3 (operations), J4 (logistics), J5 (plans), J6 (signals and communications), J7 (doctrine and training), J8 (finance), J9 civil–military relations. In a corps headquarters, each branch is commanded by a brigadier as the assistant chief of staff. The assistant chiefs of staff answer to the chief of staff whose role it is to organise the staff so that it can produce plans in line with the directions provided by the commander. The British brigadier was in charge of operations at the Corps de réaction rapide–France.

compatible with the British-led headquarters. Senior French officers in the headquarters were explicit about this connection. For instance, when ARRC visited, the Deputy Chief of Staff (DCOS) Operations was pleased to be able to confirm that the process which they had instituted based on 'Plan–Refine–Execute–Assess' accorded with the ARRC's own process. However, at the same time the DCOS Operations also highlighted the sensitivity of the Corps de réaction rapide–France to the ARRC's assessment. Describing the process of assessing the plan, he said that the headquarters had merely instituted an informal *ad hoc* process: 'We meet and discuss this pragmatically'. 'But when the British came, they said "Have you got any organisation or tool for this?" It was a wet finger on the nose.'[35] The Corps de réaction rapide–France had to admit that such a tool had not yet been developed. Although the details of the interaction are not in themselves significant, the exchange reveals that the Corps de réaction rapide–France has actively sought to develop their expertise through engagement with other national centres of operational expertise such as ARRC. It is evidence of the exchange of information and expertise across national borders and indicates that a transnational network is developing between rapid reaction corps and their staffs.

In addition to strengthening national rapid reaction corps headquarters, the NRF has driven a process of convergence; it has facilitated the formation of this transnational operational network because, on recurrent exercises, these headquarters are tested to a common set of criteria. They have to demonstrate competence around established shared planning and command procedures. The NRF has become a part of a wider process which is producing an 'operational complex'. This operational complex constitutes a new network of expertise in Europe. It does not mean the end of national military culture or state sovereignty over the armed forces. On the contrary, the new operational community consists precisely of strengthened headquarters, connected closely with their states, engaged in closer co-operative relations with peer rapid reaction corps in other European nations. The NRF has precipitated the emergence of this new transnational operational network, consisting of nodes of military capability linked in a condensing nexus. The NRF is part of the wider transformation of European forces at the operational level. Thus, while it has

---

He was tasked with implementing the plans provided by the J5 branch, while monitoring and directing the immediate activities of subordinate troops. The operations post at any level of command is vital because it realises the commander's concept of operations.

[35] Brigadier, Deputy Chief of Staff Operations, Commander Corps de réaction rapide–France, personal interview, 4 May 2007.

failed programmatically, it is part of a new complex of military institutions that represents a re-configuration of Europe's armed forces.

Industrial sociologists have noted a compatible move to network alliances (Castells 1996; Dyer 2000; Gerlach 1992; Gomes-Casseres 1996; Sassen 1991; Womack *et al.* 1990). In place of Fordist vertical integration, corporations now co-ordinate a network of suppliers in non-marketised relations. Networks share knowledge and assist each other's industrial development to their mutual benefit while retaining flexibility which is lost by vertical integration. Dyer has demonstrated how this strategy of co-operative action and network configuration has been central to the success of Toyota for four decades and the re-vitalisation of Chrysler in the 1990s (2000). Castells usefully summarises the situation:

The new production system relies on a combination of strategic alliances and *ad hoc* cooperation projects between corporations, decentralised units of each major corporation, and networks of small and medium enterprises connecting among themselves and/or with large groups of corporations or networks of corporations ... What is fundamental in this web-like industrial structure is that it is territorially spread throughout the world and its geometry keeps changing, as a whole and for each individual unit. (2000: 260)

The perspectives of scholars like Sassen and Castells are useful for understanding the emergent reality of Europe's new military headquarters. Significantly, European rapid reaction corps seem to be assuming a network form. They are concentrations of nationalising military competence and resourcing, simultaneously allying with each other on a sometimes informal basis. As the development of the Corps de réaction rapide–France demonstrates, these headquarters are actively seeking to exchange knowledge and expertise. They do not constitute a vertical command structure, but are forming themselves into a European military network in which horizontal relations enabling operational performance are vital. Moreover, individual staff officers circulate around the emergent network, encouraging organisational coherence and unity. The contrast with command structures in Europe during the Cold War is profound. During the Cold War, NATO command was strictly hierarchical, oriented eastwards towards the Soviet threat; each subordinate level of command fulfilled the directive of its superordinate. NATO standardised certain procedures, but there were few common practices between headquarters and limited interrelations between corps headquarters. In the last ten years a network of nationalised rapid reaction corps has emerged, four of which have commanded ISAF while the others have all provided staff officers and commanders for NATO missions to the Balkans, Afghanistan and other NATO headquarters. They are actively seeking to develop common forms of operational practice to facilitate their interactions (see Chapter 7).

The rapid reaction corps community might be seen as a network of concentrated nodes central to contemporary military transformation. However, the actuality of operational command in Europe is intricate. In commercial and industrial sectors, the move to network capitalism has involved increasingly multipolar complexity. A rise of complexity is similarly evident in the military sphere at the operational level. Mark Duffield's analysis of liberal intervention is illuminating here. Taking his cue from Castells' work on the network dynamics of informational society, Duffield has advanced the idea that global governance today, itself implicated in new wars, is actually enacted through 'strategic complexes of liberal peace' (Duffield 2001: 13). In contrast to the twentieth century, the international system is no longer organised on 'Newtonian' lines as Duffield calls it (2001: 10), where events can be understood in relation to a relatively few causal international factors; 'the liberal peace is not manifest within a single institution of global governance' (2001: 12). The traditional patterns of North–South relations have been reformed. States no longer monopolise international politics, rather, state authority has been compromised by the appearance of new actors that are often transnational or global in nature. States have become increasingly interdependent, addressing regional issues in concert. In addition, non-governmental organisations (NGOs) or supranational institutions, like the UN or the International Court of Justice, global corporations, including the media, and new ethnic and religious groups have all begun to appear on the international scene. All these forces coalesce to create and define the nature of any particular crisis. Any state or state coalition must recognise the influence of these agencies on the mission in which they are involved. There has been a 'move to polyarchic, non-territorial and networked relations of governance' (Duffield 2001: 11). For Duffield, then, we live in a post-Newtonian world of intense complexity, contingency and randomness. States do not rationally pursue an independent strategy, rather, events emerge in a 'strategic complex' of interconnected, mutually influencing institutions.

Following Duffield's term, it might be argued that an 'operational complex' is emerging in Europe. The rapid reaction corps have become an important part of this complex. However, the reality of operations is more complex. These headquarters do not receive direction only from ACO or JFCB or JFCN, nor do they interact exclusively with each other; the reality of the operational level is far more elaborate. Rather in each nation, the rapid reaction corps, even if they are formally declared to NATO, have necessarily developed close relations with their respective national land command headquarters which are tasked primarily with the generation of forces. This is particularly true in France where the Corps de réaction rapide–France's headquarters at the Citadel in Lille is a very short distance from the Commandement de la force d'action terrestre, France's land headquarters, also located in Lille. However, there are also close relations between Land Command in Britain and the ARRC. This connection seems to have been strengthened with the ARRC's move to Innsworth, Gloucester in 2009, less than 100 miles from Land Command in Wilton, Salisbury. The national land headquarters exerts an influence over the manning, direction and policies of the rapid reaction corps, though it is not always easy to identify the precise nature of this influence. It is often diffuse, but more often deliberately or accidentally concealed or officially secret. However, the operational complex in which the rapid reaction corps are nested involves additional elements that form an important part of the emergent operational complex.

In parallel to the emergence of NATO HRF HQs, Britain, France and Germany have created their own national operational headquarters: the Permanent Joint Headquarters (PJHQ, UK), Centre de planification et de conduite des opérations (France) and Einsatzführungskommando (Germany). These headquarters have a formally similar function: namely, organising the deployment of forces globally. There are, in fact, some differences between them. In particular, while PJHQ has accrued much authority, the Centre de planification et de conduite des opérations and Einsatzführungskommando have played a less important role in current operations. The French headquarters has played an important role in connecting deployed forces with strategic commanders, but in-theatre French commanders have typically bypassed the Centre de planification and spoken to their service chief or the Chef d'état-major himself. Einsatzführungskommando is not really an operational headquarters but, as its officers describe it, a 'supporting headquarters' which ensures the imposition of caveats and which requests forces for missions from the services.[36] Nevertheless, despite their differences, these national operational headquarters have also played an important role in the emergent operational complex, interacting with and influencing the rapid reaction corps.

The influence of these new national operational headquarters and established land headquarters is particularly evident when the rapid reaction corps have been on operations; national headquarters have exerted

---

[36] The different size of the respective headquarters illustrates their distinctive power and role; PJHQ has 600 staff, the Centre de planification and the Einsatzführungskommando approximately 120 each.

pressure on them to steer the NATO operation in a way which is most convenient to the national headquarters. The influence has not always been benign. The most obvious example of this was the contradictions which developed in Afghanistan in the course of 2006. Nominally, NATO operations were controlled by the ARRC as ISAF IX in Afghanistan. Thus, British forces in the Helmand Task Force were supposedly commanded by NATO's Regional Command South which in turn was subordinate to ISAF: General Richards, as commander ISAF, commanded Brigadier General Fraser, Regional Command South, who commanded Colonel Knags, Helmand Task Force. Operational realities were significantly more complex. Since the mission was militarily dangerous and politically sensitive, PJHQ retained close control over 16 Air Assault Brigade as it began to deploy in April 2006 and throughout its tour. The headquarters provided direction to the commander of the Helmand Task Force, even though it held no formal NATO position, and substantially influenced the nature of operations in the province. Even more problematically, PJHQ deployed Brigadier Butler, the commander of 16 Air Assault to Afghanistan, as Commander British Forces. There was a clear conflict of interest between Butler and Knags. Not only was Knags subordinate to Butler, but he nominally controlled Butler's own 16 Air Assault Brigade troops in Helmand. This was an unworkable situation and PJHQ began to pass orders and instructions to Brigadier Butler.

In effect, PJHQ and Brigadier Butler, both unrecognised in the NATO chain of command, actually orchestrated the initial campaign in Helmand. Accordingly, PJHQ blocked the use of British assets, especially helicopters, from use by other NATO forces because Britain was so overstretched in Helmand. Indeed, 16 Air Assault Brigade were unable to contribute to Operation Medusa, the crucial defence of Kandahar in August 2006 when the Taliban mounted a major offensive against the city. Even though British officers continually complain about the national agendas of other NATO members, PJHQ actively undermined the unity of NATO in Afghanistan, ironically operating against its own national commander and HRF HQ and the chain of command it was trying to create. Thus, under PJHQ's guidance British troops became involved in very intense, but ultimately unwinnable struggles in towns in northern Helmand, especially Musa Qala, which went actively against General Richards' own strategy of focused 'Afghan Development Zones'. Indeed, Richards had to broker a deal with local elders and the insurgents to facilitate an honourable withdrawal of British troops from Musa Qala in October 2006 (Fergusson 2008; Rayment 2008). PJHQ's entanglement in Helmand and ISAF IX was an extreme and nefarious example of the operational complex at work, though it is noticeable that PJHQ has in collaboration with other UK Government departments produced an independent 'Helmand Roadmap' which is not recognised by and barely references NATO and ISAF. The conflicts between a PJHQ, as a national operational headquarters, and ARRC as a British-led NATO rapid reaction corps are unusual. However, the very extremity of this example illustrates the organisational complexity of military operations today.

The transformation of Europe's armed forces at the operational level is complex. The apparently straightforward NATO hierarchy of strategic, operational and tactical commands is in reality an intricate web of interconnections, some of which are mutually contradictory, between nations and NATO, rapid reaction corps and national operational headquarters. However, although the operational complex is certainly elaborate and intricate, the rapid reaction corps represent important, even decisive, nodes within it. They are concentrations of operational authority, resourcing and expertise and they have contributed most to the planning and command of Europe's military operations in the last decade. It would seem plausible to suggest that they will become increasingly important in the coming decades.

Conclusion

The rapid reaction corps represent the organic development of a new military command structure within the shell of a formally revised operational hierarchy. The 2004 NATO reforms with its eleven commands was an attempt to create a coherent command structure, but even this reform, radical by NATO standards, is compromised. It invests commands located in Europe and established in the Cold War with far too much status given their actual contribution to NATO operations. As General Py argues, the majority of NATO's current structure is 'useless'. In reality, NATO missions are organised through strategic direction from ACO, which is then enacted in-theatre by commands in Bosnia, Kosovo and Afghanistan. Rapid reaction corps are important here because they have provided the commands for these theatres or personnel for composite headquarters as they have consistently demonstrated in the Balkans and Afghanistan. The emergent transnational military network consists of a concentration of command at the strategic level of ACO and among the rapid reaction corps and the in-theatre commands as the genuine operational commands. The reality of NATO command structures contradicts the publicly stated hierarchy. More interestingly, as NATO develops it is informally and organically developing the structure of other transnational organisations. Like Sassen's corporations, command authority is being concentrated in a single empowered headquarters located, not like most commercial multinationals in a global city, but in Mons some 80 km south-west of Brussels.

Although Mons is no cosmopolitan environment itself, ACO's location situates it at the heart of Europe with easy access to some major military commands in Lille, Rheindalen, Strasbourg and Münster. At the same time, new national operational headquarters, the PJHQ, Centre de planification et de conduite des opérations and Einsatzführungskommando, interact and influence these rapid reaction corps to form an 'operational complex' in Europe. Significantly, this complex does not represent a dissolution of the nation, but rather an affirmation of national principle. The emergent operational network in Europe consists of concentrated national and NATO headquarters in key locations in Europe.

European military forces are undergoing a profound transformation. At the level of operational command, a radical reform has been instituted in the last ten years, accelerating in the last five. In the face of the need to deploy globally against new strategic threats, a new command structure has been developed. Command authority has been concentrated into empowered joint headquarters at strategic and operational levels. In NATO, ACO now commands operations through a network of rapid reaction corps and in-theatre composite commands. At the national level, there has been a move in Europe to invest military authority into new joint operational headquarters, such as the PJHQ, Centre de planification et de conduite des opérations and Einsatzführungskommando. As in NATO, the powers of these national headquarters reflect historical political settlements between civil society and the military and between the services. Nevertheless, although it is vital to recognise these national differences, it is equally important to note the speed and scale of current transformations. In the space of just over a decade, an international military hierarchy directed to a mass threat in Eastern Europe has sought to transform itself for global deployment against complex ethnic insurgencies. In order to fulfil this mission, the armed forces in Europe, under the aegis of the United States, have adopted a strategy which has been identified very widely in globalising organisations. Large hierarchical organisations have been concentrated into nodes of command authority which now co-ordinate a network of subsidiaries. Similarly, in Europe, for all the compromises and failings of NATO and national militaries, the outline of a new transnational order is visible: concentrations of localised military resourcing and expertise in increasingly close contact and co-operation with similar concentrations in other nations. While NATO's ACO co-ordinates the activities of in-theatre troops and rapid reaction corps with the assistance of JFCB, national joint headquarters are similarly assuming control over a range of forces to conduct operations globally. The operational structure of Europe's forces has changed dramatically.

5   The operational renaissance

Introduction

Europe's operational network, in which the rapid reaction corps head-quarters hold a decisive position, represents a concentration of military capability and authority. However, the fact of concentration does not reveal precisely what role these new headquarters perform. As described in Chapter 4, the operational level refers to the co-ordination of tactical military activity into a coherent campaign in order to achieve strategic goals. The operational level refers, then, to the planning and command of these campaigns and operational art refers to the skilful design and organ-isation of military activity. Rapid reaction corps were created in order to address the new strategic pressures which NATO – and Europe – faced in the post-Cold War period. They were specifically designed to plan and command the new requirement to deploy troops at short notice to areas potentially outside those of traditional NATO responsibility. Although designated as tactical level commands, rapid reaction corps headquarters, therefore, represented an operational approach. They were specifically developed to plan operations, selecting how, when and where to deploy forces in line with strategic goals. Europe's operational network and, especially, its rapid reaction corps represent the institutional embodiment of operational art. It is necessary to explore the precise nature of this practice.

In the 1990s, the US armed forces underwent a self-proclaimed 'revo-lution in military affairs' (RMA) which generated a significant academic literature. There was extensive debate, but even scholars hostile to the concept broadly agreed that the RMA consisted of three essential develop-ments: new intelligence and target acquisition systems; precision-guided munitions; and digital communications. In his fine assessment of the concept of a military revolution, Andrew Latham identifies decisive omis-sions and elisions in that literature. The central flaw of the analysis of the RMA is that it a-historically focused on certain specific aspects of the current transformation. Scholars focused too much on technical aspects of developments in the 1990s but, crucially, they have ignored the wider historical origins of the current revolution. Latham has sought to demonstrate the evolutionary nature of the so-called RMA by utilising a Braudelian approach. In his famous works on historical change, Fernand Braudel proposed that history might best be analysed by reference to three perspectives or levels of development. Thus, Braudel maintained that history could be understood in terms of 'events time' (histoire événementielle), conjectural time of between ten and fifty years and, finally the longue durée, referring to centuries or epochs (Latham 2002: 235). For Braudel, historical explanation must trace the way in which specific events have become possible due to the social dynamics of the conjunctural situation, itself a product of the longue durée.

Accordingly, Latham seeks to re-interpret the 1990s RMA, situating it within a wider trajectory of military and social history. Thus, for Latham the shift from manoeuvre warfare to precision destruction amounts to a histoire événementielle. Yet the RMA is itself a consequence of the long-term decline of mass war and mass industry, which are themselves products of the formation of nation-states and the institution of a particular kind of war fighting within the Westphalian system. That international social order is fragmenting and as it does so a new kind of conflict is appearing. Thus, although sceptics deny that the RMA is a manifestation of 'fundamental *transformation* in the nature of war as a politico-cultural institution' (original emphasis) (Latham 2002: 259), it is difficult to maintain such a position from the perspective of the longue durée. Latham concludes: 'Viewed on this temporal plane, the contemporary RMA appears as a transition from the combined arms war fighting paradigm that emerged as decisive in World War II to a new paradigm based on concepts such as "information dominance", "non-linear operations", "dominant manoeuvre" and "precision engagement"' (2002: 263). Decisively, Latham sees the RMA not ultimately as a revolution, and certainly not a technical one in the 1990s, but as the manifestation of changes initiated in the 1970s; it represented a long-term institutional and conceptual evolution.

This chronology is directly pertinent to the question of operational art in Europe today. Although the rapid reaction corps headquarters and the kinds of stabilisation operation for which they had to plan were novel departures in the 1990s, the operational approach institutionalised by the rapid reaction corps had a much longer historical origin. In particular, the refinement of operational art in the rapid reaction corps in the last decade should be seen as the outgrowth of developments initiated in the 1970s. The rapid reaction corps drew upon existing military doctrine and practice and, indeed, they might be understood as an accentuation of an operational orientation which was already becoming well established by the end of the 1980s in NATO. In order to understand the position of the rapid reaction corps in the historic development of the operational approach, it is necessary to trace the origins of 'operations' in NATO – and European – military doctrine.

'AirLand Battle'

In the 1960s, the Soviet Union experimented with new forms of deep battle, utilising what Marshall Ogarkov called the revolution in technical affairs (Glantz 1996: 137). In the face of the developments in Soviet doctrine, NATO commanders worried that in any conventional land engagement on the West German plain they would be overwhelmed. In fact, as John Mearsheimer (1981, 1982) has argued, NATO's attritional defence strategy and their force ratios against the Warsaw Pact were not as catastrophic as often assumed at the time. Against appeals to 'manoeuvre warfare' which Mearsheimer showed were unspecific and difficult to execute within a multinational alliance, he maintained that, in fact, NATO's best defence lay in attrition. The Warsaw Pact had to advance across terrain, including substantial 'urban sprawl' (1981: 116), and, in most scenarios, the number of NATO divisions at least matched their opponents, if the standard 3:1 advantage was accorded to the defender. Mearsheimer was surely correct when he maintained that NATO would be unwise to surrender the advantages of attritional defence and, indeed, there is little evidence that they did so. General Rogers, SACEUR in the early 1980s, never professed to give up attritional defence, which he believed was the best means available to the West of countering the first echelon of Soviet forces. However, Rogers was concerned that NATO forces would be unable to resist the subsequent echelons which were a central part of the new 'operational manoeuvre groups'. The prospect of defeat by these follow-on echelons stimulated a fundamental re-conceptualisation of Western military doctrine. The United States was, of course, at the forefront of these changes which would have a fundamental impact on Europe's armed forces.

The recognition of the inadequacy of NATO force structures in Western Europe coincided with the defeat of the United States in Vietnam and the subsequently major reformation of the US Army of the early 1970s (Lock-Pullan 2003: 487; Swain 1996). Substantially in response to the poor performance of many units in Vietnam, the US Army became an all-volunteer force in 1973. At the same time, the US armed forces were actively looking to develop a new doctrine to remedy the deficiencies which were evident in Vietnam and to re-invigorate its newly professionalised forces. The US Army was impressed by the distinctive approach of the IDF in the Yom Kippur War in 1973. The IDF did not mass their forces in order to attrit the Egyptian forces from the front as the latter advanced, but attacked the rear Egyptian echelons. The IDF's strategy suggested a means by which a smaller but professionalised US Army might be able to maximise its combat effectiveness. In 1973, the Training and Doctrine Center (TRADOC) was established under the command of General Depuy to institutionalise the Army's new approach to war fighting, and to train US ground forces to conduct these operations. In 1976, Depuy issued the Army's new doctrine Field Manual (FM) 100-5 *Operations*, which proposed the concept of 'active defence', utilising the lessons of the 1973 Arab–Israeli war (Leonard 1991: 130–1). Active defence emphasised counter-attack over established attritional US doctrine. Depuy also inaugurated a 'training revolution' which developed the levels of professional competence required to engage in the more demanding operation of active defence (Lock-Pullan 2003: 503).

FM 100-5 (1976) was an important doctrinal development, but it was subsequently severely criticised by both civilian and military analysts (Bronfield 2008; Lock-Pullan 2003, 2006; Swain 1996: 154). The central problem was that active defence divided the campaign into a series of independent battles at battalion, brigade and divisional level (Leonard 1991: 132). It oriented the US Army to a series of tactical engagements, each of which were won by local manoeuvre, but it did not unify these actions into a coherent 'operation'. Corps merely positioned their forces; they did not actively co-ordinate their tactical actions into a united campaign. There was no unifying purpose which connected the tactical action. Indeed, William Lind maintained that it was an attritional doctrine: it sought to wear the opposition down at the point of their greatest strength (Swain 1996: 154). Depuy's successor at TRADOC, General Donn Starry, addressed these criticisms and in the late 1970s sought to revise US doctrine fundamentally. Starry was an innovative thinker and sought to re-orient the US conception of battle space. Donn Starry, a pivotal figure in the development of US doctrine in the late 1970s and early 1980s, was deeply impressed by the battle which his close friend, Major General Moshe Peled, commanded on the Golan Heights in 1973. Starry visited Peled in August 1977 and, although the role of civilian reformers like William Body, William Lind, Steve Canby and Edward Luttwak must be recognised (Coram 2002; Lock-Pullan 2003; Luttwak 1981), this meeting has been plausibly identified as one of the critical moments in the reformation of US doctrine (Bronfield 2008: 115, 116): 'I tried to transpose what they [the Israelis] were describing onto V Corps terrain east from Vogelsburg to the Thuringerwald in East Germany'

(2008: 116). Under Starry's influence, active defence was revised. This doctrinal reform is often dated to the publication of the revised FM 100-5 in 1982; 'AirLand Battle'. AirLand Battle prioritised deep and simultaneous assault on follow-on enemy formations. In the context of Europe, the US V and VII Corps, facing the Fulda Gap, sought to delay the first Soviet echelon in the close battle on the West German border so that the 3rd Army could be defeated at distance in-depth. Instead of attriting the Soviet forces sequentially as they entered killing zones in Germany, Soviet forces would be engaged in-depth as the first echelons assaulted NATO lines. Although some mobile land forces would be employed for this action, AirLand Battle, as the name implied, primarily envisaged the integration of air assets into the land battle. Aviation – and the Apache helicopter was explicitly developed for this role – fast air and rockets were tasked to penetrate deep positions in order to engage and destroy the enemy pre-emptively.

Despite criticisms (Leonard 1991), AirLand Battle represented a departure from the established US and Western way of war. It constituted a reconceptualisation of the battle space and where and how engagements should be organised. Although US forces might have struggled to implement AirLand Battle fully in practice, it represented an intellectual paradigm shift from the mass lineal combined arms warfare which typified the twentieth century. A number of developments were critical. AirLand Battle prioritised expertise and technology over number; it effectively made a virtue out of a necessity. Small but highly trained and well-commanded forces were preferable to large cumbersome armies. The doctrine also distinctively highlighted concepts of depth and simultaneity over lineal and sequential operations. Finally, AirLand Battle was the first systematic step towards a joint approach to military operations where air and land assets mutually and directly support each other in the pursuit of campaign goals. As House (2001) has demonstrated, combined arms warfare was the central phenomenon of the twentieth century. In the Second World War and the Korean War, there was limited tactical usage of air power. Vietnam began to suggest the potential of tactical air power, especially with the use of helicopters. However, AirLand Battle established joint action as a principle of war fighting. At the same time, although never explicitly discussed, AirLand Battle implied an 'operational' approach. Western forces could no longer fight a series of independent tactical battles. Tactical confrontations in the close and deep battle had to be united by the operational commander into a single coherent whole so that actions in the close land battle on the West German border were co-ordinated with simultaneous air strikes deep into Soviet territory.

Follow-on forces attack

Following the publication of Field Manual (FM) 100-5 *Operations* in 1982, NATO itself underwent a parallel reformation. In 1984, NATO introduced and implemented its follow-on forces attack (FOFA) doctrine, though, as General Rogers emphasised, it was really a 'sub-concept' (Rogers 1984: 1–2). Instead of attritional defence, NATO forces re-oriented themselves to a mobile battle in which they held the Soviet advance, while striking deep against rear echelons by counter-attacks and especially with air power: 'Our FOFA sub-concept is designed to attack with conventional weapons those enemy forces which stretch from just behind the troops in contact to as far into the enemy's rear as our target acquisition and conventional weapons systems will permit' (1984: 2). According to Rogers, FOFA allowed NATO to add depth to the battlefield without voluntarily surrendering 'any more NATO territory than is absolutely essential' (1984: 5). Rogers was careful to distinguish FOFA from US Army AirLand Battle. He claimed that SHAPE staff began to work on a new NATO doctrine in 1979, concurrently and even before AirLand Battle, and that FOFA, unlike AirLand Battle, did not envisage the use of nuclear or chemical weapons (1984: 7). It may be unwise to interpret FOFA merely as a European version of AirLand Battle. Nevertheless, it is difficult not to suspect some significant US involvement in the development of FOFA given their evident similarities, as well as the fact that the United States was the major partner in NATO, supplying two corps to the Central Front in Europe, and the SACEUR was American. NATO doctrine had at least to be compatible with the way in which these US corps were going to fight. Indeed, it was always expedient that the SACEUR should emphasise the independence of NATO doctrine for European Alliance members. From 1984, all European nations revised their military doctrines in line with NATO's new FOFA doctrine, procuring new equipment in order to be able to mount deep strikes and develop reaction forces capable of offensive counter-strikes against the enemy. Allied Command Europe's Mobile Force, which was a multi-national reaction formation, was developed to provide some of this theatre-wide intervention capability.

For other European land forces, Northern Army Group (Northag, Rheindalen) and, especially its commander, General Nigel Bagnall, played a decisive role in implementing the new FOFA doctrine into actual military practice. Northag provides a privileged view into the doctrinal changes at this time. As the commander of Northag in the early 1980s, with British, German, Belgian and Dutch corps under his command, Bagnall was able to reform Northag's plans, prioritising the operational level in this new concept of warfare. In 1984, in an important article he noted that 'there is no such thing as a Northag concept of operations in isolation. There can only be a joint Land/Air battle which means a joint Northag/2 ATAF [2 Allied Tactical Air Force] battle' (Bagnall 1984: 59). The problem, as Bagnall saw it, was that there was no concept of operations to unite air and land forces into a joint campaign. Northag merely organised national corps for tactical battle. Bagnall insisted, however, that 'unless we are ready to fight a truly joint Land/Air battle on the Central Front from the outbreak of hostilities, we will have failed in our peacetime duties' (1984: 59). However, Bagnall noted that as they were currently organised Northag forces could not fight such a battle: the British corps 'is encased in minefields', the German corps 'has not seriously considered offensive action' and 'has no minefield breaching capability' (1984: 62). Bagnall saw it as a prerequisite that under his command Northag should develop a concept of operations which co-ordinated all his corps into a unified campaign:

Without an agreed concept of operations, there is inevitably a conflict of ideas and overall priorities cannot be identified while four in-theatre corps each conduct their own battle independently. Another problem has been what I always describe as an over literal interpretation of forward defence ... This inevitably results in linear deployment and allocation of resources more or less equally along the entire front, regardless of where the main threat may lie, terrain, or considerations as to capability. Corps are allocated their areas of responsibility and told to fight a corps battle. This in turn leads to a tendency to perpetuate an allocation of territory throughout the chain of command with divisions, brigades and even BGs (battle groups) being given areas to defend without any direction as to the overall design for battle. (1984: 60)

In contrast, Bagnall wanted a concept which would unify control of the entire campaign involving four national corps under Northag in order to create 'the necessary degree of operational flexibility' (1984: 60). Bagnall proposed a Northag concept of operations consisting of three main elements: selection of priorities; the generation of stronger reserves; and the identification of vital ground, accepting elasticity elsewhere (1984: 60):

Once a concept of operations has been developed, and I am not talking about a detailed plan, then the role of the air forces in implementing this concept becomes clearer and the allocation of our invaluable but limited air resources is simplified. My first priorities for air support would initially be to keep the enemy off our backs. As the battle developed, however, I would ask for concentrated use of airpower in support of land operations ... My third request would be to impose the maximum delay on selected Soviet follow-on forces in order to create a vacuum between them and those leading the assault. (1984: 60)

As the same time as Bagnall revised Northag's concept of operations, he simultaneously initiated a parallel reform of the British Army. At the national level, NATO FOFA doctrine became known as the 'manoeuvrist approach' and, as such, it has been central to Britain's armed forces, especially the Army, since that time.[1]

General Martin Farndale succeeded Nigel Bagnall as Commander Northag in 1984, affirming and extending FOFA and the centrality of the operational level in order to achieve it. Farndale rejected attrition: 'A defender who remains static and faces such an [numerically superior] enemy head-on is almost certain to lose in the battle of attrition. If the defender commits his whole force to the defence of his forward area his line will be penetrated at the enemy's point of main effort and he will be powerless to deal with it' (Farndale 1985: 7). Following Bagnall, Farndale called for manoeuvre and deep strike, but he noted that 'A counter-stroke can only be decisive at the operational level' (1985: 6). 'It is at this level that one or more armoured divisions can be committed with real impact, provided the Commander has planned it from the start' (1985: 7). In order to implement a manoeuvrist defence in which numerical superiority was offset by deep strike, the operational commander at Northag had to assume greater control over tactical forces in order to conduct a coherent battle. Indeed, Farndale's operational innovations involved a quite radical reformation of the traditional NATO layer-cake: 'training must also cross international boundaries so that it is possible to launch the forces of one nation into the operating area of another. It will be necessary to co-ordinate the fire of artillery of more than one nation in such an operation and to co-ordinate the operation of engineers, electronic warfare (EW) and armed helicopters across Corps boundaries' (1985: 8).

In 1987, Farndale was able to test the new Northag concept of operations in an important exercise called Certain Strike. This exercise was part of the Reforger series which pitched Northag, the 1 (German) Panzer Division and US 3 Corps against brigades from the Netherlands, the United Kingdom and Belgium. The exercise involved a complex passage of line in which 3 Corps passed through 1 Panzer Division's lines in order to mount a counter-attack across the River Aller (Adshead 1987). The two formations were commanded by Northag which co-ordinated their manoeuvres. The exercise was extremely successful and represented the culmination of Northag reforms, demonstrating the validity of the new

---

[1] See Chief of the Defence Staff, *Design for Military Operations – the British Military Doctrine* (1989). This document represented a reformation of British military practice from attritional warfare to manoeuvrism. Crucially, it institutionalised mission command as a means of sustaining tempo and co-ordination on the battlefield.

concept of operations. It affirmed the importance of the operational level in manoeuvrist warfare. Soviet military representatives were allowed to observe the exercise which, it was reported, they viewed with some concern. NATO, and the European forces under it in Northag, had actualised a new approach to warfare.

The Bundeswehr, which operated in accordance with NATO doctrine as the Basic Law determined, adopted FOFA and the new doctrine was disseminated widely throughout Europe, demonstrated most notably in changes to French military concepts. Although outside NATO's integrated military structures and not involved in the development of FOFA, France effectively adopted their version of FOFA (Palmer 1987). The Armée de terre was assigned a role of the territorial defence of France rather than the forward defence of West Germany after 1966. Accordingly, the Second French Corps was removed from the NATO layer-cake after 1966, although divisions from both this and the First Corps remained stationed in rear areas in West Germany near the French border. However, France re-oriented its defence plans around the concept of counter-strike and deep attack in the 1980s. To that end, France developed its Force d'Action Rapide in 1984. Although the geographic remit of this force was potentially wide, it was specifically seen as a means by which France could intervene in aid of its ally, the Federal Republic of Germany, against Soviet aggression (Flanagan 1988: 52; Palmer 1987: 473). For instance, Exercise Kecker Spatz/Moineau Hardi in 1987 deployed the German 2 Corps and the Force d'Action Rapide on West German territory proving the Force d'Action Rapide's ability to intervene some 1,000 km from its base within 48 hours (Forray 1988: 28). Force d'Action Rapide was seen as an integral part of the move to a more flexible manoeuvrist defence forwarded by the FOFA doctrine, adding 47,000 men to the French engagement in central Europe (Palmer 1987: 488). French Army re-organisations in the 1980s also aimed at re-orientating its three corps to 'armoured counterattacks designed to disrupt the progression of the enemy's leading echelon and force it to mass for the time necessary to execute a massive tactical nuclear strike against that main body of enemy forces that most threatens French territory' (Palmer 1987: 493). There were significant difficulties about how to integrate France's new approach into NATO's plans, however. NATO's FOFA doctrine has been unfavourably compared with AirLand Battle, where critics have noted a lack of air power, communications assets and the persistence of a tactical orientation (Naveh 1997: 305). Indeed, despite the efforts of Bagnall, Flanagan has questioned whether such a doctrine was really fully implemented in Europe: 'The fact remains that below corps level at least, there is no ACE doctrine; only collective national doctrines dictated by national traditions' (1988: 90). Yet a very significant transformation had taken place. European forces primarily under NATO had adopted a new doctrine. A new approach to operations began to emerge in Europe.

Field Manual (FM) 100-5 *Operations* (1986)

Under FOFA and AirLand Battle, corps level headquarters should not simply organise divisions which conducted their own tactical battles. Corps headquarters should plan and actively command tactical manoeuvre on the battlefield, co-ordinating the actions of their land forces with air power. In Europe, the 'operational' co-ordination of tactical forces was evident in Bagnall's and Farndale's reformation of Northag; Bagnall himself emphasised the need to think in operational terms. Both generals aimed for the production of a coherent campaign, the individual battles of which were oriented to in-theatre goals. However, as the critics of AirLand Battle and FOFA noted, the concept of operations, although implicit in new doctrines, was substantially underdeveloped.

In his important work, Shimon Naveh has described the conceptual origins of operational art in distinctive but extremely useful terms. For Naveh, operational art is to be distinguished from attritional approaches by its focus on the system. Attritional, linear approaches did not conceive the enemy in holistic terms but remained wedded to the tactical level: 'The destruction [of enemy forces] thus appears as the supreme and universal aim of all wars, operations, engagements and battles' (Naveh 1997: 74). Focused on the tactical fight, which it regarded as decisive, attritional warfare aimed to increase mass so that the enemy would be broken by firepower at the point of strength; attritional approaches sought to defeat the enemy in detail (1997: 33, 40, 83–4): 'Due to the linear nature of the firefight the amounts of losses on both sides roughly correspond, and so it becomes almost imperative that, in order to acquire an advantage, one has to employ larger quantities of soldiers than the adversary' (1997: 79). While even General Depuy recognised that 'although 100-5 is called operations, we were thinking tactics' (1997: 11), according to Naveh the 1986 Field Manual represents an important development: 'The introduction of the term "operational art" in the 1986 Field Manual marked a definite recognition of *creativity*' (original emphasis) (1997: 12). Indeed, 'the 1986 manual was a perceptual breakthrough' (1997: 12). Other scholars have also noted that the 1986 edition of FM 100-5 represents the maturation of this conceptual evolution (English 1996a: 16); it 'officially introduced the operational level of war' (Lefebvre et al. 1996: 180). For Naveh, the concept of operations is distinctive because it understands armies as complex systems: 'systems do not behave exactly like individual components or even quantitative sum of individuals' (Naveh 1997: 79). Indeed, a system cannot really be destroyed in the sense that all its decisive parts can be eliminated. Rather, systems are fragmented, dislocated or frozen. According to Naveh, operational art takes this higher systemic approach. It does not seek to achieve strategic ends through the maximisation of destructive power against the enemy's strength with a view to gradual erosion of the opposing force. It aims to inflict a shock on the system as a whole by identifying its critical functions and aiming decisive force at those points: 'One can rightly claim that the operational level is the implementation of the universal system in the military sphere' (1997: 9). Specifically, FM 100-5 (1986) includes a novel section at the very beginning of the document defining operational art as essential to current planning:

Operational art is the employment of military forces to attain strategic goals in a theater of war or theater of operation, through the design, organization, and conduct of campaigns and major operations. A campaign is a series of joint actions designed to attain a strategic objective in a theater of war ... Operational art thus involves fundamental decisions about when and where to fight and whether to accept or decline battle. (FM 100-5 1986: 10).

It was the first time that the operational level was explicitly identified in Western military doctrine in the Cold War.

Naveh noted that in order to implement an operational approach, the decisive elements of the hostile system needed to be identified and a series of missions conceived against them in order to achieve the strategic goal. Crucially, the centre of gravity was highlighted in FM 100-5 as the key concept for operational planning: 'the concept of centers of gravity is the key to all operational design' (FM 100-5 1986: 179). Naveh affirmed the point: 'operational art involves fundamental decisions what, when and where to fight. Its essence is the identification of the enemy's operational centre of gravity' (English 1996b: 167; FM 100-5 1986: 10; Naveh 1997: 306–7). The concept of the centre of gravity united tactical missions around the identified strategic goals in order to unify the campaign. Accordingly, FM 100-5 (1986) defined the concept at some length: 'The center of gravity of an armed force refers to those sources of strength or balance. It is that characteristic, capability, or locality from which the force derives its freedom of action, physical strength, or will to fight. Clausewitz defined it as "the hub of all power and movement", on which everything depends' (FM 100-5 1986: 179). The isolation of the centre of gravity was a decisive moment in the renaissance of operational art. However, the definition of the concept articulated in 1986 was multiple and imprecise. For instance, numerous entities could be defined as a centre of gravity under the 1986 definition. For instance, FM 100-5 identifies 'a key command post' or 'a key piece of terrain' as tactical centres of gravity, while operational centres of gravity might be 'the mass of the enemy force, the boundary between two of its major combat formations, a vital command and control center, or perhaps its logistical base or lines of communication' (FM 100-5 1986: 179). FM 100-5 identifies the town of St Vith as the American centre of gravity during the Battle of the Bulge in 1944. At a strategic level, FM 100-5 again records locality as well as a key economic resource as centres of gravity.

Similar imprecision could be identified in European military doctrine at this time. NATO Allied Joint Publications (AJP) and British doctrine were equally catholic in their understanding of what could be a centre of gravity. In 1989, General Bagnall issued British Army Doctrine, for the first time institutionalising his 'manoeuvrist' approach which prioritised deep, simultaneous strikes rather than attrition. The definition of the centre of gravity in that publication accords almost exactly with FM 100-5 (1986); it referred eclectically to forces, localities or institutions like governments. In the context of the 1980s, when NATO was facing the mass divisions of the Warsaw Pact, the potential imprecision of the concept was irrelevant. Certainly, NATO forces needed to unify themselves more closely around a concrete campaign goal in order to facilitate the co-ordination of tactical battles, but this goal was still a large target; typically it was a rear enemy echelon in the deep battle. It was relatively massive and, in practice, coterminous with a location.

Recent developments in operational art

The renaissance of operational art in the 1980s constituted the enabling conditions in which current innovations should be understood. However, the concept of operational art, forwarded by senior figures such as Starry and Bagnall, still prioritised conventional, armoured warfare. In the face of new strategic circumstances in the 1990s – Europe's new wars – NATO began to develop new methods for operational planning informally in order to deal with non-Article 5 deployments. Out of this initially *ad hoc* process, the *Guidelines for Operational Planning* (GOP) emerged in the late 1990s. However, after the Kosovo campaign it went through a long and difficult process of re-drafting and was finally re-issued in June 2005. A senior general who was party to the development of GOP before the Kosovo conflict provided an illuminating account of its development:

The Operational Planning Process represents a transformation in planning. All planning in the Cold War was pre-fabricated. All German defence planning for instance was agreed by the German government and it was only for Article 5 missions. But now we have non-Art 5 missions. In the past we had off the shelf products. These plans were pre-prepared. They were routinely updated and adjusted to new equipment, new structures or force withdrawals. There was no requirement for more. The need for ad hoc planning was simply not there. Plans were there and they were simply executed. Ad hoc planning was not foreseen. No thought was necessary as to what would happen if the plan was obsolete. There was no planning mechanism for operational planning in today's sense. There was tactical planning up to Corps level. NATO was in a layer-cake structure. And each nation had its national planning system. This is where we came from. Early in 1994, I received a call from SACEUR; I was then CINC [Commander in Chief] of AFCENT at Brunssum. He had talked to [the] Secretary General the night before and [the] Secretary General had tasked him to create what was effectively a CJTF [Combined Joint Task Force] to be sent to Ngorno-Karabak: 50% NATO and 50% Russian. He told me to see him with the outline of a plan on Wednesday; it was then Monday. He was seeing the Secretary General on Friday in a secret meeting. I had turned it round in morning session with my deputy, an RAF three star, and my COS [Chief of Staff], a Belgian two star. I organised a 10:00 am meeting for tasking. On the spot, they told me it cannot be done. The systems and mechanisms were not there. It cannot be done. Between 1990 and 1994 nothing had developed but it became clear that we needed a doctrine for planning. Later we got similar tasking. A working group had developed a planning system and this gave birth to the present OPP [Operational Planning Process]. This was developed by SHAPE which is now the GOP. The requirement came up from strategic demand. There was no rational plan. On the contrary, the tide had turned and demanded this requirement from us. It was more or less done informally. Up to Kosovo, even then, SHAPE did not use the OPP. They had their own system. From the outset the whole thing was totally informal. When this course [NATO School Operational Planning Course] started it began as an experimental Operational Planning Course at The Hague in 1997. We did not then have the GOP or OPP. We applied a system that was informally developed. It was approved as the working basis for this course. It came out of a requirement to structure planning. The effort for the deployment to Bosnia in 1995 generated the official-isation of the planning process. The GOP working group at SHAPE was tasked to formalise the process. It was a case of the normative power of facts. Informally it was done here and there. Common sense dictated the pace and that we should eventually formalise the process. NAC approved the system and to my satisfaction. The EU applied the GOP and OPP. The integrity of the system has been main-tained. EU SHAPE and NATO are all singing from the same song-sheet. NATO has been extremely successful in developing techniques and doctrine that actually arose from individual initiative, which caused the development of these things. Then they became official doctrine. The process was bottom up. The development of planning especially was not top down.[2]

---

[2] NATO four-star general, personal interview, 26 April 2006.

The 2005 version of GOP lays out a single, established structure and method for operational planning, from initial situational analysis to the eventual issuing of the commander's directive. GOP (SHAPE 2005) represents the appearance of common operational concepts and practices. It has been disseminated formally through European staff colleges, the NATO School and the Joint Warfare Centre, and practically through NATO operational headquarters, especially the new network of rapid reaction corps (e.g., ARRC, German–Netherlands Rapid Reaction Corps, Corps de réaction rapide–France). GOP involves five stages: initiation; orientation; concept development; plan development; and plan review.[3] The GOP lays out the concepts and the methods to be used and establishes a format for mission statements, operational plans and operational orders. Decisively, it draws upon many of the innovations introduced in the 1980s. Above all, the centre of gravity, originally identified as critical in FM 100-5 (1986), is crucial to GOP. GOP has become a critical common resource around which European staff officers and commanders are uniting in order to plan and conduct operations together.

Significantly, a parallel process of planning refinement is observable at the national level. Germany has always followed NATO doctrine and currently employs the GOP at national level. Thus, the Einsatzführungskommando (Potsdam) employs the GOP exclusively to structure its planning, and the operational headquarters which was created for the EU Congo mission in 2006 developed a plan on this basis. However, in the last decade national planning processes developed in Britain and France have been closely related conceptually to the development of the GOP. Thus, in Britain during the 1990s, British operational planning moved away decisively from the format laid down during the Cold War towards a process which is very similar to the GOP. The 'Appreciation' of the 1980s, which was purely military in orientation, was superseded by the 'Estimate' in 1988, which introduced the 'Commander's Intent' in order to allow for mission command:

In 1996/7, there were further changes: jointery appeared. This was forced on the military and on the single services. They had to develop the Joint Services Command and Staff College (JSCSC) and become more joint. Out of this move to jointery the new estimate process developed which involves the following stages: Mission Analysis, Evaluation of Factors, Formulation and Development of COAs [courses of action], Commander's decision. For Army and warfare officers in the Royal Navy, mission analysis involved massive work but little on the evaluation of

---

[3] The GOP itself is restricted; it includes some sensitive material on NATO command structures. However, the central elements of the GOP are recorded in Allied Joint Publications AJB-01 (2002) and, especially, Allied Joint Publications AJP-5 (2006).

factors. For RAF and specialists in Royal Navy, it was the opposite. This eventually led to 2005 and the present Estimate Process which has six stages: The Mission analysis bit, weighted differently for different services, has become Steps 2a and 2. The point of all this was to solve *operational problems* by logical method.[4]

In the past five years, the British forces have elaborated the new operational planning method in published doctrine, and specifically in Joint Warfare Publication (JWP) 5.00 – *Joint Operational Planning*. This document describes the six stages of the estimate process in depth, discussing all the concepts and methods while providing examples of how they should be used. Britain adopted JWP 5.00 rather than GOP because, although there is a close conceptual relation between the two, the estimate is an expression of the distinctiveness of British command culture. It gives more latitude to the commander to exercise intuition. However, the concepts, methods and practices envisaged by GOP and the estimate process are very similar.

In France, a similar pattern is observable, despite France's own scepticism towards planning. Although the GOP is not cited as a source, in the last five years the French armed forces have developed and codified their own operational planning procedure. In 2004, France's Joint Doctrine Centre issued the *Méthode Interarmée d'Appréciation et de Raisonnement sur une Situation Militaire* (MARS). The second edition of MARS was published in 2005 under the title *Méthode de planification opérationnelle* (Collège Interarmées de Défense 2005). Although French, the *Méthode de planification opérationnelle* explicitly highlighted that it 'incorporated different aspects from British methods' and JWP 5.00, in particular (2005: 2). Specifically, taking the pragmatism of the British, the logic of the Germans, the *Méthode de planification opérationnelle* avowedly constituted a French version of the GOP (2005: 2). However, this document was intended only as a training publication, specifically for the French Staff College: the Collège Interarmées de Défense. The French armed forces have committed themselves to NATO's *Guidelines for Operational Planning*. Unsurprisingly, therefore, and in line with the GOP, the *Méthode de planification opérationnelle* involves five stages: 'l'initialisation' (initiation), 'l'orientation' (orientation), 'l'élaboration du concept d'opération' (concept development), 'le dévelopement du plan' (plan development) and 'la révision du plan' (revision), and utilises the same concepts and methods (2005: 9–10).[5] The codification of operational

[4] British lieutenant colonel, Joint Services Command and Staff College, personal interview, 4 May 2005.
[5] In order to demonstrate the close convergence of European military thinking, the *Méthode de planification opérationnelle* is discussed throughout this chapter.

planning in the 1990s and 2000s in Europe is a significant organisational development, particularly since the planning techniques are so deliberately similar.

For all the minor national discrepancies, one element of NATO and all national doctrine remains indistinguishable: the centre of gravity, the importance of which has been re-affirmed in current doctrine. As NATO and national doctrine emphasise, the definition of the centre of gravity remains 'one of the most important steps' or 'keys' in NATO, British and French doctrine (Collège interarmées de défense 2005: 33; SHAPE 2005: 3–8). In all these operational planning processes the concept of the centre of gravity is regarded as critical. Indeed, in the light of operational demands, the centre of gravity has been substantially refined as a planning concept. Consequently, it provides an apposite focus for plotting transformations at the operational level in the face of new missions.

The centre of gravity

The centre of gravity, of course, plays a significant role in Clausewitz's thoughts about strategy and has been a standard military concept since the mid-nineteenth century. However, in the face of dramatic strategic changes, Western armed forces have explicitly sought to re-invent their shared concept of the centre of gravity in the last decade. The re-interpretation of the centre of gravity is directly related to the rise of the doctrinal revolutions of the 1980s and 1990s, when it was used as a way of uniting the campaign on a single overarching objective.[6] The refinement of the concept continues today. This conceptual refinement of the centre of gravity is a direct response to new strategic conditions. In the later half of the twentieth century as the Cold War ossified Western forces along the Rhine, there was little need to define the enemy forces very precisely. The threat which Western forces faced was obvious and any element of the Warsaw Pact forces constituted part of the centre of gravity. To attack and destroy any element of the Soviet forces was to degrade its centre of gravity. Even with the development of AirLand Battle, when the precise identification of the primary enemy target became important, hostile forces presented a large and obvious mass. In the context of contemporary operations, this re-invention has been institutionally essential.

---

[6] It is no coincidence that the re-interpretation of the concept of the centre of gravity occurred at the same time as the publication of a new translation of *On War* by Michael Howard and Peter Paret. This translation had significant influence in the US military as it reformed itself after Vietnam.

Today, Western forces conceive themselves to be fighting on dispersed battlefields in which once contiguous mass formations are now replaced by small, specialist units scattered geographically and co-ordinated by digital communications. It is often difficult to identify an enemy which engages in asymmetric, guerrilla warfare. Yet in this complex environment, it is essential that a clear collective goal is identified. Diffuse, diverse and dispersed opponents must be precisely identified if forces are to be effective and, more specifically, if civilian casualties are to be avoided by the obtuse use of military power. In the past, if the armed forces could strike any part of the mass of the opponent's forces, they would be attacking the centre of gravity. Martin van Creveld has captured the reality of mass in the Clausewitzian era when the concept of the centre of gravity was first conceived:

Since armies normally stayed close together, and since the power and range of weapons were limited to the point that a hostile force more than a couple of miles away might, for all its ability to inflict damage, as well be on the moon, there was a very real sense in which wars only got under way when the two sides' main forces, each normally under the direct orders of its commander in chief, confronted each other. (Van Creveld 1985: 27)

The rise of dispersed and asymmetric warfare has, by contrast, necessitated an accurate definition of the opponent's forces. Specific guerrilla groups, such as the Taliban or al Qaeda, can be identified independently of the populations in which they swim. In the face of elusive threats, the armed forces have self-consciously realised that they need to unify themselves around a specific collective goal at the outset of an operation.

There are two passages in Clausewitz's work which have been the focus of particular attention in recent discussions and which are drawn upon directly in military doctrine. The most important characterisation of the centre of gravity occurs in book VIII, chapter 4 when Clausewitz states: 'One must keep the dominant characteristics of both belligerents in mind. Out of these characteristics a certain centre of gravity develops, the hub of all power and movement, on which everything else depends. That is the point against which all our energies should be directed' (Clausewitz 1989: 595–6; Strange 1999: 11). The centre of gravity refers to the decisive force of an opponent's armed forces around which all other elements orbit and upon which a nation's military power depends. A further passage has become particularly important. In book VI, chapter 27, Clausewitz notes that 'a centre of gravity is always found where the mass is concentrated most densely. It presents the most effective target of a blow; furthermore, the heaviest blow is that struck by the centre of gravity' (1989: 485; Strange 1999: 9). During the Napoleonic Wars, Clausewitz's concept of mass has a resonance which it has lost today.

The decisive forces at that time were almost invariably located where the largest body of a force was physically gathered. When the speed of an army was limited to marching and its firepower had an effective range of between 200 yards (182.88 m) for muskets and half a mile (804.5 m) for artillery, the massing of forces was critical to military success. In the age of gunpowder, biomass was essential.

The centre of gravity first started to attract substantial attention with the publication of FM 100-5 *Operations* (1986). Since the mid-1990s, however, there has been extensive discussion about the centre of gravity and an attempt to refine what the concept signifies. Joe Strange, an academic at the US Army War College, has been central to these discussions and, along with other scholars (Echevarria 2004, 2007), he has highlighted problems in US doctrine, including Field Manual 100-5. Specifically, he has shown how the common attribution that the centre of gravity can be applied to a locality is false. For instance, he cites US Operations Doctrine, Joint Publication 3.0 which defines the centre of gravity as 'those characteristics, capabilities or locations from which a military derives its freedom of action, physical strength or will to fight' (Strange 1999: 95). This formulation has not only been standard in US doctrine, but has become the doctrinally accepted definition of the centre of gravity in NATO and European forces (and, in fact, remains so to this day). Yet 'by this definition a military force (and by implication any other force, moral or physical) can never be a CG [centre of gravity]' (1999: 95). Using the example of the Gulf War, Strange maintains that 'neither Saddam Hussein nor the Republican Guard, nor any other Iraqi military force, were the centre of gravity during the late Persian Gulf War(!)' (1999: 95). The exclamation mark at the end of the sentence is intended to denote the absurdity of US doctrine. When applied strictly, its definition of the centre of gravity contradicts all the presumptions of military thinking. Clearly, in the Gulf War, Hussein's Republican Guard was a critical military capability. The Republican Guard was the centre of gravity, not the capabilities or locations from which this formation putatively took its strength: 'It takes considerable imagination to regard any of those military formations or leaders as "characteristics, capabilities, or localities," while they are undoubtedly centers of gravity' (Strange and Iron 2005: 24). For Strange, then, despite the evident interest of Western militaries in the concept of the centre of gravity from the 1980s, as they sought to develop operational art, they were still a long way short of a coherent definition. Consequently, from the mid-1990s, a number of Western military institutions and individuals, Joe Strange among them, sought to re-interpret Clausewitz in order to create a concept of the centre of gravity which was internally consistent and transparently applicable to current operations.

Clausewitz illustrated his conception of the centre of gravity with a series of examples: 'For Alexander, Gustavus Adolphus, Charles XII and Frederick the Great, the centre of gravity was their army. If the army had been destroyed, they would have all gone down in history as failures' (Clausewitz 1989: 596). These sentences have been central to contemporary interpretations of the concept and, on the basis of them, the concept of the centre of gravity is now used to refer only to entities which act as the 'sources of strength, power and resistance' (Strange 1999: 12). In military terms, this refers to the field army, and especially its offensive forces, but it could also refer to 'the capital', 'the totality of "State" political power', 'the head of state' or 'the King and all his agents of power from bureaucrats to regional tax collectors' (1999: 13). A centre of gravity has become a concrete entity; it is a military force, an institution or person capable of acting decisively or impelling others to do so.

A common understanding of the concept of the centre of gravity has now been accepted by Western militaries, then, which is assumed to be the definitive interpretation of Clausewitz's work: 'There is no doubt that Clausewitz meant the center of gravity as the main strength of the enemy' (Strange and Iron 2005: 24). In fact, there is significant ambiguity in *On War* about the centre of gravity. There are a number of other passages in which the centre of gravity refers not to a military force or leader, but to the vortex of battle created by the clash of forces (1989: 260). This violent maelstrom constitutes the very heart of war, around which all combatants orbit; this vortex is the 'hub of all movement'. This is an analytically profound way of conceptualising war, but in the current context it is organisationally less useful for the armed forces. Accordingly, a convenient interpretation has been prioritised. Moreover, Western doctrine still typically records the centre of gravity as those characteristics, capabilities or locations from which a military force derives its freedom of action, physical strength or will to fight. Nevertheless, although the centre of gravity is still often defined incorrectly in formal doctrinal terms as a capability or location, European staff officers and commanders now try to apply the concept in a manner which is consistent with Strange's intervention.

Extrapolating from Clausewitz, the centre of gravity has been accepted by all European militaries to mean a concrete military or political power. The definition of a centre of gravity as being 'characteristics, capabilities, or localities from which a nation, an alliance a military force or other grouping derives its freedom of action, physical strength or will to fight' (SHAPE 2005: 3–8) is still typically present as an initial definition. However, as the definition develops it becomes clear that the centre of gravity refers to the force itself. Indeed, the point is made explicit in contemporary European doctrine. Decisively, the GOP cites Clausewitz's phrase that the centre of gravity is 'the hub of all power and movement, upon which everything depends' and goes on to state that the centre of gravity 'is a principal source of strength'. Military doctrine recognises a diversity of possible centres of gravity: 'Strategic COGS [centres of gravity] provide the power, will or freedom of action to achieve strategic objectives. At the strategic level, COGS may be found in the power of a regime, the will of the people, ethnic nationalism, economic strength, the armed forces or a coalition structure' (SHAPE 2005: 3–9). This definition of the centre of gravity is itself not optimal (by Strange's criteria), but it is clarified later in the document: 'At the operational level COGS are likely to be the physical means for achieving operational and strategic objectives, such as a mass of offensive forces, air power, maritime power projection capabilities, WMD etc.' (2005: 3–9). A clear distinction is drawn between geography and the COG: 'An operational COG may be concentrated in a geographic area or dispersed' (2005: 3–9). A centre of gravity is situated in a locality; it is not the locality itself.

A compatible definition is evident in British doctrine. There, for instance, the centre of gravity refers to 'an element of the adversary's military system upon which his plans should depend', typically 'something that hurts', 'a force, someone or something that controls a force' (JWP 5.00 2004b: 2.15–16). It is 'likely to be something physical, something real that can be attacked, an ability to project power into theatre or the ability to command' (2004b: 2.16; JWP 01 2004a: 2.11). Eliminating the possibility of any misinterpretation, British doctrine stresses that the centre of gravity 'is not a rail network, nor a port, nor an ability to do something' (JWP 01 2004a: 3.12).[7] France has similarly institutionalised a concrete definition of the centre of gravity: 'the operational centre of gravity gives freedom of action and the means to attain objectives'. 'It can be constituted by physical means to attain strategic or operational objectives. It can be concentrated in a geographic area or be dispersed' (Collège interarmées de défense 2005: 34). Imitating the GOP exactly, *Méthode de planification opérationnelle* rejects the connection between locality and the centre of gravity which had been conflated in the 1980s. Europe's armed forces are all consciously seeking to adopt a common concept of the centre of gravity, which has been refined in the light of current operations.

The current concept of the centre of gravity has moved significantly beyond a mere definition; it now involves an analytical tool – a 'matrix' – which is universally employed by staff officers. The development of this

---

[7] Operational art also involves identifying the friendly centre of gravity, which must be protected. This element of operational art is omitted here for reasons of space.

tool is important in itself, but it also demonstrates very clearly that military forces today have refined the centre of gravity in order to be able to apply military force more precisely. Armed forces have developed a four-element definition of the centre of gravity (Strange 1999; 43). The centre of gravity (CG) refers to a force, military or political. Its critical capabilities (CC) refer to what this force can do. To these Strange has added the critical requirements (CR) and critical vulnerabilities (CV). Critical requirements refer to the 'essential conditions, resources and means for a critical capability to be fully operative' (Strange 1999: 43). Critical vulnerabilities refer simply to all the 'critical requirements or components thereof which are deficient, or vulnerable to neutralization, interdiction or attack' (1999: 43). From his definition of the 'CG–CC–CR–CV concept', Strange has developed a simple matrix for application in planning:

Centers of gravity: primary sources of moral or physical strength, power and resistance.
Critical capabilities: primary abilities which merits a Center of gravity to be identified as such in the context of a given scenario, situation or mission.
Critical requirements: essential conditions, resources and means for a critical capability to be fully operative.
Critical vulnerabilities: essential conditions, resources and means for a critical capability to be fully operative. (1999: 43)

As they plan operations, Strange has proposed that staff officers follow (and fill in) the categories, and the bulk of his book demonstrates how to do this with a number of historical examples.

In NATO and national doctrine in Europe, the armed forces have converted Strange's schema into a 'centre of gravity' matrix which now appears in all Western planning doctrine, including the GOP (Figure 5.1).

1. Centre of gravity *A focal point from which the enemy draws its strength*	2. Critical capabilities *That which makes it a CoG*
3. Critical requirements *That which it needs to be effective as a CoG*	4. Critical vulnerabilities *How can I attack these CRs? In what ways are they exposed?*

Collège interarmées de défense 2005: 35; JWP 5.00 2004b: 2.15; SHAPE 2005 3–10.

Figure 5.1 Centre of gravity matrix

Having identified the centre of gravity (the enemy's decisive military force), the critical capabilities of this force are ascertained. The powers and capacities of this military force are recorded in Box 2 (JWP 5.00 2004b: 2.14). In every case, certain conditions must be met for these critical capabilities to be exercised; normally, these refer to communications, logistics or mobility. For instance, in order for an armoured brigade to attack it requires extensive logistical infrastructure, appropriate terrain on which to advance and protection from air attack. Critical capacities will always therefore depend upon critical requirements, and staff officers will try to elucidate as many requirements as possible and fill in Box 3 accordingly (JWP 5.00 2004b: 2.14–15). Finally, and most importantly, the centre of gravity schematic identifies the 'critical vulnerabilities' of the centres of gravity; these refer to the exposed points of the centre of gravity on which its offensive capability rests. There is a direct relationship between the critical requirements of Box 3 and the critical vulnerabilities of Box 4. The more requirements a centre of gravity has, the more vulnerable it is. In line with Strange's argument, current doctrine describes how critical requirements 'become the Critical Vulnerabilities, the things that can be exploited to bring down an adversary's COG' (JWP 5.00 2004b: 2.14). Thus, if a centre of gravity requires long lines of communication, large amounts of logistic supply and columns of vehicles to move those supplies, then the identified centre of gravity is extremely vulnerable. Staff officers direct their plan at these vulnerabilities in order to undermine the enemy in the most effective way. Strange's concept of the centre of gravity – and the matrix which accompanies it – has become institutionalised into Western military thought and practice. It is recognised to be central to operational art.

In order to unify themselves, the armed forces have followed a nearly universal social strategy. They have re-invented the concept of the centre of gravity, interpreting Clausewitz in a manner which is consistent with contemporary organisational needs (Hobsbawm and Ranger 1986). This concept has been disseminated until it has now become established as a shared understanding among all Western staff officers and commanders.[8] The concept is a decisive element in operational art today, orienting staff and commanders to the critical element of the operation. Significantly, the current definition of the centre of gravity and its method of application has a relatively long history. Its emergence is not primarily a product of

[8] European staff colleges, which are themselves forming an educational network, have been very important in the dissemination of operational art. It is possible to see common definitions of the centre of gravity being taught and employed at these institutions across Europe.

digitalisation in the 1990s, but the reformation of Western concepts of warfare which began to crystallise in the 1970s.

Conclusion

Discussion of contemporary military transformation has often focused on technological innovations and has tended to identify the decade after the mid-1990s as decisive. There is no denying either the importance of technology or the importance of innovations undertaken, especially in the United States, in the 1990s. However, the operational renaissance, which is central to contemporary European transformation, is not primarily a technical innovation; it is conceptual and cultural adaptation, changing the way in which the armed forces understand and conduct operations. This conceptual reformation was not sudden; it was not ultimately a revolution. Rather, it was a slow evolution which should be situated in the longue durée. In particular, it should be seen as part of a wider organisational and conceptual transformation of Europe's armed forces; it should be seen as an intensification of the operational renaissance first conceived in the late 1970s and implemented in Western Europe in the early to mid-1980s. These concepts and practices have been essential to the current transformation of Europe's armed forces. They have allowed European forces to define missions more precisely and, crucially, to orient themselves collectively around these operations. During the Cold War, until the mid-1980s, national corps developed their own concept of operations. The convergence of European staffs on a common form of the operational art, and above all a shared definition of the centre of gravity is an important moment of unification. It signifies the dissemination of a refined form of military expertise. In the development of operational art, the network of rapid reaction headquarters, as part of the operational complex, has been critical. It has become the 'milieu of innovation' in which concepts like the centre of gravity have been disseminated, utilised and refined.

6   Operational art

ISAF IX

Rapid reaction corps headquarters constitute an important part of the new 'milieu of operational innovation'. However, in order to demonstrate how this milieu operates and how these headquarters are in fact innovating, it is necessary to examine them in action. It is not easy to do this comprehensively. The headquarters are geographically dispersed, conducting exercises and operations at different times and places, to which it is not always easy to gain access, especially as a foreign national. Borders have become porous in Europe but they still operate and, especially in the military sphere, issues of state sovereignty can be sensitive. Consequently, in order to provide a detailed picture of operational art in practice, it has been necessary to focus on one rapid reaction corps in action: the ARRC.

In 2006, ARRC took over command of the International Security Assistance Force (ISAF) Headquarters in Kabul. ISAF was originally established in 2002 primarily on peace support missions in the north and east of the country, eventually becoming a NATO command in 2003. As part of NATO's strategic plan, the south and east of the country, originally under United States' command as part of their Operation Enduring Freedom, came under unified ISAF control between July and October 2006. ARRC was tasked to form the core of the new ISAF headquarters and to administer the transition to full NATO responsibility for Afghanistan. It was a complex mission, involving thirty-seven NATO and non-NATO nations, the government of Afghanistan under President Karzai and his subordinate ministers, a diversity of warlords currently allied to NATO, numerous NGOs, international organisations, the UN and the international media. Clearly, the ARRC as a British-led headquarters had its own cultural peculiarities; it cannot stand for rapid reaction corps generally. Indeed, no such generalisation is possible: each of the rapid reaction corps demonstrates a different organisational culture and orientation. However, as a member of the emergent network of rapid reaction corps with close connections to the other commands, the ARRC may show how new forms of operational expertise are being established. It may signify more general developments in this milieu. Significantly, the concepts and practices of operational art were utilised by the ARRC in the planning of the ISAF mission. The centre of gravity featured prominently in their planning.

The 'Commander's Intent'

When ARRC took over ISAF headquarters, General Richards produced his 'Commander's Intent' in which he laid out his operational priorities as the new ISAF commander. One of the most important aims of the Intent was to identify ISAF's centre of gravity for Richards' command: 'We are to focus on action that actively assists the GOA [Government of Afghanistan] in nurturing and further developing the consent of the people to the GOA (our centre of gravity) and its international peers, not least NATO' (Richards 2006: 4). It was interesting that Richards identified not the Taliban as the centre of gravity, but rather the government which ISAF was tasked to support. In this way, he inverted the priorities of NATO's mission from mere destruction of enemy forces into reconstruction and stabilisation. On this model, the Taliban became a critical vulnerability for the government of Afghanistan, capable of undermining and de-stabilising it, but not a centre of gravity itself. Richards tried to select a centre of gravity which was militarily apposite, but also politically palatable to all thirty-seven troop contributing nations and their governments as well as governmental and non-governmental civil organisations in Afghanistan.

Richards' Intent and his designation of the centre of gravity were prominently positioned in every office in the ISAF. It focused the attention of all the staff on a single goal: the government of Afghanistan. Within the headquarters, staff officers actively drew on the Commander's Intent to explain and co-ordinate the activities of the different branches of the headquarters.[1] Richards' centre of gravity was also disseminated more widely. In order to orient all these agencies to the centre of gravity, Richards' Intent was published on the ISAF website and circulated to all the major agencies and governments with which ISAF was operating. The chief of the ARRC's planning branch, 'combined joint cell 05' (CJ05), emphasised how important Richards' Intent was to the unification of the headquarters. CJ05 needed to co-ordinate the activities of the regional commands to ensure the progress of the mission. It was inappropriate

---

[1] Interview, army major, ISAF HQ, 14 July 2006.

and inefficient for CJ05 to give the regional commands specific tasks for them to fulfil. The regional commands had a better tactical awareness of their areas of operation and how to forward the mission in them. However, Richards' Intent with its designation of the centre of gravity became crucial in uniting the regional commands and generating operational momentum. Consequently, two weeks before the ARRC took over command, one of the staff officers from CJ05 went round the regional commands to explain Richards' Intent to them, emphasising that this was what ISAF, and CJ05 in particular, wanted to achieve. 'For me, the big take-away was the Intent. It proved the idea of having a mission statement. And having an Intent out there worked. I always knew what the general wanted to achieve. The Intent allowed the staff to focus on what the Commander wanted'.[2] There is evidence that the Intent had the unifying effect beyond the headquarters. For instance, the commander of 3 Commando Brigade, Brigadier Jerry Thomas, who took over Helmand in October 2006 and was part of Regional Command South, explicitly connected his mission in southern Afghanistan with the overarching ISAF campaign. 'Our priority remains assisting the legitimate Government of Afghanistan to move forward with reconstruction and the development of democracy across the country.'[3] He referenced the centre of gravity as the framing principle for his own command.

Of course, given the complexity of the mission and the diversity of national interests, Richards spent much of his time encouraging unity through a series of discussions, visits and briefings which were aimed at reinforcing his centre of gravity among contributing nations and their forces. A television programme recorded the skilful way in which Richards utilised informal interaction with his subordinate commanders to engender unity among NATO's forces.[4] The visit to Herat may have had little obvious operational effect and Richards' purpose was not to give them any precise guidance. Nevertheless, although Richards was affable and charming to his hosts in Regional Command West, he revealed on his journey over to the Command that the apparently social visit had a serious purpose: 'You do have to massage national and individual egos a bit to make sure they remain together as a team.' The aim of the visit was to encourage ever greater levels of commitment and co-operation from the Italians and the Spanish through personal contact with them, uniting them around his definition of the centre of gravity.

[2] Colonel, CJ05 chief, personal interview 28 November 2007.
[3] http://nds.coi.gov.uk/content/detail.asp?NewsAreaID=2&ReleaseID-233603.
[4] 'The General's War', directed by Olly Lambert, broadcast 28 February 2007, BBC2.

Graphics

Richards' centre of gravity was communicated to his headquarters and his subordinate commands through his Intent and a series of social engagements in which he affirmed its relevance. His headquarters also drew upon other techniques which have been developed in Western military doctrine to promote a common understanding of the centre of gravity among staff in Kabul and subordinates around the country: graphics. ISAF IX was a large and complex organisation. There was huge potential for dislocation and misunderstanding. Defining the centre of gravity was clearly critical to operational art. Without that initial clarity of definition, the complex organisation of current military headquarters would become disjointed. At each point, the staff aimed to link their decisions about specific tasks to the campaign as a whole. Among Western armed forces, graphics have become central to this process of re-affirmation, and a standard format has been developed for illustrating an operational plan: a campaign schematic (Figure 6.1). From the centre of gravity, the staff develop 'a series of co-ordinated actions' which must be achieved in order to undermine the opponent. Each of these actions is known as a decisive point (Collège interarmées de défense 2005; JWP 5.00 2004b: 2.16; SHAPE 2005 3–10). Decisive points typically involve the mustering, transporting and

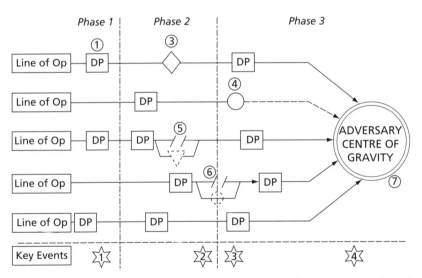

From JWP 5.00 2004b: 2B3-1. See also Collège interarmée de défense 2005: 48, 62–3, 67–8, 69; SHAPE 2005: 3–16).

Figure 6.1 Campaign schematic

disembarkation of troops and material and their deployment to specific locations in-theatre, the seizing of key points or the achievement of certain goals, such as air superiority or media blackouts. The centre of gravity matrix is crucial to this process of delineating decisive points, since the latter are derived from the identified critical vulnerabilities: the staff work out where they need to apply force and from that assumption deduce what actions need to be taken in order to achieve those decisive points. Having thus arrived at a series of decisive points, the staff then link the various these points in time and space to create 'lines of operation': 'lines of operation are planning tools that establish the inter-relationship, in time and space, between DPs [Decisive Points] and the COG [centre of gravity]' (JWP 5.00 2004b: 2.17). Once the staff have established all the decisive points and located them on lines of operations, they are able to diagrammatise the whole campaign.

This schematic depicts the centre of gravity on the right-hand side, typically as a circle (Figure 6.1). The lines of operation interspersed with decisive points, usually depicted as a triangles and numbered in sequence, run towards the identified centre of gravity. The campaign schematic originates from the operational plan of the Napoleonic era. Then, the centre of gravity denoted the location of the critical enemy force, and the lines of operation, developed as a concept by Henry Lloyd, represented the routes along which different corps would march. The decisive points represented 'fixed and determined points' where provisions and munitions were stored or transported to the army (Echevarria 2007: 14). The lines of operation and decisive points were geographical locations – roads and magazines – along and to which troops proceeded in time and space; the graphics represented a connected spatial and temporal sequence. The original campaign plan of the late eighteenth century depicted the route and duration of troop movements along roads, punctuated by a series of decisive junctions. In these campaign plans, time and space were united and could be easily represented.

In today's operations, the lines of operation have become conceptual, referring not to the geographic–temporal axis of advance, but to a kind of activity which will occur in a number of locations. For instance, headquarters will organise campaigns into 'lines of operation' defined as deterrence, stabilisation or information operations. However, the temporal element of the campaign schematic remains critical. In order to undermine an opponent's centre of gravity certain conditions have to be met, and, therefore, a sequence of activities and tasks has to be undertaken in a more or less logical order. Accordingly, staff officers are trained to phase the operations temporally and to sequence the decisive points in a chronological order along the lines of operation. Conceptually, the left-hand side of the campaign schematic represents the present, moving forward in time, as forces approach the enemy's centre of gravity, exerting more and more pressure upon it. The campaign schematic innovates on the methods of modern warfare to establish a clear collective understanding of the operation so that headquarters, staff officers and forces understand what they are trying to achieve. The schematic growing out of the centre of gravity remains essential to the co-ordination of military operations today. The production of a common form of campaign schematic can be seen at all staff colleges in Europe (Figure 6.1).

In line with emerging military doctrine, schematics, often in the form of graphics displayed by Power-Point during meetings, played an important role in ISAF. However, ISAF had great difficulty in developing a suitable campaign schematic. The complexity of their mission, with numerous interrelated activities dispersed over time and space, exceeded existing schematics described in doctrine and originally developed for a very different kind of lineal military operation. Because of the complexity of the mission, it was extremely difficult to depict these in standard fashion. Before the ARRC deployed, the Combined Joint Planning Branch (CJ05 or 'Plans') had invested significant effort in developing a campaign plan, utilising the standard campaign schematic. The commander of Combined Joint Planning Branch[5] was able to produce a rough campaign schematic quickly. He sketched on a piece of paper (which he still possesses) three overlapping phases of the mission: stabilisation; transition; and re-deployment. In each phase, certain activities were identified as essential. Thus, in the stabilisation phase the build-up of the Afghan National Army and border security were (and remain) critical, and these objectives might be listed as decisive points or as decisive effects. Plans identified a number of other 'achievable milestones' around which the command of ISAF would be focused. Without achieving these decisive effects, NATO could not make the transition from a leading security role into an advisory capacity and, therefore, from stabilisation to transition and final withdrawal. The broad outlines of the campaign were clear.

The problem was representing the specifics of this campaign with conventional schematics. In particular, Plans found it difficult to prioritise decisive effects or, indeed, to differentiate between 'broad order effects' and 'second order effects' (the intended and unintended consequences of activities). There was also the problem of the timescale. The mission in Afghanistan is manifestly a long one and, consequently, it was difficult to define a precise plan with sequenced decisive points when the length of the

---

[5] From now on, this branch will be called 'Plans' for simplicity.

operation was unclear. ISAF identified four lines of operation: security; governance; development; and co-ordination. The development of the border police and border security could easily be placed in chronological sequence on the security line of operation. The problem came when these decisive points or effects were connected to others. The development of an effective border police presumed the creation of a coherent ministry of the interior on the governance line of operation, but it was also intimately related to economic issues; without border control the Afghan Government lost a significant part of its revenue. These interrelations between the lines of operation in which each mutually presumed and promoted the other meant that it was almost impossible to diagrammatise the Afghan campaign in the standard manner. The sequencing was too complicated and, indeed, any attempt to order dynamic and mutually supporting processes was hopelessly simplistic: 'Then it becomes really difficult.' The Plans chief, a full colonel, joked that 'if you give me a week in a dark room', he might have been able to develop a lucid schematic.[6] However, in practice it proved extremely difficult to schematise the Afghan campaign. The Afghan campaign conceptually exceeded the doctrinally established campaign schematic, originally conceived for conventional wars in which armies physically marched along the lines of operations against their enemies.

Conventional schematics were, therefore, inadequate. However, ARRC's plan needed to be diagrammatised in some way. Without a simple collective representation for all the staff and for the other agencies outside the headquarters, it was very difficult to unify the disparate activities in Afghanistan. Significantly, Plans had to adapt in-theatre to overcome the inadequacy of existing doctrine. Plans attempted to diagrammatise what they were doing in-theatre so that they could communicate their intentions to subordinate commands. They innovated with new kinds of representation. On each of its lines of operation, ISAF were trying to create different effects, such as border security, the reconstruction of infrastructure, in different provinces to synergise all their effects in support of the government of Afghanistan. However, so numerous were the effects which ISAF were trying to achieve that the staff in Plans struggled to produce a clear and concise graphic of the operation. For instance, one overly complex graphic produced within Plans was rejected by the senior major there precisely because it confused rather than co-ordinated the staff.[7] The rejected diagram omitted reference to the centre of gravity (the government of Afghanistan) and did not use the

---

[6] Personal interview, 28 November 2007.
[7] Interview with Army major, Plans Branch, ISAF, 13 July 2006.

standard format for campaign schematics. Effects were not arranged on coherent lines of operation, instead, they were represented as four nodal points and positioned in isolation in respective corners of the graphic, unconnected to any common centre of gravity or to each other. Effects, depicted as arrows, darted around them, pointing almost randomly from one effect to another and to other nodes of operation. The graphic fragmented because it tried to signify too many effects (and the complex interrelations between them) and, decisively, it was not organised around a single collective goal: a centre of gravity. It served no useful organisational purpose. Consequently, for the most part, Plans used a simplified campaign schematic for planning purposes and during meetings. These diagrams consisted of the four lines of operation running towards the government of Afghanistan as the centre of gravity and pointing to an end-state of government autonomy and national stability. To avoid problems of sequencing and interrelations, decisive points or effects were omitted.

In the absence of a doctrinally available model, Plans developed another technique for illustrating their campaign design. They avoided the problem of sequencing by pinning decisive 'effects' or points to geographic areas. The origins of this mapping of the plan rather than schematising it can be traced back to preparatory work which the ARRC conducted before deploying to Afghanistan:

When we did the mission analysis for General David [Richards] in May last year (2006), the first Campaign Plan wasn't usable. This wasn't going to happen. So we needed a way forward. This is where the ADZ [Afghan Development Zones] comes from. It wasn't rocket science. There were few resources and, therefore, we could only hope to have limited effects. Consequently we decided to secure certain hamlets in the first instance. We came to them from a similar starting point to others.[8]

The Plans commander illustrates the institutional origins of a need for a concept like the Afghan Development Zone (ADZ). There were some important external sources for this concept. In particular, Richards derived the concept of ADZs from General Templar's 'ink-spot' strategy, devised in Malaya in the 1950s, in which British forces developed havens of stability against communist insurgents that were gradually expanded. Similarly, Richards sought to bring security and economic growth to limited areas, expanding out until the entire country – or at least the decisive parts of it – were covered. The concept of ADZs was not only an effective strategy in the light of limited resources, but it proved expeditious in terms of the planning process. It simplified the Afghan mission in

[8] Colonel, CJ05 chief, personal interview, 28 November 2007.

planning terms. While it was difficult to sequence decisive points for the entire Afghan campaign, which was predicted to last decades, it was eminently possible to identify shorter-term goals in specific areas: 'It was easier to plonk an ADZ on a geographic area such as on a border province near Kandahar like Spin Boldak.'[9] Plans could then develop a detailed strategy which specified what tasks needed to be undertaken in that ADZ during their time as ISAF IX in order to improve the situation. Indeed, the Plans chief called the ADZ an 'effects bubble'; it was delimited space in which operations could be mounted to improve conditions. Other officers in the ARRC confirmed the point:

The ADZ covered security, governance, development and co-ordination. It was different to the inkspot idea but that was the kernel of the idea. It is a coordination tool to make governance answerable to the people and to give it any relevance to the people. Operation Oqab[10] was important because it was aimed at an ADZ in Phase I and II on the border. It brought the ADZ concept together subconsciously across the lines of operation. It created an interagency effect.[11]

The ADZs became enduring decisive points or effects, which overlapped across lines of operations but were united in support of the centre of gravity: the government of Afghanistan. During the course of the command of ISAF, the ADZ served precisely the purpose which the Plans commander suggested. They became the concrete focus of attention from which a variety of objectives and tasks could be developed and measured. The concept of the ADZ, as an elaboration of ISAF's centre of gravity, became a common referent in the headquarters by which staff officers unified the plan and co-ordinated their own work in relation to it.

The definition of the government of Afghanistan as its centre of gravity and the subsequent innovations with schematics demonstrate operational art at work in a rapid reaction corps today. During its time as ISAF IX headquarters, the ARRC conveniently demonstrated in practice some important aspects of the planning process. As ISAF IV commander in 2004, General Py had struggled to unite his staff and there was little evidence of coherent planning during the headquarters tour of Afghanistan. The ARRC, by contrast, developed a robust plan and demonstrated a highly developed capacity for operational art. All the doctrinally established concepts were utilised actively to inform the

---

[9] Colonel, CJ05 chief, personal interview, 28 November 2007.
[10] 'Operation Oqab was the first pan-Afghanistan synchronised mission designed to facilitate more focused and visible reconstruction and governance,' General Richards, available at: www.iiss.org/whats-new/iiss-in-the-press/press-coverage-2006/november-2006/i-will-build-more-and-kill-less-says-general.
[11] Brigadier, Joint Influence Branch, personal interview, 28 November 2007.

campaign in 2006: the centre of gravity; lines of operation; decisive points. Moreover, the ARRC actively improvised on existing doctrine, switching the centre of gravity from enemy to friendly groups and developing a new way to represent the campaign graphically. Instead of a conventional schematic, ISAF IX returned to the old Napoleonic practice of planning an operation in close reference to the map; to real geography. The concept of the ADZ focused the headquarters and ISAF more widely on specific places where NATO needed to achieve some defined successes. This innovation is potentially important in itself and may lead to doctrinal changes in the future in terms of campaign schematics. It also illustrates the capability of ARRC as a rapid reaction corps. The ARRC did not passively implement existing doctrine, but instead actively improvised when established practice was inadequate to the complexities of the mission in 2006. This demonstrated a level of institutional creativity and flexibility which was unusual and seems to be absent from headquarters like JFCB.

The ARRC's flexibility raises the question of why it was able to innovate in Afghanistan so successfully. The appointment of good commanders and staff officers to the ARRC is not irrelevant here. However, as General Richards emphasised, one of the critical strengths of the ARRC rested on the fact that it was a framework nation headquarters. It consisted of a dense core of British officers, sharing language, military culture, training and often past operational experience. It seems plausible to suggest that the density of shared British military culture allowed Plans to adapt existing doctrine with such facility. It could improvise upon a doctrinal theme, knowing that other officers in the headquarters, cued into a common approach, would understand the rationale and purpose of their new planning practices and concepts. In a headquarters with little shared experience, it is difficult to unify officers around already established practices, as ISAF IV demonstrated. Improvisation typically leads to fragmentation. Of course, the importance of the collective expertise of the ARRC suggests a reconsideration of the merits of the individual British officers. They are competent not because they are necessarily individually talented, but because they are part of a co-ordinated and coherent organisation.

As the Plans commander eloquently illustrated, ISAF IX has to be creative in applying concepts like the centre of gravity or decisive point. They had to interpret the situation which confronted them in Afghanistan and manipulate existing doctrinal concepts until they fitted the situation at hand. The headquarters displayed a high level of reflexivity in developing the concept of the ADZ. They were sufficiently confident that they rejected doctrinally established schematics which constrained rather than facilitated the planning effort. Moreover, once the ADZ had been accepted in July 2006, General Richards was then able to implement this concept into the headquarters very quickly, even though some external agencies were sceptical.

The importance of the ARRC's organisational culture to their innovativeness was displayed graphically by the way quite informal uses of humour assisted in the development of the ADZ concept. Irony is a well-recognised feature of British military culture whose importance is affirmed by British personnel across the ranks. Indeed, even British doctrine emphasises its importance, especially for successful command: 'And last but not least, it is highly desirable that they have a sense of humour; the importance of this in maintaining morale and motivation should never be downplayed' (JWP 0-01 2001: 7.3). JWP 0-01 continues:

Many of those who have no personal experience of the UK's modern, volunteer Armed Forces tend to assume that their efficiency and ability to achieve success is due to a rigid, disciplinarian's approach to getting things done. Nothing could be further from the truth. Ultimately, in the tightest and most demanding operational circumstances, orders need to be given and carried out with a sense of urgency and without question. However, those circumstances are few and far between and the essence of sound military organisation is achieved by instilling in people a discipline based on co-operation and team-work. (2001: 7.3)

In the first instance, humour is seen as a means of sustaining morale in difficult circumstances. However, the use of irony by British officers is much more significant. Irony has become established as an institution in the British forces allowing commanders and their subordinates to question each other without either losing face. Irony brackets a potential challenge, allowing an opportunity for what Erving Goffman would call 'role distance' (Goffman 1961: 115). At these moments, social actors can separate themselves from the roles which they have been designated to fulfil. Goffman emphasised that the process of role distance is not 'introduced on an individual basis' (1961: 115). On the contrary, 'role distance is part (but, of course, only one part) of a typical role' (1961: 115). Role distance is an institutional reality sustained collectively by members of a community. The role-distancing irony employed by British officers was not only the spontaneous wit of a single individual, it was also a manifestation of British military culture deliberately developed and sustained by the armed forces as a means of engendering organisational cohesiveness. Through the legitimate use of humour, the rank structure, official decisions and individual commanders themselves become open to criticism and transformation. Officers can begin to see the elements of a role which are necessary and those which are merely the formal status appendages which have coalesced around it. The British are not unusual in their use of humour, but their irony is distinctive; it draws upon deep linguistic and cultural understanding. It presumes a dense corpus of shared understanding.

Interestingly, in July 2006, just as he was introducing a quite radical innovation in the concept of the ADZ, General Richards used a distinctive type of British irony to stimulate understanding and acceptance of this term. He sought to use the shared cultural resource of humour to introduce a new practice coherently. Pronounced in American English, the acronym 'ADZs [A-D-Zees]' sounds like 'a disease' and Richards used this homonym for humorous effect in a number of meetings.[12] His play on the sound of the ADZ had a useful effect. The joke usefully united the staff by focusing their attention on the concept of the ADZ, which was central to ISAF strategy. Away from the meeting, staff officers drew on the same joke in their own internal discussions. The joke oriented members of the headquarters to Richards' unifying intent as effectively as his designation of the Afghan Government as the centre of gravity. However, the joke was able to have this unifying intent only because of the dense shared national culture of the ARRC officers; they were highly attuned to British irony and the wit of their commander. This cultural unity extended beyond merely 'getting' General Richards' jokes. Because there was an embedded institutional culture sustained by personnel who were very familiar with each other, the headquarters could adapt and innovate in the face of new demands without major ruptures appearing within the organisation. Members of the organisation shared a sufficiently common culture that they could apply existing concepts like the centre of gravity in a new way with apparent ease. The organisation was sufficiently united that members were already oriented to particular kinds of solutions without having to engage in fundamental debates about roles and duties. Since the core of ARRC's officers shared a single national professional culture, they are able to unite themselves around established planning concepts, apply them collectively to new situations and, indeed, manipulate them in the light of current operations while at the same time remaining united and coherent as an organisation.

The ARRC's flexibility in Afghanistan in 2006 seems to affirm the trajectory of operational transformation in Europe. The trend is towards a condensation of national expertise, authority and resourcing at the operational level. In six out of eight cases, rapid reaction corps have adopted a framework nation format. These headquarters seem to be

---

[12] Fieldnotes, Planning Review Meeting, 11 July 2006.

crystallising into a set of military nodes, located at the national level, but increasingly incorporated into a transnational operational network. To date, they have contributed most to NATO military operations, and it would seem likely that in the coming decade they will contribute most to the planning of Europe's future campaigns under NATO or, possibly, under the EU.

Effects-based approach to operations

As NATO has become more deeply engaged in Afghanistan, it has become increasingly obvious that twentieth-century military paradigms are no longer adequate. Conventional inter-state conflict has become the exception rather than the norm for European forces and, consequently, Europe's armed forces have had to re-conceptualise the nature of conflict and their role in it. It has now been almost universally accepted that autonomous military action, aimed primarily at the destruction of the enemy, cannot bring success in Afghanistan. The armed forces, both NATO and national militaries, need to develop a 'comprehensive approach' to armed conflict in which the military dimension is but one, mainly supporting, element in a wider political project which addresses the fundamental social and political causes of state failure and insurgency. All the concepts which originally appeared in operational planning doctrine derive from the conventional warfare of the twentieth century. The revised concept of the centre of gravity de-territorialised operational planning: the objectives and decisive points were increasingly political rather than geographic. The armed forces no longer aimed to seize certain strategic points in order to defeat an army. They sought to create the social and political conditions in which a stable regime could be established. However, in the 2000s, further re-conceptualisation of the operational planning process has been necessary. In order to connect military operations with wider political projects, the armed forces have actively sought to revise their concepts in order to understand the purpose of military action more clearly. A decisive new concept in this new era is the concept of the 'effect'. The armed forces no longer focus bluntly on maximising firepower or seizing geographic objectives, but on the political and social impacts of their activities. The concept of the effect refers to those broad conditions which are essential for campaign success. Once they have identified the political, economic or social conditions on which the mission depends, the armed forces deduce a series of implied activities and tasks which have to be accomplished in order to achieve each effect.

The concept of the effect can be historically traced back to the air force's use of the term. In the 1970s, precision-guided munitions began to appear in Western, and above all US, armouries. With the appearance of accurate bombs, missiles and rockets, the US Air Force (USAF) began to consider more closely what effect the attacks they were being tasked to conduct were designed to have. New munitions allowed the USAF to consider precisely which target they needed to destroy or which might be interdicted or disabled by the use of alternate weaponry. In the mid-twentieth century, air forces might be tasked to destroy a railway yard which they would achieve through the use of squadrons of bombers. Increasingly, given the task to interdict a transport system, air forces could designate a particular point on it which they could eliminate precisely. The concept of the effect appeared in Western doctrine as a result of this shift in the way that air forces conceptualised their mission. Instead of being given a task which was achieved through techniques of mass bombing, they sought to elucidate the precise effect which their assaults were intended to have and to arm planes with the specific munitions which would achieve it. This was a more efficient and effective way of conducting air operations. Indeed, in the United States, the effects-based approach has been propelled by heavy reliance on quantitative operational analysis where missions are assessed through computerised analysis of metrics. The desire to demonstrate the success of a mission and, therefore, to be able to quantify it has encouraged an effects-based orientation.

Since the 1990s, the effects-based approach has transcended its air force origins. There are several elements to the effects-based approach, some of which remain purely military. At one level, the effects-based approach is designed to encourage the armed forces to utilise all their assets to achieve their goals. The effects-based philosophy is a palliative to single-service orientation. In the Cold War, air, land or maritime formations were given a specific task to achieve with their own organic assets. Effect-based philosophy encourages planners to think laterally and to use all the available assets to achieve an objective in the most efficient way. Consequently, a bridge might be destroyed by a special forces raid, an air strike, Tomahawk Land Attack Missiles (TLAM) or naval gunfire. At the same time, the effects-based philosophy has been a means by which the armed forces have encouraged the mission command which is essential to effective operations. Subordinate commanders are given an effect which the commander is trying to achieve and are empowered to achieve it by whatever means they are able to develop: 'Conceptually, it [effects-based approach] is no different to the way the British are trying to operate. It is mission command in a different format'.[13] The point is affirmed in

---

[13] Colonel, CJ05 chief, personal interview, 28 November 2007.

formal British doctrine: 'This philosophy ensures that individuals, at all levels, are provided with an understanding of the context in which they are operating; awareness of the principal consequences of their actions; and the essential guidance that will allow them to contribute positively to the outcomes required' (Joint Doctrine Note 7/06 2006: 1–2).

However, the effects-based approach is explicitly tied to the rise of new stabilisation missions in the post-Cold War era. In contrast to most of the twentieth century, Western armed forces have increasingly realised that traditional military activity – organised violence to eliminate the armed forces of another state – are insufficient for conducting new missions. While the ability to deter and eliminate opponents remains central to the armed forces, as Afghanistan has demonstrated, military means have to complement peaceful means of state-building. Effects-based operations represent the institutional recognition that military actions have to be co-ordinated with other civil lines of operation. The armed forces need to consider the wider political and social conditions that the actions are trying to promote. Immediate military action should be conducted in the light of this wider impact, and overall operational planning should connect the military with other civil authorities. British officers are explicit that the effects-based approach is intimately linked to the so-called 'comprehensive approach' in which the military is but one lever of a co-ordinated cross-ministry strategy: 'To think of effects is to try and coordinate different agencies for strategic success.'[14] British doctrine affirms this definition: 'The UK effects-based philosophy recognises that the military instrument needs to act in harmony with the diplomatic and economic instruments of national power in taking a long-term view to address both the underlying causes, and the overt symptom of a crisis' (Joint Doctrine Note 7/06 2006: 1–2).

In the last five years, but especially since the official activation of ACT in 2004, NATO has tried to implement an effects-based approach to operations (EBAO) and to disseminate it to European militaries:

For instance, EBAO is the current way that NATO have amended the planning system. This has not been well managed. It has taken the top-down approach. NATO ACT has not been successful in implementing these things top-down. ACT has not been good at taking people by the hand and generating ownership at the lower levels of the innovations. NATO has been very successful when the bottom-up system is driven by requirements generated in the field: for instance, when experiences from Kosovo or Afghanistan have fed these developments. But with the example of EBAO it has not been successful from top-down. There is a lack of ownership and NATO is currently in big trouble. I talked with SACEUR

[14] Lieutenant colonel, JSCSC, personal interview, 11 May 2005.

about it. At one level he xwants to be at the forefront of current developments but on the other, a key aim is interoperability. These are potentially incompatible. For instance, Brunssum uses the OPP but Naples uses EBAO. Two Joint HQs have a different system. This is mismanagement. The management is miserable. I was talking with John Reith, the DSACEUR, and he said that the SACEUR had said we had reached experimental stage 4, out of 7 stages being foreseen. But there is no coherent doctrine being produced by ACT. It makes no sense to develop like this; before you have the experiences, you don't know what you need or the best way to operate. I was talking with 2 people in Istanbul (NRDC-Turkey). It has now become clear that EBAO cannot provide for a new planning system. The only way to introduce new systems is to introduce elements of them into the OPP and the GOP. Instead of introducing the EBOA system into the GOP they are developing a whole new planning system. How is this being managed? Miserably. John Reith is currently trying to convince SACEUR that guidance is required and is not being implemented.[15]

The general was condemnatory about the introduction of EBAO into NATO. In the last year there may have been some improvement in the process. In 2006, General Jones ordered all NATO operational commands to use the GOP. This was explicitly directed at JFCN, which had begun to introduce its own effects-based approach. More recently, further decisions have been taken which may have regulated the process. Against fears that the GOP, itself only recently ratified and disseminated, should be replaced by an unknown process, NATO has recently announced that EBAO constitutes an amendment and, it is planned, as an improvement to the GOP rather than its elimination. Indeed, between June 2006 and February 2007, NATO conducted a study of operational planning capabilities based on an analysis of five NATO case studies: ISAF expansion; response to the Pakistan earthquake; support to the African Union mission in Sudan; NRF generic contingency plan; and Exercise Allied Action in 2005. This study provided a number of recommendations regarding significant aspects of EBAO, including effects taxonomy, knowledge development, assessment and civil–military interaction. The GOP underwent a process of revision from 2008, which was eventually implemented in February 2010 with the promulgation of the Allied Command Operations' new Comprehensive Operations Planning Directive (COPD-trial version).

The GOP and its successor, the COPD, will be important in the dissemination of effects-based thinking, but it is likely to be supported and even preceded by developments at the national level. It may be possible to gain an insight into the likely trajectory of conceptual change. In British doctrine, the concept of the effect has been introduced by

---

[15] NATO four-star general (retired), personal interview, 26 April 2006.

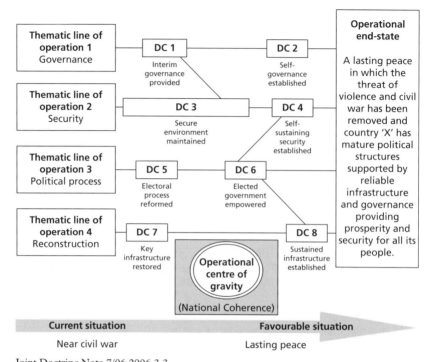

Joint Doctrine Note 7/06 2006 3.3.

Figure 6.2 Proposed effects-based campaign schematic

replacing the term decisive point with decisive condition in order to communicate the idea that the armed forces are helping to create the wider civil setting for campaign success, not merely to eliminate a force or seize a strategically valuable point; a decisive condition is defined as 'a combination of interrelated changes and circumstances that contribute to a favourable end-state' (Joint Doctrine Note 7/06 2006: 1.5). Decisive conditions are created through achieving supporting effects, which are defined as 'the changes brought about by the interplay of deliberate activities and dynamic circumstances'. Decisive conditions are themselves achieved through influencing 'capability and capacity' (physical effects) and 'will and understanding' (cognitive effects) (2006: 1.7; Farrell 2008: 793).[16] In order to capture the more conceptual orientation of the effects-based approach, the British have explored new ways of schematising the campaign plan (Figure 6.2).

[16] See Farrell (2008) for a longer discussion of the introduction of effects-based thinking into British doctrine.

By 2010, NATO had re-written and ratified a revised GOP which incorporated specific aspects of EBAO into the process of operational design, while maintaining the basic concepts and methods of the original GOP. Clearly, NATO and the other European forces will not simply adopt the British approach to effects-based operation. However, it seems likely that the GOP will be revised in a manner at least broadly similar to the way in which the British are currently revising their estimate process. Decisive points are likely to become decisive conditions of some kind with an amended procedure for producing campaign schematics.

Theoretically, the development of an effects-based process has been assigned to ACT in collaboration with ACO (Mons) and especially JFCB, which has a lead on the effects-based approach. However, although the NATO doctrinal process is not irrelevant and the institutions involved are working hard to produce a coherent effects-based approach, ACT and JFCB have serious organisational shortcomings which undermine their ability to create a unified doctrine for Europe's armed forces. The weaknesses of JFCB and its lack of legitimacy have already been discussed, but these problems are even more extreme at ACT. ACT is based on the old Supreme Allied Command Atlantic (SACLANT) in Norfolk, Virginia. That command, dual-hatted with the US Atlantic Fleet, was always regarded 'as second team' to the US Navy and has continued to suffer comparison with Joint Forces Command today.[17] ACT has limited direct relations with NATO operations or to NATO nations. Consequently, it has difficulty in communicating let alone enforcing its concepts on NATO countries. Moreover, as a highly multinationalised staff, ACT demonstrates the frictions and inefficiencies which are typical of such organisations. It expends significant organisational effort trying to create internal cohesion rather than developing doctrine and concepts. It is highly likely that the formal production of NATO doctrine will be overtaken by events and, more specifically, by innovations at the level of the rapid reaction corps or in-theatre headquarters demanded by current operations. It is likely that innovations at this level, where there are condensations of national expertise in close interaction with each other, will produce a new effects-based doctrine. The ARRC is a particularly apposite example here, especially since its deployment to Afghanistan propelled the introduction of effects-based thinking into the headquarters.

The ARRC developed some novel approaches to military operations in Afghanistan which have superseded contemporary Western doctrine.

---

[17] US Marine Corps Officer, Allied Command Transformation, personal interview, 18 April 2007.

In particular, they developed a Joint Effects Board which sought to co-ordinate activities from across the branches. This branch related kinetic effect from the use of firepower with softer effects of media, information and intelligence campaigns to ensure that the overall campaign in support of the centre of gravity was not undermined by the overuse of military force. In-theatre, the Joint Effects Branch was reconstituted as a Joint Influence Branch (JIB). Re-constituted as the JIB, this cell sought to refine ISAF's understanding of the mission and Afghan social dynamics. Thus, JIB developed an influence model which is reminicent of actor network theory. JIB identified the individuals whom they needed to influence and then traced back the social relations in which that individual was nested in order to ascertain where influence operations – whether military, humanitarian or informational – should be applied in order to gain the support of that person. Individuals were located in a series of concentric social circles, the contours of which ISAF had to understand. The brigadier emphasised that it was not soldiers that ISAF needed, conducting standard military intelligence work about enemy activity, but sociologists, psychologists and anthropologists who could help the command formulate an effective influence plan: 'If we don't understand the culture deeply. If we don't understand, we can't have influence in the right place.'[18] Critical to influence was not mere military force, whose co-ordination was conceptually easy if practically delicate, but strategies by which leaders might be co-opted. 'The Mullahs can be paid to communicate the message. The Taliban are paying, we need to pay more. That is crude and it rankles with our psyche but we need to recognise that the tribal leaders are influenced by the Taliban.'[19]

The significance of the ARRC, as an example of innovation with a rapid reaction corps, is that it demonstrates the dissemination of a common pattern of military expertise across Europe. However, the concepts and practices upon which it has elaborated especially in Afghanistan, such as the centre of gravity, the campaign schematic and the effects-based approach, are all increasingly shared by, and disseminated to, other headquarters in Europe. Indeed, although the ARRC is a British framework nation headquarters, European officers hold key positions in the organisation both at home and when it was deployed in Afghanistan. The ARRC actively encourages European military unification around a concept of operational art. The ARRC is successful substantially because it is a framework nation headquarters. Consequently, it has organisational

[18] British brigadier, personal interview, 28 November 2007.
[19] British brigadier, personal interview, 28 November 2007.

unity, based on common professional presumptions, which allow it to innovate coherently.

Conclusion

Europe's armed forces are under-resourced in comparison with those of the United States and, perhaps more seriously, they lack the political will to engage in high-intensity operations. However, despite these difficulties, Europe's armed forces are undergoing significant development. In terms of operational art, a common approach is being disseminated across Europe. National sovereignty remains paramount, but European officers are increasingly converging on common professional practice. A colonel at the German staff college noted the importance of the process:

> We have only been doing the GOP on the General Staff Course for 6 years. It is very new. However, this is creating an 'operational community'. There are only a very small number of officers who work in operational international HQ and these are converging on similar processes and knowledge. The GOP means that we can work together very quickly and efficiently when operations begin. And we know that they will begin quickly.[20]

The term 'operational community', with its felicitous reference to the more traditional European Communities, is extremely useful. In contrast to the Cold War, when national militaries operated substantially independently of each other, fighting their own tactical battles, a dense transnational network sustained by common forms of expertise is emerging at the operational level. An operational renaissance, initiated in the 1980s, intensified from the mid-1990s as European armed forces engaged in new missions in the Balkans. A new operational network has crystallised yet further as a result of operations in Afghanistan. This nascent network has begun to develop new shared concepts and practices, new forms of collective expertise, in order that Europe's forces can co-operate with each other. Certainly, this expertise cannot offset the lack of resources and the will to participate in missions which carry risk. However, without this expertise it would be impossible for Europe's forces to operate globally. The emergence of a transnational operational community at least begins to create a framework in which multinational operations are possible for Europeans. Independent of the development of any mental acuity, the mere familiarisation of European officers with the concept of contingent missions, in which forces have to be deployed and sustained at short notice, is crucial. It has altered the collective perspectives of

---

[20] German colonel, personal interview, 6 September 2006.

Europe's armed forces and provided a critical step in moving towards genuinely capable expeditionary forces.

However, although there has been a transnationalisation of operational art so that officers in Europe share concepts and practices and are able to co-operate with each other ever more closely, no European officer corps – nor any European army – is remotely in sight. As the rapid reaction corps demonstrate, there is a tendency towards the concentration of military capability which affirms the importance of national military culture and the connection between the government and the armed forces. The development of military competence has, ironically, intensified the professional linkages between officers at the national level. At this level, officers are now working together at a new level of intensity, especially in their in national rapid reaction corps. They are drawing on shared concepts like the centre of gravity and utilising them in their interactions with each other as they plan and command increasingly demanding missions. These experiences are affirming not weakening national identities. In this way, the ARRC demonstrated the strength of the emergent network of rapid reaction corps. Since the majority of these headquarters are built around a framework nation they share the same dense national culture as the ARRC. There is already a well-established culture around which they are able to operate more efficiently and innovate more coherently. There is an irony to contemporary military transformation in Europe. While common concepts have been disseminated transnationally, they are best applied and implemented nationally by rapid reaction corps as centres of planning expertise. The unified national cultures of these headquarters facilitate the application, adaptation and development of these concepts. Current operations are actually promoting rapid reaction corps as national centres of military excellence, while stimulating their convergence on common concepts and practices. Operational art is becoming a transnational form of professional expertise, condensed in decisive military headquarters in Europe, but disseminating around the operational headquarters to allow co-operation and collaboration.

Part III

Tactical transformation

7 The empowered brigade

Introduction

The appearance of a transnational operational complex is both a notable and novel development for Europe's armed forces. This new network of military expertise is likely to be profoundly significant for Europe's military capabilities in the future. Yet operational headquarters in themselves serve only a co-ordinating and directing function. However sophisticated their plans and however brilliant their commanders and staff, they require tactical forces to prosecute their campaigns. Ardant Du Picq noted the priority in his famous treatise on combat in the nineteenth century:

> Is it the good qualities of staffs or that of combatants that makes the strength of armies? If you want good fighting men, do everything to excite their ambition, to spare them, so that people of intelligence and with a future will not despise the line but will elect to serve in it. It is the line that gives you your high command, the line only, and very rarely the staff. (Du Picq 2006: 178)

European military capability and effectiveness are, therefore, not solely determined by operational level developments. Operational developments are a necessary but not sufficient dimension of military reform. The success of Europe's military operations relies on the troops actually conducting operations in theatres from the Balkans to Afghanistan. Transformation at the 'tactical' level among those forces that actually engage with hostile and friendly populations is indispensable. The development of these military forces is central to any account of European military development. Ultimately, transformations at the operational level are critical enablers for decisive innovations among tactical forces.

The transformation of Europe's tactical forces is potentially a huge topic. Europe's armies, air forces and navies are all tactical forces that engage with potentially hostile opponents. Each one of these forces is undergoing transformation which could usefully be analysed to illustrate the dynamics of military transformation today. In stark contrast to the Cold War, the primary mission of Europe's air forces is no longer interdiction and nuclear attack, rather, they are now increasingly oriented to tactical close air support missions for ground forces, originally in the Balkans and now in Afghanistan. At the same time, European air forces are bringing the Eurofighter into service – although its precise role is unclear – and the new transport plane, the A400M, will presumably eventually appear. Digital communications are also altering procedures in the air forces. These procurements will alter the way in which European air forces operate. European navies have been similarly re-constituted from their Cold War role. During the Cold War, the surface fleets were tasked to interdict the Soviet navy at critical strategic points to maintain and gain sea control, while the mainly US nuclear submarine fleet threatened to deliver nuclear weapons. Because of the long life of naval vessels, Europe's navies are still using their Cold War shipping for new missions, protecting globally strategic points on the ocean and supporting deployed ground forces ashore. However, they have also begun to procure new shipping, weapons and communications systems. Particularly notable has been the move to brown (littoral) water fleets with an emphasis on amphibious shipping and aircraft carriers to project power ashore.

The transformation of tactical air and naval forces constitutes a critical part of current military transformation. They are not discussed here, however. It is methodologically impossible to discuss all these changes in depth in the context of a single monograph. Some focus of analysis is necessary. Rather, the focus here is on land forces; principally the army but also the marines. Land forces are the focus of this analysis because, while air and maritime innovations have been important, deployed troops are the decisive element of all current campaigns on the ground. In the Balkans, Africa and Afghanistan, European militaries are involved in stabilisation and counter-insurgency campaigns which have been prosecuted through the deployment of significant numbers of soldiers. Air forces have played an important role in the Balkans and Afghanistan, but it is a supporting function. These campaigns cannot be won by the performance of the air force, no matter how impressive. Even the Kosovo campaign demonstrated the primacy of land forces (Daalder and O'Hanlon 2000). Although NATO was able to compel the Serb government to withdraw forces from Kosovo after a six-week bombing campaign, the campaign did not disprove Robert Pape's (1996) well-known argument that strategic bombing can never be strategically decisive. The Serbs withdrew only when the threat of a ground offensive became credible (Byman and Waxman 2000). Moreover, the withdrawal of Serb troops constituted only the beginning of the Kosovan campaign. The stabilisation mission has manifestly depended upon NATO ground forces, with air assets once again relegated to a supporting role. The over-used phrase 'boots on the ground' is intended to communicate the current strategic priority of ground forces over maritime and air forces. Admittedly, the ability of the West to deploy forces globally is itself dependent on the often ignored fact of strategic US maritime and air domination. However, because of their immediate relevance to current operational success, the focus of analysis here is Europe's ground forces and, in particular, the armies of Britain, France and Germany.

Yet the armies themselves cannot be analysed comprehensively. Every aspect of army operations in Britain, France and Germany has undergone a profound reform since 2000. Logistics, communications, medical care, reserve forces have all been transformed in the face of strategic and financial pressures. There have been important innovations in armoured and mechanised warfare, although none of these interesting developments is discussed here. Rather, this study focuses on selected rapid reaction brigades in Britain, France and Germany: namely, Britain's 3 Commando Brigade and 16 Air Assault Brigade; France's 9 brigade légère blindée de marine (Light Armoured Marine Brigade); and Germany's Division Spezielle Operationen (Specialist Operations Division). All of these formations are highly specialist, entry forces and the research focuses on the infantry battalions within these brigades; since they are at the forefront of innovation among ground forces in Europe today. The distinctiveness of these formations must, of course, be recognised; they are organised in a different way to armoured or mechanised forces and demonstrate quite different attributes to a logistic brigade. However, there are a number of reasons for focusing attention on these specialist brigades, and their infantry units in particular. These brigades have featured prominently in post-Cold War operations and are central to defence planning and force structure in Europe today; they have participated in national and multinational operations in the Balkans, Africa and Afghanistan. They are accordingly at the vanguard of European military transformation around which the adaptation of the army as a whole is being organised. They have become strategically pivotal in the current era. Not only can many of the changes to these brigades be traced across to other formations, but other formations are being forced to adapt in line with these brigades or to co-operate with them. In Britain, for instance, 19 Brigade has been transformed into a light brigade on the lines of 3 Commando and 16 Brigade (but without the level of resourcing required to attain the capabilities of those formations).

Size

Military capability cannot be reduced merely to size. There are numerous conflicts in which the smaller combatant has triumphed. Indeed, emphasising the point, Napoleon himself emphasised that morale is to materiel as three is to one. Nevertheless, especially after 1796, his successes lay substantially in the prodigious size of his Grande Armée. Size does not define military power but it is, minimally, a useful index of it. Indeed, in his magisterial work on military history, Hans Delbrück emphasises the point, noting that the best starting point for the analysis of the armed forces must be their size:

Wherever the sources permit, a military-historical study does best to start with the army strengths. They are of decisive importance not simply because of the relative strengths, whereby the greater mass wins or is counterbalanced by bravery or leadership on the part of the weaker force, but also on an absolute basis. A movement that is made by an organisation of 1,000 men without complications becomes an accomplishment for 10,000 men, a work of art for 50,000 and an impossibility for 100,000. In the case of the larger army, the task of providing rations becomes a more and more important part of strategy. Without a definite concept of the size of the armies, therefore, a critical treatment of the historical accounts, as of the events themselves, is impossible. (Delbrück 1975: 33)

It is difficult to gain a true appreciation of a military force without some awareness of its numbers and, therefore, the scale of its operations. Size serves some other useful heuristic purposes. Decisively, changes in the relative and absolute size of a regiment, an arm or service normally indicate an alteration in strategic significance and political favour; size usually reflects investment and, therefore, the operational importance which a formation is accorded. Consequently, although size is certainly not presumed to be definitive, the current transformation of Europe's armed forces at the tactical level can begin to be illustrated by examining the changing relative and absolute size of the identified rapid reaction brigades.

In the mid-1980s, European land forces consisted of mass, substantially conscript forces, organised into heavy armoured and mechanised divisions; the light brigades (which would be designated as rapid reaction brigades after the Cold War) represented a numerically small part of this force structure. Their diminutive size reflected their strategic subordination. A similar profile is identifiable in all three major European powers. Britain was unusual in Europe in that it possessed an all-volunteer force for most of the Cold War. Following the 1957 Sandys Report, which recommended a reduction in the size and cost of the armed forces as Britain retreated west of Suez, Britain phased conscription out between 1960 and 1963. However, even with the abolition of conscription and the concomitant reduction of force size, Britain's forces, and especially its land forces, remained extremely large. In 1964, Britain's forces consisted of 425,000 personnel with 190,000 in the

Army. In 1983, even after numerous further cuts, the Army still comprised nearly 160,700 personnel (Cordesman 1987: 133). These forces
were committed to NATO and to the defence of the West German
plains. British defence plans prioritised European defence. Moreover,
the central element of those land forces were the three armoured divisions of 1 British Corps, with its headquarters in Bidefeld (the British
Army on the Rhine) and its area of operation, Central Region, as part
of Northag (Cordesman 1987: 137). As Cordesman noted, 'the bulk of
the British Army is now committed to the Central Region' (1987: 137).
The British land forces consisted of eighteen armoured regiments and
fifty-nine infantry battalions, including the Special Air Service (one
battalion), the Parachute Regiment (three battalions) and the Royal
Marines (three commandos) (1987: 138). Britain's elite light forces,
the Parachute Regiment, providing the three core infantry units of
5 Airborne Brigade, and the Royal Marines, central to 3 Commando
Brigade, represented a small proportion of the total land forces; in 1988,
there were 7,800 marines and 5,000 paratroopers in an army of approximately 160,700 (1987: 133). Strategically, these forces remained
peripheral, tasked with defending NATO's flanks and to act as a reaction
force, even with the move to FOFA doctrine.

Twenty years later, force size and especially the relative balance
between light and heavy forces had been substantially revised. In 2008,
the British Army consisted of 108,000 personnel. The number of armoured and infantry battalions was reduced after the Conservative Party's
Options for Change in the early 1990s; just forty infantry battalions were
retained. Following New Labour's *Strategic Defence Review*, further reductions, particularly in heavy armoured and mechanised forces, were made
but infantry battalions were also reduced in 2004 to thirty-six, excluding
the Special Forces. However, both the Parachute Regiment and the Royal
Marine Commandos have retained their post-1960s strength of three
battalions each. In relative terms, these regiments have nearly doubled
in size. The Royal Marines, at 6,000, and the Parachute Regiment, at
2,500, are now the largest infantry regiments in the British armed forces.

In addition to the relative numeric increase in paratroopers and
marines, the brigades of which they are part have been augmented.
During the Second World War, Britain fielded two airborne divisions,
1 and 6 Airborne Divisions, in north-western Europe. In the 1950s,
the two divisions were reduced in size and finally amalgamated into
16 Parachute Brigade, the number referring to the original divisional
designations. 16 Parachute Brigade was itself disbanded in 1977 following
defence cuts, although the Parachute Regiment was preserved to form a
battle group-sized Airborne Field Force. Substantially as a result of the

performance of the Parachute Regiment during the Falklands War, a new airborne formation, 5 Airborne Brigade, was re-established in 1983 from 5 Infantry Brigade, which, following the structure of 16 Parachute Brigade, had included two parachute battalions in its order of battle. In 1999, 5 Airborne Brigade was merged with 24 Airmobile Brigade to form 16 Air Assault Brigade; the designation 16 was deliberately intended to reference back to the original post-war Parachute Brigade. The Brigade's order of battle consists of two Parachute Regiment battalions as its spearhead infantry force, and two other line infantry 'air assault' battalions. Since its establishment, 16 Air Assault Brigade has become the focus of Army investment and attention.

The creation of 16 Air Assault Brigade constitutes an important moment in the reformation of Britain's forces. It moves the centre of gravity away from heavy forces on the Rhine, to strategically and tactically mobile forces capable of high-intensity intervention around the globe. More specifically, it represents a prodigious concentration of resources in a once small and relatively weak infantry brigade. 5 Airborne Brigade comprised approximately 3,000 personnel, including two Parachute Regiment battalions, an airborne artillery battalion (7 Royal Horse Artillery) with supporting light reconnaissance, airborne engineer, logistics and signals squadrons: it consisted of four units and four additional sub-units of company strength. 16 Air Assault Brigade currently includes two Parachute Battalion regiments, two Air Assault infantry regiments, an artillery battalion, three army air corps regiments, a signals squadron, a logistics battalion, a Royal Electrical and Mechanical Engineers (REME) battalion, an engineer battalion, a light reconnaissance squadron and some other supporting units: twelve units and six company-sized sub-units in all. 16 Air Assault Brigade now consists of 8,000 personnel. Members of the Brigade, as well as outsiders, have observed that 16 Air Assault Brigade is no longer so much a brigade as a division:

Conventional doctrine suggests that the optimum span of command is five major units. 16 Air Assault Brigade has twelve major units. With the limited number of opportunities within the British Army all the regular Brigade commanders are of the highest quality and arrive in post with substantial experience and maturity. It is likely that a larger span of command would be well within their capacity. The contemporary definition of a Division is changing. On [Operation] Telic [the invasion of Iraq in 2003], the Joint Task Force Headquarters spanned the grand strategic, operational and tactical levels. At JSCSC, I asked General Jackson whether the days of the divisional formation were over? He was surprised at my suggestion that a span of command of ten units might be feasible. This was before I arrived at 16 Brigade – with its 12 major units.[1]

---

[1] Chief of Staff, 16 Brigade, personal interview, 28 July 2005.

The evolution of 3 Commando Brigade displays a parallel process. Although the Royal Marines, as part of the Royal Navy, have been protected from much of the Army's regimental politics, the amphibious assault capability, owned by 3 Commando Brigade, is expensive and has come under periodic review. 5 Airborne Brigade was created after the Falklands and similarly the performance of 3 Commando Brigade in the Falklands demonstrated the utility of an amphibious capability to defence planners. In the late 1980s, 3 Commando Brigade consisted of three Royal Marines commandos (battalions), an artillery regiment, an engineer squadron, a logistics regiment (which was unusual for a brigade) and a signals squadron; in all, it fielded approximately 4,000 personnel. In the last five years, the Brigade has expanded in size. The 59 Engineer Squadron with 120 soldiers has been expanded to a regiment (24 Regiment Royal Engineers, 600 soldiers), a regular infantry battalion (6 The Rifles, 600 soldiers) has been attached to the Brigade to complement the three existing Royal Marines commandos and a light armoured reconnaissance squadron (ninety soldiers and six armoured reconnaissance vehicles) has also been added to the Brigade's order of battle. The Brigade has increased to over 6,000 in strength. Like 16 Air Assault Brigade, 3 Commando Brigade has become more of a division than a brigade.

Clearly, it is important to recognise the distinctive national trajectories of military development. National force structures are a product of the wider political and institutional dynamics and, consequently, military forces are never entirely commensurate. Britain's historical orientation to deployment and its history of involvement in post-Second World War conflicts have moulded its defence posture, facilitating the rise of its two 'empowered' brigades today. Nevertheless, although national differences must be recognised, the growth of elite forces in Britain has its parallels in the rest of Europe. In 1988, France's forces had a total strength of 296,480, including 189,000 conscripts. Following reforms in 1984–5, which were partly instituted in response to changing NATO doctrine, the First Army consisted of three corps and a rapid reaction force (Force d'Action Rapide); 147,500 personnel in total with 102,500 in the corps and 45,000 in the reaction force. The main strength of the 1st Army consisted of six armoured divisions, two light armoured divisions and two motorised rifle divisions. The Force d'Action Rapide consisted of airmobile, airborne, light armoured, alpine and marine divisions; 11 Paratroop Division had a complement of 13,500, while the other divisions had approximately 6,000–8,000 troops each. In addition, the Foreign Legion had 8,000 men. In short, France possessed ten heavy and five light divisions, as well as the Foreign Legion.

In 1999, the French Army was re-organised in response to the end of the Cold War and as part of the process of creating an all-volunteer force. Divisions were disbanded and France re-organised its forces into eight deployable combined arms brigades which include two armoured, two mechanised, two light armoured and two infantry brigades. These brigades are organised in pairs of heavy and light forces. France's armed forces seem, as they have professionalised, to have undergone a radical down-sizing; divisions have been replaced by brigades, traditionally a force a third of the size of a division. There has been some significant reduction in force size as France abolished conscription, but as in Britain, there has been a relative growth in the size of light forces. France's three Cold War corps have shrunk disproportionately.

One of the most interesting formations in the French forces is the 9 brigade légère blindée de marine (9 Light Armoured Marine Brigade or 9 Marine Brigade) which provides a useful parallel to 3 Commando Brigade in Britain, though certain important differences need to be noted. 9 brigade légère blindée de marine is part of the Armée de terre, not the navy, and its battalions (regiments) are smaller than Royal Marine commandos: 400 personnel to over 600 in a commando. The 9 brigade légère blindée de marine was re-constituted in 1963 having been disbanded after the Second World War. In 1976, the Brigade was augmented to form a Marine Division which became part of the rapid reaction force in 1984–5. The Marine Division, like the Foreign Legion, was an all-volunteer professional force from its conception. However, following the 1999 reforms, the Marine Division was itself reduced to a single brigade: the 9 brigade légère blindée de marine. In fact, although the formation is described as a brigade, it is, like its peer formation, extremely large numerically. 9 brigade légère blindée de marine consists of 6,000 personnel and over 600 vehicles: 'French brigades are all 5–6,000. We changed the name from Division to Brigade but we kept the people. Our brigade is the equivalent of a division in other countries.'[2]

---

[2] Deputy commander, 9 brigade légère blindée de marine, personal interview, 14 November 2007. This reformation of the divisional level and empowerment of the Brigade is reflected at the level of tactical command. In the Cold War, France was organised into a series of territorial divisional organisations. This system of organisation enabled the Army to administer a large number of troops and was appropriate to the Cold War, where territorial defence by mass divisions was primary. France's divisions were concentrated on the French–German border in the region of Strasbourg. However, in the current era, the divisional organisation system was regarded as inflexible and poorly adapted to the demands of deployment. Consequently, these standing divisional organisations were disbanded and replaced by four état-major de force (EMF) headquarters in 2002, each of which is capable of controlling two to four of the reconstituted brigades. The EMF 2, based at Nantes, shared the same

The Marines have grown in relative size in France. In the late 1980s, 9 Division d'Infanterie de Marine consisted of 8,000 troops out of a total strength of 147,500: just over 5 per cent of the French Army. The new 9 brigade légère blindée de marine has been reduced to 6,000 troops, but the French Army has also shrunk to a size of 110,000; relatively, the Marines have remained at just over 5 per cent of the force. However, while the division was one of fifteen in the French Army in the 1980s, 9 brigade légère blindée de marine now constitutes eight brigades of the French Army. In terms of relative combat power, 9 brigade légère blindée de marine is significantly stronger. In the 1980s, France's main combat power was provided by six armoured divisions; the light Force d'Action Rapide divisions had less density than France's armoured forces. With the disproportionate loss of armoured forces, 9 brigade légère blindée de marine now constitutes an increasingly large part of France's combat power. The other mountain and airborne divisions in the old Force d'Action Rapide have similarly increased not only in personnel size but in relative combat power.

Following the latest *Livre Blanc*, there have been significant additional developments which further advantage light intervention forces. The État-major de force headquarters, the reformed divisional commands tasked to act as joint task force headquarters after the 1999 reforms, have been disbanded and the staff from them are likely to be re-assigned to NATO commands in line with France's re-integration into NATO military structures. 9 brigade légère blindée de marine is currently undergoing a further development. One of the light armoured regiments (battalions) is being removed from the Brigade's order of battle, leaving it with two infantry and one light armoured battalion. Although this represents a reduction in absolute size of the division (consonant with a further reduction of France's forces overall), the concept behind the reduction is to improve the Brigade's flexibility and the adaptability of France's land forces more widely. The *Livre Blanc* has emphasised the need to create a more 'polyvalent' (multi-purpose) force structure, each brigade in which is capable of a diversity of interventionist operations. Heavy and light armoured battalions are being re-assigned so that more brigades are deployable. In terms of 9 brigade légère blindée de marine the *Livre Blanc*'s removal of an armoured regiment from its order of battle is intended to make the Brigade more deployable and agile by reducing the logistics and command burden on it. The Brigade will be smaller, but the plan is that it should be more capable. At the same time, under the *Livre Blanc*, the

barracks as 9 brigade légère blindée de marine headquarters, although there was no formal command connection between the two headquarters. They were tasked to command battle group and company group interventions.

headline goal size for the French Army is 88,000. Even with the loss of an armoured battalion, 9 brigade légère blindée de marine will have increased in size relative to the French Army as a whole.

In 1986, the Bundeswehr numbered 485,800 and was 'the keystone to NATO's conventional defence' (Cordesman 1987: 82). Once the Struck reforms have been implemented by 2010, the Bundeswehr will be 252,000 strong; in just over twenty years, it has halved in size. Indeed, since the East German People's Army mustered 300,000 troops, it could be argued that forces of the re-united Germany are almost a quarter of the size of those which East and West Germany fielded in the Cold War. During the Cold War, the West German Army (Bundesheer) numbered 266,000 with a further 49,400 men in the Territorial Army (1987: 93). These forces were organised into three corps. 1 Corps, headquartered in Münster, included 1, 3 and 7 Armoured Divisions and the 11 and 6 Armoured Infantry (Mechanised) Divisions, with a total of fifteen brigades. 2 Corps was headquartered in Ulm, commanding 4 Armoured Infantry Division, 1 Airborne Division, 1 Mountain Division and 10 Armoured Division. 3 Corps was based in Koblenz and had 5 and 12 Armoured Divisions and 2 Armoured Infantry (1987: 93). Germany's land forces were dominated by heavy armoured and mechanised forces which comprised nine of the army's eleven divisions or thirty-two of its thirty-eight combat brigades; one mountain, three airborne and two home defence brigades completed West Germany's order of battle. The East German Army, consisting of some 200,000 troops, was similarly geared to mechanised warfare.

The current and future structure of the German Federal Army (Bundesheer) reflects the changes which have occurred in Britain and France. The Bundesheer is significantly smaller than it was during the Cold War. From just under 300,000 troops (including territorial forces) in 1998, the Bundesheer is currently scaled to approximately 150,000 soldiers, although it still possesses considerable armoured and mechanised forces. The current Bundesheer consists of seven divisions, with five armoured or mechanised divisions. However, under Struck's plans elaborated in the *Outline of the Bundeswehr Concept*, the Bundesheer will be structured into five divisions, two armoured, one mechanised, one 'specialist' (formerly airborne) and one air mobile division. As in France and Britain, the German Army has re-focused its resources on its light, specialist forces. While six Cold War divisions – most of them mechanised or armoured – have disappeared, the airborne division has been retained and a significant element of the old mountain division also remains. From being two divisions out of twelve, there are now two light divisions [the Division Spezielle Operationen and the Division Luftbewegliche

Operationen (the air mobile division)] and a brigade of mountain troops (half a division) out of five. These light forces now comprise 40 per cent of Germany's land forces, whereas in the past they comprised 15 per cent of the Bundesheer.

The Division Spezielle Operationen is an especially important and interesting example of concentration here. It was established on 1 April 2001, with its headquarters in Regensburg, and was based on the old airborne division. While one of the brigades of the old airborne division was disbanded, 26 Airborne Brigade (based in Saarland) and 31 Airborne Brigade (based in Oldenberg) were assigned to the Division Spezielle Operationen. These brigades display many of the qualities typical of airborne forces, but they are no longer simply airborne infantry. In April 1994, 200 Europeans, including eleven German citizens, were trapped in Kigali, Rwanda during the genocide. Belgian para-commandos undertook the rescue mission but, from that moment, the German Government decided to create a specialist unit for evacuation operations which was deployable to crisis regions.[3] In the first instance, the Kommando Spezialkräfte (Special Forces Command) was created for this role, but the capability has subsequently been developed with the airborne divisions being re-organised in 2001 (Scholzen 2009b: 38–42). At that point, 26 Airborne Brigade was designated as the specialist brigade for non-combatant evacuation; the two battalions in the formation have trained to conduct evacuation operations worldwide. 31 Brigade specialises in stabilisation and counter-insurgency operations. The designation of the Division Spezielle Operationen as a division is potentially misleading, concealing the full significance of the current development. Although organised for administrative and efficiency purposes as a division, the Division Spezielle Operationen actually consists of two independent intervention brigades. The two brigades are not trained to operate as a divisional organisation and, indeed, even their deployment as full brigades under the Division Spezielle Operationen headquarters is unlikely for political and resourcing reasons. Indeed, up to now parachute units have tended to deploy as companies. The Division Spezielle Operationen is called a division, but since each brigade consists of only two paratroop battalions it may in fact be more accurate to describe it as a rapid reaction brigade with manoeuvre units specialised in particular roles. Significantly, as a brigade, the Division Spezielle Operationen currently consists of 8,000 personnel, but this will be increased to 10,600 under the current reforms.

[3] www.bundeswehr.de/portal/a/bwde/kcxml/04_Sj9SPykssy0xPLMnMz0vM0Y_QjzKL d443DnIDSYGZASH6kTCxoJRUfV-P_NxUfW_9AP2C3IhyR0dFRQB5dv4D/delta/ base64xml/L2dJQSEvUUt3QS80SVVFLzZfQ180Nkc!?yw_contentURL=%2FC1256 EF4002AED30%2FW26U7DJ2655INFODE%2Fcontent.jsp.

As armoured and mechanised formations decline, the Division Spezielle Operationen is expanding. In Germany, as in France and Britain, it is possible to identify a trajectory of military adaptation. In each case, in differentiated ways, as the mass divisions of the Cold War decline, elite forces are expanding. Marines and paratroopers, in particular, are increasing in relative and sometimes absolute size.

Resourcing

Light forces and the brigades of which they are part are growing in size. However, this is only one aspect of the current development. It is not simply that there are relatively more marines and paratroopers in the armed forces today – and fewer tanks – rather, the brigades of which they are part have enjoyed high levels of investment in the last decade, quite radically changing their capabilities. This is particularly clear in Britain with the creation of 16 Air Assault Brigade. One of the principal rationales for the creation of the 16 Air Assault Brigade was that it provided a formation in which the sixty-seven new Apache helicopters could be lodged. The Apache helicopter represented the most significant of the Army's procurements in the post-Cold War era, costing £4 billion (North 2009: 137). Significantly, although Apache was originally designed by the US Army for a deep-strike role under AirLand Battle doctrine, it was not assigned to Britain's heavy armoured forces still stationed on the Rhine. Rather, given the new strategic environment, political forces within the Ministry of Defence favoured the introduction of Apache through the British Army's 16 Air Assault Brigade, its only interventionist formation at that time.[4] The US 101 Airborne Division, which seems to have been the model for 16 Air Assault Brigade, features this mixture of attack and support helicopters with elite assault infantry. The result is that, although the Army Air Corps have been awarded the Apache, 16 Air Assault Brigade and the Parachute Regiment, in particular, has been the indirect recipient of the largest investment by the Army: 'As the backbone of the new 16 Air Assault Brigade, the WAH-64 is intended to work alongside units like the Paras to hold and seize objectives and attack enemy tanks and other armour from a distance of more than four miles.'[5] Less spectacularly, but no less significantly, the Parachute Regiment has been exploring the possibility of procuring vehicles. In 2005, the Parachute Regiment were considering the question of improving their tactical mobility, though the concept was not at that point seen

---

[4] In 2005, following *Future Army Structures*, 19 Brigade began to be converted to a light role.
[5] www.globalsecurity.org/military/systems/aircraft/ah-64-fms.htm.

as a critical requirement. In the event, operations in Helmand from 2006 resulted in the urgent procurement of new tactical vehicles by the Army. Having been at the forefront of these operations, the Parachute Regiment has been able to develop its tactical mobility, significantly extending its traditional light infantry role through the use of weapons mount installation kit (WMIK)[6] Land Rovers and a range of new land vehicles (including Jackal).

A similar increase in resourcing is evident for the Royal Marines. For instance, on 30 September 1998, the 20,000-tonne HMS *Ocean* was commissioned into service exclusively as a commando carrier for the Royal Marines and was crucial to the deployments of 3 Commando Brigade in Afghanistan and Iraq. *Ocean* is capable of accommodating a Royal Marine commando (the equivalent of a 600-man battalion), twenty-four helicopters and fifteen combat aircraft. It complements the earlier procurement of two landing platform docks, HMS *Albion* and *Bulwark*. There have been other important maritime procurements, including new fast riverine boats and assault hovercraft. With these ships and boats, 3 Commando Brigade is able to conduct amphibious operations globally as it has demonstrated on operations to Sierra Leone and Iraq and on exercises in Norway, the United States and Oman. In 2004, the Royal Marines also received the new Viking All-Terrain Vehicle, a lightly armoured tracked vehicle capable of carrying marines and equipment over almost all terrains, at an initial cost of £96 million. The Viking has transformed the Royal Marines into a mobile force capable of both medium (vehicular) and light (non-vehicular) deployment. The Viking was originally procured to ensure that the Royal Marines would not be excluded from peacekeeping missions like those in Bosnia in the mid-1990s where protected mobility was paramount. There was huge scepticism in the Royal Marines about their introduction. They were seen as a threat to the commando ethos of the marines and were difficult to resource and man. The Royal Marines had to produce drivers and mechanics from their existing troop numbers, which, in 2006 during their introduction, resulted in the temporary reduction of infantry sections in 42 Commando from eight to only seven marines. That was regarded as extremely problematic. Indeed, one senior Royal Marine rejected Viking outright and advocated that the best thing for the Brigade would be 'if they were pushed off the back of HMS *Ocean* into the sea'. Viking undermined the effectiveness of the Brigade without bringing sufficient capability. In Afghanistan from 2006, however, the Viking has proved to be a capable and, indeed, essential new asset, like the Apache. It

---

[6] This refers to the structure, welded to the chassis, which allows heavy machine guns to be carried and fired from the vehicle.

has allowed the Royal Marines and the Army forces relieving them to move rapidly and relatively more safety around Helmand:

Every Royal Marine believes himself to be a heavily armed commando soldier who relies on intelligent fieldcraft, cunning, speed, surprise, subterfuge, guile, superior training, supreme physical fitness and endurance to take the fight to the enemy. If he had to go to war with armoured vehicles – inside which he could gain no situational awareness as he approached his objective – he would have joined some other branch of Britain's Armed Forces. Simply, the Viking was not for him. By the tour's end, opinions were to change, even among the most Luddite, and as one of 3 Commando Brigade remarked, 'The most hardened marine can become quite armour-friendly when the RPGs are flying around.' With experience and a growing understanding of the Viking's capabilities – and its limitations – it soon endeared itself to the commando brigade and was, truly, to become not only a life-saver but a battle-winning asset. (Southby-Tailyour 2008: 89)

3 Commando and 16 Air Assault Brigades have been substantially advantaged over their peers by the early introduction of digital communications. 3 Commando Brigade was the first land formation to be digitalised in 2005–6, so that when it deployed to Helmand it was fully networked. Although it cost the Brigade significant effort in retraining signals operators and augmenting elements of the headquarters, the Bowman digital communications system was functional throughout the tour. Digital communications, like Bowman, are superior to former analogue systems as they allow for closer connection between higher and lower command; higher command can plot in real time the exact location of their sub-units on the basis of this communication. At the same time, digital communications have facilitated greater horizontal communications between sub-units improving levels of tactical co-ordination (in theory, at least). The 3 Para Battle Group was provided with secure digital communications while in Helmand in 2006, and the Brigade was itself digitalised (Bowmanised) in the course of 2007 so that on its return to Helmand in April 2008 it was able to conduct network operations with the Bowman system.

The increased resourcing which 3 Commando and 16 Air Assault Brigades have enjoyed constitutes a very significant development. It represents a concentration of tactical military power. During the Cold War, the division of 15,000 to 20,000 was the primary operational formation. Only at the very end of the Cold War, with the move to the FOFA doctrine, was there any attempt to try and conduct corps level operations. Even then, as Farndale's Certain Strike exercise in 1987 demonstrated, the division remained fundamental. The brigade has now superseded the division as the prime tactical formation. It is important to recognise that the emergence of the brigade is not simply a matter of reduction. Significant resources, once distributed across the divisional level, have migrated to selected brigade formations. Accordingly, the status of the brigade has undergone a radical change; today's brigades are far bigger, more potent and more mobile than the Cold War brigades:

As a nation we can still deliver a division on to the field of battle. But what would its role be? Divisional operational art translates strategy through effect into tactical action. But in the contemporary dispersed battlefield, which is not linear but asymmetric and 360 degree, the concept of a front line is no longer relevant. This is 'war amongst the people' as Rupert Smith explained. What is the best unit of effect in this context? I would contend that the optimum formation is the 'empowered' brigade: such as 16 Air Assault or 3 Commando Brigades. Empowered refers to their organic combat support and combat service support as well as the strategic air and sea lift capabilities.[7]

The concept of the 'empowered' brigade is useful here, summarising an important shift in defence policy and military priorities. In place of the heavy divisions of the Cold War, Britain has developed two smaller, but in many ways more potent, formations. Of course, the empowerment of 3 and 16 Brigades reflects the similar prioritisation of the brigade or the regimental combat team in the United States. There a systematic attempt was made under Rumsfeld to eliminate divisions[8] as a fighting formation, replacing them with modular brigade-sized forces. The appearance of the empowered brigade in Britain has been a more *ad hoc* process. Yet the ultimate effect has been similar. The empowered brigade is more deployable and sustainable than the division, and on current operations is a force of sufficient power to deliver and co-ordinate a diversity of effects. Affirming the growing importance of brigades, following *Future Army Structures*[9] in 2004, 19 Mechanised Brigade was converted to a light brigade in 2005; 52 Brigade and 11 Brigade, both deployable headquarters with no organic troops, were created in 2006 and 2007 to act as Helmand Task Force Headquarters. Crucially, in the context of defence cuts, the brigade is the largest force which a medium-sized power like Britain can feasibly deploy quickly and sustain.

In France, there have been significant investments in 9 brigade légère blindée de marine, where, unlike Britain, there is limited experience of genuine amphibious operations. France's strategic situation, in which

---

[7] Chief of Staff, 16 Air Assault Brigade, personal interview, 28 July 2005.
[8] The division remained as a headquarters, which often commanded single regimental combat teams (RCTs). In order to co-ordinate the joint assets upon which these RCTs relied, larger headquarters have become necessary in comparison with the ratios which existed in the Cold War between command posts and tactical troops.
[9] *Future Army Structures* was the name of an internal Army review process focusing particularly on the combat arms. It was initiated in 2004 by the then Chief of the General Staff, General Sir Mike Jackson.

colonial Africa has been the main focus of attention, has rendered the development of such an interventionist capability unnecessary. The unimportance of an amphibious capability explains why 9 Marine Division was, and its successor, 9 brigade légère blindée de marine is, part of the army and not the navy as in Britain or the Netherland. The old Marine Division was capable of some low level maritime insertion, but it functioned primarily as an elite and professional infantry division dedicated to global operations, while the rest of France's conscript army focused on territorial defence. 9 brigade légère blindée de marine is still underdeveloped as an amphibious assault formation. Nevertheless, although not the assault force represented by 3 Commando Brigade, 9 brigade légère blindée de marine has recently developed its maritime intervention capabilities, having been the recipient of significant defence investment. The Brigade now possesses two amphibious assault ships, the *Mistral* and *Tonnerre*,[10] providing it with global reach and allowing genuine amphibious capability for the first time:

In our new ship we have a huge room, 800 square metres, for the command post. We can fit 150–200 people in that command post. We have communications assets and huge capacity for satellite transmission to send data. We have two like that: the *Mistral* and *Tonnerre*.[11]

Although a major development in capability, the ships are not ideal as savings were made on their construction, as a result of which 9 brigade légère blindée de marine's amphibious ambitions have been somewhat blunted:

They are built like civilian ships and therefore vulnerable. Now we do not have a lot of money so we built a system which was the most cost effective. But when we might have to go to war, we haven't considered the question of losses. And we don't have the ability to take losses. We would lose expertise and if we lose one technician that can be irreplaceable. With the ships it is the same. We pay for the ships but not for the different systems of capability. They are too expensive. The problem is that if we are committed it could be difficult.[12]

There are further problems with the shipping:

We work on amphibious issues but we don't have our own boats. Our amphibious ships are in Toulon. For the amphibious issue, nothing has changed since 9/11. In

[10] www.defense.gouv.fr/marine/base/articles/le_tonnerre_depart_en_mission_usa_afrique_2009.
[11] Deputy commander, 9 brigade légère blindée de marine, personal interview, 14 November 2007.
[12] Deputy commander, 9 brigade légère blindée de marine, personal interview, 14 November 2007.

our doctrine, our amphibious doctrine is the same. We assault where the coast is feebly defended.[13]

As a result of these compromises, French amphibious doctrine is underdeveloped and 9 brigade légère blindée de marine has not developed its own autonomous approach to amphibious operations: 'We don't write our own doctrine or conops [concept of operations]; that is done by CFAT [Commandement de la force d'action terrestre, i.e., Land Command] – for the two amphibious brigades – this one and the 6th. We then provide input for Paris.'[14] More specifically, because the shipping is vulnerable, 9 brigade légère blindée de marine has scaled its amphibious doctrines for benign, unopposed interventions: 'We don't do Omaha or Anzio. But otherwise it [our amphibious mission] is determined by the policy of France. But there could be other amphibious operation: e.g. French Guyana or against hostile territory.'[15]

British amphibious doctrine also eschews frontal assault on enemy positions of the type which occurred in Normandy. Nevertheless, although 9 brigade légère blindée de marine's amphibious capability is deliberately pitched at a lower level than 3 Commando Brigade, it has developed an interventionist capability where its predecessor had no specialist capacity at all. This capability represents a significant investment.

9 brigade légère blindée de marine has always been a light armoured brigade and so it has never lacked protected mobility, unlike 3 Commando Brigade. Nevertheless, 9 brigade légère blindée de marine has also sought to improve its mobility; the Brigade wants to procure a lighter, protected assault vehicle:

Our equipment is not exactly what we want. We have an assault vehicle and a recovery vehicle. It is possible we will get Viking. The decision will be taken in three to four years for this kind of asset. But it looks like they will equip mountain troops with Viking. To have enough economy of scale, we would have one company per brigade. It is not what we want. We want the US AAAV [Advanced Amphibious Assault Vehicle] as Viking is not an assault vehicle.[16]

The outcome of these debates is unclear. However, it emphasises the fact that 9 brigade légère blindée de marine is envisaging new kinds of missions for itself in which not only will they have to deploy amphibiously

---

[13] Brigadier general, commander, 9 brigade légère blindée de marine, personal interview, 13 November 2007.
[14] Brigadier general, commander, 9 brigade légère blindée de marine, personal interview, 13 November 2007.
[15] Brigadier general, commander, 9 brigade légère blindée de marine, personal interview, 13 November 2007.
[16] Deputy commander, 9 brigade légère blindée de marine, personal interview, 14 November 2007.

but, once on the ground, greater tactical mobility will be necessary. In Britain, 3 Commando and 16 Air Assault Brigades were the first formations to digitalise. In France, 9 brigade légère blindée de marine was one of the formations to digitalise early. France has developed a quite distinctive digitalisation programme where different communications systems operate at different levels. The tactical formations, like 9 brigade légère blindée de marine, operate on a different network to the operational headquarters and the integration of both systems has caused some frictions. However, 9 brigade légère blindée de marine is moving towards a full digital capability. The Brigade is becoming more capable than the Marine Division which it superseded; investment and capabilities are being concentrated in it.

In Germany, the Division Spezielle Operationen has also been the recipient of substantial investment. As the former commander of the Division Spezielle Operationen emphasised, his division is not merely an increasingly large element of Germany's land forces but it is also the best resourced: 'I am the only division in Germany with enough money. Scarcely a divisional commander would say they have enough money but I belong to them. We have the most modern equipment. We don't have a beautiful staff building but we have the best equipment.'[17] Crucially, the higher level of resourcing has allowed the formation to train extensively. These two new missions have demanded the procurement of new equipment in the Division:

I have one brigade which has specialised in NEO [non-combatant evacuation] worldwide: it could be for Europeans, Germans or to protect other people. They fly in and use vehicles to evacuate people. The second mission is counter-insurgency. We use dogs; that is new. Also we have our Unmanned Aerial Vehicles [UAV] for ISTAR: that is new. We must intensify military operations in urban terrain; this is the battle space. The jungle of Vietnam is today the city. We must oppose this and it demands a totally new quality. We must react quicker. There is a man on the street who must decide who is the bad guy. He cannot ask colonel 'What shall I do?.' The colonel is busy. He must decide. We have new methods – new shooting methods, for instance. We have new sensors. We need new signal and intelligence systems.[18]

As part of this technology, the Division Spezielle Operationen is also beginning to digitalise, although full digitalisation was not achieved until 2010 under the Struck reforms. Unusually, the Division has no organic artillery. The former commander of the Division Spezielle Operationen explained that deployed forces would draw on air assets to provide the

---

[17] Commander, Division Spezielle Operationen, personal interview, 19 June 2006.
[18] Commander, Division Spezielle Operationen, personal interview, 19 June 2006.

necessary supporting fire. The lack of artillery means that the Division is a lighter formation than its British and French counterparts. The Division Spezielle Operationen is not the only light interventionist formation which has been the recipient of major investment. At present, the German Army is establishing a new Air Mobile Operations Division (Division Luftbewegliche Operationen) (Schreer 2006: 184–5). At the heart of this division is the Air Mobile Brigade, based on the former air mechanised brigade. This brigade was established in Fritzlar on 1 April 1999. It is described as an air mobile brigade but, in fact, it is very similar to Britain's Air Assault Brigade. It is planned to be able to provide a stabilisation framework force and headquarters on the basis of the framework nation or core principle; other forces will be attached to it for stabilisation operations (Schreer 2006: 185). It has been explicitly developed to ensure the Bundeswehr's compatibility with its allies: 'As the beacon project to the army, Luftbewegliche (literally air mobile but actually air assault[19]) Brigade 1, the armed forces are catching up again with our allied partners' (Wolski 2006: 17). Whether 16 Air Assault Brigade (or the US 101 Airborne Division) are the explicit models for Air Assault Brigade 1 has not been made entirely certain by the Bundesheer, but it seems likely that defence planners in Germany may have been influenced by these new formations. The Brigade consists of newly acquired NH90 Tiger attack helicopters, support helicopters and the elite Jäger Regiment 1 (Schreer 2006: 184). The word 'jäger' is very difficult to translate accurately into English. Literally, the word means 'hunter' and, in a military context, usually refers to light troops originally tasked with foraging, skirmishing and sniping in front of the line infantry. In the twentieth century, the word has come to refer in German to light infantry who similarly act as reconnaissance or as initial raiding or assault forces in front of the main army, especially in difficult terrain. In Britain, the word 'commando' is used in a similar fashion, although that term has become associated with marine forces and the special forces. Jäger does not have either connotation, but the function they are trained to perform as light specialist infantry and the standards required are commensurate with marines, paratroopers or legionnaires in Britain and France. In line with contemporary doctrine, Germany's Air Mobile Brigade 1 is tasked with deep independent strike, supported by air and maritime assets reconnaissance, intelligence and combat recovery (Wolski 2006: 16).

Highlighting the rise of 'jäger' forces, the Bundeswehr has recently invested heavily in Gebirgsjägerbrigade 23, which specialises in

---

[19] Air mobile refers to the use of helicopters to transport troops in a benign environment from which they will advance to or await battle. Air assault means that air transport will lift troops directly into contact with the enemy.

mountain warfare. This specialism brings the formation close to the Royal Marines and, indeed, indicating this functional similarity, the Brigade is equipped with the same Viking vehicles as 3 Commando Brigade. Gebirgsjägerbrigade 23 is also regarded as the most specialist and highly trained Brigade in the German Army (Stier 2006: 52–3). The Division Luftbewegliche Operationen is also interesting in that it has been constituted as a framework nation headquarters, capable of being deployed on stabilisation operations. The Bundeswehr has no framework nation rapid reaction corps, but it is possible that at this lower level a German-led reaction headquarters is being developed. It is possible that the Bundeswehr will gain the same benefits from the developments which have been apparent with the ARRC and France's Rapid Reaction Corps. The appearance or consolidation of the Division Spezielle Operationen, Air Mobile Brigade 1 and Gebirgsjägerbrigade 23 represents a transformation in Germany's armed forces away from their traditional Cold War posture of territorial defence by mass armour. They have been identified as the key formations in the current era, in contrast to the armoured divisions of the twentieth century, and have enjoyed significantly higher levels of investment than other formations. National trajectories are clearly different, but in Britain, France and Germany it is possible to trace the emergence of at least commensurate empowered brigades.

The special forces

Empowered brigades represent a concentration of military power. Yet they are not the only kind of troops which have been favoured in the current era. On the contrary, the process of concentration is most extremely demonstrated by the rise of special (operations) forces in post-Cold War Europe. In Britain, France and Germany, the special forces have become an increasingly important element of Europe's armed forces. Their growth can be similarly plotted by reference to the indices of size and resourcing.

The development of the Special Air Service (SAS) in Britain is the most obvious example of this localised growth. The SAS was established in the Second World War (closely linked to the commandos and, especially, paratroopers), but was disbanded soon afterwards. The Regiment was re-formed during the Malaya conflict in the early 1950s and went on to play a small but significant role in a series of post-colonial conflicts (Geraghty 1980). However, the Regiment was peripheral to the Army and viewed with hostility by many senior commanders (1980: 216). Since the end of the Cold War, by contrast, the Regiment has assumed a new position in British defence posture. Concurrent with significant reductions in infantry, the Regiment has preserved its full complement of four 'sabre' squadrons (companies), despite the ferocity of its selection process. Indeed, over the last decade it has been substantially augmented by the addition of attached supporting organisations. The SAS signals squadron which provides its communications has been expanded to battalion size to provide global communications for deployed forces. In 2004, a new regiment, the Special Reconnaissance Regiment, based on the surveillance agency, the Joint Communications Unit Northern Ireland (J14) (Urban 2001), was created to provide dedicated intelligence to the SAS (Rayment 2004). In addition, under *Future Army Structures*, a new Joint Special Forces Support Group – a 'Ranger' battalion – structured around 1 Battalion, The Parachute Regiment, was formed which has augmented the special forces community in Britain. Finally, since the late 1990s, the Special Boat Service (SBS), originally a small and exclusively Royal Marines organisation, has also increased in size to four 'sabre' squadrons, while integrating with the SAS to produce a more unified and larger special forces capability in Britain.[20] The two special forces units had had some interaction with each other in the Falklands and the Gulf wars, and the post of Director Special Forces was created in the late 1980s to unify their activities (Harclerode 2000). However, close operational connections first appeared in the late 1990s. These relations were particularly notable on Operation Barras in Sierra Leone in 2000, when a third of the British special forces assault team, which freed five British Army soldiers held hostage by the West Side Boys, consisted of SBS men (Lewis 2005: 575). In addition, Britain's special forces now have their own exclusive air assets, the Joint Special Forces Air Wing, including 8 Flight Army Air Corps, 657 Squadron (RAF), 7 Squadron (RAF) and 47 Squadron (RAF) which provide rotary and fixed-wing strategic and tactical mobility. While the number of SAS troopers has been preserved and, therefore, the SAS has increased in relative size as the rest of the British Army has shrunk, the special forces cluster – the Special Forces Signals Battalion, the Special Reconnaissance Regiment, the Joint Special Forces Support Group and the SBS which support and collaborate with the SAS – has more than tripled in size to approximately 2,000 personnel (excluding the supporting air personnel)

---

[20] This connection is symbolised by the SBS' new cap badge and motto. In the past, the SBS' badge featured a frog and parachute wings with the motto 'By guile, not strength'. This badge was replaced in 2004 by a sword rising out of the seas, with a new motto ('By guile and by strength') furled around the handle of the sword. Although the badge is nominally based on a Second World War SBS squadron, it matches the SAS' winged dagger almost exactly. The introduction of the new badge through the heraldic committee in the Ministry of Defence was explicitly designed to unite the special forces.

(Lewis 2006: 164). Effectively, Britain has created a special forces 'brigade'; indeed, it has the same standing as a division in British defence policy. In 2007, the post of Director Special Forces was re-designated from a one-star (brigadier) to two-star (major general) status. The SAS – and the special forces more widely – have increased in relative and absolute size in the last two decades.

In France and Germany, the emergence of the special forces has taken a different route. In Germany, for instance, the counter-terrorist role was assumed by elements of the civil police. After the Munich Olympics, the German Government established a specialist police unit, the Grenzschutzgruppe 9 (Border Security Group), to act as a counter-terrorist organisation, and in 1977, Grenzschutzgruppe 9 successfully ended the hostage crisis on Lufthansa 181 at Mogadishu, storming the plane with two SAS colleagues and killing three of the four Palestinian Popular Liberation Front hijackers (Harclerode 2000). Grenzschutzgruppe 9 remains as Germany's internal and covert counter-terrorist organisation. However, during the 1990s, the Bundeswehr began to recognise the new salience of military special forces for conventional reconnaissance, rescue and deep missions. Initially, the crisis in Kigali in 1994 was the catalyst for the formation of a special forces capability. On 20 September 1996, the Bundeswehr formally inaugurated the Kommando Spezialkräfte. The force, based on US Delta Force and the British SAS, consists of approximately 1,100 soldiers arranged into four specialist companies (Pflüger, 1998: 94–5). The Kommando Spezialkräfte comes under the command of the Division Spezielle Operationen, further enhancing the Division's already enviable position in terms of resources and capabilities. Indeed, in 2008, under the new conception, the Kommando Spezialkräfte was further increased to 1,300 troops.

In response to international terrorism in the 1970s, France also developed a specialist counter-terrorist unit, Groupe d'Intervention de la Gendarmerie. Groupe d'Intervention de la Gendarmerie, as part of the Gendarmerie, was much closer to Germany's Grenzschutzgruppe 9 than Britain's SAS; it was not part of the Army and did not conduct any conventional military tasks. During the Cold War, the French Army possessed elite commandos units, but these troops did not constitute a genuine special forces capability. Serious shortcomings were revealed in the doctrine, training, equipment and command structure of these forces in the Gulf War, when US and UK special forces began to emerge as a central element of military operations. 'While many assets were available for use at the time – Special Forces units from the three services (French Army, Air Force and Navy), the FAR [Force d'Action Rapide – the French version of Rapid Reaction Forces] and the DGSE [Direction

Générale de la Sécurité Extérieure – French Intelligence Service] units –
these did not form a coherent group of military operational assets'
(Micheletti 1999: 8). Accordingly, Major General Le Page chaired a
commission which examined existing capabilities in France in comparison with US and British special forces:

> The idea was to attain a balance of our Special Forces. They had to be large enough
> to be taken seriously, capable of joint operations and they needed to have trans-
> portation assets of all types at their disposal. We didn't want them to be too large; we
> emphasised quality and training over numbers. After inspecting several special
> operations commands and groups in the Western hemisphere, we felt that the
> British concept of about 1,000 man units with joint operations capability was the
> most appropriate for the French armed forces. (Major General Jacques Saleun, first
> commander, Commandement des Opérations Spéciales, in Micheletti 1999: 8–9)

Accordingly, France granted legal status to the Commandement des
Opérations Spéciales (Special Operations Command) at Taverny outside
Paris on 24 June 1992 to imitate the new strategic role of special operations forces in Britain and America, and this headquarters now constitutes a critical part of France's high intensity force posture (Palmer 1997:
104, 108). Denoting the growing importance of the special forces in
France, the Special Operations branch enjoys a central position at the
Centre de planification et de conduite des opérations in Paris, with an
officer opposite to the commander's office and adjacent to the J3 and J5
branches. Commandement des Opérations Spéciales has been assigned
a number of elite units: 1 Régiment Parachutiste d'Infanterie de Marine;
Les Commandos Marine [including units Jaubert, de Penfentenyo,
Trepel, Kieffer, Hubert and the Groupe de Combat en Milieu Clos
(close quarters combat team) which is part of the Commandement des
fusilier-marin commandos]; and Commando Parachutiste de l'Air No. 10.
The Division Aérien Opérations Spéciales provides dedicated air support to
these special forces units (Micheletti 1999: 9).
    The creation of Commandement des Opérations Spéciales and the
designation of these units as France's special forces has created an elite
military cluster which is reminiscent of the emergence of special forces
in Britain. However, although the designated units are available to
the Commandement des Opérations Spéciales on a mission basis, they
remain simultaneously part of their separate services. This has caused
some problems especially in the 1990s:

> The early years were difficult because, through a lack of communication, we were
> perceived as trouble-makers and competitors. Gradually through dialogue, pre-
> sentations and observation of COS [Commandement des Opérations Spéciales]
> units operating in the field, the other chiefs of staff were able to see the need for

Special Forces during operations and how each service could use them for specific missions. This way we found our niche. Our experience wasn't unusual: it took nearly ten years for the American command, USSOFCOM (US Special Forces Command), to establish itself, and almost fifty years for British Special Forces to attain a foothold in the command staffs of the various services. (General Saleun in Micheletti 1999: 12)

While increasingly unified, France's special forces have retained a distinctive form: small specialist units, dedicated to particular functions, comprise the special forces capability. The dense, highly distinctive and covert special forces community which has appeared in Britain, almost entirely separate from the conventional Army, is not so evident. In France, covert missions are the realm of the French secret service, which often recruits from the special forces but has a separate command structure. This may be observable in terms of the relative capabilities of French special forces. The French special forces have been described as the equivalent of a British 'close observation platoon': highly trained but conventional reconnaissance soldiers, as opposed to genuinely covert special forces on the British model conducting deniable operations.

Like the rapid reaction brigades, Europe's special forces are not simply increasing in size. In Britain, for instance, the SAS is the recipient of a significantly higher level of investment than the rest of the British Army. On the basis of its counter-terrorist role, the Regiment was very effective in expanding its resourcing much more widely. The disparity of resourcing has become even more obvious since the 1990s. As the Ministry of Defence has recently stated: 'We are increasing the strength of our Special Forces and investing in new equipment for them. These are significant enhancements, but the details of these changes must remain classified.'[21] Members of the Regiment emphasise the importance of this institutional investment: 'Make no mistake, though, the Special Air Service is the best equipped regiment in the British Army. No other unit has better kit than we have. The system is brilliant; in effect, the Regiment has carte blanche on weapons purchase, and on all sorts of other equipment besides. Thus whatever the SAS wants, the SAS gets' (Ratcliffe 2001: 90). Peter Ratcliffe, the Regimental Sergeant Major of the SAS during the first Gulf War, described how the SAS' procurements have unusually gained the status of 'urgent operational requirement'. The Kommando Spezialkräfte are, by far, the best equipped in Germany. Similarly, in France, the special forces enjoy high levels of investment. Commandement des Opérations Spéciales have their own research and development office, the Equipment Innovation and Development

[21] See www.mod.uk/issues/security/cm6269/chapter2.htm.

Bureau, which provides the special forces with new types of equipment (Micheletti 1999: 32).

Operations

As resources have been concentrated on Europe's light forces, empowering these brigades, they have begun to monopolise missions, especially high status intense, theatre-entry operations. This is extremely significant because in the armed forces, operational status is critical to future funding. Formations which can demonstrate their operational utility have been consistently able to defend and, indeed, augment themselves at the expense of their less operationally active rivals in defence planning debates. Accordingly, in Britain, the Parachute Regiment and Royal Marines have conducted numerous operations over the last decade, but, more specifically, they have conducted the operations which have attracted the most attention and been defined as critical. The 1 Battalion the Parachute Regiment was deployed successively into Kosovo in 1999 and Sierra Leone in 2000 to be relieved by 45 and 42 Commandos, Royal Marines, respectively (Connaughton 2001: 228, 253–7). 3 Commando Brigade was deployed in Afghanistan in 2002, and performed the most important missions in Iraq 2003, including the initial seizure of the Al Faw Peninsula. 16 Air Assault Brigade was the first to be deployed to Helmand. By September 2011, both brigades will have done three tours of the province, taking responsibility for Helmand for thirty-six of the sixty-six months that British forces will have been in the province. This has given the formations a visibility far above those of regular line infantry, even though Fusiliers, Gurkhas, Guards and Royal Anglians have performed important roles in the province.

Significantly, both 16 and 3 Brigades' assets have supported 12 and 4 Mechanised Brigades and 52, 11 and 19 Brigades, which have succeeded the Marines and Paratroopers in Helmand. Even when 3 Command and 16 Air Assault Brigades have not been deployed, their organic assets are critical to the operations of other brigades: Apache helicopters have continued to support British troops who rely heavily on the Royal Marines' Vikings (and their drivers) for transportation. Indeed, an Army Air Corps Regiment and the Royal Marines Armoured Support Company (its Vikings) have been formally assigned to Helmand until at least 2010. As these brigades have enjoyed the greatest level of investment of any of Britain's land forces, other formations are becoming operationally dependent on them for assets.

France's 9 brigade légère blindée de marine has been similarly active in the last decade in the Balkans and Africa. It was deployed in Rwanda during the genocide in 1994, where its performance, as part of Operation Turquoise, was controversial. It played an important role in Bosnia, taking control of Mostar. The Brigade also provided the core of the force for the ESDP mission to Congo in 2003, when its commander, Brigadier General Thonier, assumed control of forces in-theatre. In 2008, the Brigade was heavily deployed. In addition to providing a force for the EU mission to Chad, it has other troops deployed in more regular roulements to the Ivory Coast and elsewhere:

This brigade consists of 6,000 people. We are sending 4,500 abroad during this year. 85% of troops will be sent during this four-month period of projection, between February and June. 15% will be sent in other months of the year. The people staying in France are the logs and admin people ... Our main projection will be to Chad. 2 Battle Groups are going to east Chad [as part of the EU mission]. We will send 500 to replace others, plus another 1,300. This is about 2 Battle Groups which will be stationed on the other side of the border because we already have UN and African forces in Sudan. France will be on the other side. We are not implicated in Sudan but we will secure the Chad side.[22]

The Brigade has featured heavily on NRF and EU battle group rosters:

In the past we have committed forces to the amphibious capability but not presently ... At the beginning of the year we were the QRF [Quick Reaction Force] for Kovoso and Afghanistan. Different countries build a multinational force with different units. Currently we don't have assignments to the NRF. We have the Guépard [rapid reaction rotation] system. During the alert stage, we have provided troops for deployment under this system. If the EU 1500 is superimposed on Guépard, there is a multiplication of people on alert. That is inefficient and, in fact, not sustainable. We want the same troops on alert for all three reaction forces: on Guépard, EU 1500 or NRF. Not three guys: one on each. We are experienced in reacting rapidly. We can leave the garrison in two days. First units leave in twelve hours: the first battalion in twenty-four hours and the heavy forces within forty-eight hours. Logistics takes longer. For heavy forces, we need more time and assets. The main problem with projection is the assets; we don't have strategic planes. We rent Russian Antonovs.[23]

Germany's Division Spezielle Operationen has been disproportionately prominent in recent operations. German commanders explain this activity in terms of the importance of light troops in the current era:

What can 60 tank brigades do? We have new a scenario. We must break through this conceptual mechanism and industrial production. We still buy planes – Eurofighter – designed to fight vs enemy airforce. But there aren't any. And

---

[22] Deputy commander, 9 brigade légère blindée de marine, personal interview, 14 November 2007.
[23] Deputy commander, 9 brigade légère blindée de marine, personal interview, 14 November 2007.

tanks designed to fight tanks; there aren't any ... We have phenomenon in Afghanistan – we are in the middle of the population. The mission is to bring justice, to bring water, etc. We must help; we must do CIMIC. And someone turns up in a Toyota or has an IED, or a bike-IED or even a donkey-based IED; or totally subtle methods – a pregnant woman blowing themselves up with belt.[24]

With this change in strategic orientation, the Division Spezielle Operationen, and 26/3 Battalion in particular, has been prominent in recent interventions: '150 soldiers under the command of 4 Company from the battalion were deployed to KFOR between June and October 1999 as well as providing force protection troops for ISAF, predominantly from 3 Company from October 2003 until January 2004.'[25] While it was on EU battle group stand-by, the battalion deployed a company to Congo in 2007. In 2008, 140 soldiers deployed again to Afghanistan, returning in January 2009, having had three troopers killed by a suicide bomber.

Reflecting their high level of investment and capability, Europe's special forces have played an important role, especially in current operations in Afghanistan. One of the reasons why the special forces have been preferred by European governments is that they have allowed military intervention to occur out of sight of the global media. Consequently, governments have been able to prosecute foreign policy by military means while obviating domestic political reaction. The covertness of the special forces has increased their operational deployments disproportionately. They have been used frequently on missions, such as the assaults on cave complexes in Afghanistan in 2002, which might have been conducted by conventional forces (Rayment 2008: 25). Accordingly, the SAS have been operating at a high level of tempo in Iraq and Afghanistan. The Kommando Spezialkräfte have been engaged in high intensity operations such as Operation Enduring Freedom in Afghanistan. Kommando Spezialkräfte troopers were also part of the ill-fated Operation Anaconda in March 2002. Acting alongside British, Australian and Canadian special forces, they provided a blocking force to prevent the retreat of fleeing Taliban and al Qaeda operatives (Ryan 2007: 46). More reports from British allies record the successful performance of Kommando Spezialkräfte troopers on a multinational mission in the east: though illustrating the extent of political oversight, they were withdrawn from future operations by the German Government immediately after the mission.[26] Since the formation of Commandement des Opérations Spéciales in 1992, France's special forces have deployed on

---

[24] Commander, Division Spezielle Operationen, personal interview, 19 June 2006.
[25] www.deutschesheer.de/portal/a/dso/kcxml/04_Sj9SPykssy0xPLMnMz0vM0Y_QjzK
LN3SOdzQ2AcmB2ZZhXvqRcNGglFR9X4_83FR9b_0A_YLciHJHR0VFAMusT
TU!/delta/base64xml/L3dJdyEvd0ZNQUFzQUMvNElVRS82XzFDX0EzNQ!!.
[26] Anonymous British source (special forces aviator), interview, 28 November 2007.

a number of operations, mainly to Africa. They successfully opposed the coup conducted by Bob Denard's mercenaries on the Comoros, were involved in operations in Somalia in 1993 and provided forces for Operation Turquoise in Rwanda. More recently, France has deployed special forces to Afghanistan, where they have engaged in a number of high intensity operations. In Helmand in 2006, two French special forces soldiers were killed while they were patrolling in the area around Kajaki. Unconfirmed reports suggest they were captured, tortured and mutilated. During 16 Air Assault Brigade's deployment to Helmand, French special forces accompanied a convoy from Kajaki to Sangin; they reported taking fire from every village and, indeed, every building as they drove through the valley.

Conclusion

Europe's armed forces face new threats in the current era. They must conduct new global missions in an increasingly strained budgetary context. The armed forces are becoming smaller, but they are not merely downsizing. They are not reduced versions of their Cold War structures. Rather, resources are being concentrated on professionalised elites: marines, paratroops, jägers and special forces. As the armed forces have declined as a whole, selected forces within them have grown in relative, and sometimes absolute, size and have been invested with new capabilities; empowered brigades have emerged. In contrast to the Cold War, these forces have become strategically decisive, dominating current operations especially in Afghanistan and, thereby, justifying further augmentation and investment. They represent a parallel process of concentration at the tactical level, which has already been identified at the operational level. The emergence of empowered brigades which deploy to conduct missions is part of the same organisational dynamic which has promoted the higher readiness force headquarters at the operational level. Indeed, higher readiness force headquarters, especially in Afghanistan, have commanded these forces in-theatre. In each country, empowered marine and airborne elites are emerging as the primary force for Europe's new missions commanded by the operational network.

There is a self-generating dynamic to current developments. As Europe's armed forces diminish, European states and their armed forces are increasingly dependent upon each other. Consequently, they must generate collective defence for themselves, once substantially delivered by nations independently, through transnational co-operation. As a result, Europe's armed forces have converged on common organisational patterns in order to facilitate co-operation. The emergence of the empowered brigade may then accord with current strategic and budgetary conditions, but nations have not transformed their militaries independently. On the contrary, they have actively sought to imitate each other. This is particularly obvious with the special forces where the Kommando Spezialkräfte, in particular, and France's special forces have modelled themselves on the SAS' structure and techniques. It is impossible to ascertain whether the current trajectory of transformation is optimal, but, certainly, the convergence towards common patterns has tangible collective benefits for states and their armed forces.

8   Elitism

Introduction

Since the end of the Cold War, empowered brigades have become a
central element in defence postures across Europe. The rise of these
elite forces seems almost self-evident. In the face of new wars around
the world, Europe's armed forces need troops that can deploy rapidly
to potentially hostile situations. The requirement for rapid deployment
disadvantages heavy armoured forces that can be transported by plane at
best only with great difficulty. Light forces are easier to deploy and sustain.
In many of the stabilisation situations which European forces have
encountered, heavy armour has been unnecessary. Consequently, light
forces have offered European governments the opportunity to insert a
robust early presence in crisis regions and, consequently, their steady
advance in military importance is explicable in rational operational
terms. The advantages of light forces in the current era seem clear.
Moreover, with strained public finances elite forces seem to represent
the best value for money; they provide the most capabilities, especially the
critical ones of deployability in an era of global operations for the least
investment. For instance, New Labour's *Strategic Defence Review* in 1997
stated: 'In the Cold War, we needed large forces at home and on the
Continent to defend against the constant threat of massive attack. Now,
the need is increasingly to help prevent or shape crises further away and,
if necessary, to deploy military forces rapidly before they get out of hand'
(Directorate of Defence Policy 1998a: 21). The *Livre Blanc* (2008) prioritises intervention as one of the critical military capacities in the twenty-
first century. The appeal to deployability has been used by defence
planners to justify investment in these forces and, of course, elite brigades
have used precisely these arguments to legitimate themselves and attract
funding.

Yet despite the apparently favourable strategic context, it is not self-
evident that elite light forces should have attained a position of dominance
in contemporary military doctrine and planning. Marines, paratroopers

and the special forces are expensive to train. Moreover, a significant part of their training and role is not relevant to current operations. These forces are trained for offensive, and even spectacular, theatre-entry – amphibious, mountain or airborne assault. However, on stabilisation or counter-insurgency operations these capabilities are more or less irrelevant. Britain has employed its amphibious capability three times in the last thirty years (the Falklands in 1982, Sierra Leone in 1999 and Iraq in 2003), and it has not conducted an operational parachute jump since 1956 (Suez). There is no prospect of either amphibious[1] or airborne operations in Helmand. France has never conducted an amphibious assault and, despite its large airborne forces, last conducted an operational parachute jump in Africa in 1977. Its previous jump before that was in 1956 at Suez with the British. The Bundeswehr has never employed paratroopers operationally.

In a period of severe financial constraint, it is strange that the most expensive forms of infantry, highly trained in insertion methods which are, at best, infrequently used, should have attained a position of such dominance. It would seem to be more cost-effective to maximise the number of regular line infantry available for current stabilisation operations. All European forces currently claim that they suffer from overstretching. Yet by investing in specialist infantry, defence planners have reduced the number of soldiers available to them. Indeed, it is not entirely clear that light forces are ideal for current operations. Certainly, heavy forces are more difficult to deploy; however, only in the initial stages of operations in the Balkans and Afghanistan was any intervention capability required. Thereafter, NATO and the European forces contributing to the NATO mission were involved in long-running stabilisation or counter-insurgency operations. In the Balkans, armoured personnel carriers have been vital. Indeed, the Royal Marines procured Viking precisely because they were excluded from these missions because of their lack of protected mobility. As the Afghan mission has developed, armoured vehicles and tanks have become increasingly useful, especially in the decisive urban areas and populated valleys. Indeed, elite light infantry is increasingly no longer technically light. These forces are now almost always mounted on, often armoured, vehicles. Consequently, they are less deployable than might be assumed. The deployability and expertise of these forces is typically employed to justify the concentration of resources on them. However, these factors are an inadequate explanation as to why these

---

[1] The use of rigid inflatable boats on the Kajaki reservoir during Herrick V demonstrated Royal Marine initiative, but cannot be considered as a genuine example of amphibious operations.

forces have been promoted in the current era. Other factors must be recognised in order to understand the increasing prominence of elite and special forces in force structures today.

Selection

It is important to recognise the institutional patronage which elite forces have enjoyed, allowing them to monopolise resources and dominate current operations. The political aspects of concentration will be discussed below. However, whatever the political factors, there are some evident military reasons why elite forces are so favoured at the moment. Empowered brigades have begun to dominate land operations because since the end of the Cold War they have demonstrated their capability through a series of successful operations. Having observed Royal Marines Commandos in Kosovo, Bellamy came to the potentially surprising conclusion that 'the toughest and most professional British troops were also the best at stabilisation operations which required the sensitive handling of the population' (Bellamy 1996: 6). These forces display some distinctive and advantageous capacities.

In one of the most famous and poetic paragraphs in his treatise *On War*, Clausewitz described the qualities of a true army:

An army that maintains its cohesion under the most murderous fire; that cannot be shaken by imaginary fears and resists well-founded ones with all its might; that, proud of its victories, will not lose the strength to obey orders and its respect and trust for its officers even in defeat; whose physical power, like the muscles of an athlete, has been steeled by training in privation and effort; a force that regards such efforts as a means to victory rather than a curse on its cause; that is mindful of all these duties and qualities by virtue of the single powerful idea of the honour of its arms – such an army is imbued with true military spirit. (1989: 187)

A true army exists, according to Clausewitz, insofar as it is collectively dedicated to a single goal; that is, the demonstration of its military prowess (its honour) against its rivals. This unity – this common dedication to a single idea – demands extraordinary sacrifices from individual soldiers. The 'one idea' transforms a group of soldiers into more than the sum of their parts; it turns them into an army.

Clausewitz's definition of military virtue raises the question of how armies inculcate a single unifying idea – a sense of honour, purpose and common destiny – into all the thousands of soldiers who comprise them. A variety of answers are possible here. Omar Bartov (1992) has identified political ideology as critical to the performance of the German Army on the Eastern Front in the Second World War and, certainly, revolutionary ideals were not irrelevant to the performance of Napoleon's armies. Moskos emphasised the role which 'latent ideology' could play in motivating soldiers. In Europe's empowered brigades, more prosaically practical processes seem to be more important. Professional skills inculcated through selection, training and operations seem to be decisive to the tactical performance of Europe's troops. Training and the inculcation of drills will be discussed in Chapter 9. Here, I want to examine the connection between elitism, selection and the special capabilities of Europe's empowered brigades.

It seems plausible to suggest that the selection tests which members of these organisations must pass play a crucial role in inducing this sense of unity to which Clausewitz alludes. The centrality of selection to the increasingly dominant position of elite forces is evident in the British, French and German armed forces. In Britain, all commando and airborne forces must undergo a series of endurance tests, assessing physical and mental stamina. The tests are designed to eliminate unmotivated candidates or others who are susceptible to physical and mental pressure. For instance, in Britain, the Commando Course and Pegasus Company, which are the selection tests for 3 Commando Brigade and the airborne forces in 16 Air Assault Brigade, seek to identify and to inculcate individual characteristics deemed essential to the role of theatre-entry. Both courses principally involve long forced marches and assault courses. These tests select for individuals who are more robust and determined than the average soldier. Typically, approximately half of the candidates fail the Commando Course and Pegasus Company.

Similarly, in Germany airborne and jäger forces are submitted to stern entry tests. Indeed, the Division Spezielle Operationen effectively imposes an annual test on its members in the form of mass parachute drops to sustain the airborne capability. Although it is unlikely that the Division Spezielle Operationen would actually parachute operationally, the annual parachuting has been important to engendering elitism in the formation:

From 20 to 24 August the Saarland Brigade (26) conducted their traditional para-drop week. 1,400 paras in total were dispatched. In addition, there were also guests from the international community of paratroopers. The fostering of camaraderie among the paras was at the forefront of the event. From 20 August 2007, everyone anticipated the evocative and beloved instruction for every para – 'Ready to Jump' – in the skies about Saarlandish Saarlouis. For the audience on the ground, the drone of planes and the whirring of helicopter blades is even more evocative. For everyone knew the paras would jump over the next five days with their green-grey canopies from so-called static lines out of the transport plane Transall C-160 and an armoured support helicopter, Type CH-53 GC (equipped with additional petrol tanks). In spite of the sometimes poor weather, 1,400 paras were eventually able to exit from the two airframes during the course of the jumps weeks as a whole.[2]

In France, the marines of 9 brigade légère blindée de marine do not undergo specific entry tests. However, the Brigade selects only the best officers from St Cyr and, given its history as the first professional and one of the most highly respected formations in the French Army, it attracts a higher quality of soldier than in the rest of the army. As one French colonel, who was a marine, put it: '9 Brigade is without doubt *the* best brigade in the French army'.[3]

The process of selection is particularly ferocious among the special forces in Europe. In Britain, for instance, candidates for the SAS undergo a four-month selection process which includes a month of forced marches in the Welsh mountains, a month of jungle training in Brunei and a month of combat survival. Of the professional soldiers who go forward for the SAS, 90 per cent fail selection. In France and Germany, comparably ferocious selection processes have been developed. Recruits for 1 Régiment Parachutiste d'Infanterie de Marine, for instance, are pre-selected candidates with good performance records, who then undergo a nine-month training programme with an attrition rate of 50 per cent. The programme involves basic, airborne, commando and finally specialist training. Once accepted into 1 Régiment Parachutiste d'Infanterie de Marine, the candidate undergoes a further fifteen months of continuation training (Micheletti 1999: 44–6). The navy commandos, Groupe de Combat en Milieu Clos, are among the most highly selected in the French forces: 'Only the best get through the selection process – about four per year. For one week, applicants – all experienced commando qualified personnel – are subjected to extreme conditions, day and night, including rucksack marches, physical training, face-offs with attacks dogs to assess reactions, handgun qualifications and other tests, all of which assess the candidates' ability to react quickly and correctly' (Micheletti 1999: 74). Candidates for Germany's Kommando Spezialkräfte are submitted to a two-year programme of training and probation, after which they commit themselves to four years in a special forces company.[4] In the selection phase at the testing centre (Versuchzentrum)

---

[2] Translated from: www.deutschesheer.de/portal/a/dso/kcxml/04_Sj9SPykssy0xPLMnMz0
vM0Y_QjzKLN3SOdzQwA8mB2ZZhXvqRcNGglFR9X4_83FR9b_0A_YLciHJHR0V
FAB78g50!/delta/base64xml/L2dJQSEvUUt3QS80SVVFLzZfMUNfQTRU?yw_content
URL=%2F01DB050500000001%2FW276RAYF380INFODE%2Fcontent.jsp.

[3] Personal interview, 20 July 2005.

[4] www.bundeswehr.de/portal/a/bwde/kcxml/04_Sj9SPykssy0xPLMnMz0vM0Y_QjzK
Ld443MXMHSYGYxgEh-pEwsaCUVH1fj_zcVH1v_QD9gtyIckdHRUUAK2vjUw!!/
delta/base64xml/L2dJQSEvUUt3QS80SVVFLzZfQ180Nkc!?yw_contentURL=%2F
C1256EF4002AED30%2FW26U7DJP733INFODE%2Fcontent.jsp.

which (like the SAS) runs twice a year, candidates undertake a series of tests which culminate in a week-long exercise in which they must perform military tasks under extreme psychological and physical duress, culminating in a 160-km march (Pflüger 1998: 97; Scholzen 2009a: 62–79); 60–80 per cent fail (Scholzen 2009b: 126). Selection and training processes are tests for individual capabilities to ensure that only the most motivated and robust individuals are accepted into these forces.

The special forces are an extreme case, but the process of selection is important for the other empowered brigades. With higher quality personnel, elite formations are able to attain higher standards of performance. However, it is important not to individualise the organisational impact of selection tests for military elites. One of the most decisive effects of the selection process is the performative role it plays in collective self-definition; it has a sociological effect. Whatever the actual merits of the selected individual and, however relevant the tests themselves to current operations, the process of selection creates in and of itself a social group which believes itself to be elite. Members of these organisations share a feeling of election. As a result, they enjoy a distinctive status which, in and of itself, improves their levels of performance. The self-expectation that elite forces should perform becomes a self-referential reality. For instance, a former commanding officer of 3 Para described how his battalion had been tasked to fix a barbed wire fence on the border in Armagh between Northern Ireland and the Republic of Ireland on a tour to Ulster. The task was tedious. However, by explicitly referencing the fact that they were paratroopers and that 'they would do the job better than anyone else', the contingent which was sent to carry out the mundane duty ensured that they performed excellently; even on a tedious duty their pride as paratroopers and their desire to prove themselves to be superior impelled a higher level of performance.[5] Indeed, as he briefed his troops on the final exercise in Britain in January 2006 before deploying to Helmand, the commanding officer explicitly referenced their identity as paratroopers to encourage the highest levels of performance: 'We are paras. If it is best to go up a river in minus 5 [degrees Celsius]: we go up the river. If there is a right hard way and a wrong easy way, we will take the right way every time.'[6] Merely because they are expected and expect themselves to perform to a higher standard, elite regiments seem to perform better. Interestingly, the very fact that tests exist for elite forces may actually attract stronger applicants to these regiments. This is particularly the case in Britain where the Royal Marines and Parachute Regiment recruit

---

[5] Personal interview, 30 January 2006.   [6] Fieldnotes, 30 January 2006.

nationally, using their entry tests as a means of advertising themselves to fit and adventurous young men, in contrast to line regiments which draw recruits from specific regions.

Elite insignia: berets and badges

Elite selection processes typically culminate in the award of a special, coloured beret. In the Royal Marine Commandos and the Parachute Regiment, new members are awarded distinctive green and maroon berets on passing the entry tests. The history of these berets can be traced back to the Second World War when Britain established commando and airborne forces. In response to Churchill's demand for the raising of raiding forces to harass the Continent after the debacle of May 1940, the first commando units to be raised consisted of volunteers from all regiments and corps. A commando training centre was established in northwestern Scotland and eventually based at Achnacarry Castle near Fort William. In turn, in order to denote their distinctive status, the new commandos adopted a distinctive green beret in 1941. The first commandos chose a green salamander passing (unscathed) through fire as a badge which they wore on their arm, and it is believed that the selection of green for the commando beret is a reference to the original salamander. The green beret has subsequently been adopted internationally by commando forces as their headdress. For instance, Free French forces underwent commando training at Achnacarry during the Second World War and a French company of commandos in 4 Commando landed under the command of Captain Kieffer at Juno beach in 1944. Consequently, France's naval special forces (marine commandos, 'les bérets verts') wear a green beret, which has the same origin as the Royal Marines' beret, while the commando dagger on their cap badge is further reference to Achnacarry (Micheletti 1999: 68). Their cap badge also consists of a cross of Lorraine which is a significant marker of distinction. The performance of French forces in the Second World War is still a matter of contention, with only the Free French forces and the mountain troops escaping the opprobrium which was attached to the capitulation to the Nazis. Significantly, the cross of Lorraine was the symbol of the Free French in the Second World War, and 9 brigade légère blindée de marine's appropriation of it is a deliberate attempt to distinguish themselves from an ignominious past. Through the symbol, the Brigade differentiates itself from the rest of the French Army, contaminated by that defeat.

The British Parachute Regiment shared a common origin with the Royal Marines Commandos. Recognising the potential for airborne assault, 2 Commando was assigned to parachute training in 1941, and both the

SAS[7] and the Parachute Regiment, as airborne commandos, arose from this new method of entry.[8] As it separated from Britain's marine commando forces, creating its own selection and training programme at Hardwick Hall in Derbyshire, the Parachute Regiment was given a new maroon beret. The maroon beret was originally brought into service in 1942 by Major General Browning, the first GOC of the 1 Airborne Division, although it was actually selected by General Sir Alan Brooke (Harclerode 1993: 25). Since that time, the maroon beret has become a symbol for airborne forces worldwide. German and French paratroopers also wear the same maroon beret. For instance, 1 Régiment Parachutiste d'Infanterie de Marine were allowed to wear the beret by George VI in recognition of their contributions during the Second World War. The connection with the Second World War is evident in the Division Spezielle Operationen which has essentially retained the original Wehrmacht insignia for airborne forces: an attacking eagle in a laurel wreath, but dispensing with the swastika which the original eagle carried in its talons. The Kommando Spezialkräfte also retain the airborne maroon beret, but have their own special insignia: in place of the paratrooper's screaming eagle, the Kommando Spezialkräfte are designated by a sword inside a laurel wreath (in possible reference to the winged dagger of the SAS). In addition, they have a regimental flash consisting of a black arrow on a blue background to signify deep, precision strike.

9 brigade légère blindée de marine is not a commando organisation and does not wear a distinctively coloured beret. However, because of its early professionalisation, the Brigade considers itself an elite brigade. Accordingly, although the French marines wear the standard blue beret of the French Army, their distinctive regimental insignia, a gold anchor, serves a similarly distinctive function in France. 9 brigade légère blindée de marine has also adopted the cross of Lorraine as its insignia. Like the naval commandos, the selection of the cross references its use by de Gaulle's Free French Forces in the Second World War, of which 9 brigade légère blindée de marine's predecessors, the 9 Division d'infanterie coloniale, were part. The symbol has an historical significance which distinguishes its members from other formations in the French Army.

The coloured berets of commando, airborne and special forces are arbitrary symbols. In themselves, they are simply pieces of material.

---

[7] Having passed through Achnacarry, David Stirling, a lieutenant in the Scots Guards, conceived the idea of a deep raiding force in North Africa. The SAS emerged from this force.

[8] 2 Commando was renamed the 11 Special Air Service Battalion in November 1940 (Harclerode 1993: 20).

They have become organisationally important because they signify a distinctive elite community. The green and maroon berets have become indivisibly connected to a military selection process. Because all members of these organisations wear the same distinctive and coveted berets and have, therefore, passed the same tests, there is recognition of a common status even among individuals unknown to each other. In a recent contribution to the debates about cohesion in the armed forces, Ben-Shalom *et al.* (2005) have forwarded the concept of 'quick trust'. Israeli soldiers who do not know each other personally are able to unify themselves around particular tasks with great facility. They are able to do this because the IDF has instilled common tactical practices among its forces, the members of which are operationally experienced. Consequently, unknown soldiers have access to highly elaborated and well-established shared concepts and practices.

The selection process and distinctive berets of elite forces have a similar effect. Independently of personal acquaintance, members of these regiments already share common reference points: a shared selection process. There is a common presumption about the qualities and standards which an individual wearing these berets should display.[9] Signifying a common selection process, they are able to engender organisational unity and coherence even among members who are personally unknown to each other. There are other organisational benefits to military elitism. Unlike line regiments, who do not endure the same entry ordeal, elite regiments often display greater social unity. Typically, there is less distance between officers and soldiers. Selection creates a sense of distinction which enjoins higher levels of performance from elite forces. The higher levels of unity among elite formations have been self-consciously recognised by its members. This is particularly clear in a recent memoir of a British paratrooper in Helmand. His explanation of the title of his book, *Blood Clot*, is illuminating:

As you know 'blood clot' means blood cells coming together to form a strong clot that forms and sticks together to keep the wound sealed enabling it to repair. The Parachute Regiment's 'blood clot' acts the same, whether downtown scrapping or in some far away country fighting alongside each other. Our maroon berets come together, they stick together, they close ranks forming the blood clot and fight against anything that comes their way … Without even knowing the other person, if you catch sight of another maroon beret, you close in on each other … The trust

[9] In 16 Air Assault Brigade, there has been extensive debate about the policy of beret wearing since all members of the brigade are allowed to wear the paratroopers' maroon beret. This has angered many paratroopers who believe that the right to wear the beret should be reserved for those who have passed P Company. The organisational implications of this policy will be discussed in Chapter 10.

in each other's abilities is there automatically, as well as the mutual respect ... We are also all put through the same rigorous selection tests and have the same pride and passion in the regiment. (Scott 2008: 165)

Scott elides the selection process and the regimental symbol (the maroon beret) to demonstrate that the elite status of paratroopers is a fundamental resource for enjoining unity.

Collective memory

The maroon and green berets of British marines and paratroopers have been explicitly tied to the collective memories of these regiments. Although the Royal Marines were founded in 1664, the current commando status is only sixty years old. In 1941, volunteers from the Royal Marines formed a new commando unit, designated A Commando, later to be re-named 40 Commando. Royal Marines Commandos in the Second World War wore the green beret, but most marines remained in conventional roles and continued to wear the traditional blue beret of the sea soldier. Later, in the 1960s, following the Sandys Report, blue-bereted marines disappeared and only the Royal Marines Commandos remained. The Parachute Regiment, as already mentioned, was founded in 1942. Accordingly, for both regiments the Second World War represents the critical institutional memory; indeed, it provides the organisations with their myths of origin. Both the Royal Marines and Parachute Regiment have been involved in a multiplicity of operations since their creation in the early 1940s, but each regiment has identified certain operations as definitive. Of course, especially with their commitment to Afghanistan, new operations are likely to become central to institutional memories. The green and maroon berets connote these operations. For the Royal Marines, the Normandy landings and the Falklands represent idealised collective memories in which the commando attributes were demonstrated in hostile amphibious operations. The importance of these memories for the Marines was demonstrated in 2007 when 42 Commando commemorated the 25th anniversary of the Falklands War and its latest operations in Helmand simultaneously. Although the Falklands has been taken to signify commando ethos at its most developed, past members of 42 Commando who had fought in the Falklands emphasised that, in fact, the current tour to Helmand involved more intense and more prolonged war fighting.

For the Parachute Regiment, Arnhem has been central to their definition of themselves. The centrality of Arnhem to the Regiment usefully demonstrates the way collective memories are mobilised by elite forces in

Europe today. The battle for Arnhem was part of the Allied airborne operation (Market Garden) mounted in September 1944 to seize a series of bridges across the Low Countries in order to facilitate an early seizure of the Ruhr region (Harclerode 1993: 92–124). Arnhem in the Netherlands was the last bridge across the Rhine before Germany. Britain's 1 Airborne Division were tasked to seize this bridge so that the armoured 30 Corps could penetrate the Ruhr. The operation was a disaster, although elements of 2 Battalion the Parachute Regiment reached the bridge at Arnhem which they held for three days. The salience of Arnhem in Regiment mythology is instructive. The memory of Arnhem emphasises courage at the lowest tactical levels and extraordinary levels of sacrifice. As such, Arnhem has become central to the Parachute Regiment's self-image. This has had evident operational effects. It is noticeable that on the second day at Goose Green during the Falklands War, Major John Crosland the officer commanding B Company successfully referred to Arnhem to motivate his battered company:

Look, we've done bloody well today. Okay, we've lost some lads; we've lost the CO. Now we've really got to show our mettle. It's not over yet, we haven't got the place. We're about 1,000 metres from D Company; we're on our own and [the] enemy has landed to our south and there's a considerable force at Goose Green, so we could be in a fairly sticky position. It's going to be like Arnhem – Day 3. (Fitz-Gibbon 1995)

Similarly, during the battle, 2 Para's adjutant declared 'Let's remember Arnhem!' moments before he was killed (Harclerode 1993: 18). The commemoration of Arnhem remains central to this day. British para-troopers have tailored their uniforms so that this connection to Arnhem is constantly asserted. During the Second World War, British airborne forces were issued a special rimless, steel helmet because the standard British helmet was unsuitable for exiting from planes. Airborne soldiers typically cover this helmet with netting to which strips of cloth or leaves are attached to provide some rudimentary camouflage. Today, British para-troops still cover their helmets with scrim-netting in explicit reference to their forebears; photographs of paratroopers in Helmand demonstrate that the practice is all but universal among them. Even when deployed to the Arctic, when there is not even a theoretical possibility of using the scrim-netting for camouflage, British paratroopers doctor their helmets in obstinate reference to Arnhem. Arnhem has become an important collec-tive memory, mobilised by all members of the Parachute Regiment and represented physically on their equipment as a means of denoting their distinction. The Arnhem memory has unified members of the Parachute Regiment into a cohesive organisation.

Conveniently, the Arnhem myth of origin has also served the Regiment's political needs. Arnhem is a story of how a parachute division, surrounded and alone, fought off a superior enemy until it was overwhelmed or was able to escape back across the Rhine. The memory reflects the political position in which the Parachute Regiment found itself over the last five decades. From the 1960s, the Regiment was surrounded by detractors in the Army who could not see the validity of the airborne role and were intent on reducing or cutting the beleaguered Regiment. They almost succeeded. In 1977, 16 Parachute Brigade was disbanded. The collective memory of Arnhem did not just record a feat of arms, then; the Parachute Regiment might well have chosen the successful Normandy campaign for that purpose. It spoke to the Regiment's immediate predicament in the 1960s and 1970s.

The Parachute Regiment's commemoration of Arnhem illustrates an important point. Collective memories do not accurately record those events which were decisive in the formation of an elite regiment. Rather they are continually invented and re-invented to embody the central understandings of the social group in the face of contemporary threats and opportunities. Collective memory actively seizes upon and manipulates its past in order to mobilise the social group in the present. The most successful organisations are able to create invented traditions for themselves – however fictitious – to inspire allegiance. In this the Regiment followed the practice which is typical of all social groups and is evident among other elite forces in Europe.

For France's 9 brigade légère blindée de marine, collective memories have been equally significant. The brigade's cap badge and cross of Lorraine motif are themselves tied to collective memories by which the Brigade actively defines itself. 9 brigade légère blindée de marine self-consciously traces its origins back to the Division Bleue (Marine Division) which served during the Franco-Prussian War. Cardinal Richelieu created the first troupe de la Marine in 1622 to perform a similar function to the Royal Marines, founded in 1664. They acted as musketeers, snipers and gunners on French ships. These troops, like the Royal Marines, were subsequently used to garrison colonial outposts and to defend ports ashore both abroad and in France. As Prussia began to pose a greater threat to France in the middle of the nineteenth century, the French Army augmented itself by assuming control of the marines garrisoning ports in France. They were formed into a Division Bleue in reference to their maritime origins. Their performance during the Franco-Prussian War remains central to 9 brigade légère blindée de marine's current self-definition:

They fought at Sedan. That is very important for us. It is a proud achievement. We lost but it was federative for us as a unit. We maintain the concept from that war: we are good soldiers who do our duty until death. This battle: Bazeilles is our main annual commemoration for us. It is very important – it is in October. We were defeated but only because we had no more ammunition. The cartridges were made by a Belgian factory one of the owners of which was the son of Wilhelm II. He stopped the supply of ammunition.[10]

The story of Bazeilles contains all the elements of an heroic narrative in which soldiers fought against the odds only to be undone by a cowardly foreign capitalist. The Brigade's formal briefing includes an historical section featuring an oil painting of the Brigade's 'heroic' defence of Bazeilles between 31 August and 1 September 1870.

For the French Army, the Second World War is a deeply problematic memory as the ultimate victory of the Allies was preceded by the ignoble military collapse of France's army and the capitulation to and, indeed, collusion of its forces with Nazi Germany. Raised in Africa and committed to the North African campaign in the first instance, 9 brigade légère blindée de marine, by contrast, has been able to employ the Second World War as a resource. The current formation cites its heritage back to the 9 Division d'infanterie coloniale which fought in Africa, helped to seize Toulon and then took part in the Operation Torch landings against the Vichy in the south of France in 1944. The Division campaigned through France and into Germany, reaching Lake Constance by the end of the war. Interestingly, when the Division d'infanterie coloniale arrived in France, its predominantly African soldiers were replaced by white Frenchmen, whose liberation of their fellow white citizens was deemed more politically appropriate. The Division d'infanterie coloniale was eventually deployed to Indochina to be disbanded in 1948.

9 brigade légère blindée de marine have used similar creativity to the Parachute Regiment in creating a collective memory. There is little formal organisational connection between today's 9 brigade légère blindée de marine and its marine predecessors. The current formation can plausibly be traced back to 1963 when the marine division was re-formed. At this point, the French Army deliberately endowed the new formation with a long and honourable (but invented) heritage; the designation – 9 – did not accord with any extant institutional connection but was a performative act of self-definition. The Brigade was given the old emblem of the 9 Division d'infanterie coloniale, the cross of Lorraine, in order to consolidate this act of historical invention. The link to Bazeilles and the pathos of the

---

[10] Deputy commander, 9 brigade légère blindée de marine, personal interview, 14 November 2007.

marines' stand at that village may be uncorroborated historically and may have no real connection with today's formation, but members of 9 brigade légère blindée de marine actively invoke them in order to define themselves and to engender unity within the organisation. The collective memory has a manifest social effect, even if the memory itself was invented in 1963. Crucially, the Brigade has been able to affirm its invented collective memory in action since its formation, deploying to Chad in the 1970s and engaged in an increasing number of operations since the 1990s.

The French special forces consciously evoke their historic origins. The French Army's special forces invest great significance in their berets and badges. For instance, not only do 1 Régiment Parachutiste d'Infanterie de Marine wear the same maroon beret as that worn by British paratroopers and, in northern Europe during the Second World War, by the SAS, they adopted the same motto as the SAS ('Qui Ose Gagne', 'Who Dares Wins'), while the regimental badge, with sword and parachute, imitates the SAS' insignia. 1 Régiment Parachutiste d'Infanterie de Marine's origins in the Africa campaign in the Second World War have become particularly important for it in the current era as it begins to conduct missions in Afghanistan, alongside the SAS, which have evident parallels with the raids they performed in the Second World War. Similarly, France's marine commandos name their five companies after commanders or soldiers killed in past conflicts. One of the companies is named after Lieutenant Augustin Hubert who, under the command of Captain Kieffer, was killed on Sword Beach on 6 June 1944; another is named after Kieffer himself.

Collective memories can be invented; convenient events can be appropriated. Their periodic evocation does not return participants to the pristine act, but rather unifies them around a renewed signifier which references contemporary circumstances and enjoins appropriate action in the light of that context. Collective memories are, therefore, critical to the coherence and effectiveness of social groups and organisations. The unity of the French and British elite forces is substantially dependent upon the self-defining creation of institutional memories. Despite their evident expertise, the Bundeswehr, especially the Bundesheer, is severely compromised in the archive of collective memories upon which it can draw. The decisive memory for European armed forces today is typically the Second World War because this is the largest major conflict these forces were involved in within living memory. The Second World War can be utilised as a potent collective resource for resources which affirm the formation's coherence today, especially since the Second World War has been de-politicised for the French and British; it is no longer a source of international grievance. Yet for the Division Spezielle Operationen and the Bundesheer more widely, memories of the Second World War are problematic (Schulze and Verhülsdonk, 1998; Sünkler, 2007). Airborne operations in Sicily in 1941 are commemorated by the paratroopers in the Division Spezielle Operationen, but these memories are politicised by their necessary association with the Nazi atrocities of that era. Despite the fact that the purely operational performance of their land forces was outstanding (Dupuy 1977; Van Creveld 2007), it is very difficult for the German Army to utilise these memories. For Germany, the shameful memories of the Second World War are instructive as a negative prescription for the Bundeswehr. The Bundeswehr has limited collective operational memories upon which to draw.

The problem is compounded by the Cold War experiences. German forces prepared extensively to fight a conflict which never broke out and whose nature was quite different to current operations. Unlike British and French forces, however, German forces were constitutionally unable to engage in any operations outside Europe and, therefore, have no historical resources away from the European theatre. The Bundeswehr has few collective memories which it can evoke in order to engender the dense social unity which is essential for military operations. The German Army has institutional doctrines, procedures and practices, but fewer collective memories to inspire organisational unity. There have been some attempts to address this problem in the Bundeswehr by appealing to longer-standing Prussian military traditions. The problem with these traditions from the eighteenth and nineteenth century is that they are so far beyond the span of existing organisational memory, activity and membership that they have little resonance with forces today.

Political and military leaders have been well aware of the lack of institutionalised memory. Indeed, General von Baudissin sought to overcome this problem when the Bundeswehr was re-established in 1952 (Clement and Joris 2005: 88). He developed the concept of Innere Führung (literally meaning 'inner direction', but sometimes rendered as 'leadership and civic education'), where soldiers were 'citizens in uniform'; Innere Führung bound soldiers to the same ethical and legal codes as citizens (Bald 2005: 49). Crucially, it was a soldier's duty to refuse to carry out an illegal order; in stark contravention of the standard defence utilised by those who had recently been on trial at Nuremberg. Innere Führung was often associated with von Stauffenberg's plot to kill Hitler in July 1944; he demonstrated precisely the inner moral conviction embodied by Innere Führung avant la lettre. Innere Führung was institutionalised as the invented tradition of the Bundeswehr. It seemed to unite the Bundeswehr as a coherent military organisation while preventing any reversion to Nazi barbarism. Innere Führung was a new collective memory, cleansed of Nazi corruptions, around which the armed forces could unite. Indeed, it remains critical today. In his Bundeswehr reforms, Peter Struck explicitly referenced this history. He identified the courage of men and women resisting the Nazis as a fundamental part of the Bundeswehr's traditions.

During the Cold War, Innere Führung was broadly successful. It legitimated the Bundeswehr, while having little apparent impact on operational performance. This seemed to be substantially due to the nature of the conflict. For the Bundeswehr, geared wholly to conventional war, the conflict was simple: it was a conventional military struggle in which politics were excluded from the battlefield. The only problems German officers had to consider were tactical. Since the end of the Cold War, the usefulness of Innere Führung has been called into question as missions have become more complex and intensely politicised even at the lowest levels. At this point, Innere Führung seems to offer little specific content or direction to German soldiers; it did not unite them in pursuit of collective projects, but was a negative prescription about what not to do. Moreover, not only was it an individual principle rather than a collective resource, it was also a misnomer. In order to prevent any regression, the Institute of Innere Führung the Bundeswehr established an ombudsman (Vertrauensamt). This institution functions as a complaints bureau for the German armed forces. Independent of the chain of command, individual soldiers are free to write to the institute criticising their commanding officers on almost limitless grounds. The officer is then required by the Vertrauensamt to answer those charges; effectively, the charges are *prima facie* treated as plausible. Innere Führung is not primarily actually about internal moral direction. On the contrary, it refers to an organisational structure external to the individual soldier, to which rightly or wrongly aggrieved parties can appeal. It is an institutional method by which the Bundeswehr surveills its middle ranking officers who are in tactical command of troops; it is, in fact, Äussere or Obere (external or superior) Führung. In private many German officers have major reservations about Innere Führung. Indeed, some reject the concept furiously:

Innere Führung is a dogma. It is an ideology. Other armies have operational readiness; we have Innere Führung ... An army, where the principle of an army actually exists, is based on the orders and obedience. Nothing else works. The Bundeswehr – I believe it to be the only army, which tries next to the principle of order and obedience to insist upon the insight of the so-called responsible citizen in uniform inspired by the spirit of Innere Führung.[11]

[11] Personal interview, anonymous German officer, 2006 (full date withheld to protect identity).

According to this officer, of the new Bundeswehr generals only General von Baudissin regarded the concept as workable. The officer agreed that in every army there were scandals in which soldiers were abused but, he asserted, these unfortunate events were not necessarily systemic: 'Because of this, I say the following, this so-called Innere Führung is a singularly large lie.'[12] Indeed, the officer's perspective is just an extreme articulation of the intense debates in the Bundeswehr since 2004 about Innere Führung (after the controversial performance of the Bundeswehr during the riots in Kosovo, particularly in Prizren). Many senior officers have questioned its viability in a professional army. Army Inspektor (Chief of the General Staff) Gudera shocked Peter Struck and Generalinspekteur Schneiderhan when he used the opportunity of his retirement to question Innere Führung as part of a series of rightist–nationalist political interventions (Bald 2005: 184). Similarly, Brigadier General Günzel, eventually sacked from the Kommando Spezialkräfte for a letter of support he wrote to an anti-Semitic politician, argued that Innere Führung made neither good citizens nor good soldiers (Bald 2005: 184). Indeed, he maintained that the concept of a citizen in uniform was 'a homunculus', created out of fear of the military and with no connection to German military tradition. It was the institutional equivalent to planting a 'tree without roots' (Günzel 2006: 85).

There is no implication that the officers who reject Innere Führung are correct. However, the debates have demonstrated a fundamental crisis in the Bundeswehr in which new operations have demanded an alternative organisational culture that is at odds with the military–political consensus established in the 1950s. Typically, senior officers, who are no longer under threat of being reported by subordinates, have learned to appreciate the benefits of the concept; a *post factum* justification has been established:

It is very important and you would love to have it. In organisational terms it involves a Vertrauensamt – an ombudsman – and an educational organisation. We have our special procedures with claims. A military person at my level in the field can be written about by a draftee to the Ombudsman. I had this happen to me – it stays on my record but it did not affect my career. I have made general. It is a beautiful system. Once you know how to handle it. You must explain yourself to your troops. You must talk to them. You must explain: 'Look I am now being a bit nasty, please understand the reasons.' In Britain, it is different. Officers give a command and then they retire. With Innere Führung [IF] we are trained to lead by example and it is not just a military matter. It is how we live and how we behave. The draft system has presented difficulties for men when commanding. But we must care for him. There must be comradeship from both ends. I, as a general,

---

[12] Personal interview, anonymous German officer, 2006 (full date withheld to protect identity).

have a claim on his comradeship. It is not only about management but about personal authority. The boys accept me as a human being. IF has a lot of politics behind it too. It provides training for the right kind of courage. There is a boundary between comradeship and camaraderie: IF [is] about comradeship. We are going places – where there is 'Umgang mit Angst, Verletzung und Tod' ['the presence of fear, injury and death']. We deal with these things in IF. How can our ethics, for instance, and Basic Law prepare us for potentially fighting with child soldiers in Africa. IF explains where they are and gives them cultural orientation. It all goes along with IF. I love it. It comes out of our anxiety about our history. IF is very difficult to define and if you ask five different people you will get six different answers. And they would all be valid. IF is very important, it supports the transition from a soldier who does it because he is paid to a man serving his country. The British do not fight for the Queen, they fight for money. With the help of IF we help them to develop that feeling. It may take some years to persuade them that you do it for God and your country . . . The older and more senior you get the more interesting it becomes. For young officers it can be something of a pain – an irrelevance. But as you get more senior you get more and more interested and involved in it. I love it.[13]

It is possible that Innere Führung inspires unity, as the German brigadier general suggests; it may unify officers and soldiers. Officers may, indeed, have to engage more personally with their soldiers through Innere Führung. It may also encourage a broader, less militaristic approach which is actually better suited to current missions (Hoffman 2005: 51). However, as it is currently constituted, Innere Führung tends to obstruct the formation of operationally relevant memories of Germany's armed forces, just when they need these shared imaginings the most. It focuses the Bundeswehr on the political shame of the Second World War. German forces conspicuously lack the vivid traditions of British and French militaries whose members can unite themselves around concrete, if imagined, memories. The unifying self-conception of the German armed forces is a non-military legal principle enforced by a complaints institution; the authority of senior officers is always open to question. It does not enjoin soldiers to commit themselves to common military endeavours in order to promote the honour and status of their regiment or brigade, as Clausewitz described. It does not focus the soldiers' attention on collective military practice. Rather, it emphasises the individual rights of the soldier, while blunting the tactical commander's ability to lead and make decisions.

Nevertheless, paratroopers in the Bundeswehr have still sought to sacralise their role through historical reference (Scholzen 2009a; Schulze and Verhülsdonk 1998). The British and French armed forces

---

[13] Brigadier general, personal interview, 19 June 2006.

are traditionally politically conservative. Indeed, there have been some politically dubious elements within Britain's forces. For instance, especially in the 1980s, a group of soldiers, NCOs and some junior officers in the Parachute Regiment formed themselves into a militaristic sub-culture with extreme right-wing tendencies (Jennings and Weale 1996). The appearance of deviant military sub-cultures has been apparent in Germany. The Wehrmacht was the first army to employ airborne forces and conducted some successful assaults especially during the fall of France. Throughout the Second World War, the German airborne formations distinguished themselves militarily. These events are obviously attractive and potentially potent collective memories for today's paratroopers in Germany. Reports suggest that, in addition to some more or less legitimised commemorations such as those relating to Crete, some Wehrmacht operations have been illicitly established as the collective memories of these forces, providing a focal point for regimental identity.[14] Indeed, some commentators have criticised the creation of the Kommando Spezialkräfte because it has historical links to units within the Wehrmacht's old 78 Storm Division, which was the spearhead of Hitler's Wehrmacht and implicated in many Nazi crimes (Pflüger 1998: 101). Indeed, there has been some evidence that the Kommando Spezialkräfte has been self-consciously linked to these formations by their members (Bald 2005: 185). Illustrating the problem, its disgraced former Brigadier General Günzel has recently published a book with the former commander of Grenzschutzgruppe 9, Brigadier General Wegener, called *Secret Warriors* (in German) which traces the history of the Kommando Spezialkräfte, Grenzschutzgruppe 9 and Wehrmacht Brandenburg Division, using some of their own personal photographs. By aligning the three formations in this way, Günzel and Wegener have, whether intentionally or not, invented a potentially dubious history for Germany's special forces today (Günzel *et al.* 2006). There has been understandable anxiety in Germany about these connections between the Bundeswehr and the Wehrmacht and the SS. That certain formations within the Army are incipiently fascist is worrying, and some researchers have found a correlation between right-wing views and paratroopers (Tomforde 2005).

It might be possible to interpret the invocation of these memories in a different way. Paratroopers and other soldiers in the army may not

---

[14] Even legitimate memories like Crete are ambiguous because of civilian massacres which occurred during the operation, perpetrated by German paratroopers. Indeed, a German colleague described the whole issue of collective memory in the Bundeswehr as a 'thick, swarming wasp's nest' (email communication, 14 October 2008).

necessarily invoke this connection to the Wehrmacht because they are political extremists. Rather, in order to unify themselves for difficult and dangerous operations, it is necessary that German paratroops provide some collective narrative to themselves. They need to invest their membership of their regiment with special significance in order that bonds of sufficient strength can be established so that soldiers can jump out of planes and go on operations together. With the lack of officially sanctioned collective memories, members of these regiments have independently sought to create their own illegal traditions. Germany's armed forces have been legally restricted as a result of history, and many of their European peers point to the German Constitution as central to the performance of the Bundeswehr in the post-Cold War era. There is little doubt that the close constitutional control over the Bundeswehr has obstructed its performance since the end of the Cold War. Less obvious is the fact that the shameful history of Germany's armies during the Second World War cuts the Bundeswehr off from a potent cultural resource which is pertinent to organisational unification and, therefore, military performance: collective memory. The Bundeswehr has few resources available to it to define what it actually is and, therefore, how it should perform the new operations being asked of it.

Since the late 1990s, there may have been some minor reformations of this culture. German troops have begun to use operational experience as a status marker in the Bundeswehr. In a recent article, Maren Tomforde has analysed the experience of deployment in terms of Van Gennep's concept of a three-stage ritual process: separation; isolation; and re-integration. She has argued that this ritual process has altered the status of the deployed troops in the Bundeswehr, which has been denoted symbolically by both formal and informal techniques. For instance, in Afghanistan German ISAF troops have developed a method of signalling their experience. While in-theatre, the experienced wear a light tropical uniform, which assumes a slightly pinkish hue after vigorous washing. In this way, they demonstrate their membership of the 'in-group' of operationally experienced soldiers to others in their contingent (Tomforde 2005: 111–12). The Bundeswehr has itself institutionalised techniques which have signified the professional importance of operations. They have introduced deployment medals for new missions: bronze for 30 days' deployment; silver for 360 days; and gold for 690 days. These medals, featuring the Federal Eagle in a laurel wreath, are a recognised national award from the Bundespräsident. They are awarded at formal 'medal parades' after operations and soldiers are entitled to wear them on their uniforms. Tomforde has observed the important role which medal ceremonies have played for the troops, not only in recognition from the fellow professionals but also in terms of their promotion (Tomforde 2005: 116). One soldier noted the centrality of operations to current professional self-definition: 'You have to have been there at least once, otherwise you can't really talk, when your comrades discuss operations. And operations get talked about a lot' (2005: 116). Indeed, there have been reports of senior field officers actively seeking deployments, which are unnecessary in military terms, as a means of advancing themselves. The new focus on operations, symbolised by medals and discoloured uniforms, may be institutionally important for the Bundeswehr. 'Foreign missions are creating a mission oriented, military identity which deployed soldiers understand as an important transition from the "classic" trained soldier to a deployable trooper in a newly structured Bundeswehr. In other words, operational experiences have had a collective effect and have contributed to a new self-understanding in the direction of deployable military professionals' (2005: 118). It is possible that this individual pursuit of status within the Bundeswehr may have an effect on its institutional culture, creating new collective memories about recent or current operations which are useful in uniting troops around new or continuing missions.

The politics of concentration

Elite forces demonstrate certain advantageous organisational capabilities – selection and distinctive insignia and memories – but it would be wrong to ignore the intense political activity which has facilitated their current position. Intense political lobbying has also been necessary to establish them in their current position of dominance. In France, Britain (in particular), but also in Germany, there is a notable correlation between elite status and high rank. In Britain, paratroopers, marines and the special forces are over-represented at the highest levels of the military. Similarly, in France senior ranks of the military are dominated by officers from the marines, paratroopers, legion and cavalry. Accordingly, ambitious officer cadets at St Cyr will select these services in order to maximise their chances of promotion.[15] In Germany, where high intensity operations have not been primary and where mechanised forces still dominate, the connection is less decisive, but there are nevertheless some prominent senior generals from the airborne divisions (e.g., General Budde and General Domröser).

---

[15] Personal communication Claude Weber, 11 September 2008.

Some British examples will illustrate the intensely political process involved in concentration. As the most favoured regiment in Britain, the SAS is a particularly apposite example demonstrating the contingent politics of concentration. The rise of the SAS to its current position of dominance was in no way inevitable or even an optimal solution to Britain's defence problems since the 1970s. In the face of strategic and budgetary constraints, other organisational possibilities could have developed. Certainly, many of the counter-terrorist roles which the SAS assumed and, on the basis of which they enjoyed government patronage, could have been performed by the police, as they were by the Grenzschutzgruppe 9 in Germany, specialist elements of the Gendarmerie in France and the Federal Bureau of Investigation's SWAT team (SWAT) in the United States. On the contrary, the strategic role which the SAS has now appropriated for itself is the result of intense political lobbying. The SAS' current indispensability is a political achievement, involving institutional alliances and strategically significant personal relations. It is not the optimal product of rational institutional adaptation.

The rise of the SAS in Britain illustrates the politics of concentration very clearly. As a result of their sensitive role in Northern Ireland, in the 1970s new institutional links began to develop between the SAS, the highest levels of the Ministry of Defence and Downing Street (Urban 2001). The SAS offered a conveniently covert and deniable military option for the government and the Ministry of the Defence for the new threat posed by the IRA. After the Palestinian terrorist assault on the Munich Olympics in 1972, the British Government identified the need for a specialist counter-terrorist capability. The SAS skilfully appropriated the counter-terrorist role. The commanding officer, Peter de la Billière, wrote a well-regarded paper outlining the development of a counter-revolutionary wing in the SAS, which was adopted by the government. Consolidating this emergent alliance, Brigadier (later General Sir) Peter de la Billière, who was Director of Special Forces between 1978 and 1982, cultivated a close personal relationship with Margaret Thatcher, especially after the Iranian Embassy operation (Connor 1998: 399). Enjoying privileged personal access to the Prime Minister, de la Billière was able to convince Thatcher of the SAS' centrality to the re-capture of the Falklands and to all future British operations (1998: 399–401). De la Billière's personal relationship to Thatcher facilitated his selection as the commander of British forces in the Gulf War. Once in post, he used his authority as commander to promote the SAS to General Schwarzkopf, the supreme coalition commander. At the outset of the war, Schwarzkopf himself was sceptical about the use of special forces (1998: 469). He had seen them perform poorly in Vietnam where valuable assets had been consistently expended in rescuing them from failed missions, but de la Billière persuaded Schwarzkopf to deploy the SAS into the desert to hunt scud missiles. Although there were, in fact, a number of serious problems with SAS missions in Iraq and their activities were dependent upon total air superiority, their performance was widely praised in the United Kingdom and the United States and was decisive in promoting them in defence planning. Similar processes can be identified for both the Royal Marines and the Parachute Regiment.

In Germany, where there is more political oversight over defence planning and where elite forces, such as the Kommando Spezialkräfte and the paratroopers, are looked on with suspicion, senior generals have been unable to wield the influence which has been evident among the senior cadre of Britain's officer corps. However, in France a similar promotion of the elite marine, légionnaire and special forces is evident, sponsored by senior generals like the former Chief of the Defence Staff, General Henri Bentégeat, who once served in formations like 9 brigade légère blindée de marine.[16] In both countries there is an important supporting process which has benefited elite paratroop, marine and special forces. In their work on organisational sociology, DiMaggio and Powell (1983) argued that in any sector, institutions will imitate the leading actor. Thus, subordinate institutions will actively imitate the structures of the dominant organisation in a process DiMaggio and Powell called 'mimetic isomorphism'. For DiMaggio and Powell this process is not about rational adaptation, but primarily about status competition and assertion. Institutions imitate each other in order to demonstrate their status and to legitimate themselves. Christine Demchak (2003) has taken up this argument in reference to the dissemination of network-centric operations, which she similarly argues is the irrational pursuit of status which has nothing to do with rational state policy. However, in an era of transnationalisation when states are increasingly

---

[16] It is difficult to prove. However, it does not seem impossible that the fascination of the global media with war may have also promoted elite forces in the current era. In the 1990s, a number of scholars (Baudrillard 1995; Der Derian 2001; Ignatieff 2000; McInnes 2002; Virilio and Lotzinger 1997) explored the way in which the media were spectacularising war in order to attract global audiences. Precision-guided munitions and elite special forces warriors, transformed into digitalised cyborgs, were among the central images which dominated the new representation of war. The primacy of elite forces in contemporary representations of warfare may have assisted in promoting elite forces more widely. There is some evidence of this in Britain where the announcement of *Future Army Structures* in 2004, involving the disbanding of some famous Scottish regiments, was deflected by transforming 1 Para into a Joint Special Forces Support Group. Advisers rightly inferred that the media would be distracted from the issue of regimental mergers by headline references to the special forces. It may be that Europeans are beginning to make war in line with the way in which they are imagining war in films, video games and news footage.

interdependent she may have overstated the point. The status dimension of military mimesis should not be dismissed, but in many cases the armed forces have imitated each other – and especially the United States – in order to be able to co-operate. Political and military leaders are well aware of the fact that only by being able to co-operate with the United States will they benefit from the collective security and defence goods which alliance with America offers. The great efforts which the French and German militaries have made to create special operations forces, on the model of the SAS and Delta Force, and to produce rapid reaction forces, similar to Britain's intervention brigades, is substantially a product of this calculation. France and Germany are not insensitive to status pressures – and elite forces, especially special operations forces, enhance a state's credibility – but crucially the generation of these forces has allowed them to co-operate with the United States and with other European forces, like the British, on new missions. It is no coincidence that in structure, techniques, selection and insignia, special forces in Germany and France parallel British and US forces almost exactly. There is transnational political pressure on France and Germany which explains the development of these forces. As in Britain, the generation of special and elite forces is a political matter not a purely rational response to an objective strategic threat.

The elevation of elite forces in European defence posture more widely has been a political process involving the coalescing alliance between governments, defence ministries, the services and the empowered brigades themselves, enacted by strategically located individuals. As a result of these alliances, these elite forces have been able to seize opportunities and promote themselves. This self-promotion does not deny the military effectiveness of these forces. However, it is important to recognise that the current position of the elite forces at the heart of Europe's defence posture, as a result of concentration, has not been a neutral and objective process. The very capabilities and successes of these forces are the result of intense lobbying and contestation which has increased their profile and, therefore, their resourcing. The claims that these forces are the most deployable and capable are not statements of fact which then explain higher levels of resourcing. These claims operate as self-referential statements, promoting the importance of these forces in the eyes of defence planners, service chiefs and politicians and who, therefore, provide them with the very resources which are essential to demonstrate their superiority. The current status of elite forces is, therefore, rather like Bruno Latour's description of a scientific fact. Once established, a scientific fact appears self-evident and objective; the institutional networks, interests and disputes which brought it into being are effaced (Latour and Woolgar 1987). Similarly, the rise of elite forces in Europe seems to be a rational and optimal institutional response to the strategic environment. Like a scientific fact, elite forces hide the political contingencies of their production. Elite forces have become a critical defence asset not because they were always self-evidently the most appropriate military capability for current operations. Rather, they have become a potent military force because they have successfully convinced key figures that they are – or could be – a critical capability. In Britain, the SAS have skilfully used their role in Ireland to leverage their position, while in Germany and France the political imperative of transnational co-operation has encouraged their generation and augmentation, quite independently of whether they are objectively the best kind of forces for national defence missions. Their rise has been a self-referential process where the very acceptance of their importance has led to a level of resourcing and institutional favour which has made them indispensable. Their current indispensability is an achievement, not an inevitability. Consequently, because these forces have been resourced to train for the demanding role of theatre-entry, they have gained certain organisational advantages over regular forces. These forces are, therefore, able to conduct current operations more effectively than regular infantry.

Conclusion

The higher level of performance of elite forces and their greater operational visibility is partly a result of intense institutional politics within and between the services. The empowerment of elite brigades was a product of intense negotiation in which they played a major role in defining the criteria of performance, at which they, of course, excelled: deployability; agility; high intensity. However, the success of elite formations in these debates was not completely arbitrary. Crucially, these brigades were substantially successful because they were able to point to concrete evidence of why patronage of them was justified. The selection processes, berets and collective memories of Europe's elite forces can begin to explain why it is that they have been favoured with high levels of investment in the current era. The selection processes have ensured that a higher calibre of individual becomes a member of these elite formations with evident organisational benefits. However, the success of these organisations is not due merely to individual talents. Rather, the creation of elite units with selected individuals (even if they are not objectively the best) generates a high level of institutional unity. The very status of these formations is a self-referential fact where their claim to be elite engenders elite performance. They are, consequently, robust, innovative and flexible. The performance of the Royal Marines in Kosovo, which so impressed

Bellamy, was a demonstration of the organisational potential of elitism. Elite formations are highly unified; they display dense professional solidarity, demanding greater commitment from their members. Consequently, they are able to perform to a higher level and it is that greater unity and, therefore, higher level of performance that has been promoted in current defence planning; it has proved that the investment in them is justified. The elitism of these formations is a reality, but it is achieved through the complex interaction of institutions and interest groups inside and outside the armed forces themselves.

9 Cohesion

The problem of cohesion

Selection processes, insignia and collective memories are all central to the military effectiveness of Europe's empowered brigades; they are signifiers of elitism. Yet elitism alone seems unable to explain the level of performance which is typical of effective military organisations. It does not, in itself, constitute military competence, it merely enables operational performance, which encourages greater effort from members of these organisations and stimulates higher levels of unity. The empowered brigades are not effective organisations simply because they are symbolically united or because they feel themselves to be elect. Rather, they are able to conduct operations which other forces, especially Europe's old conscript armies, could not perform. They have been successful in performing military operations. The question is how are relatively large-scale organisations, such as these empowered brigades or the small sub-units of which they comprise, able to perform the new missions on which they are being deployed. In this, the performance of these brigades connects with long-standing concerns in military sociology about the issue of cohesion.

Military institutions depend on a level of social cohesion which is matched in few other social groups. In combat, the armed forces are able to sustain themselves only as long as individual members commit themselves to collective goals even at the cost of personal injury or death. The point about the armed forces, which perhaps differentiates it from civilian spheres, is that cohesion in and of itself is critical to this prosecution of violence. United combat units are able to overcome opponents and achieve their mission. Cohesion is fundamental to the question of task performance, competence and finally military expertise itself. The prime goal of all military organisations is to unify their troops into a single, uniform, self-supporting entity.

Social scientists have sought to explain the processes that produce social cohesion and they have often emphasised the personal bonds between soldiers as being decisive.[1] The importance of Janowitz's and Shils' famous article on the German forces in the Second World War has already been mentioned in Chapter 1. It is useful to explore it further here (Janowitz and Shils 1975). In their article, Janowitz and Shils describe the exceptional performance of the Wehrmacht by reference to the strength of small 'primary groups'.[2] For them, primary groups were held together by bonds of comradeship produced by 'spatial proximity, the capacity for intimate communications, the provision of paternal protectiveness by NCO's and junior officers, and the gratification of certain personality needs, e.g., manliness, by the military organisation and its activities' (1975: 216). Janowitz and Shils were not unaware of the specifically military functions of primary groups. Wehrmacht soldiers were 'enthusiasts for the military life' (1975: 184) and Janowitz and Shils also noted the relevance of a disciplined hierarchy to the creation of these primary groups (1975: 196–9). Nevertheless, Janowitz and Shils prioritised personal relations within the primary groups as critical to the fighting effectiveness of the Wehrmacht. As long as primary groups fulfilled the 'major primary needs' of the individual soldier; 'as long as the group possessed leadership with which he could identify himself, and as long as he gave affection to and received affection from the other members of his squad or platoon', the German soldier would be willing to sacrifice himself in combat rather than betray his colleagues (1975: 181).

The article was a seminal contribution to military sociology, whose analysis has been consistently re-affirmed in more recent literature.[3] Indeed, although consonant with Janowitz's and Shils' work, these commentators have tended to focus exclusively on the personal and intimate relations within primary groups. More recently, social psychologists have

---

[1] In the recent literature, a division has been drawn between social cohesion and combat readiness. This chapter employs the word cohesion to refer to the collective effectiveness of military groups in combat in line with Janowitz's and Shils' original definition of the term.

[2] See Bartov (1992) for a critique of Janowitz's and Shils' argument. Bartov's argument against the existence of primary groups is itself unconvincing. He claims that casualty rates were so high on the Eastern Front that no primary groups could have endured. In fact, he fails to recognise that while primary groups of experienced soldiers underwent slow attrition, casualty rates among the replacements were inordinately high. Autobiographical accounts of the Eastern Front demonstrate that primary groups did, in fact, endure to the very end of the war; see, for example, Sajer (1999). Bartov is certainly correct in emphasising that Nazi ideology was significant in the conduct of the war against Soviet Russia and to the dense social bonding of primary groups, but ideology cannot explain why the Wehrmacht was so operationally successful.

[3] See Arkin 1978: 151–66; Ben-Ari 2001: 239–67; Cockerham 1978: 1–15; Henderson 1985; Hockey 1986; Kinzer Stewart 1991; Moskos 1975: 25–37, 1989; Rosen and Martin 1997: 221–44; Rosen *et al.* 1996: 537–54; 2002: 325–52; Stouffer *et al.* 1949; Vaughan and Schum 2001: 7–31; Winslow 1997.

explored the issue of cohesion extensively. Social cohesion is typically understood by social psychologists as a social bond which precedes specific forms of military practice (Siebold 2007). Indeed, social psychologists have distinguished social cohesion from task cohesion: 'social cohesion refers to the quality of the bonds of friendship and emotional closeness among unit members – the type of cohesion referred to by the post-World War II studies. *Task* cohesion, on the other hand, refers to the commitment among unit members to accomplish a task that requires the collective efforts of the unit' (original emphasis) (Wong 2003: 4). Accordingly, Leonard Wong has explored how cohesion was engendered among US troops in Iraq in 2003 and how it contributed to military performance in the field. He, too, stresses the importance of dense, personal bonds between soldiers.

Despite its consistent prioritisation in the social sciences, it is not clear that comradeship alone can explain either cohesion in combat or the competent military performance of Europe's elite forces. For instance, scholars are increasingly seeking other explanations for cohesion and, therefore, coherent collective performance in combat. William Cockerham's article on US paratroopers might be taken as the starting point of this practical turn (1978). He accepted Moskos' arguments about the importance of latent ideology and comradeship to military performance, but argued that 'theories of primary group relations and latent ideology are not in themselves all-inclusive explanations of combat motivation' (1978: 12). Rather, he suggests that 'identification with immediate [competent] superiors' and above all the 'strong value of teamwork' are decisive (1978: 13). Indeed, Cockerham highlights the importance of drills in uniting soldiers: 'one of the most efficient techniques which allows soldiers generally to adjust to combat is to ignore the danger by interpreting combat not as a threat to life but as a sequence of requirements to be met by an effective technical performance' (1978: 13). Citing Fehrenbach's work on Korea, Cockerham notes that, 'only knowing almost from rote what to do, can men carry out their tasks' (1978: 13). In his way, Cockerham prioritised not personal intimacy or friendship but training. Soldiers were able to conduct cohesive drills not because they were motivated by a latent ideology or because they were friends, but, rather, because they had been ruthlessly trained to perform the same drills. More recently, this emphasis on collective drills has become particularly obvious in debates (Ben-Shalom *et al.* 2005; King 2006, 2008; MacCoun *et al.* 2006).

These studies focus on current debates and use contemporary examples. However, in fact, the practical orientation which they promote, focusing on the specifics of military activity and how it is enjoined, echoes the classical texts of military studies closely. Clausewitz, Machiavelli and Du Picq all prioritise training and discipline as essential to effective military performance. The cohesion of a platoon is not the same as the unity of friends or colleagues. For instance, as noted in Chapter 8, Clausewitz emphasises the indispensability of cohesion in military forces – he praises those forces which never lose their 'cohesion even under the most murderous fire' – but nowhere does he suggest that solidarity is based on personal comradeship. On the contrary, Clausewitz is very clear about the way to develop this special moral unity – the honour in its arms – in military forces:

One should be careful not to compare this expanded and refined solidarity of a brotherhood of tempered, battle-scarred veterans with the self-esteem and vanity of regular armies which are patched together only by service regulations and drill. Grim severity and iron discipline may be able to preserve the military virtues of a unit, but it cannot create them. These factors are valuable, but they should not be overrated. Discipline, skill, good-will, a certain pride, and high morale are the attributes of an army trained in times of peace. They command respect, but they have no strength of their own. They stand or fall together. (Clausewitz 1989: 189)

Surprisingly, Clausewitz seems to disparage training – 'service regulations and drill' – to prioritise operational experience as the decisive unifying factor for effective armies. Soldiers themselves have consistently emphasised the importance of experience to successful military conduct. For Clausewitz, experience seems to be the foundation of cohesion and, therefore, all military competence. Clausewitz's apparent disparagement of training might be related to the historical condition of warfare at the time of writing. During the Napoleonic era, infantry tactics were relatively simple. The infantry was armed with muskets and, in order to maximise their fire power, they were drilled to march in rank and file. Although the French revolutionary army favoured the shock of the infantry column, the infantry was typically organised in lines (normally of three ranks) which sought to generate continuous fire through successive volleys by the different ranks. The individual drill of loading, 'levelling' (musketeers did not aim in the modern sense) and firing was simple and, even the co-ordination of the entire battalion was not especially complex, though, of course, the tension of combat induced confusion and incompetence (Collins 2008). Cohesion was substantially aided by the fact that soldiers stood physically together in rank and file. That proximity induced unity and aided the individual soldier in co-ordinating his drills with his fellow soldiers.

Yet, although battlefield tactics in the Napoleonic era were in some senses simpler than in the present day, soldiers did not automatically dress in lines to present and fire their weapons together. Effective Napoleonic armies displayed highly unified drills even in the face of enemy fire, and such discipline evidently required extensive training. Poorly drilled forces would break, never to be reformed and, therefore, never to gain operational experience. It is perhaps more coherent to interpret Clausewitz as not disparaging training – service regulation or drill – *per se* but only unrealistic parade ground exercises. Indeed, there is some evidence that this is what he did mean in his discussion of the difference between bravery and military virtue. Crucially, in order to create an effective military force, individual bravery was important but, for Clausewitz, 'the natural tendency for unbridled action and outbursts of violence must be subordinated to demands of a higher kind: obedience, order, rule and method' (1989: 187). At this point, it is possible to understand Clausewitz's position on cohesion. While true military virtue cannot be inculcated on the formal parade ground, realistic military training and exercises in which troops are bonded in hardship and conduct drills under arduous conditions are crucial. When combined with operational experience, a genuinely cohesive unit can be forged. For Clausewitz, then, the bonds of unity in the armed forces are distinctive. They are not the same as bonds of friendship in the civilian population. Soldiers unite around military practices and organisational relations. They are unified by drill and method which they are taught to enact in response to an order.

Many other military commentators have affirmed the point historically. For instance, in the early modern period, in his famous treatise on war, Machiavelli ([1520] 1965) disparages mercenary forces in comparison with the virtue displayed by a civil militia inspired by urban patriotism. Yet the virtue of an effective military force cannot be solely dependent on patriotism; broad social unity which inspires fellow feeling is insufficient for competent military performance. Utilising classical examples, Machiavelli highlights rather the importance of drills and training as essential to the production of military virtue; he affirms Clausewitz's basic intuition. For Machiavelli, the Roman legion with its complex drills and ruthless discipline represented the highest point of Western military achievement and constituted the model that the Italian city-state should follow, even as it moved into the gunpowder age. The discipline of these formations would unite the citizen soldiers within them.

Ardant Du Picq is particularly pertinent in these discussions because he analysed warfare in the late nineteenth century just as close order drill and musketry was being superseded by rifles, machineguns and the need for tactical dispersion. In this context, Du Picq recognised that soldiers had to know each other or they would not be able to assert mutual moral pressure over each other in the line of battle (Du Picq 2006: 91). However, merely knowing each other, while necessary, was not sufficient for military success on the dispersed battlefield: 'We are brought by dispersion to the need of cohesion greater than ever before' (2006: 38). Du Picq accordingly affirmed the centrality of training in the formation of effective fighting forces. In order to induce the level of social unity required for the intense arena of combat, soldiers must be unified through arduous regimes of training in which their collective drills are affirmed and re-affirmed: 'a rational and ordered method of combat, or if not ordered, known to all, is enough to make good troops, if there is discipline be it understood' (2006: 123). Without the implementation of such an order, Du Picq observes that an army 'degenerates rapidly into a flock of lost sheep' because 'troops come to the battle field entirely unused to reality' (2006: 123). In particular, Du Picq was very sensitive to the differential effects of tactical deployment on the morale of forces in combat. For him, combat was not so much a fight to the death as a series of bluffs in which the collective commitment of opposing forces was mutually tested. Warfare, the crash of guns and the drum-roll of rifles, were all symbols, signalling the collective resolve of one force against another. Armies were defeated not because so many of their troops had been killed in the line of fire that they could no longer fight effectively but, rather, because panic had spread among them. Their morale had collapsed. Because morale – cohesion – was decisive in warfare, Du Picq discussed the use of reserves at length. Their surprising appearance on the battlefield could be decisive in breaking the morale of the enemy, whether or not they were, in fact, militarily superior. For Du Picq, the ability to deliver effective fire (and therefore to signal resolve), to resist the fire of others and to be sufficiently disciplined to hold back and then deploy a reserve, required prodigious levels of training. This discipline was the basis of tactical competence. Machiavelli and Du Picq accord closely with Clausewitz: military effectiveness depends upon the tactical co-ordination of the fighting force. That cohesion can be generated only through intense training; military personnel are unified around singular collective practices.

In his recent and highly relevant work on military power which carries forward the central themes of the work of Machiavelli, Clausewitz and Du Picq, Steven Biddle explores how military virtue was developed in the twentieth century. He identifies what he calls the 'modern system' which he believes emerged in the First World War, especially among Germany's storm troopers (Biddle 2004: 33). The modern military system refers to the organisational and tactical adaptations which armies (Biddle's focus is on land forces) have made in the face of the realities of an industrial battlefield with its machineguns, long-range artillery and air support: 'The modern system is a tightly interrelated complex of cover, concealment, dispersion, suppression, small-unit independent manoeuvre and combined arms at the tactical level and depth, reserves and differential concentration at the operational level of war' (2004: 2). Biddle dismisses the notion that mere numerical preponderance is fundamental to military success. Against advocates of the RMA, Biddle insists that this modern system still defines military effectiveness today. More importantly, he rejects the notion that technology alone can explain military superiority: 'Of the sixteen wars for which data are available, only eight were won by the technologically superior side' (2004: 24). For Biddle, the key to military success still relies on 'force employment' (2004: 30). Modern armies require highly developed operational commands in order to be able to co-ordinate large numbers of soldiers, as we have seen with the discussion of operational art. However, crucially for Biddle, the tactical units of modern armies need to be highly trained so that they can engage in complex combined arms warfare. In a modern army, the artillery are trained to suppress enemy activity as infantry and tank units, themselves employing sophisticated fire-and-manoeuvre drills or concealment, advance or defend. Modern armies rely not on numbers or technology but on expertise, one of the central forms of which is the ability of forces to co-ordinate their fire and manoeuvre from the highest level of a corps down to the platoon.

In order to demonstrate the validity of the modern system and the centrality of 'force employment', Biddle uses the examples of Operation Michael, the final German assault in March and April 1918; Operation Goodwood, Britain's failed offensive east of Caen in July 1944; and Desert Storm in Kuwait and Iraq in January to February 1991. In each case, Biddle demonstrates that the professional competences identified as the modern system were fundamental to military success or, in the case of the British, failure. Interestingly, Biddle examines the US SOF campaign in Afghanistan in 2001–2 to demonstrate his point. While the 'Afghan model' has been used frequently in the United States to promote the RMA and, indeed, was exploited by Rumsfeld to drive troop numbers down for the Iraqi invasion, Biddle takes a quite different conclusion from Afghanistan. Initially, precision strike called in by SOF troops in support of the Northern Alliance was effective. However, against concealed Taliban positions during Operation Anaconda and at Bai Beche, precision-guided munitions failed and the US SOF had to utilise their tactical acumen, co-ordinating fires and engaging in seamless fire and manoeuvre tactics (Biddle 2005: 169–76). For Biddle, collective military skills especially at the tactical level are the fundamental basis of operational performance. Indeed, Biddle, entering into policy debates about US military posture, warns against 'modernisation at the expense of readiness'; 'readiness cutbacks that have allowed today's combat skills to decay would not only forfeit the ability to exploit current technical advances against skilled opponents, but they would also enable future challengers to turn the tables by acquiring better technology themselves' (2004: 203). Biddle's argument is highly suggestive. He maintains that the organisational success of Western armed forces is not to be based ultimately on their technologies but on their cohesiveness. A successful army consists of a multitude of highly competent small groups, united around specific drills and co-ordinated through a coherent common structure. For Biddle, as for Clausewitz, 'order, rule and method' is the decisive feature of a competent military force, for without it any technological advantages will be irrelevant. Hans Delbrück has usefully summarised the point: 'The art of war has need of weapons, but it is not composed essentially of weapons' (1975: 211). On the contrary, it depends upon the unity of troops and their ability to engage in co-ordinated tactical activity. Drills are the apparently prosaic, but quite critical, institution here.

Drills

A successful army consists of a multiplicity of smaller units performing different 'combat functions'. It would be impossible to analyse all these functions or to trace the way in which Europe's empowered brigades are changing the way they do logistics, signals, artillery and so on. Rather than such a comprehensive approach, this study will examine one kind of activity – one drill – in Europe's elite forces today: infantry tactics. More specifically, it will analyse small unit (fire team, section and platoon) fire and manoeuvre assault tactics. These tactics are specialist drills conducted by relatively few personnel in the armed forces – members of infantry rifle companies and the special forces. However, since the success of an armed force finally rests on its prosecution of violence – its ability to assault opponents – these small group tactical drills are particularly important. No matter how impressive an army's logistical system, if it lacks competence in combat it will fail. Small unit tactics have other advantages as a focus for the investigation of cohesion. Small unit tactics represent the elementary form of combat; they are the grammar of war. The section attack is the smallest collective drill which infantry soldiers perform. It involves a limited number of actions which are clearly definable. Unlike much military activity, these practices can be observed in a small geographic area over a short space of time. Nevertheless, eight soldiers must perform a significant number of actions together. Each action is itself simple in individual terms, but the co-ordination is necessarily demanding. Clearly, in the infantry there are a huge number of other drills. Attacks rarely involve only one section and, indeed, even for infanteers outright assault is a rare drill in reality. In the artillery, signals, cavalry or the support services drills are quite different. However, the section attack might usefully serve a heuristic purpose. As an elementary form of military practice, it might demonstrate how troops – especially professional troops in empowered brigades – engender and sustain cohesion among themselves much more generally. The section attack is therefore taken here as a useful illustration of the problem of cohesion, because it reveals how infantry soldiers co-ordinate their activities under the intense pressure of enemy fire – and, therefore, potentially how soldiers generally unite themselves around the 'honour of their arms'.

In contemporary Western military doctrine, an infantry section consists of eight to ten soldiers and is divided into two 'fire teams', known as the Charlie and Delta teams.[4] Charlie and Delta teams are matching units armed with the same or similar weapons. As it advances on its objective, the whole section fires on to the objective to 'suppress' the enemy; the weight of fire will force the enemy to take cover. Then, while Charlie team lays down further covering fire, Delta team will move forward to assault the position. Section fire teams need to co-ordinate themselves and the actions of their individual members. At the same time, sections must themselves synchronise their fire and manoeuvre with the platoons and companies of which they are part. Building upon the grammar of the section attack, a successful infantry assault involves the integration of hundreds of soldiers, alternately firing and manoeuvring in support of each other, often through difficult terrain, at night, in poor weather under fire from the enemy. It becomes an extremely complex and demanding form of activity.

Steve Biddle usefully punctured the rhetoric surrounding SOF operations in Afghanistan by demonstrating that conventional offensive tactics, initially developed in the twentieth century, remain essential to success in the twenty-first. Nevertheless, he recognised the potential significance of SOF in contemporary warfare. SOF are important for Biddle not because they are the most technological resourced forces, but because through intense training they have developed the highest levels of collective expertise: they have the best tactical drills. Biddle recommends that all infantry forces be trained up to the level of special operations forces. It is notable that training is central to Europe's special forces; the British special forces, the Kommando Spezialkräfte and France's

---

[4] The term 'four-man team' is used here because in the British, French and German force, only males are allowed to serve in combat units which will perform the drills described here.

para-marine commandos are all the most highly trained forces in their nations. The SAS' seizure of the Iranian Embassy in 1980 was substantially the product of intense and realistic training as their commander recognised: 'These men had been superbly trained, and they had so often practised the kind of task they were about to carry out that it had become almost an everyday event' (de la Billière 1995: 330). Indeed, the SAS themselves recognise the centrality of training to their professionalism, altering their motto informally from 'Who Dares Wins' to 'Who Trains Wins'. Recognising the operational success of the SAS, the Kommando Spezialkräfte and French special forces have instituted training regimes which are extremely similar to those of the SAS. Indeed, both have developed close links with the SAS. For instance, in 1997 the Bundeswehr established a dedicated special forces training base at Pfullendorf, which has so far been attended by troops from Germany, Denmark, Belgium, Greece, Italy, the Netherlands, Norway, Turkey and the United States, though most of the trainees are from the Kommando Spezialkräfte or the Division Spezielle Operationen (Scholzen 2009a: 57). Training at Pfullendorf involves survival, special operations planning, sniping, advanced patrolling, first aid and, significantly, close quarter battle. The school seeks to develop the collective tactical drills which are evident in other special forces (Y Magazine 2005: 32–3). Special forces are trained there for deep insertion, reconnaissance and raiding. The training is intended to be realistic. Indeed, a reconnaissance company trained at Pfullendorf took up a position in the Division Spezielle Operationen in 2007 on completion of their course (Y Magazine 2005: 33). French and German special forces have institutionalised a training programme modelled on the SAS. In his recent account of the Kommando Spezialkräfte, Reinhard Scholzen (2009a) has discussed their training at length, emphasising both its connection to other Western special forces, the SAS, and its attempt to inculcate not only individual skills but, above all, collective drills among Kommando Spezialkräfte teams.

In his analysis of US SOF, Rune Henriksen argues that these troops display individual martial virtuosity. In his famous work on the US Army in the Second World War, S. L. A. Marshall claimed that only one in four riflemen ever actually fired his weapon (Marshall 2000). For Henriksen, the SOF warrior is the contemporary manifestation of Marshall's one in four 'firers'. Henriksen has to qualify this definition since, with the professionalisation of the armed forces, firing rates have become very high in the infantry since the mid-twentieth century. They were 95 per cent in Vietnam and, in current operations, they seem to be almost total. There is, according to Henriksen, still a difference between a soldier and a SOF warrior, however: 'Warriors are more balanced, informed and cautious when it comes to combat decision-making, political sensitivity and intellectual acuity, but nevertheless more ruthless at the decisive point' (Henriksen 2007: 211). SOF warriors are existentially and psychologically oriented to combat; they are more tactically and politically astute than mere soldiers. They may be more reluctant to fire than soldiers but when they do, they shoot to kill. Significantly, Henriksen asserts that these attributes are intrinsic to the individual soldier and are identified in selection: 'The SOF approach to warrior selection implies that warriors are revealed and that they cannot be made' (2007: 210). Henriksen cites the example of Dave Nelson, who served as an extremely successful sniper during the Vietnam War (2007: 205). He was an individual killer, who was oriented to combat from childhood; his SOF selection and training merely demonstrated inherent personal capacities. For Henriksen, the SOF represent a collection of individual virtuosos.

Henriksen's analysis is interesting and suggestive. However, it is not clear that it is completely accurate. Beyond the initial processes of selection, special forces training does not seem to be simply or even primarily about revealing individual martial talent, as Henriksen claims. As Randall Collins has emphasised, training is primarily dedicated to collective unification: '"Training" is not simply a matter of learning; it is above all establishing identity with the group who carry out their skills collectively' (2004: 91). Training aims to inculcate collective practices in all the members of the group so that they become unified rather than provide a forum for individual self-expression. This seems to be particularly true in the special forces. In the infantry, military success relies not primarily on the individual, whose mobility, vision and firepower is limited, but on the fire team, the section or the platoon. Consequently, military training is collective. It does not seek to encourage individual virtuosity in the first instance; indeed, there are active attempts in training to eliminate individual practices. Training seeks to inculcate standardised drills, co-ordinating the complex actions of many individual soldiers (King 2006). Through intense training cycles, the special forces seek to develop high levels of collective expertise, synchronising individual action into coherent drills. They try to inculcate fast and co-ordinated fire and manoeuvre tactics so that when special forces make an assault, opponents are overwhelmed by the speed of the attack and immobilised by the accuracy and weight of fire which the troops generate.

Training serves an important purpose in facilitating these highly sophisticated team performances. Through repeated training, members of Europe's special forces become so familiar with each other's drills that they know instinctively what others will do in response to contact.[5] This is not because these soldiers are naturally more intuitive than other soldiers, as Henriksen suggests, but because, having trained for long periods together, the same collective drills are more deeply ingrained in all of them; members are united around common practice and are finely tuned to even small cues from their colleagues. The shared experience of past training instinctively induces common responses from these troops when they are on operations. Since they know how they and their colleagues will respond to combat, the special forces have removed a major cause of anxiety and, therefore, incompetence from their military performance. Special forces in Europe select for soldiers who are robust, but they are organisationally successful because their members train together intensely and realistically. Decisively, they, therefore, develop the best collective drills. Critically for a military group, they are likely to respond collectively fastest and most coherently to unforeseen circumstances. Individuals in the special forces will adhere to collective patterns of behaviour at extreme moments when other military groups will fragment. The special forces' expertise might be most effectively explained not by reference to prior individual qualities, as Henriksen claims, but rather by reference to insti-tutionalised processes of training.

The SAS is particularly useful here because other European special forces have imitated their training regime very closely. Having been awarded the counter-terrorist role in 1972, the SAS instituted an intense regime of training, building their own facility, 'The Killing House', in which they repeatedly practised hostage rescue. The cohesion which this training engendered was central to the assault on the Iranian Embassy in May 1980. However, the SAS training regime has been consistently central to their successful operational performance. In August 2000, eleven British soldiers were seized in Sierra Leone by a notorious local militia, the West Side Boys. Tasked with their rescue, the SAS trained intensely for this complex mission (Operation Barras). Dividing them-selves into six-man fire teams, each was assigned particular targets within designated areas within the village; they were tasked to eliminate the enemy within those bounds. The co-ordination of the fire teams was then refined through repeated training and practice. As a result of this training, on the operation itself the West Side Boys, used to confronting untrained militia or poor government troops, were surprised by the highly attuned fire and manoeuvre drills of the SAS troopers. Accurate fire was co-ordinated with rapid and aggressive assault so that a number of West

[5] Interview SBS officer, 15 January 2004.

Side Boys were killed, while others were driven into the jungle (Lewis 2005: 455–8). British special forces have used the same tactics in Afghanistan.

France's specialist naval commando unit, Groupe de Combat en Milieu Clos, have drawn upon the SAS' method and display similar capabilities. This unit is specifically trained for the assault of ships especially in the event of an act of terrorism. The group consists of sixteen personnel divided into two eight-man teams. The Groupe de Combat en Milieu Clos seeks to develop the highest levels of collective skill and co-ordination so that it can assault a vessel and conduct an assault through the complex structure of gangways, holds and cabins before opponents can react (Micheletti 1999: 74–7). These drills have been demonstrated in practice. In 1994, French special forces stormed a plane at Marseilles airport when two GIA (Groupement Islamique Armé) terrorists threatened to seize a Lufthansa plane and, anticipating 9/11, fly it into the Eiffel Tower.

Training is not just important for Europe's special forces. Professional armed forces recognise the centrality of training to operational performance. British doctrine highlights the importance of training: 'Collective performance is only achieved through an understanding of common doctrine combined with collective training and exercising to rehearse and sharpen the ability to apply it . . . There can be no compromise on this, for the ability to deploy fully prepared for combat is at the core of fighting power' (JWP 0-01 2001: 4.6). French and German doctrine also recognises the centrality of training to military performance. Accordingly, the intense regime of training which is observable among British special forces is evident among empowered brigades in Europe more widely. Very high levels of training separate these professional forces from their conscript forebears in the twentieth century. Accordingly, in Britain, the Royal Marines and Parachute Regiment develop high levels of collective skill which are often comparable to those of the SAS precisely because they train in the same way. Indeed, at levels above the platoon (or squadron) of twenty to thirty soldiers, regular British infantry are often more effective than the SAS precisely because they are trained to operate in company groups. In Afghanistan, the SAS complained that they were being misused as conventional infantry in offensive actions against cave complexes. As one squadron commander noted: 'This was not one for us – 1 Para could have done it better' (Rayment 2008: 25). Confirming the point, ex-SAS troopers have stressed the potential weakness of the SAS' conventional infantry drills. The SAS recruit from the Army as a whole, not just the infantry, so it is not unusual for troopers and sergeants to have little experience in conducting conventional infantry tactics: 'I was surprised to discover that many of the senior ranks had never operated as infantry in their lives; the majority of the troopers were more qualified in this than the senior ranks. Most of my own sergeants didn't have a clue about infantry battle-drills. They couldn't give section or platoon orders and, consequently, would be dangerous to have around in a fire-fight' (Horsfall 2002: 195).

Training and drills have been fundamental to the performance of other elite forces in Britain. Descriptions of the British marines and paratroopers in Helmand demonstrate these drills at work, with close co-operation between soldiers being evident. 3 Para deployed to Helmand in April 2006 and was quickly involved in intense fighting in which drills came to the fore. For instance, on 4 June 2006 A Company 3 Para conducted a heliborne operation (Operation Mutay) which aimed to seize identified Taliban leaders in a compound outside of Now Zad. The paratroopers were ambushed as their helicopters landed in a wadi and they had to fight their way out of an intense predicament. In order to extract themselves, one paratroop section conducted an assault on a Taliban position. A Parachute Regiment corporal, Quentin Poll, took command. In the face of enemy fire, Poll 'decided to get on top of them' and bounded forward in line with British tactical doctrine. He split his men into two fire teams for the real life execution of the drill called 'fire and manoeuvre':

'I got the blokes spread out into a single line and four of us moved forward while the other four fired', he said. 'Then they would start firing and we would move forward so there was always the fire going down and we were gaining ground on the enemy position. When they reached, it, they saw the Taliban fighters retreating into the orchard.' (Bishop 2007: 69)

He is describing the elements of a section attack, as laid out in infantry doctrine.

Early in 3 Commando Brigade's tour of Helmand in 2006, an unexpected contact with the Taliban demonstrated not only the importance of training, but also its close connection to actual tactical action. Because it was manning static defence of observation posts around Kajaki, the reconnaissance platoon of M Company 42 Commando were concerned that they were 'losing basic counter-enemy ambush techniques' (Southby-Tailyour 2008: 64):

To address this concern a training package was drawn up which involved moving off the mountain to the Forward Operating Base at the bottom of the peak, where a 'patrol-shoot' exercise was planned in a relatively safe area that had not been attacked for some time. This involved the section, under [Royal Marine Corporal] Tom Birch's command, practising anti-ambush drills along a 200-metre track. Once they were on the track, however, the Taliban – who had, in practice, set up an ambush – attacked. Instantly the drills now became the real thing and the enemy was successfully rebuffed, but the Taliban must have been surprised at the speed with which they were countered, not realising that the team were specifically training at that moment for this very eventuality. (2008: 64)

The importance of training has been emphasised by British troops who describe how under the duress of combat, 'training takes over'. Tactical drills are so deeply ingrained that troops follow them routinely in the face of uncertainty; soldiers collectively fall back on shared practices which are most familiar to them. They begin to enact their training. Indeed, one of the major complaints among British soldiers deploying to Helmand is that the training has simply not been realistic enough. Health and safety regulations and the size and structure of training estates have hampered the ability of troops to train properly with live ammunition.

In his work on elite swimming, Chambliss (1989) disparages the claim that athletic excellence could be the product of inherent personal talent. On the contrary, sporting excellence is achieved as athletes submit themselves to a routine of training rituals: 'The best swimmers are more likely to be strict with their training, coming to workouts on time, carefully doing the competitive strokes legally (i.e., without violating the technical rules of the sport), watch what they eat, sleep regular hours, do proper warm-ups before a meet, and the like' (1989: 73). Focusing on every detail of their performance, individual swimmers develop new abilities through a regime of reiterated, collective rituals. Yet swimmers are only able to participate in these routines if they are already members of the elite group. Crucially, for Chambliss, excellence arises through the thorough integration of the individual into the social routines of the elite group. As a result, individuals are able to integrate a number of small skills into a unified whole which together constitutes elite performance. Chambliss calls this the 'mundanity of excellence'. In fact, excellence arises through the sacralisation of the mundane; the sanctification of detail. For Chambliss, the origins of sporting virtuosity are social; excellence is ultimately a collective property. It is a product of teams who develop drills. In order to become an Olympic swimmer, it is necessary to be a member of an elite athletic community and to engage in its practices. Today's professional soldiers are becoming like Chambliss' elite swimmers, united around highly developed collective drills.

Similar processes are observable in France and Germany, especially among the Division Spezielle Operationen and 9 brigade légère blindée de marine. In the Division Spezielle Operationen, there has been considerable innovation in training. Parabataillon 26/3, tasked for non-combatant evacuation operations, have trained in highly realistic scenarios (Scholzen 2009b). They have been inserted into training areas, populated by groups playing neutral, hostile and hostage roles, with whom they must interact. The parachute battalions in the Division Spezielle Operationen have undergone very similar tactical training to elite forces in Britain. The old training rituals of the Cold War have been replaced; German troops no longer engage in formal static training shoots, adequate for prepared defensive positions, but engage life-like targets in simulated tactical situations (Scholzen 2009b: 44). Indeed, the same drills are observable among these troops; in his book, Scholzen reproduces a photograph sequence of contact drills which are enacted when a small patrol meets an enemy. He describes, in language very reminiscent of Lewis' description of the SAS in Sierra Leone, the 'choreographies' which the troops perform (Scholzen 2009b: 45). They train until the members of squads and platoons are integrated into a common and co-ordinated course of action. These elite forces similarly seek to develop high levels of collective performance through training (Scholzen 2009b; Schulze and Verhülsdonk, 1998; Sünkler, 2007). The training is extremely realistic, and in November 2006 resulted in the death of a Kommando Spezialkräfte sergeant in a shooting accident (Scholzen 2009b: 45).

In the French Army, fire and manoeuvre drills are currently practised at Ceito Larzac on a digitalised range. Firing positions are pre-set and targets record how many hits the troops score. In this way, a computer records how successfully the troops are performing; but they do not engage so much in the collective training and drills evident in Britain.[6] The training at Ceito Larzac is somewhere between formal static shooting and open live range work. Nevertheless, 9 brigade légère blindée de marine has been very effective on operations. Royal Marine liaison officers with the Brigade in the Ivory Coast in 2006 and in Chad in 2007 (as part of the EU Battle Group mission) confirm the competence and hardiness of the troupes de marine:

The French troops have a wealth of experience in West Africa and the average Marine will spend on average 50% of his career on this continent. I have learnt an enormous amount from them as they have a deep insight into the workings of the African mind and their 'lessons learnt' process is effective. They understand how a demonstration of force is vital here as only strength is respected and that the local militia groups will test all new battalions as they arrive to see how far they can push things. (O'Hara 2007: 120)

However, although French troops are robust, their infantry drills tend to be less developed. Moreover, having operated in Africa for decades, French infantry have adopted a doctrine of staying with the vehicles

---

[6] British lieutenant colonel, personal interview, 20 June 2005.

from which they fire their weapons; they have been able to generate sufficient firepower in this way against the rebel forces they have often encountered. Accordingly, their dismounted section and platoon drills are not practised so extensively. In addition, reports suggest that they tend to patrol in long parallel lines rather than in mutually supporting sections; such lines are easier to control but tend to be more vulnerable to ambush.[7] Some commentators have suggested it was precisely their lack of appropriately professionalised drills that played a significant role in the deaths of the ten French paratroopers in August 2008. Accordingly, the Brigade is seeking to develop its tactical skills. In the 1990s, 9 brigade légère blindée de marine signed a formal partnership with 3 Commando Brigade. This agreement has allowed the units to participate in each other's exercises and to use each other's training areas without cost. As a result, in October 2008, 9 brigade légère blindée de marine conducted an exercise in Cape Wrath in which the formation was exposed to British tactical training.[8] Interestingly, 9 brigade légère blindée de marine demonstrate somewhat different characteristics to British troops. The French troupe de marine are robust and effective soldiers who are extremely disciplined. They will carry out orders even though they involve great physical discomfort and danger. For instance, during the exercise in Cape Wrath, French troops had to endure some very poor weather conditions for a number of days. In addition, there is a much more dirigiste command culture in the French forces, so that tactical commanders will rarely innovate themselves; they follow their orders. British soldiers are clearly disciplined, but there is a greater attempt to institutionalise 'mission command' (devolved tactical authority) than in France. 9 brigade légère blindée de marine is actively seeking to develop its training programme and its level of tactical co-ordination.

Battle preparation

Elite forces emphasise not only generic tactical training, but also mission specific 'battle preparation'. This preparation involves a now institutionalised series of activities which troops conduct before they are deployed on a mission. Effective tactical performance is regarded as dependent upon this battle preparation. In order to improve tactical co-ordination, professional Western forces have introduced an additional technique – the model – which is now nearly universal among all professional troops. It is difficult to ascertain the precise historical origins of the use of the tactical

---

[7] British lieutenant colonel, personal interview, 20 June 2005.
[8] Royal Marine liaison officer, September 2008.

model. Since the end of the eighteenth century, European staffs have employed models in order to plan more effectively; models were used especially for war-gaming when different strategies would be tested. Since the First World War, models have been used periodically, typically for special missions or major offensives, by tactical units outside operational headquarters. However, by the 1990s, the model became a central part of the training and mission rehearsal process.

Before a mission, professional soldiers are given a detailed set of orders in which their commander explains the plan and his troops' role in it. NATO has established a standard method for giving orders which is evident across countries. Models have played a crucial role in this institution of the 'orders process'. The use of models has sociologically profound implications which are directly relevant to the question of social cohesion. At the highest level of command, professional model-builders are employed to create detailed dioramas of the areas in which the missions will be carried out, physically detailing the ground and the enemy positions. However, even at the lowest section and platoon levels in the infantry, models are always preferred, even by the special forces who are adept at using maps and usually operate in small numbers (Ratcliffe 2001: 354; Spence 1998: 251). The models typically consist of two shallow square 'pits' moulded into scale-relief dioramas of the area in which the mission is to take place; one of the models (the general area model) will represent the ground over which the entire mission will take place, while the other (the objective area model) represents in greater detail the decisive phase of the mission (see Figure 9.1).[9]

Troops use surprising creativity in sculpturing the earth inside the model pits to represent ridges and valleys, and improvise with stones, grass, twigs and leaves to signify woods, streams, paths and roads. In the British forces, troops will also carry with them coloured ribbons and tags specifically designated to represent these distinctive features. The models facilitate the orders process by physically representing enemy positions and ground over which the action will take place. Commanders are able to illustrate the precise movements of their troops on the ground by refer-ence to the models, highlighting specific features which will orient the action or which may pose problems for the advancing troops. The model is a graphic device aimed at facilitating communication.

There are obvious pragmatic reasons why models are employed by the British forces. It is impractical to use maps in a tactical situation. Commanders and troops must be able identify central landmarks by sight

---

[9] In environments where it is difficult to dig pits, 'ponchos' (neoprene sheets which are used as bivouac shelters) are used as models. They are pegged out flat and made into relief models by the insertion of rocks, pieces of equipment or clothing beneath them.

Figure 9.1 Model pits, showing the general area model on the left and the objective area model on the right. The relief indicating hills and valleys on the models are visible. The tape on the right-hand model represents the boundaries of fields, along which the assaulting troops will find cover, the square markers indicate enemy positions. The troops receiving orders are Royal Marines Young Officers and are arranged by section in assault order with the reserve section seated in the rear.

as they advance under fire or as they lie in tactical concealment; in these situations it will be difficult for them to examine a map. Consequently, the models represent what the troops will see as they advance on their target, preparing them with a series of visual cues. However, the models assist collective action not merely because they depict the ground as the troops themselves will see it. More importantly, models are used because this ensures that there is only a single representation of the terrain, to which the attention of all is directed. Maps, by contrast, display a multitude of extraneous and often irrelevant topographic features in extensive detail; alternatively, they lack certain critical pieces of detail. If each soldier received orders by reference to their own individual map, individual misinterpretations could occur. Soldiers could easily interpret their maps and the features depicted on them differently; they could focus on alternative geographic points, or misread the lie of the land from the contours of the map.

Models are deliberately designed to eliminate individual deviance. The soldiers who are tasked to construct the models work from a map, but they deliberately ignore subsidiary and irrelevant data which could mislead. The model is not simply a large-scale map. The model-makers are concerned with detail, but no attempt is made at a universal model which includes every feature realistically represented. Model-makers focus on those decisive points which soldiers have been trained to employ as orienting axes and reference points in tactical situations and which troops will confront on the operation. Thus, the model-makers and the commander using the model will emphasise wood lines (which stand out clearly even at night), roads, rivers and pylons, which are unmistakable physical features. The result is evident. All are knowingly oriented to a single collective representation which consists of clear and distinct symbols. In this way, the chances of misinterpretation and deviancy are minimised. The models also serve another important purpose. Precisely because troops are oriented to common objectives, signified by the model, they are more able to improvise during the mission itself. Since troops all understand the primary objective, expressed in orders as the Commander's Intent, and know the ground on which they will be operating, the models are intended to allow the troops to pursue this objective in alternative ways, as the situation demands. The models have become a means of institutionalising collective flexibility.

The function of the model as a collective representation, enjoining co-ordinated action, is equally observable on operations. For instance, during their deployment to Helmand, British forces have employed models before each operation. In early December 2006, Zulu Company 45 Commando under the commander of the Information Exploitation Group were planning on operation south of Garmsir, the first of a series of missions called Operation Glacier:

As with all operations, the colonel ensured everyone understood what he wanted from them by constructing realistic models in the dry desert earth based on photographs supplied by the RAF; in other circumstances, the men would be called round a table to see the layout of the ground they would be fighting across. Shallow trenches were dug to represent the river and its tributaries; pebbles and sticks stood for the buildings, with blue counters to show the compound walls while white and orange tape marked out the start line and the objectives it was expected the marines would reach. (Southby-Tailyour 2008: 133–4)

One photograph (see Figure 9.2) usefully records the officer commanding Zulu Company briefing his company before Operation Glacier 5 in March 2007. The model, built from cardboard inside the base at Garmsir, represented the compound which the marines were tasked to assault and

Figure 9.2 Orders for Glacier 5. The officer speaks to the model with
'Reporting Line Taunton' marked diagonally on the floor with tape.

their complex line of approach across some wide irrigation ditches. The
model acts as a collective representation inspiring coherent action on the
ground and sustaining group coherence.

In training, troops are taught to give features on their models distinctive
and evocative nicknames which consciously refer to existing institutional
memories. In Figure 9.1, the objectives were called 'Globe', 'Buster' and
'Laurel' referring to the Royal Marines' regimental badge. This procedure
is not simply a way of inculcating institutional loyalty among new members of a regiment, it is also self-consciously used by soldiers on operations. In Helmand, nicknames, which have now become established in
all the areas of operation, have oriented troops to decisive features, facilitating collective situational awareness. Names have been deliberately
selected which signify important collective memories. One of the important co-ordinating references on Operation Glacier 5 was a 'Reporting
Line Taunton' which referred to a large ditch between the River Helmand
and canal on the outskirts of Garmsir. The assault across the canal and
into Garmsir was launched at the junction of 'Taunton' and the canal.
Significantly, Taunton is the town in which 40 Commando is based and
with which many marines are very familiar. Perhaps most evocatively,

paratroopers named one of the spot heights around the Kajaki dam, 'Arnhem' (Southby-Tailyour 2008: 50). This is a very important social procedure whose significance should not be overlooked. Decisively, the armed forces actively try to fuse immediate tactical activity with wider regimental identity in the imagination of the troops. As members of a regiment who have a common experience of training and selection and share intense collective memories, soldiers are morally obliged to commit themselves to the objective depicted on the model which has now become associated with the honour of their regiment. The model simultaneously generates a sufficient level of shared knowledge for the soldiers to achieve their objective with a realistic chance of success. In this way, models unite moral and practical reasoning, engendering unity among the troops and encouraging co-ordinated military activity. Totally consistent with Durkheim's analysis of religion, moral obligation is fused with shared knowledge through the institution of models. They connect a concrete series of mundane practices in the here and now with a sacred shared idea of regimental selection, distinction and destiny.

This social process is supported and enriched by further activities. The armed forces also conduct full-scale rehearsals in which all the troops are involved in order to improve levels of collective performance. These rehearsals will sometimes occur in specially designed training areas, precisely reflecting the ground on which the mission will be conducted. Then the training ritual will produce the collective effervescence which Durkheim noted (1976), as the training sequences will involve live rounds and battle simulations to stimulate fear and excitement in the soldiers conducting the drills. Before the hostage rescue in Sierra Leone, Operation Barras, the SAS conducted dedicated rehearsals in which they imitated the precise tactical manoeuvres which they performed on the mission itself. One commentator recorded the comprehensiveness of these rehearsals: 'Repeated rehearsal – running through the assault time and time and time again – helped drill the details and the routine into each man's head. Eventually movement, awareness, synchronicity and timing all became part of a ritual, a dance, an instinctive course of action' (Lewis 2005: 297–8). Before Operation Telic (the invasion of Iraq) on 24 February 2003, the British forces underwent extensive rehearsals in Kuwait as Lieutenant Colonel Messenger, the commanding officer of 40 Commando, emphasised:

Such were the complexity and scale of the mission rehearsals that they became known as MOAR 1 and 2 (Mother of All Rehearsals). With over 40 aircraft involved and an enormously complex coordination challenge on the ground, the detail had to be just right. Dummy buildings were constructed in the middle of the Kuwaiti desert to replicate various targets, and our various battle positions and schemes of manoeuvre became quickly engrained in the men's minds. (Matthews 2003: 11; see also Rossiter 2008: 77)

Significantly, Lieutenant Colonel Messenger emphasised that the purpose of these rehearsals was to ensure that collective practices became ingrained in the shared consciousness of the Royal Marines, thereby maximising the cohesiveness of the unit on the operation itself. By rehearsing the mission, Royal Marines developed a shared understanding of what each was supposed to do in order to contribute to the collective goal. Moreover, the effervescence produced in training rituals was an important resource in unifying the group. In the rehearsal, the Royal Marines experienced a shared sense of fear and excitement. In this way, the ritualistic choreographing of bodies acted as a powerful means of encouraging group cohesion on the mission. Before the mission had begun, all the Royal Marines knew the locations and tasks of other members of their unit and similarly knew that everyone else knew their own role. In Helmand, the Royal Marines constructed a training and rehearsal area by Camp Bastion to refine tactics at the start of their tour and before each operation. Although British forces have conducted major rehearsals for operations like the invasion of Iraq, the rehearsal has become institutionally ingrained into the armed forces.

There is evidence of these battle preparations among Europe's professional forces more widely. For instance, on the EU Chad mission, members of 1 Régiment Parachutiste d'Infanterie de Marine (French special forces) conducted casualty extraction rehearsals before the mission. This suggests that the concept of the rehearsal is established in the French military. However, model-making as a component of battle preparation is not nearly so evident. For instance, despite their professionalism, 9 brigade légère blindée de marine does not seem to engage routinely in model-making for the orders process. It would be difficult to assert that models are not ever made, but they seem to be rare. Certainly, no models were used during the Brigade's recent exercise in Cape Wrath. It is possible that the absence of models could be explained by constraints of time; in a relatively short exercise, in which the focus was on amphibious insertion, it is possible that the Brigade chose not to use models.[10] The reluctance to use models may reflect French military culture more widely in which mission command has not been developed to anything like the same extent as in Britain. Soldiers in France, including NCOs, are primarily expected to follow orders. Consequently, missions are conceived and conducted by reference not to general missions which subordinates

---

[10] Royal Marine liaison officer, personal interview, 28 November 2008.

accomplish as they judge best, but under close superior supervision. Soldiers conduct specific tasks in response to orders. In such an organisational environment, the great emphasis on battle preparation – and on models and rehearsals – which has become central to the British military is not so evident.[11]

Expert military squads

The appearance of highly skilled military forces in Europe denotes a historic transformation of the armed forces. Europe's armed forces have moved from mass conscription, which developed in the nineteenth century, to small and specialist professionalism. In his famous study of the US Army during the Second World War, Marshall proposed, on the basis of interviews with combat veterans, that only one in four riflemen ever fired their weapon, even when they had an opportunity to do so. Marshall's analysis has been subsequently disparaged, normally on methodological grounds. His interview technique could not support this extraordinary claim that three-quarters of the infantry actually contributed nothing to battle in the Second World War. In fact, while the arguments against Marshall questioned his evidence, critics provided little empirical evidence themselves. They rejected his methodology and reasserted the conventional account of combat: in the face of the enemy, individual riflemen fired. Various extrinsic factors seem to motivate Marshall's critics. His findings offended rational assumptions that individual humans would always protect themselves in the face of danger. It also seemed to challenge the nationalist and democratic values of the US Army in particular and mass, citizen armies in general. The convenient political rhetoric that citizens would defend their nations and that, inspired by patriotism, they would prove the most effective soldiers was undermined by Marshall. He implied that citizen armies were poor (Glenn 2000; Leinbaugh and Campbell 1985; Smoler 1989). Divisional loyalty also have seems to have affected the reception of Marshall's work; one of Marshall's critics, General Gavin, had been a commander of the 82 Airborne Division, whose rival, the 101 Airborne Division, Marshall singled out for special praise. More seriously, Roger Spiller (1988) and Whiteclay Chambers II have shown that not only was Marshall prone to hyperbole and self-promotion, but their investigation of his archive and interviews with his assistants suggest that the demonstrativeness with which he put forward his figure of only one in four firers could not be justified: 'But without

---

[11] Royal Marine liaison officer, personal interview, 11 November 2008.

further corroboration, the source of Marshall's contentions about shockingly low rates of fire at least in some US Army Divisions in World War II appears to have been based at best on chance rather than on scientific sampling, and at worst on sheer speculation' (Whiteclay Chambers 2003: 120). Marshall may have exaggerated how systematic his findings were, but as he himself emphasised the incident on the Makin Islands, from which his whole argument germinated, when only thirty-six men out of a battalion fired their weapons against the Japanese, they were basically accurate. Moreover, the existing evidence suggests that Marshall was broadly correct (Collins 2008; Grossman 1995; Henriksen 2007; Jordan 2002). Memoirs confirm the poor performance of riflemen in mass armies, while Marshall's belief that group violence is typically enacted by a few active participants supported by many others, who do very little, has been widely observed by social scientists (Collins 2008). For instance, in E Coy 506 Regiment, the 101 Airborne Division, which Marshall himself regarded as one of the finest companies fighting in the north-western theatre (Marshall 2000: 73–4), one of the platoon commanders admitted at the end of the war to never having fired his rifle, even though he participated in three operational airborne drops and was with the company as it fought its way from Normandy, through Holland and into Germany. Other observers, such as the British training experts Major Lionel Wigram and Major General Lucian Truscott, record very similar rates of performance.

The performance of the company also vindicates Marshall's point that while the majority of riflemen merely occupied the battlefield, a small number of virtuosos dominated the action. Easy Company developed a high degree of collective skill especially by the time they reached Holland in the winter of 1944; one ambush on a German position demonstrated a level of tactical co-ordination, with the use of concurrent fire and manoeuvre, which was unusual at that time (Ambrose 2001: 146–53). A memoir from the same company also mentions the principle of 'fire and manoeuvre' (Webster 2009: 26). Nevertheless, active individuals interspersed in a passive majority still predominated. For instance, in January 1945, Easy Company assaulted the village of Foy as the Division broke out of Bastogne at the end of the Battle of the Bulge (Ambrose 2001: 209–11). The newly appointed company commander froze and a captain from another company, Ronald Spiers, was instructed to take over. He led the assault into Foy. Extraordinarily, concerned to ensure that his company co-ordinated its assault with a second company, attacking from a different angle, he personally charged through the village then held by the Germans. He held a short conference with his counterpart, and then returned through the German positions in Foy to his own lines.

Sociologically, Spiers' action illustrates a much wider organisational principle of mass and individual virtuosity. There are numerous other examples of individual virtuosity in the Second World War. For instance, on 7 June 1944, Lieutenant Wray of the 82 Airborne independently conducted his own reconnaissance patrol against the enemy near St Mère Eglise. He killed eight officers and two machine-gunners single-handedly (Ambrose 1997: 20). On returning to his lines, he then led the assault against the Germans and broke the counter-attack which allowed St Mère Eglise to be taken. He died on 19 September 1945 during the Nijmegen operation demonstrating similarly individualistic initiative.

The mass armies of this period demonstrated low levels of military skill, but tended to be united by a common identity; they were members of the same nation or the same ethnic group. These extraneous social criteria were actively mobilised to unite soldiers in these armies and encourage tactical performance. It is noticeable that the bayonet charge rather than the fire and manoeuvre drill, which has now become primary, was favoured during that period. Even in the era of modern rifles and the appearance of machineguns, Ardant Du Picq emphasised the moral effect of bayonets (2006: 117). Reflecting Du Picq's advocacy, bayonet training was an important part of military training in the twentieth century, and the bayonet charge an accepted doctrine (Bourke 2000: 89). For Bourke, the bayonet was an ideological means of infusing aggression into soldiers in order to make them more willing ultimately to risk (and, indeed, sacrifice) themselves rather than cower from the enemy by using grenades and gun: 'they were selling us charms to ward off fear' (2000: 93). There is some evidence to support Bourke's interpretation, but she seems to miss the important organisational benefits of the bayonet. The bayonet charge has many advantages as a tactic especially for a conscript army. Unlike fire and manoeuvre drills, it is extremely simple and requires minimal training. Crucially, it physically unites potentially poorly trained troops into a mass, thereby inspiring the assailants. In the bayonet charge, the charging mass provided mutual morale support for its members, discouraging wavering individuals whose cowardice is visible to their comrades. Du Picq has noted the moral effect of this loss of mutual observation on troops: 'The bewildered men, even the officers, have no longer the eyes of their comrades or of their commanders upon them, sustaining them. Self-esteem [i.e. recognition by one's peers] no longer impels them, they do not hold out' (Du Picq 2006: 136). At the same time, the bayonet charge demoralised defenders primarily not because they feared the wounds the bayonet inflicted (bullets and grenades caused worse injuries), but because a force charging with bayonets demonstrated its unshakable resolve; they would close and kill. In the light of this display of collective determination,

Du Picq claimed that no force ever withstood a bayonet charge: the defenders' morale (unity) fragmented in the face of the manifest cohesion of the attacking force.

The mass armies of the mid-twentieth century assumed a distinctive character which Marshall captures well. Most of the fire was supplied by crew-served weapons: machineguns, mortars and artillery. However, among the rifle companies which prosecuted assaults and comprised the bulk of the defensive formations, the majority of soldiers under-performed. They provided targets for the enemy and moral support for the individual virtuosos like Ronald Spiers or Lieutenant Wray. Mass armed forces were defined by a relatively passive majority punctuated by highly active individuals. The bayonet charge was a collective solution to the modern military problem of mass and individual.

As European armed forces move to all-volunteer forces, this dynamic of mass and individual is being superseded. Especially in the empowered brigade, synchronised and sophisticated teamwork is superseding the mass–individual dialectic. These emergent teams are capable of signifi-cantly higher levels of performance than their mass forebears, especially in terms of relative size. They can generate a greater level of firepower than their mass predecessor because of the institution of established drills around which all are unified. Their empowered brigades, highly resourced and increasingly expert, are capable of much higher levels of performance than the mainly conscript divisions of the twentieth century. They can generate a disproportionate level of combat power given their size. This increased performance should not be explained primarily in terms of weaponry and ordnance, although that is not insignificant. Weapons are significant only if they are used properly by forces in concert. That unity of application requires dense levels of cohesion at the lowest tactical level; it presumes the formation of coherent primary groups. These groups are then united into larger organisational units. Europe's empowered bri-gades seek to create highly cohesive primary groups of professional sol-diers and then integrate these small sections and platoons with others. In Europe today, this integration does not take place primarily by appeals to nationality, ethnicity, gender or political affiliation which were typical in the conscript armies of the twentieth century, rather, the prime means of integration is training and, therefore, drill. European soldiers unite them-selves not around ideals, but around concrete military practice.

Comradeship and collective drills

Military sociologists and social psychologists, such as Janowitz, Kinzer Stewart, Arkin, Winslow and Siebold, have emphasised the centrality of personal comradeship to military performance: friendship is the basis of cohesion. This approach has been evident in studies of European forces today. For instance, Moelker and Soeters have examined the individual perceptions of the members of the German–Netherlands Corps of each other. Paul Klein has also tended to focus on individual relations, implying that better military performance will arise in those European formations in which there are higher levels of personal trust. None of this may be irrelevant. Moreover, there is evidence that in the twentieth century, prior social bonds were critical to promoting cohesion in the armed forces. One of the most obvious and tragic examples of the importance of the extra-military bonds was the raising of Field Marshall Kitchener's volunteer armies in the First World War. Then, males from villages, neighbourhoods, factories and even sports clubs signed up together as friends to form 'Pals' battalions.

Comradeship in the twenty-first century seems to be quite different in Europe's professional forces, where the armed forces themselves seem to prioritise not personal trust but training. For them, cohesion seems to be the product of intense training regimes when collective practices are inculcated. The power of primary groups in the military rests on their ability to adhere to these collective drills even under intense pressure. No matter how familiar soldiers are with each other on a personal and informal basis, if they cannot perform collective military practices together they will lack social cohesion; they will be militarily ineffective.

This seems to be most extreme in Britain. For instance, members of the SAS emphasise that the Regiment is distinctly un-comradely:

the loyalty to one another that I had hoped to find within the SAS didn't appear to exist. Instead, I was soon to discover that the Regiment had no esprit de corps: instead, it's just a group of insecure individuals drawn from many different organisations in the Armed Forces. There's no bonding process to hold them together after selection, no infantry style buddy-buddy system that could unite friends and enemies into a brotherhood such as the one I had experienced in the Paras (Horsfall 2002: 146).

'In the Paras we used to take care of our own, but in the SAS the onus was on the individual to keep on top of his game. It didn't take me long to realise it was a selfish society' (Curtis 1998: 263). Yet Horsfall qualified the comradeship he found in the Parachute Regiment: 'We became the ultimate team. We didn't necessarily like each other, but our differences were internal; if an outsider intervened, he'd find six hundred brothers facing him. And the harder we struggled as a team, the closer we became' (2002: 47). Despite the notable absence of comradeship in the SAS, the Regiment remains extremely effective because 'when the crunch comes every member of the team had to trust implicitly the men alongside him'

(Curtis 1998: 263; see also Ratcliffe 2001; Spence 1998). This trust was not the warm comradeship found in the 'Pals' battalions. It was possible because troopers had trained so intensely together and were united around the drills to the highest standards; at that point, friendship – being prepared to socialise and look after comrades away from the business of soldiering – becomes almost irrelevant.

The priority of collective drills to military cohesion suggests that a potentially radical re-thinking of comradeship in Europe's armed forces may be necessary. Military sociologists have suggested that comradeship – especially the personal bond between males – is a prerequisite for effective military performance: comrades will be good soldiers. In fact, the relationship between comradeship and military performance may be rather different. Above all, the current emphasis on the intimacy of social relations between the members of primary groups may be misleading. Perhaps surprisingly, the basis of genuine military comradeship may not be located in private and personal exchange. In reality, the bonds of friendship may grow out of military proficiency; comradeship may be the function of collective drills not their prerequisite. Indeed, there is extensive evidence that this is indeed the case. For instance, in his account of the Falklands War in 1982, Lance Corporal Bramley of Support Company 3 Battalion, the Parachute Regiment, described how his friendship with a private in his section was undermined by the latter's professional incompetence. Bramley described how the private had stood up to put on waterproof trousers during a battle, thereby compromising the section's position: 'I felt embarrassed by him. Twice he had acted like a week-one recruit. Things were never to be the same between us' (Bramley 1991: 170). Horsfall summarised the point:

In the Paras the biggest insult that could be levelled against anyone was to accuse them of being a bad soldier. Every man prided himself on being one of the elite, and tried never to leave himself open to such a comment. He could be wet, queer, thick, an idiot or any number of other things but he could not allow himself to be called a bad soldier. (2002: 88)

In an account of his experiences in the Royal Marines, Steven Preece has affirmed the point, albeit accidentally. This work focuses almost exclusively on the masculine rituals which many military sociologists have found fascinating: drinking, fighting, and sex. However, in a revealing sentence Preece undermines the significance of his entire narrative. Although the purpose of the work is to demonstrate his masculine status in these informal realms, he records a quite different process of acceptance in the Royal Marines: 'Amongst the Marines there was always the same code of practice: don't gob off [boast] unless you can back it up with your fists, and always maintain the high soldiering standards required of a Marine or expect to be beaten up' (Preece 2004: 160). For all his discussion of the informal masculine practices, the critical criterion of membership in the Royal Marines was the ability to adhere to collective military drills. Comradeship within the Royal Marines was finally only awarded to those who had submitted themselves to established military drills and were proficient at them. Only those who had proved themselves in training and on operations were considered worthy of comradeship. Crucially, honour and shame – and therefore comradeship – is attached to collective, professional practices not to any personal qualities.

Significantly, the mechanisms of honour and shame by which professional comradeship is established among primary groups is clearly observable among British forces. In any training or operational context, there are gaps between the formal military evolutions. There are inevitable unscheduled pauses between actions as well as designated rest periods. These gaps serve a vital purpose beyond mere recuperation. In them, members of the armed forces discuss the outcome of the formal training process or the mission itself. They raise issues and consider the validity of what they have just done. They assess the performance of the group and its members. Moreover, in this informal but still military context, performances will be praised or criticised. Jake Scott repeatedly records the way in which unprofessional activity was the subject of informal censure in the Parachute Regiment. At one point, he records how he dropped into a firing position and nearly shot at a desert fox which surprised him. Had he fired, he was worried that others would have followed, causing 'panic within the convoy and locals or letting the Taliban know our whereabouts' (Scott 2008: 155). However, his greatest worry was that he would have 'looked like a tit', giving his comrades a 'big opportunity to slag me' (2008: 155). The competitive dynamic between soldiers is important to the performance of professional troops. The exchanges between them ensure that each feels obliged to reach the requisite standards demanded of them and to contribute fully to the operational capability of the unit. In these informal interstices, the honour and status of members of military forces are assessed and publicised. Effectively, in these informal periods in training and in operational environments the basis of comradeship is established. Those who are militarily proficient and, therefore, good comrades are lauded, while those who have failed to contribute to collective goals are ridiculed, defaced and ultimately excluded. As European forces are submitted to stern operational tests in Afghanistan, the primacy of immediate professional competence over established friendship is being re-affirmed. Although confidentiality has to be protected, there are a number of cases where officers, well regarded and well liked before the deploying to Helmand, were denigrated and finally dismissed because they failed to perform in line with expected standards.

It may be possible to situate this transformation in comradeship in a wider context. Analysing social conditions in Europe a century ago, Emile Durkheim was worried by the prospect of individualism and anomie. With the emergence of the market and the growth of urban populations, individuals were freed from established social bonds. Once constrained by existing patterns of social order, they were threatened by a bewildering liberation; they were free to be and do as they wished. For Durkheim, the absence of dense social groups, binding individuals to collective goals, represented a potentially disastrous situation for the individual. Significantly, the state could not begin to resolve the problem of anomie or to integrate individuals into coherent social groups: 'While the State becomes inflated and hypertrophied in order to obtain a firm enough grip upon individuals, but without succeeding, the latter, without mutual relationships, tumble over one another like so many liquid mole-cules, encountering no central energy to retain, fix or organize them' (Durkheim 1952: 389). For Durkheim, the solution to the problem of anomic dislocation was evident, if not yet fully realised, in modern society. The rise of professional status groups represented precisely the dense forms of social solidarity which he regarded as essential for individual fulfilment and social cohesion overall. Durkheim advocated that profes-sional guilds and associations could become secular churches uniting the members of modern society around common endeavours: 'The facts related show that the professional group is by no means incapable of being in itself a moral sphere, since this was its character in the past' (1957: 23).

Durkheim continues:

Within any political society, we get a number of individuals who share the same ideas and interests, sentiments and occupations, in which the rest of the population have no part. When that occurs, it is inevitable that these individuals are carried along by the current of their similarities, as if under impulsion; they feel mutual attraction, they seek out one another, they enter into relations with one another and form compacts and so, by degree, become a limited group with recognizable features, within general society. Now once the group is formed, nothing can hinder an appropriate moral life from evolving. It is at this point we have a corpus of moral rules already well on their way to being founded. (1957: 23–4)

Durkheim's promotion of professional associations may be directly rele-vant to the question of European military transformation today. In line with Durkheim's intuition, Europe's armed forces – which are increas-ingly all-volunteer professional – may be increasingly integrated not by concepts of national identity, civic duty or personal bonds, but rather by a concrete professional ethos. Military professionalism may provide the new 'moral sphere' which unites European soldiers. It provides a common resource on the basis of which they interact and co-operate, enabling them to engage in the complex struggles to which Europe is now committed around the world.

Conclusion

Europe's armed forces are moving away from a mass military model. Empowered brigades of highly trained professionals, displaying high levels of cohesion, are superseding mass armies. However, this change is not primarily about numbers. It is primarily a process of condensing military capability among relatively small expert teams. It is about the development of co-ordinated teams and improving their performance through the synchronisation of drills. As with the rise of post-Fordist production techniques in industry, it points to a paradigm shift in military activity. In particular, new training regimes have transformed organisational culture as sophisticated collective drills have been institutionalised in order to maximise team performance. The empowered brigades in Europe represent the concentration of military expertise, with skilled teams replacing virtuosic warriors, supported by a passive, mass soldiery.

The emergence of the empowered brigade is perhaps best seen not merely as a military adaptation in the face of new strategic circumstances, but, rather as representing a profound shift not simply in the Western way of war, but in Western culture and society itself. In the nineteenth and twentieth centuries, the nation-state sought to protect itself by the (sometimes voluntary) service of its citizenry. National service was part of a political settlement in which a unified and centralised state administered the lives and wellbeing of its people, who were willing to sacrifice themselves in the national interest. This arrangement has now been eroded. The citizenry do not fight the nation's wars out of a sense of duty and obligation to protect a recognised national community. Specialist professionals now prosecute distant campaigns whose connection to the national interest is often unclear. They perform this role not by appeal to ethnic, nationalist, political ideology nor even potentially masculine comradeship. They are increasingly united around a set of professional drills which are inculcated in training and through ever more refined systems of battle preparation. Comradeship now arises out of, and is a manifestation of, this systemisation of training. Comrades are no longer those whom the individual soldiers necessarily initially like because they share a common background; appeals to nationalism, political ideology, ethnicity, race or gender may all be less pertinent. In the twenty-first century, professional European soldiers may be increasingly extending comradeship to those who can perform their drills properly. Friendship may be a manifestation of practical capability and, in particular, the individual contribution to the military team through the performance of collective drills. Cohesion is becoming a function of professional practice, not so much a prior condition of it as it seems to have been in the mass conscript armies of the twentieth century. The bayonet charge of the twentieth-century citizen-soldier has been replaced by the seamless fire and manoeuvre of the twenty-first-century professional.

10 Co-ordination

Network operations

By the end of the 1980s, an operational renaissance was apparent in Europe. Twentieth-century mass, lineal combined arms warfare had, at the intellectual level at least, been displaced by a 'manoeuvrist' approach, prioritising operations which sought to fight deep, simultaneous battle in the enemy's rear. In the 1990s, the American forces, already oriented to a manoeuvrist approach, underwent a so-called 'revolution in military affairs' (RMA) promoted primarily by Admiral William Owens and Andrew Marshall, director of the Department of Defense, Office of Net Assessment (Metz 1997: 185; Owens 2002). The term RMA was enshrined in the 1997 *Quadrennial Defence Review*. Despite the very significant criticisms of the concept of the RMA (Biddle 2002; Farrell and Terriff 2002; Freedman 1998; Gray 1997), scholars have broadly accepted that in the 1990s fundamental military reformation was evident in the United States. This transformation is generally conceived to consist of three elements: intelligence, surveillance and reconnaissance technology (ISR): command, control, communication, computers and interoperability (C^4I); and precision-guided munitions (PGMs) (Gray 1997: 14; Latham 2002). Through new ISR technology, the US armed forces aspired to gathering near perfect and immediate situational awareness of the battle space throughout its depth. The development of C^4I capabilities then allowed commanders to co-ordinate their forces across time and space. Above all, the new C^4I capabilities allowed US forces to disperse across wide areas, converging on designated points. Finally, by the 1990s, America had developed PGMs to a high degree. Instead of massing divisions to create the desired weapons effect, accurate and devastating firepower could be generated from a distance by smaller, dispersed forces. Enemy targets in the battle space could be engaged from outside and because the munitions were accurate, fewer platforms were required

(Freedman 1998: 13). Through the development of intelligence, communication and weapons assets, the US armed forces sought to maximise their effectiveness while minimising their own vulnerability by dispersing their forces and increasing the tempo of operations.[1] The *Joint Vision 2010*[2] describes this situation as 'full spectrum dominance'.

Although significantly behind the United States in technological capability, Europe's armed forces have sought to digitalise themselves so that they too can conduct dispersed, network operations. Britain has sought to engage in network warfare on a dispersed battle space. Having established the 'manoeuvrist approach' in the 1980s, Britain's armed forces have explicitly followed the United States in radicalising their use of depth and tempo: 'By manoeuvring to surprise the adversary, by using firepower selectively to attack that which underpins his cohesion (i.e., critical Command and Control systems (C2) and vital logistics and industrial facilities), and harmonising these with attacks on his will to continue to struggle, his cohesion can be broken apart' (JWP 5.00 2004b: 2.2). Significantly, the British manoeuvrist approach, like the US model, identifies simultaneous and deep assault as the ideal: 'Although they can achieve a significant effect on their own, the synchronised use of firepower and manoeuvre has devastating potential' (2004b: 2.3). Digital communications are regarded as a central facilitator for deep and dispersed operations: 'More flexible arrangements for C2 across functions, environments and within a coalition will inevitably lead to the alteration of existing methods, particularly in relation to traditional hierarchical planning, execution and communication' (Development, Concepts and Doctrine Centre 2007: 2.2). By means of digital communications, British forces aspire to 'self-synchronisation' between tactical forces unified on an identified objective by a 'clear and consistent understanding of Command Intent' (2007: 2.2). Digital communications are being exploited to accentuate adaptations already institutionalised as Mission Command.

The Bundeswehr is still under closer political supervision than any other military force in Europe. Reflecting this political dependence and the historical need to tie the force into international structures, the Bundeswehr has not yet produced its own doctrine; it has instead followed NATO doctrine. In the last five years, however, the Bundeswehr has begun to recognise that it needs to articulate to itself how it is to

---

[1] Taking the RMA to its logical conclusion, American doctrine is currently developing the idea of a 'battle swarm' where numerous, small units are co-ordinated over a large area to create the necessary weapons effects (see Arquilla and Ronfeldt 1997: 476–7).

[2] *Joint Vision 2010*, a US military publication outlining a joint concept of operations for the digital era.

implement the radical potential of new technology. The Bundeswehr has no autonomous doctrinal institution, although elements within the Führungsstab at the Bundesministerium der Verteidigung (Ministry of Defence) and the Zentrum für Transformation der Bundeswehr are beginning to draft network doctrine. It seems highly likely that this doctrine will be closely compatible with existing US, British and NATO doctrine. Führungsstab V, for instance, has attempted to create communications with the Development, Concepts and Doctrine Centre. No doctrine yet exists. However, Peter Struck's Defence Policy Guidelines and the *Outline of the Bundeswehr Concept* illustrate the current direction of military thinking in Germany and the likely form which autonomous German doctrine will take once it is published. The very cover of the document illustrates a convergence of doctrine. The title page features a digital image of friendly (blue) units distributed around an operating area; 'locations of exercising units are displayed in real time on the monitors of the Letzling Heide Training Centre'. The image denotes that the Bundeswehr has already made a crucial conceptual shift and understands warfare in terms of a network of forces operating simultaneously in a dispersed area, to be co-ordinated in real time by a higher headquarters by means of digital communications. There is clear evidence that such a concept of operations has now become widely accepted in the Bundeswehr. Patrick Fitschen has noted that the Bundeswehr concept of operation is substantially dependent upon the US network-centric warfare model (Fitschen 2006: 168). This involves new digital technology. The Defence Ministry have decided to create a strategic satellite communications system for the Bundeswehr and, at the tactical level, 'FAUST' digital communications have been introduced to create interoperability with French forces, among others, in the context of the NRF. This development is part of a wider programme which will see the introduction of new ISTAR assets, aircraft (Puma and the A400M) and support vehicles, such as the Dingo and Wiesel and a version of the British Future Rapid Effects System (Schreer 2006: 186–7). The Bundeswehr is also developing an 'infanteer of the future', equipped with an individual global positioning system (Fitschen 2006: 175–6). At least as important as these procurements is the conceptual transformation. The Bundeswehr has been heavily influenced by the ideas which inspired the US RMA. For instance, Captain Boyd's concept of the 'observe orient decide act' loop, where the force that acquires, shares and acts fastest upon information will be the most effective, has been heavily drawn upon by the Bundeswehr (Fitschen 2006:169).

Indeed, a quite new understanding of contemporary operations is appearing among senior officers. For instance, the commander of the

Division Spezielle Operationen described contemporary operations as fundamentally different from the Cold War. Instead of lineal operations, he illustrated the nature of current operations by drawing a series of circles on a piece of paper, each representing a military force. Instead of facing forward they looked to dominate space outwards in all directions. Pointing at the diagram, he said: 'We operate like this – like little blobs of activity which work outwards.'[3] In order to operate in this kind of environment, the Bundeswehr has actively sought to imitate the United States. Explicitly referencing US developments, the concept prioritises Bundeswehr 'transformation'. The term refers to the introduction of digital technology and its implications for the structure and practices of the Bundeswehr:

The revolutionary developments in the field of information technology offer the possibility to gather, transmit and process large amounts of data quickly and in a secure way ... NCW [network-centric warfare] enables armed forces to conduct operations based on comprehensive and current information quickly precisely and successfully with the least possible commitment of force. (Bundesministerium der Verteidigung 2004: 15)

The concept identifies the key threats as conflict prevention and crisis management and seeks to apply network-centric warfare capability to address these threats. Significantly, 'the increased demands necessitate unrestricted application of jointness in thinking and acting. The Bundeswehr's military capability as whole therefore takes priority over the capabilities of the single services and organisational areas' (Bundesministerium der Verteidigung 2004: 17). In addition to digital communications, the concept stresses the need for precision munitions. The aim is to maximise the capabilities of the Bundeswehr while minimising the risk to its small deployed forces. Yet all these technical developments presuppose the doctrinal reformations of the 1980s and demand further investment at the operational level.

France remained outside NATO military structures from 1966 and did not contribute to NATO doctrinal developments in the 1970s and 1980s. However, it has already been noted that France was influenced by the changing approach to 'operations' in the 1980s and, in the last decade, France has sought to develop network capabilities in a manner consistent with its allies. France has focused on the issue of how to utilise the potential of digital communications and precision weapons for war fighting in a globalising era. Its capstone army doctrine demonstrates French exceptionalism. It is a florid historical piece which seeks to establish fundamental principles, featuring recurrent criticisms of the United

---

[3] Commander, Division Spezielle Operationen, personal interview 19 September 2006.

States' overly technical and kinetic approach to operations. Nevertheless, the document is remarkable to the extent that it demands a thorough reform of the French armed forces, substantially in line with US transformations; 'Laissez faire will condemn the Armée de Terre to become the army of the Second Empire again' (Centre de Doctrine d'Emploi des Forces 2005: 14). The invocation of Sedan is evidence of how seriously the French Army takes contemporary reform. Significantly, the document describes the distinctive nature of contemporary warfare, noting the centrality of insurgency and ethnic conflict. This has changed the geography of war. In place of lineal warfare, 'modern war is a game of go'; it is multidimensional and 'nebulous'. French military doctrine disparages the over-technicalisation of warfare; conflict remains human. Yet digitalisation is essential: 'joint, combined, technological, flexible, digitalization . . . these themes are at the heart of all thoughts for those of us who are planning the future of our armed forces' (Centre de Doctrine d'Emploi des Forces 2005: 30).

As the new doctrine publications emphasise, following the United States, Europe's military now understand themselves as fighting on a dispersed, non-lineal battle space. In place of fronts, the battle space consists of independent 'lozenges' of discrete tactical activity. Decisively, the empowered brigade has been identified as the prime tactical formation in this new battle space. These brigades operate substantially independently of one another against threats which may come from any direction. Western militaries no longer possess enough forces to fight a lineal battle, even if they wanted to. Instead of massing divisions to create the desired weapons effect, the armed forces seek to generate accurate firepower from a distance with smaller, dispersed forces using PGMs. Network-centric technology has been a critical enabler, but network warfare refers not simply to the weapons and communications system but also to the dispersal and co-ordination of forces. In order to implement this doctrinal change, major European militaries are currently undergoing a digitalisation process (Adam and Ben-Ari 2006).

The most insightful critics of the RMA do not deny the significance of the introduction of digital communications or PGMs. Rather, they claim that it is wrong to understand contemporary military transformation primarily in technological terms: 'The picture of "revolutionary" change – whether past or present – that emerges in much of the literature tends to be one of technical and tactical innovation' (Latham 2002: 232). This is particularly true of the empowered brigades tasked to conduct network operations in-theatre today. The new technologies are significant only insofar as military organisations have been able to restructure themselves and develop the competences in order to be able to exploit them.

During the Cold War, land formations drew primarily on their own organic firepower; some limited close air support was developed especially after FOFA was introduced, but brigades relied primarily on their own artillery. One of the most empowering developments for Europe's elite brigades today is the increasingly close co-operation with the other services; as they engage in network operations, they are becoming 'joint' (tri-service) organisations. Empowered brigades utilise air and maritime assets in order to multiply their combat power and mobility. They do not draw on air or maritime assets merely for insertion, but are closely integrated into the other services which provide them with critical support. Indeed, their 'empowerment' substantially relies on their ability to draw on joint assets. The emergence of joint brigades, where assets from air or maritime components have been assigned to these formations, is a significant moment. However, the utilisation of air and maritime assets in these brigades requires very significant organisational adaptation in order that these additional forces can be co-ordinated within existing structures and practices. New concepts of operations, new staff and command procedures and, in some cases, reformations of the structure of the headquarters itself have been necessary. In order to exploit the potential of these new assets, the headquarters of the empowered brigades have had to innovate new planning and command techniques and, in many cases, have simply had to increase in size in order to incorporate new personnel.

Headquarters

Jointery has demanded very significant augmentations to the headquarters of Europe's rapid reaction brigades. It is very apparent in Britain, where 16 Air Assault Brigade and 3 Commando Brigade are among the most joint tactical formations in Europe. In the Cold War, 16 Parachute Brigade and 5 Airborne Brigade had a small RAF staff which organised planes for airborne drops. They liaised with the RAF which provided the airframes and organised the air corridors to and from the drop zone. However, once the paratroopers exited the planes the RAF had only a small subordinate role in the brigade organising re-supplies. Today, the brigade's concept of operations is quite different. It does not merely insert paratroopers from the air, but seeks to have an effect on the theatre of operations through the simultaneous use of support and attack helicopters. Air manoeuvre is central to the brigade throughout their operations not merely at the beginning. 16 Air Assault Brigade's concept of operations is not simply to drop troops on a target which is seized. Rather the forces are to be moved by support helicopter around the dispersed battlefield, supported by Apache helicopters and bombers. By providing an 'air recognised' picture (a current map of where all aircraft are in-theatre), the RAF personnel in the headquarters allow this co-ordination of land and air assets, the helicopters of which are owned by the Brigade. It is a critical and continuous role which requires total integration into the headquarters in order to assure de-confliction. Consequently, 16 Air Assault Brigade has a headquarters, which includes twenty RAF personnel, including non-commissioned officers and clerks, out of a standing staff of fifty-three in order to co-ordinate the aviation and air assets. The complexity of air operations makes this augmentation essential. However, when deployed on operations the brigade headquarters staff has been expanded to 150, with a proportionate increase in RAF personnel. This complement of RAF personnel exceeds the size of a normal army brigade headquarters in total and is almost bigger than 5 Airborne Brigade's entire headquarters in the 1980s and 1990s. As senior members of the Brigade recognise, the integration of air and land elements within the headquarters is very challenging:

With air manoeuvre, we are removed from the physical friction of the ground, and the attendant restrictions to tempo. We enter the big blue. However, this brings with it new and substantial logistics and battle space management friction, frequently with much more significant consequences. There are very good reasons the Air Force prefer to 'programme' their movements for ease of deconfliction. An alien concept to land warriors bred on a diet of physical and enemy-induced unknowns that make programming a distant aspiration.[4]

The co-ordination of air and land operations is further complicated by the very different organisational cultures of the RAF and the British Army:

The air community have a different ethos to the land. It is a different service. As a COS [Chief of Staff] I was keen to educate our new Army staff officers that although we were the majority shareholder in the HQ we didn't need the RAF to swallow our ethos whole. Many of their practices were far more suitable for air manoeuvre than our land-centric culture. We had to be especially attuned to the vagaries of the air environment. You need time to plan; and instinctively assume air manoeuvre is fast in the conventional sense as result of aircraft speed in the air, although one is in real danger of rushing to logistical failure. The RAF are there-fore understandably platform-centric. The complexity of their environment means they have to be. There are considerably fewer variables than on land. As a result some air staff can underestimate the complexity of the tactical ground situation and its attendant frictions. The Army focuses on delivering a single activity or effect – that has been designated as critical – in extreme conditions. The Army therefore breeds a different attitude where the human is the key. It is about will, not money or equipment. This inculcates a leadership ethos where the human resource is the primary asset and the proverbial 'enemy vote variable' is

[4] Chief of staff, 16 Air Assault Brigade, personal interview, 28 July 2005.

always uppermost in their considerations. Of course, frequently the final effect is normally in the land environment amongst the people. 16 Brigade attempts to marry the two philosophies together for the optimum solution but there are still occasional RAF/Army disagreements![5]

During the Cold War, 3 Commando Brigade was an early example of the kind of joint co-operation which has now become typical among reaction brigades. The organisation sought to fuse the land power of the Royal Marines, and attached Army units, with the Royal Navy. In contrast to airborne operations, the offensive amphibious operations for which 3 Commando Brigade trained required far closer integration with the Royal Navy. Since amphibious assault involved a longer transition phase than an airborne assault, this connection between naval and marine elements within the Brigade was always necessarily closer. 3 Commando Brigade conducted the first British heliborne assault when elements of 45 Commando were inserted during the Suez operation (Speller 2001: 59). The Brigade seemed to anticipate future developments and was significantly ahead of the Army in developing air assault – a necessarily joint venture – as a concept (Waddy 2003). The Falklands campaign in 1982 seemed to demonstrate the early jointery of 3 Command Brigade. In fact, the frictions between the naval and marine elements during that campaign were prodigious: 'A lot of lessons which we should have known were unlearnt but eventually we reached a point of co-operation.'[6] While 16 Air Assault Brigade obviously represents a profound transformation of 5 Airborne Brigade, it is easy to presume that during the Cold War 3 Commando Brigade was already a joint brigade consistent with the aspirations of today's intervention formation. In fact, at that time 3 Commando Brigade's joint capabilities were limited.

Today, 3 Commando Brigade is seeking to integrate both maritime and air assets, especially in the post-9/11 missions to Iraq and Afghanistan. Reflecting these changes, amphibious doctrine – the brigade's concept of operations – has been fundamentally revised. A British amphibious assault now involves simultaneous assault by sea and air; two Commandos are landed by boat, while the other two manoeuvre units are inserted by aviation. Indeed, 3 Commando Brigade has developed a concept of 'ship to objective manoeuvre' in which forces are inserted inland on to the target and withdrawn from it by helicopter. Its very concept of amphibious operations now involves not merely maritime activity, but also the organic use of aviation assets. Its concept of operations has, in fact, converged with 16 Air Assault Brigade's. In order to organise this integration, the

---

[5] Chief of staff, 16 Air Assault Brigade, personal interview, 28 July 2005.
[6] 3 Commando Brigade's commander, Brigadier Julian Thompson.

headquarters of 3 Commando Brigade, like 16 Air Assault Brigade, has been further enlarged in terms of size and expertise. Senior figures in that organisation recognise that the Brigade has been unusually favoured in this transition:

We have an advantage. We never had the traditional Cold War experience. We were always expeditionary; like 16 which came from 24 Brigade, we are not a big army. In addition, amphibious operations are defined by complexity. You need to plan in detail. That is not necessary on the West German plain. This is reflected in the structure of the headquarters. I am a Lieutenant Colonel and I have a very senior DCOS [Deputy Chief of Staff]; he will be appointed to full Colonel on leaving this job. So in running complex operations, my planners are the equivalent of army chiefs of staff; they are staff trained, good majors. So the horsepower is greater here. This is because we have always been working with the Navy with no divisional HQ above us. We needed that oversight. That paid dividends in Helmand. On ops in Helmand, my planners were with the US in Kandahar developing the Kajaki project. I would be with ISAF – discussing targeting etc. – while the J3 team were conducting operations. I had the level of experience and a greater pool of cerebral capacity to be able to do all these things.[7]

The fact that the Royal Marines and the Brigade are part of the Royal Navy has ensured that it has been favourably resourced in comparison with normal army brigades; they have more senior officers in the headquarters. Indeed, as the chief of staff's statement clarifies, it is well staffed even in comparison with 16 Air Assault Brigade. Moreover, precisely because the Marines have always had to interact closely with the Royal Navy, they have adopted a more open approach to other services. Indeed, RAF personnel who have recently begun to work with 3 Commando Brigade have emphasised this inclusive ethos: 'The Marines are completely different. They [The RAF] have sent people to 3 Commando Brigade and the attitude and willingness to learn has been completely different.'[8] Emerging out of the ferociously independent 5 Airborne Brigade, 16 Air Assault Brigade initially found this transition to jointery more problematic. The airborne, parachute-trained members of the organisation often found it difficult to treat others members of the Brigade as equals.

9 brigade légère blindée de marine and the Division Spezielle Operationen have also changed their concepts of operations. 9 brigade légère blindée de marine now conceives of itself as a genuine amphibious brigade, while the Division Spezielle Operationen has organised itself for rapid insertion for evacuation operations. They are organised for amphibious or airborne or air assault insertion operations of a type compatible

[7] Chief of staff, 3 Commando Brigade, personal interview, 17 October 2007.
[8] RAF flight lieutenant, 16 Air Assault Brigade, personal interview, 1 February 2006.

with 3 Commando and 16 Air Assault Brigades. However, it is not clear that they yet have headquarters of sufficient size and expertise to conduct joint operations at a high intensity tempo. The headquarters of 9 brigade légère blindée de marine consists of sixty officers, but has less capability to conduct brigade size offensive operations. Some of this may be due to the historical legacy of the French Army which is still scarred by the mutiny in 1961 over the war in Algeria. In order to avoid a repetition of such events, the French prefer to deploy smaller forces, often from different forma-tions, dissipating an organic culture which might mutate into opposition to Paris. 9 brigade légère blindée de marine headquarters is organised for smaller force packages, delivered perhaps by amphibious insertion but with little need to co-ordinate with air assets. The Division Spezielle Operationen's headquarters is understaffed for genuinely joint offensive action. There seem to be insufficient staff officers to oversee the details of air–land co-ordination to ensure that the concept of insertion and exclu-sive fire support from the air can be realised in practice. The problem for the Division Spezielle Operationen, as an aspirationally joint brigade, is that it has not yet conducted a genuinely joint operation and therefore its integration with air assets has not been properly tested.

Fires

Since the advent of gunpowder, armies have sought to maximise their firepower, and since the artillery has always produced the most devastat-ing effect on the battlefield, this arm has always been critical to the armed forces. Artillery 'fires' remain a core concern for these organisations, despite the introduction of PGMs delivered by advanced jets and new unmanned aerial vehicles. The artillery not only remains a central element of these brigades, but is also a useful focal point to highlight the central features of current transformations. During the twentieth century, mod-ern forces became adept at combined arms warfare in which artillery was co-ordinated with the manoeuvre of infantry or armoured forces (House 2001). The Forward Observation Officer (FOO), supported by a signal-ler, played a crucial role in orchestrating these fires. Artillery remains central to contemporary operations because brigades have tried to fuse air and maritime assets – close air support from jets and attack helicopters with bombs, rockets and cannon fire, naval gunfire and TLAMs – with existing supporting fires.

During the First and Second World Wars, fires were increased by massing artillery and designating targets more precisely. From the Second World War it was not uncommon to employ air strikes before the artillery bombardment in a sequential fires plan. For instance, in July

1944, the British Army launched Operation Goodwood to the east of Caen, aiming at breaking the German defence in that sector. The armoured assault was preceded by the heaviest tactical air bombardment in Allied history, followed by artillery support (Biddle 2004; Keegan 1992). In the current era, 16 Air Assault Brigade and 3 Commando Brigade have sought to organise their fire control system so that they are able to synchronise a multiplicity of fires. Both were influenced by their observation of the US Marine Corps during the Iraq War,[9] whose formations were uniquely able to co-ordinate their fires simultaneously principally because the US Marines provide their own air, maritime and land assets. However, this co-ordination requires a clear identification not only of the target, but also of different air corridors in which artillery shells, mortar rounds, missiles and planes and helicopters travel. Without this de-confliction of air space, helicopters and jets can be struck by 'friendly fire'.

Arquilla and Ronfeldt (1997) have discussed the current change to command structure. Drawing a parallel with the commercial sector, they have argued that the old industrial–military hierarchies suitable to mass armies have been replaced by networks which are more flexible and responsive to the current strategic situation. They describe these new military structures as 'networks' in which horizontal relations between formerly discrete formations and services are now critical. Arquilla and Ronfeldt do not suggest that military networks have totally displaced former hierarchies. There is still a chain of command in the military. Rather, military command structures have become 'hybridised', as Arquilla and Ronfeldt subsequently call it (1997: 461–5). In place of the rigid twentieth-century hierarchy with its clearly defined jurisdiction, today's headquarters draw on a diversity of resources on an often *ad hoc* basis. Crucially, for such 'hybridised' organisations to operate coherently, participants need to be able to interact and co-operate with each other horizontally, sometimes independently of the explicit direction of their commanders. This requires a profound shift not simply in structures, but in the training, expectations and professional practices of members of these new hybrid organisations. This transformation in organisational culture is evident in the empowered brigade.

The role of the FOO and his party has been critical in this hybridisation, not only to the co-ordination of a diversity of fires in the current era but

---

[9] The Royal Marines have had a close relationship with the US Marine Corps throughout the Cold War period, training with them. It is probably not irrelevant that in developing a concept of synchronous fires, a battery from 16 Air Assault Brigade was assigned to 1 Marine Expeditionary Force for the invasion of Iraq, where it provided significant fire support for the Marines.

also to the development of self-managing horizontal linkages. In order to perform this role, in both 16 Air Assault Brigade and 3 Commando Brigade, the old FOO party has been substantially reformed and augmented. In particular, the FOO party has been fused with the once independent Tactical Air Control Party (TACP) tasked with co-ordinating close air strikes. The concept of the TACP had been invented in the Second World War when close air support had become a significant, if subordinate, factor on the battlefield. During the Korean War, the UN forces employed some limited close air support which were called in by a TACP, usually consisting of an officer, a signaller and perhaps one other soldier. Nine TACPs were assigned to each of the US divisions comprising some 15,000 combat and support troops. This was not an arbitrary figure: one TACP was assigned to each battalion. This was a small number, but it was sufficient for operational purposes. Battalions generally held static positions in a circumscribed area with a limited front, on which the TACP called air strikes. The number of TACPs has multiplied in Britain's intervention brigades. There are now TACPs for every company, although TACPs are regularly attached to sub-units as small as a platoon or even a patrol. In addition, in order to co-ordinate air and artillery fires, the TACPs have themselves been attached to existing FOO teams to create new fires teams.

In 16 Air Assault Brigade, the Apache helicopter has been very important in driving these changes, because without an effective mechanism of calling in Apache strikes and integrating with other fires, the capabilities of the new helicopter could not be exploited. The task of creating a system of co-ordinating fires was given to G Battery, 7 Royal Horse Artillery. This battery created the concept of Close in Fire Support (CIFS) teams, which fused existing TACP with FOOs teams in a larger team of seven or eight personnel attached to a company, developing new tactical doctrines about how Apache, as a new fires asset, was to be called in. The Dutch Army, which has also procured Apache, experienced a number of problems because they had not designated a specific individual for the role of co-ordinating Apache. G Battery designated one individual within the new CIFS Team who was given the authority to cue attack helicopter.

3 Commando Brigade undertook a concurrent adaptation, somewhat differently to 16 Air Assault Brigade, though the Brigade has organised its TACP and FOOs into Fire Support Teams (FST), partly as a result of its access to naval gunfire:

The Fire Support Team concept was developed by 29 Cdo Regt. It consisted of a FOO party with the officer in charge. He is the conductor and forward air controller and each FST terminally guides all the assets. The reason for developing the FST concept on the basis of a FOO party was a question of size. If we were co-ordinating an air component, we would have had to attach a four man air team, a TACP, to the FOO party. You would then end up with a ten-man team which could theoretically lead to friction. So instead of that increase in size, we have increased the skill of our FOOs teams, allowing them to keep their small four man size. The officer is a FAC [forward air controller] and a FOO. By good fortune, we have more forward air controllers than 3 Division. 148 Battery which specialises in Naval Gunfire [NGF] provide a lot of additional links and expertise for us. Consequently, every FST has an NGF expert and one half to two thirds of them have an air controller. The officer in the FST is not the terminal controller but the co-ordinator. The captain of the FST is responsible to the commander but he is able to take work off the commander, co-ordinating fires at the tactical level. We have a different doctrine here; we don't have a particular FST dogmatically attached to one company as in other formations. We chop FST up according to need. If you pre-assign teams, four terminal guidance fire support teams could be doing nothing, attached to companies which are not in action. We are no longer on a lineal battlefield and so we have to be more flexible where and when we need joint fires and therefore to which subunit we assign our FSTs.[10]

In the face of new missions, 3 Commando Brigade has preferred smaller joint fires teams, comprising fewer personnel with more skills, and to organise them on a task-by-task basis, rather than assigning them to a particular company.

Each solution reflects internal institutional factors. However, in effect, the two brigades have undergone a parallel institutional evolution; they have enlarged or empowered existing FOO teams and TACPs to

[10] Commanding officer and field officers, 29 Commando Artillery Regiment, personal interview, 9 January 2006. 'Since 2006, the FST concept has been substantially developed. The captain or warrant officer who now commands it no longer does the terminal guidance of any munitions as previously. However, he takes the key decisions: whether to engage or not, through an intimate knowledge of the targeting directives and tactical directives pushed out from both national (PJHQ) and theatre (HQ ISAF) sources, the Rules of Engagement and his own ethical principles. If he is to engage, he then does the weapon-to-target matching – what to engage with – fast air, AH, guns, precision rockets, mortars or small arms – all the time in discussion with his ground commander (a company commander) to weigh up the best options. He then instructs and oversees one or more of his experts in the target engagement process – these are the FAC (fast air), the close combat attack controller (AH), naval gunfire observer (NGS), artillery observer (guns), mortar fire controller (mors), or anyone capable of creating a precision grid to call for guided multi-launch rocket systems fire. The FST commander also ensures his airspace is clear (rockets won't hit AH as they come into the target area etc.) – de-conflicting one weapon system with another. Every FST would have all of these capabilities on paper (they all now have an FAC, for example – this is where 29 are years ahead of the rest of the Army as it continues to lead on FST development) – however, there are never enough FSTs to go round. Thus, FSTs would be broken down and bespoke teams created for specific tasks – but always with the aim of rejoining, or at least remaining in contact with the commander – whose role is so crucial. Again, 29 deployed to Afghanistan in 2008 with more FSTs than any other regiment – it had seen the demand coming and aimed for it and its still very much the future.' (artillery colonel, personal communication, 8 January 2010)

synchronise a wider range of available fires. The increase in fires has altered the role of the commanding officer of artillery battalions in 3 and 16 Brigades. During the twentieth century, the commanding officer of an artillery regiment parcelled out his four batteries to infantry battalions: one battery of six guns would be assigned to a battalion. The commanding officer controlled his batteries vertically, creating fire plans for them to de-conflict their activities and provide ammunition to them. The command-ing officer of 29 Commando Artillery Regiment now has a quite different role. He does not supervise, he devolves missions downwards to his batteries and FSTs. His role is to co-ordinate horizontally with the various fires which Brigade forces might draw upon:

There have been little changes to the guns or technology. The changes are at [the] level of joint effects. Our role is to co-ordinate fires – no matter where it comes from. We are about precision attack. That is, the terminal guidance of all assets: naval gunfire, AH [attack helicopter], rocket artillery and so on. We are able to do it much better now than before. The result is a change in organisational structure. The Joint Fires Centre at Brigade level is now the hub of the wheel co-ordinating assets drawn in from a wider range: rockets, fast air, TLAM and so on. And they are pulled in from a longer distance, at less notice and with greater precision than ever before. We have to give precision to the fire-missions.[11]

As a result, 3 Commando Brigade was able to draw on a diversity of fires during its first tour to Helmand.[12] A former Brigade commander in 3 Brigade noted the difference between the commanding officer of his artillery regiment and that of another, then more traditional infantry brigade in Britain: 'By contrast I saw an artillery regiment with the CO [Commanding Officer] sat in the battalion HQ occasionally visiting the brigade from time to time. The CO of 29 is networked into Brigade. He is looking to link his unit into other assets. His second-in-command orders artillery fires.'[13] In 3 Commando Brigade, the commanding officer acted precisely as the hub which his field officers described. He sought to co-ordinate assets both across the Brigade and outside it into a unified fires plan. In the then relatively under-resourced 19 Brigade, by contrast, with less assets, the commanding

[11] Commanding officer and field officers, 29 Commando Artillery Regiment, personal interview, 9 January 2006.
[12] 'The key has been the realisation of Joint Fires. It was the first time we have delivered fires as joined up as that. In World War II or maybe in Korea we did, but we haven't had that level of jointness for a long time. And certainly not in the modern era. In the air, we had available B1 Bombers which would be there for 10 hours: with 10,000 lbs worth of bombs. We had US-A10s which are good ground attack aircraft. We had F15s, French Mirage 2000s, British GR7s, Dutch F16s and other US aircraft. We had all the strike aircraft available and we came to fully understand and utilise their capabilities' (Lieutenant colonel, commanding officer, 29 Commando Artillery, personal interview, 8 June 2006).
[13] Brigadier, commander, 3 Commando Brigade, 29 September 2005.

officer controlled his artillery batteries, parcelling them out according to need in a manner consistent with twentieth-century practice. The high level of resourcing which 3 Commando Brigade enjoys may have assisted in the creation of this network structure. However, the elite commando status of the organisation does not seem to be irrelevant either. The commanding officer of 29 Commando is a commando-trained soldier, united to his men by his right to wear a green beret having passed the commando course. He, therefore, shares an important unifying experience not only with the Royal Marines, but with other Army commandos in 3 Commando. Their elite status potentially facilitates the empowered brigades to develop themselves into more horizontally-oriented network organisations. They already have shared experience, a sense of mutual expectation and, therefore, professional trust, independently of personal knowledge. Commando status unites the organisation and facilitates unusual forms of co-operation. In his work on the innovations in American forces in Iraq, James Russell (2009) has observed a similar process. He analysed the different way in which the US Marines and an army armoured regiment conducted counter-insurgency operations in Anbar province between 2005 and 2007. He emphasised the way in which formal hierarchies were revised by the investment of authority in selected junior commanders, who had proved themselves to be particularly adept at interacting with locals. At the same time, independently of superior direction, soldiers communicated their experiences and innovations horizontally across the organisation by means of digital communications, often email. Interestingly, while Russell notes the adaptability of the army regiment, he implies that the Marines were particularly advantaged in these innovations. The fact that all marines were united around a single allegiance to the corps, as an elite military formation, facilitated new practices which transcended existing doctrine and command structures.

16 Air Assault Brigade is an elite organisation, dominated by airborne personnel. This elitism seems to have assisted the organisation to adapt, as the innovations made by 7 Royal Horse Artillery demonstrate. However, 16 Air Assault Brigade has also experienced some organisational difficulties which seem to demonstrate the adaptiveness of military elitism. In this Brigade, not all personnel are airborne. However, in order to create a sense of unity, all members of the Brigade are allowed to wear the maroon beret.[14] This has, in many cases, outraged airborne personnel in the

---

[14] This policy was first introduced by 5 Airborne Brigade in the early 1990s in order to stop the harassment of (the small number of) non-airborne personnel. Interestingly, various units within the Brigade, including the Army Air Corps Regiments and the REME squadrons attached to them, prefer their own regimental headdress.

Brigade, who regard the extension of privilege as a corruption. Indeed, the universalisation of the maroon beret seems to have had little effect on diluting the solidarity of the airborne status group. Since the maroon beret no longer denotes an airborne trained soldier, the signifier of the elite paratrooper has migrated from the head to the parachute wings displayed on the right sleeve of combat smocks and shirts. Individuals in 16 Air Assault now regularly check to see if an individual displays parachute wings (showing they are airborne). Airborne soldiers will interact much more willingly and easily with other para-trained personnel (who have therefore passed P Company) than with non-paras. Indeed, the commanding officer of 3 Para regarded the apparent acceptance of non-airborne staff in the headquarters as unacceptable.[15] As 3 Commando Brigade expands, with the admission of a new army manoeuvre unit and an engineer squadron, the majority of which personnel will not be commando-trained, similar tensions may appear in that organisation. The frictions within 16 Brigade are not necessarily disastrous. However, they demonstrate how elitism may be a useful form of social mobilisation and facilitation in an era of dramatic organisational transformation. Elitism – as a common status honour – facilitates co-operation outside established command hierarchies.

16 Air Assault Brigade and 3 Commando are among the most advanced and innovative formations in Europe today as a result of the levels of investment in them and the operational experience they have accrued over the last decade. However, the other intervention brigades in Europe have begun to make some similar adaptations. 9 brigade légère blindée de marine have their own organic artillery; they have a choice of whether to deploy with 105 guns or 120 mm mortars. Consequently, they have developed some FOO teams with expertise to control these artillery fires. However, their co-ordination of fires is still substantially under-developed. 9 brigade légère blindée de marine have found it difficult to train officers and soldiers into an equivalent of the FST which is observable in 3 Commando Brigade:

The Fire Support Team is a universal observer. They co-ordinate artillery fire, aviation, fast jets and naval gunfire. There is a problem with the FST here. The Lieutenant who commands it is mostly recruited direct from St Cyr. He only has 3 years in the grade. To get all the qualifications it is difficult. He has no more than 3 years in the regiment before he goes overseas. If we want an observer who can co-ordinate all air, art and naval assets when he has the qualification, they will leave the regiment. A former NCO could become Lieutenant but the problem is that they don't speak English and cannot do their air co-ordination. The aim is to

---

[15] Personal interview, February 2006.

stabilise people in the job and provide instruction. Maybe we could increase them in size. Maybe we could bring in an aviator who would be helped to survive. But the problem is not solved yet. We are a marine unit but we are not a marine brigade like the Royal Marines. We belong to the army. Amphibious operations are only one mission among others. In 3 Commando Brigade, there is longer stability with people. The name 'Marine' came from the colonial troops. Amphibiosity was only a little part of that. We are like other army brigades in France. This explains the higher level of professionalisation in Britain. We change around too much. For instance, with FST [First Support Teams] we can't have the same level of training. A lieutenant is in the job here for two years – but you need five . . . The problem is that when they are a captain, they leave. A lieutenant must have an idea of how to be an observer but he must also know more than one part of rear operations. He must also be in the rear. He does not have a lot of time as an observations officer. Then he becomes chief of an artillery platoon and then in the future a lieutenant colonel. We have currently a preference for short experience of different jobs.[16]

In fact, British officers command FSTs or equivalent specialist groups for less time than their French counterparts. Officers spend a maximum of two years in such appointments, but it is frequently only a year. The structure of the professional career, organisational expectations and the training demands have militated against 9 brigade légère blindée de marine creating the necessary expertise and structures to generate the co-ordinated fires which the British intervention brigades are now capable of delivering. With their formal partnership with 3 Commando Brigade, it seems likely that 9 brigade légère blindée de marine will be influenced by the way in which the Royal Marines are developing into a joint organisation, utilising assets from air and maritime forces.

The Division Spezielle Operationen is reliant on air support and, consequently, they have invested in developing new TACPs in order to co-ordinate air strikes:

We have a special operations task manager who calls in air. We are entering a different environment. We use naval artillery. And we are training TACPs. And this whole concept must be ready by 2008. I must reach FOC [full operational capacity] then. I have a lot of work in the next two years to get there.

Author: are you optimistic you will get there?
Yes we have very good personnel.[17]

The commander is confident and it is possible that the Division Spezielle Operationen will be able to integrate air assets into its operations unproblematically. However, extrapolating from the British experience,

[16] Deputy commander, 9 brigade légère blindée de marine, personal interview, 14 November 2007.
[17] Commander, Division Spezielle Operationen, personal interview, 19 June 2006.

there may be organisational difficulties which confront the Division Spezielle Operationen. For 3 Commando and 16 Air Assault Brigade, the key site of joint innovation has, in both cases, been the Brigades' artillery regiments. The joint fires function has been fused on to the existing FOO structure. The artillery has provided the concepts, the personnel and the expertise for the development of joint fires. The lack of any artillery in the Division Spezielle Operationen potentially obstructs the development of a truly co-ordinated joint brigade, because there is no dedicated organisation within the division linking manoeuvre to supporting fires (Scholzen 2009b). There is also an underlying institutional tension which echoes frictions in 16 Brigade. In the Division Spezielle Operationen, the old airborne brigades, consisting of parachute-trained soldiers, have been augmented by non-airborne personnel. As in 16 Brigade, this inclusion and the ability of non-para-trained individuals to wear the maroon beret have led to hostility. The Division Spezielle Operationen's headquarters is located in a barracks in Regensburg, which was formerly occupied by a mechanised division. Many of the staff officers in the Division Spezielle Operationen come originally from this division and there is resentment that these outsiders, wearing a beret they have not earned, have excessive influence over the division. German paratroopers, like their British peers, at best tolerate the presence of non-airborne personnel. The status tensions in 16 Air Assault Brigade and the Division Spezielle Operationen illustrate a paradox in contemporary military development. The empowered brigade based on elite troops has become the favoured formation for military transformation. However, in order to empower the brigade, allowing joint assets to be attached, it has been necessary to introduce new personnel, many of whom are not elite. The development has been necessary, but it has inevitably introduced problems and undermined the cohesiveness of these organisations. The frictions do not seem to be fatal; typically they are negotiated in the micro-dynamics of interaction by small snubs and insults or by behind the scenes grumbling by paratroopers. However, these difficulties illustrate the impediments to military development.

The special forces may demonstrate these organisational transformations at the most extreme, although it is difficult to confirm their current modes of operations since little material is in the public realm, especially in France and Germany. However, it is widely known that special forces patrols are trained to identify targets against which they are able to call in air and maritime assets. In Afghanistan, British, French and German special forces are all likely to have co-ordinated the use of strategic air assets, fast air, using PGMs against hostile forces. Certainly, NATO procedures have been developed for these operations (Ryan 2007: 79). Although it is dangerous to draw direct parallels, the British special forces, whose activities are more prominent in the public domain, may usefully illustrate the appearance of joint land formations. Following the 9/11 attacks, British special forces deployed to Afghanistan as part of Operation Enduring Freedom. They were involved in a number of actions which demonstrate the close co-ordination between the special forces and other formations and services. One of these actions is particularly useful since, extraordinarily, it was broadcast by British news teams who were present and has subsequently been described at a level of detail which demonstrates this jointery very clearly. On 24 November 2001, 600 Taliban prisoners were imprisoned in the Qala-i-Janghi fort near Mazar-i-Sharif by Northern Alliance General Abdul Rashid Dostum. Almost immediately, there was unrest among the prisoners, in which one prisoner killed himself and a Northern Alliance commander with a grenade. The next day the Taliban overpowered their guards, armed themselves and threatened a mass break-out from the fort. Two CIA men, who had been interrogating the prisoners, were trapped in the fort, although, as it subsequently transpired, one was killed in the initial uprising. As the fighting continued between the Taliban in the fort and the Northern Alliance soldiers outside it, an SBS patrol arrived in white Land Rovers and engaged the Taliban from the battlements with small arms in an effort to locate the CIA men. The patrol called in a series of successful 'danger-close' air strikes on the fort, identifying the central gateway to the fort and Dostum's stables as the decisive enemy positions. They lased the two structures with laser targeting devices in order to record their co-ordinates, which were then relayed to the approaching jets (Lewis 2006: 205). The forward air controller in the SBS patrol then talked the pilot on to the target, identifying orienting landmarks on his bomb-run and lasing the targets again for him as he approached (2006: 207–9). The bomb struck the target precisely.

The special forces are an extreme case. However, they affirm a general observation about the empowered brigade. The new brigade no longer functions as an independent element in a vertical hierarchy. It has become a node in a network organisation, interacting, integrating and collaborating with other institutions across old service lines. In order to integrate a diversity of assets from other formations and services, the headquarters of the empowered brigade is enlarging and other co-ordinating elements within it are being augmented. The traditional FOO and the TACP have been critical here. The role of the artillery officer and his signaller calling in indirect fire has become a small team, co-ordinating a diversity of fires. As a result of improved co-ordination, tactical capabilities are coagulating around these new concentrations of military competence in Europe.

The combined brigade: transnationalisation

European rapid reaction brigades have been increasingly empowered by drawing upon assets from other services in order to conduct their missions. At the same time they are co-operating ever more closely with other forces. Brigades within Europe have become not only joint or cross-service but also 'combined': they are multinational. In order to prosecute current operations, with declining resources, multinational brigades have appeared in Europe since the 1990s: units and sub-units have been organised into combined formations. Multinational task forces appeared for the first time in Bosnia and Kosovo to control designated areas of responsibility. These multinational formations were bi- or multilateral, with contingents of equal national size under the command of one designated nation. They persist in the Balkans today. For a stabilisation operation at a relatively low level of intensity, multinational formations have been successful. For instance, the German–Netherlands Corps had performed adequately in the Balkans on tours since the 1990s. However, as the level of intensity has become higher and the deployments more stressful, the fragility of this organisational form has become apparent. There are some notable examples of this fissuring. One of the most obvious examples of this is the performance of the German–Dutch Multinational Brigade at Camp Warehouse in Afghanistan in 2003 when the German–Netherlands Corps acted as ISAF III. Although this formation had been successful in previous exercises and deployments to the Balkans, the Afghan operation proved contentious. The Dutch battalion accused the German command of administrative bias: the Dutch were accommodated in tents rather than huts like the Germans and received fewer luxuries than the Germans. Operationally, they claimed that they were forced to mount guard duty more often than the German contingent and, because of stringent German caveats, where the Germans deployed only in armoured vehicles, the Dutch troops were given the most dangerous patrolling tasks (Moelker and Soeters 2004: 373–4). Dutch soldiers infamously summarised the situation: 'We do not have a problem with the Afghans. We have a problem with the Germans' (2004: 368). The Brigade illustrated the political and organisational problems of multinationality. In multinational formations where contingents are more or less equal, a genuine consensus is required which unites the parties at a higher collective level. It is extremely difficult to attain this level of unity, but failure to do so engenders bitterness and recriminations between the groups, which assume rightly or wrongly that they are being disadvantaged.

Close tactical relations began to develop between French and British soldiers in the Balkans on UN and NATO missions in the mid-1990s.

Since that time, and especially from 2001, empowered brigades have been increasingly co-operating with other military forces from other nations, particularly other elite forces. However, the preferred format for the 'combined' brigade is not multinational. Rather, empowered brigades seem to prefer to operate on a framework nation basis. The French Army – and 9 brigade légère blindée de marine, in particular – have demonstrated this approach very clearly. They have provided the core of the deployed forces on which other national elements are attached, avoiding the rivalries evident at Camp Warehouse. In the EU mission to the Congo in 2003, for instance, small European contingents, including a troop of Swedish special forces, were commanded by 9 brigade légère blindée de marine. In the recent deployment to Chad on the EU mission, the framework nation approach has again been utilised by the French. They provided the core of this force, the tactical troops coming from 9 brigade légère blindée de marine, with contributions from Sweden, Finland, Austria, Poland and Italy, including special forces from France and a number of other nations.[18]

In the light of the intensity of the mission, especially in the south, a framework nation approach has been adopted in Helmand, Uruzgan and Kandahar: the British have taken responsibility for Helmand; the Dutch for Uruzgan; and the Canadians for Kandahar. Each has deployed a framework nation task force of about brigade size. Britain's Helmand Task Force provides a concrete insight into how these combined brigades, co-ordinating the operations of different national contingents, have operated. The Helmand Task Force is a transnational brigade. During their deployments, 3 Commando and 16 Air Assault Brigade have had a Danish recce squadron of approximately 100 soldiers and a similarly sized Estonian contingent under their command. The Helmand Task Force is a useful example of how some of Europe's reaction brigades are adapting.

Since the beginning of the campaign in the summer of 2006, the Danes and Estonians have been involved in some intense fighting as part of the British Task Force. From 26 July until 16 August, the Danish recce squadron was deployed to Musa Qala, relieving 16 Brigade's Pathfinder Platoon which had been besieged in the town for fifty-six days. The Danish recce squadron was supported by the mortars platoon from the Royal Irish Rangers. This *ad hoc* force forged a close and effective working relationship in Musa Qala. The Danes positioned their vehicles in such a way that their twelve .05 Browning heavy machineguns mounted on the roofs could be fired in defence of the district centre. They provided invaluable firepower

---

[18] Royal Marine liaison officer, personal interview, 17 September 2008.

against the nightly Taliban assaults. At the same time, the Royal Irish Rangers' mortar team proved adept at delivering defensive fire. On 7 August, the mortar platoon repelled an attack with an intense barrage: 'The Danish guys came down and said: "You Guys Rock!!" [It] was the most awesome display of accurate mortar fire they had ever seen' (Bishop 2007: 231).

The Danish contribution demonstrated another important aspect of transnational co-operation. During the Cold War, national corps followed their own tactical operating procedures. The NATO Standardisation Agreement existed, but mostly referred to equipment, such as bullet calibre, and, in terms of shared military drills, there was huge variability in their application. As European forces work together in an increasingly intense environment, they are converging on common practices at ever lower levels. A British captain working for 16 Air Assault Brigade in 2006 was attached to the Danish company when they redeployed to Garmsir after their withdrawal from Musa Qala. He described how he commanded a mixed section of four British and five Danish soldiers as it advanced on a compound south of the town. The section came under enemy fire as they approached the buildings. The mixed section returned fire and, given the strength of the enemy, the British captain decided to withdraw: '"Delta, this is Charlie. When I throw smoke I want you to withdraw back across the track to me" ... The Danes scrambled across the road in pairs. When they were safely over I gave the order for withdrawal, fire team by fire team' (Beattie 2008: 265). The captain concluded: 'I was impressed with how the Danes had acted. They were disciplined and enthusiastic. The sergeant had led well' (2008: 265–6). The British captain describes how the Danes had adopted section tactics employed by the British and Americans and had become adept in their use. They moved under the cover of fire and smoke from the supporting Charlie fire team, and broke themselves down into mutually supporting pairs, according to infantry doctrine, in order to retreat across the track. The Estonians have also been increasingly integrated into the Helmand Task Force, learning British standard operating procedures: 'The Estonians: they had no caveats. They were under my command. Their only complaint was that I would not let them mix it enough. At first, I had to hold them back: they just were not ready. They would complain: you are not using us enough. But by the end, they were pretty good.'[19]

The close co-operation between Danish and British soldiers at Musa Qala was unusual and, indeed, should not be taken as the model of future transnational interaction in Europe's rapid reaction brigades. The relations between the Danes and Royal Irish troops obscured deep tensions in the

[19] Commanding officer, 3 Para, personal interview, 23 March 2007.

relations between the squadron as a whole and 16 Air Assault Brigade. Although the troops performed well in Musa Qala, the Danish military and government were extremely critical of Britain's command of them. Indeed, the Danish Government insisted on the withdrawal of their troops from Musa Qala and reduced the status of Britain's command over the recce squadron to tactical control. Following these difficulties, 3 Commando Brigade decided that the most successful way of incorporating them would be to give them precise and independent tasks which they could perform independently in accordance with national political and military expectations. In contrast to their deployment with 3 Para, the Danish recce squadron predominantly conducted mobile operations groups under 3 Commando Brigade utilising their excellent mobility:

The Battle Group was 1,500 strong. The Estonians and the Danes were integrated. With multinational troops, you have to play to their strengths. Don't misapply them; don't put them in platoon houses. The Danes were good, they had a MOG [Mobile Operations Group] in the north. The Estonians were rough around the edges but did the job.[20]

Although 3 Commando Brigade may have been more sensitive to their Danish contingent, the tensions between the Danes and 16 Air Assault Brigade demonstrate an important point. Precisely because the Danes were a small part of a much larger framework nation battle group in 2006, rather than an equal partner in a multinational one, their initial disgruntlement with the command of the Helmand Task Force could not destabilise the entire mission as Dutch–German frictions did in Camp Warehouse. Since 2006, Danish commitment to Helmand has increased from a reconnaissance squadron to a battle group which now takes responsibility for the districts around Gereshk, in an area designated as Helmand Battle Group Central. This increase in troop numbers has been matched by a compatible increase in British force numbers from just over 2,000 in 2006 to 8,000 in 2008. The Danes remain a small element within a framework nation task force, assigned their own area of responsibility quite separate from British operations in the north and south of the province.

The Helmand campaign has illustrated an important point about current and future European military transformation. National differences and national autonomy will remain and, indeed, be reinforced. The evidence of British and French rapid reaction brigades suggests that these formations will form the framework of operations, but increasingly at the lowest tactical levels national forces will co-operate with each other. Precisely because the foreign contingents are small in comparison with the

---

[20] Royal Marine officer, 42 Commando, personal interview, 15 June 2007.

British framework nation force in the Helmand Task Force, the disruption manifest in the Dutch–German brigades where two equal contingents have been able to squabble has been much less evident. Operational pressures have demanded a transnational approach to military operations from NATO troops on the ground.

Information operations

The emergence of joint and combined brigades, drawing on a diversity of fires, represents a significant military adaptation. However, the use of a diversity of kinetic capabilities and the incorporation of troops from other nations is only part of the transformation of Europe's intervention brigades, and perhaps not even the most important one. During the Cold War, the predecessors of the empowered brigade were trained to fight an inter-state war against military peers. In today's new wars, these brigades are deployed on stabilising and counter-insurgency missions. This has profoundly altered the way they conceptualise operations. On these new missions, military intelligence on the basis of which operations are planned has been radically transformed.

Intelligence in the Cold War was relatively simple. From information about the advance of Soviet forces, intelligence officers plotted the direction and speed of their projected advance. Intelligence officers were able to put a 'steel arrow' on the map against which the formation would plan a response: 'It was easy for intelligence then. We knew that the Russian Brigade was travelling at so many kilometres an hour. We tracked that on to the map and in two hours you know where they will be.'[21] Cold War intelligence has now been superseded by information operations. Military forces need a deep situational understanding of the cultural and political context in which they are operating that gives rise to the kinds of groups with and against which they are engaging. At the same time they need a strategy of how to engage with and communicate their mission to audience groups in-theatre and globally:

Now you have to have great awareness of the AOR [area of responsibility]: regional, tribes, political, economic – there is a lot of interaction. Great awareness of the general culture is required. But the difficulty is to have this awareness in spite of our military culture. We deploy very quickly and don't have time to develop this awareness. We have to have awareness.[22]

---

[21] Lieutenant colonel, G2 (Intelligence), 9 brigade légère blindée de marine, 14 November 2007.
[22] Lieutenant colonel, G2 (Intelligence), 9 brigade légère blindée de marine, 14 November 2007.

At the same time, while firepower – or the threat of it – remains essential to the armed forces, current operations cannot be successful unless they are conducted as an information operation; the armed forces are seeking to engage with hostile, neutral and friendly audiences in-theatre and at home in order to mobilise support for their activities. The armed forces are increasingly re-orienting their understanding of operations; tactical action can have strategic effect only if it is communicated to decisive audiences in the area of operations and European audiences often by means of the global media:

I often attempt to get the staff to visualize the operational area as a canvas with a complex picture. [The chief of staff draws a picture on his whiteboard with 16 Brigade as a small box in more complex operational picture including economic, political, diplomatic spheres to illustrate the point.] Traditionally, at the tactical level we automatically focus only on the military aspects and search for a definable 'enemy'. This is now a defunct philosophy. Wherever we go now tends to define the frontline as the enemy comes to us from amongst the people. 16 Brigade is a conventional force for use against another military force, although our greatest strategic impact is more likely to come from the effect on perceptions as a result of our arrival in a certain area at an appropriate time. The best example is the appearance of two British flagged attack helicopters behind the PM at precisely the right moment in time and space. This focused strategic communication impact will be felt by all actors across the spectrum and often eclipses the impact of multiple and laborious tactical actions.[23]

You need actionable intelligence. But you must also build schools etc. If people are hungry it will be bad. You need to conduct a hearts and minds campaign. That is good. That happens in the context of a multinational force; e.g. in Afghanistan, Britain has ARRC but also works with the US and other coalition forces.[24]

In effect, these brigades are reconceptualising conflict in a manner which coheres with the development of an effects-based approach to operations (EBAO) in operational headquarters. They are situating their military activity in the wider political and economic context seeking to engage with the population.

One of the most interesting examples of the effect of the information revolution in Europe is the Command Support Group of 3 Commando Brigade. In the face of the centrality of intelligence and information operations to all military missions, 3 Commando Brigade has developed a new unit, the Command Support Group (CSG), to fuse information and influence operations with kinetic effects:

[23] Chief of staff, 16 Air Assault Brigade, personal interview, 28 July 2005.
[24] Commander, Division Spezielle Operationen, personal interview, 19 June 2006.

The Command Support Group is responsible for ISTAR: for deep intelligence – not just geographic information. I am charged with producing intelligence from the deep battle. We find elements and then we run the intelligence cycle to produce J2 product. There are other elements to the CSG: decisively, the info campaign in order to influence the operation. We also aim to understand the environment. We must understand the environment – and also organise key leader engagement.[25]

The CSG was formed by fusing existing elements of the Brigade into one augmented unit in the headquarters:

Originally this unit was the HQ and Signals squadron, it was like 216 [Signals Squadron] in 16 Brigade. But we did have the Mountain and Arctic Warfare Cadre and Y troop (electronic warfare) bolted on. We parented them. We then had a communications troop and a logs troop. It was a bit more than a signals squadron in an Army brigade. We needed this because we were dealing with strategic communications and amphibious shipping. The logs burden was bigger therefore and we were bolting on the MAWC [Mountain and Artic Warfare Cadre, specialist reconnaissance troops] too. When Rob Fry was the Brigade Commander and Chris Scott was the CO, papers were written proposing renaming the unit, the Command Support Group (CSG). I can't remember how the policy was passed or whether Rob Fry simply did it by fiat. But one of the reasons was to raise the status of the CO. People had turned down the job before. And there was an expansion of size. The communications troop became a communications squadron. The MAWC provided reconnaissance in their new format as the Brigade Patrol Troop; Y troop (electronic warfare) and the Air Defence Squadron were all put under a squadron structure. Since then the task has been to fight the info battle at brigade level. We moved the TACPs to 29 because they are strike assets not info ones. We organised all the units to provide joint and integrated assets for the brigade; the commandos deliver manoeuvre, the CSG delivers information and 29 (Commando Artillery Regiment) strike. The CSG is now 427 plus 21 officers, currently running at 93% strength. The CSG is the same shape as old HQ and signals squadron in many ways. However we deploy differently. And most importantly, there has been a conceptual change. We need to win the information battle. CSG has to control ISTAR. To do this we have needed to take on a unit structure which allows us to take on other units organically under our command. For instance on Telic [the operational name for the Iraq invasion] with the addition of the QDG [Queen's Dragoon Guards, armoured reconnaissance] at one point the unit became well over 600. That was for a short period admittedly. However, if you are running a unit like that you need a HQ structure to cope with it and how you organise yourself in the field is relevant.

My predecessor argued we needed to look at information as a whole. We needed to unite ISTAR and intelligence with info ops. Who should do this? The Brigade staff is overworked. We are the only unit that does it all. In army terms we unite signals,

---

[25] Commanding officer, CSG, personal interview, 3 September 2007.

intelligence and reconnaissance. But these all have their own cap-badge interests. These are problems which we have avoided.[26]

The CSG has a number of organic and external intelligence feeds which it has to collate into a unified picture of the theatre for the brigade commander. The commanding officer aims to co-ordinate these intelligence feeds into a single information campaign and to suggest a series of activities which should take place in order to prosecute this campaign. Instead of simply focusing on enemy forces and kinetic activity, the CSG aims to assist in the creation of a holistic campaign plan in which influence activities are fused with kinetic firepower to achieve the ends which have been designated. The CSG is an innovative organisation which has proved valuable, especially in Afghanistan.

The CSG is an important development, but issues of procurement and manning remain:

It is very slow and problematic. Some things we have funded ourselves. We have done something within the limited numbers available in the HQ and Signals squadron. We cannot get more personnel – and so we are constrained in what we can do. However, this works better than the army. It is worth investing in the information capability. And we have got increased resourcing. John Rose [Brigade Commander 2004–5] was willing to take manpower out of commandos and give them to us. For the current commander, it is not so simple. Any progress is stopped by operational analysis and fleet staffing. They work out the optimal size of the commando units and then look at the ISTAR afterwards. If there is no manpower available – that is just it. But I think they need to look at it more coherently. But in fact, manoeuvre units are always seen as priority and always looked to first.[27]

Significantly, one of the biggest problems for the CSG is how to train and exercise the new unit. In Britain, exercises are still overwhelmingly oriented to traditional manoeuvre warfare:

And it is also very difficult to train. It is difficult to exercise; for example, it is difficult to produce target sets for electronic warfare. We do do formation level exercises. But manoeuvre still shapes all the exercises. We are working on synthetic training with Thales using simulations.[28]

There is little doubt that the Brigade has benefited from the CSG's independence and high level of resourcing in comparison with army brigades. The Brigade has recognised an organisational requirement and been able to resource and staff this innovation.

---

[26] Commanding officer, CSG, personal communication, 31 May 2006.
[27] Commanding officer, CSG, personal communication, 31 May 2006.
[28] Commanding officer, CSG, personal communication, 31 May 2006.

However, even in 3 Commando Brigade problems endure which exceed difficulties with training, equipment and resourcing. The Commanding Officer CSG notes that in the past its status was a problem. Officers turned down the role of commanding officer of this unit because it was seen as secondary to the command of a commando unit. Indeed, he noted that the status of the CSG would not be fundamentally revised until a brigade commander was selected who had commanded this unit. In order to attempt to raise the status of the unit, he sought to consolidate the autonomous identity of the CSG: 'I recently wrote a paper arguing that we should call this unit 30 Information Exploitation Commando Royal Marines. By giving ourselves a numeric identity we raise our profile and our status and the importance of this aspect of warfare.'[29]

The reference to 30 Commando is significant. Numeric titles like 42 Commando enjoy a high status because they denote a recognised regimental history. In relation to 30 Commando, during the Second World War a commando unit with this designation was raised in order to conduct what would now be called intelligence and psychological operations. The Commanding Officer CSG actively sought to tie the unit's current identity to the past in order to legitimate the CSG and increase its standing. He has endeavoured to alter the conventional war fighting ethos which is still dominant in the Royal Marines. There is a paradox here, for the very brigades in Europe, which have been forced to develop most rapidly, are disadvantaged by the institutional culture which favoured them in the first place. Ironically, despite the evident benefits of the elitism of the brigades in the current era, this elitism may actually be a problem in this radical conceptualisation. 3 Commando Brigade, for instance, prioritises high risk, offensive operations. They attract, select and train marines for amphibious assaults; the green beret, the central reference point for all marines, symbolises this role. Reputation within the organisation is based on the ability of an officer or marine to perform expertly on these operations; the commando ethos of the Royal Marines defines their perception of excellence and their institutional priorities. The CSG, which gathers intelligence to develop a coherent information campaign, is situated some way outside that ideal. The very organisational strength of the Royal Marines with its highly motivated, robust personnel may actually promote an adherence to traditional commando identity at a time when such concepts, prioritising firepower and physical manoeuvre, may no longer be adequate in themselves to the new operational realities. Nevertheless, despite the difficulties of asserting the status of the CSG, 3 Commando Brigade is significantly ahead of its peers in Europe.

[29] Commanding officer, CSG, personal communication, 31 May 2006. In 2010, the unit was designated formally as 30 Commando.

Following their deployment to Helmand in 2006, traditionalist attitudes prioritising manoeuvre warfare and firepower have altered in 16 Air Assault Brigade, as the commanding officer of 3 Para noted:

When I was second-in-command in 1 PARA, the LEWTs (Light Electronic Warfare Teams) would turn up on exercise; they were just another twenty-four bodies to feed. We did not include them; we did not know what to do with them. But now no 3 PARA commander would deploy without them. They would listen in to the Taliban signals and communications for us.[30]

However, even though the concepts of the members of the 16 Air Assault Brigade may be changing about the priority of intelligence and information warfare, the headquarters has been insufficiently resourced to create an equivalent of the CSG; a dedicated cell which unites all intelligence feeds in order to develop a coherent information operation. Army brigades are constrained by manpower and by numbers. 16 and 19 Brigades have expressed an interest in 3 Commando Brigade's model, but they cannot resource the development. Both army brigades recognise the new salience of information in current operations, but neither has been able to institutionalise adaptations.

Theo Farrell's recent work demonstrates how the British Army in-theatre may be organically developing institutions like the CSG. Closely related to the development of information operations, is the introduction of EBAO (effects-based approach to operations) at the tactical level. Indeed, in his insightful work on 16 Air Assault and 52 Brigade's operations in Helmand, Farrell has explored the way in which their commanders utilised an effects-based approach in order to co-ordinate military operations with other stabilisation activities (Farrell 2008):

EBAO was clearly evident in 52 Brigade's campaign when it took charge of Task Force Helmand from October 2007 to April 2008. The campaign plan was focused on generating those effects and decisive conditions necessary to produce an operational end-state, defined in broad terms of security, political stability and economic sustainability. Accordingly, the centre of gravity was conceptualized in terms of the local population rather than insurgents' will and ability to fight. (2008: 795)

Focusing on the population, the brigade commander sought to integrate 'kinetic *and* non-kinetic effects' (2008: 795). Significantly, as a result of this effects-based approach, 52 Brigade began to create development influence teams to conduct deeper assessment and intelligence gathering. In effect, 52 Brigade began organically to grow its own version of the CSG in order to develop a more coherent campaign. British Army brigades

[30] 27 March 2007.

have innovated informally around the problem of intelligence gathering and information operations.

Like British Army brigades, 9 brigade légère blindée de marine is also constrained by manpower:

It is a little different with us. We have to comply with troop allowances and in our branch, staff are organised in six areas, two officers and two NCOs in each. That is not enough. On operations we are reinforced by individuals from the higher level HQ or from the Intelligence Brigade. Last time I was with the Brigade, I was J2 [Joint Intelligence] leader for the Intell [Intelligence] Cell. The Intell cell was a big cell. Intell was reinforced by one intell gathering company from the Intell Brigade, with Humint [human intelligence] and other relevant assets. For analysis we had personnel from the Divisional level HQ. In the near future, there are more experiments. Another Brigade structure is possible. At Brigade level, we are going to receive a multi-sensor unit with a Humint platoon, some UAVs with short range (10 km) and radar surveillance. These will be our sensors. In addition, we have one company with eighty men. J2 will be reinforced by more than 10 personnel. A good cell in the Brigade HQ will be able to cope with new threats. But we only work against similar threats and brigades at the moment. G2 [army intelligence] in the brigade consists of two groups of two officers and one NCO – six people in all. We are changing the nature of conflict. Our culture is to fight against the Russians. Intelligence gives a picture of the situation in the field to understand the enemy's objectives. Currently this is material intelligence: a vehicle or a soldier is in such a location, therefore, certain military deductions follow. But intell in Kosovo and Afghanistan, it is very different. We are in the area for a long period. We need very deep intell of the area of responsibility. How many inhabitants are there? What are they are thinking? What are the links between ethnic groups? How do they earn their money? Does the alliance have secret links? This is not material/factual; it is amaterial. The soldier is not trained and equipped for it. We have cameras and drones but we need Humint – that is very important. We have to talk to people. It is not the same at all and we have some difficulty with it. We are in a period of change in terms of training, equipment and organisation. But we have not changed in some ways. Even if we increased the size of intell on peacekeeping operations, we still don't understand it all and don't use all we know. The British are very intelligent. But French officers do not have the same culture. I'll give you an example. When I was chief of staff here, I had a reserve officer who was a farmer, I told him I am interested in you because you are a farmer. Give me intelligence on that. You must help the intell cell to understand local peasant farmers because you belong to that world. If someone worked in a bank they could provide economic intelligence. It is not enough to just track the fighter who is waiting at some crossroads for instance. We have to explain economic changes. We must use a specialist. This is a long way from a traditional Brigade HQ. Britain and the US have made a lot of progress in Iraq and Afghanistan; they have made good advances in intell.[31]

[31] Deputy commander, 9 brigade légère blindée de marine, personal interview, 14 November 2007.

It is possible that 9 brigade légère blindée de marine may in the future institutionalise capabilities like the CSG: 'The experiment last summer – 2007 Aug – will carry on over 2 years. Our Chief of Staff has emphasised it is a real need for our Brigade to have this tool. The future unit implementation will be decided before end of the experiment in 2008.'[32] However, at the moment the Brigade, while recognising the transformation of warfare, has been able to adapt only on an *ad hoc* basis, drawing on the contingent expertise of members of the brigade.

In the Division Spezielle Operationen, a similar situation is observable. The brigade fully recognises the new environment in which it must operate:

At the same time, we have a new situation. We are now threatened by pre-historical threats: Islam etc. They recognised no rights for women etc. They don't fight in the clean way we used to fight: tank vs tank. A change point was 9/11: a totally conventional object – a plane – was flown into building. What can sixty tank brigades do now? We have a new scenario.[33]

Like its British equivalents, the Division Spezielle Operationen has new sensors. The Brigade has also instituted a cell dedicated to the analysis of intelligence and, more specifically, to the planning of information operations:

We have new sensors. We need new signal and intelligence systems. We need human intelligence. I have an intelligence company: 15 officers and 15 NCOs, they have specialist language and other information for the theatre. We are forming another one at the moment. There is a renaissance of intelligence.[34]

It is unclear at this point how effective this small cell is for processing new forms of intelligence. Certainly, the cell is much smaller than the CSG. Nevertheless, the very fact that the Division Spezielle Operationen has created such a branch within the headquarters is an important development.

At the moment, the CSG is a unique organisation in terms of its concept and capabilities. However, it is unlikely that it will remain so in the future. The concept of a dedicated information operations branch is likely to germinate across Europe's empowered brigades, probably beginning with some *ad hoc* staff grouping. Technology has been an important element in this move to information warfare; digital communications have facilitated new forms of hostile activity, including media campaigns against European forces. However, the shift to information operations is more

---

[32] Lieutenant colonel, G2, 9 brigade légère blindée de marine, 14 November 2007.
[33] Commander, Division Spezielle Operationen, personal interview, 19 June 2006.
[34] Commander, Division Spezielle Operationen, personal interview, 19 June 2006.

fundamental than mere technology. It represents a fundamental change in the way in which Europe's armed forces and their opponents are prosecuting war. It represents a shift in the way combatant groups are organising themselves to fight and the goals which they pursue. This change has itself demanded a profound re-definition of what war actually is – and, therefore, what the armed forces do. The armed forces have made dramatic alterations to their own self-definitions in comparison with the Cold War, but they remain overwhelmingly wedded to a conventional manoeuvre approach to warfare. For an organisation that has monopolised legitimate violence since the rise of the modern state, the difficulty with which the armed forces have had to adapt is perhaps understandable. The point remains, however, despite organisational resistance to change. The empowered brigades now emerging in Europe are not only more powerful than their predecessors, as organisations, they also are fundamentally different. They are re-organising themselves for a quite different form of conflict and developing new structures, practices and linkages with other forces in order to be successful in the twenty-first century. It is not yet clear how successful this transition will be.

Conclusion

It is dangerous to universalise about European military development; the armed forces of Europe are organised on a national basis and are a reflection of institutional history. However, Europe's armed forces are in transition. The mass, armoured divisions of the Cold War are being superseded by empowered brigades. The elite status of these brigades has been an important element in their advancement and their performance; their elite status demands higher levels of performance from their personnel and unites members of these brigades in a way which allows these formations to be more robust and flexible. There is a more unified organisational culture, allowing for greater and easier co-operation between personnel, even when they are unknown to each other. In addition, these brigades have become more capable not only as they have benefited from increased resourcing, but as the troops in them are more highly trained. In Britain, France and Germany, elite brigades have simultaneously emerged as central to defence postures, although a similar process is observable in the smaller European powers.

At the same time, these brigades, especially in Britain, have begun to change in structure. They are no longer properly light infantry brigades, but have developed into hybrid, mobile brigades capable of manoeuvring on a dispersed battlefield. At the same time, they are becoming joint organisations, with horizontal relations developing into supporting assets often from the air and maritime components. Finally, in the light of new operations, these brigades have recognised the centrality of new forms of intelligence and, indeed, information operations to the conduct of their missions. Across Europe commanders and staff officers in these intervention brigades recognise that they require deep intelligence not just in terms of space, but in terms of cultural understanding. They are developing a new concept of operations. Firepower and manoeuvre will remain essential to these brigades as long as they exist; indeed, these brigades are innovating dramatically to increase both capabilities on the dispersed battle space of the twenty-first century. However, the status of traditional warfare in the armed forces seems to have obstructed the development of information warfare. Nevertheless, the empowered brigade represents a significant transformation of Europe's armed forces. The brigade's capabilities, concepts and structure have all transformed into a quite new institution. Marines and paratroopers in Europe wear a beret which associates them with forces created in the Second World War or before. That history – often invented – is central to their organisational performance, but the organisation in which those collective memories are mobilised are fundamentally different even from their predecessors in the 1980s. The rise of the empowered brigade represents an historical transformation.

Europe's armed forces are significantly smaller than they were in the Cold War, but they have not simply shrunk. The empowered brigade demonstrates that they have undergone a profound reformation in terms of capabilities, expertise and organisation. These formations often share the same names as their Cold War forebears, but they are very different kinds of organisation. For instance, the predecessors of 3 and 16 Brigades had some joint aspects: they were amphibious or airborne formations. However, the organisations were vertical and pyramidal. The commander laid down the plan and units were given specific tasks within defined constraints. Artillery batteries were parcelled out. Today, these organisations have changed shape; they have become 'hybridised' (Arquilla and Ronfeldt 1997) with horizontal networks growing out from them and linking together previously separate divisions within them. They have become joint brigades, with increased numbers of personnel from the Royal Navy and/or the RAF. A pyramidal command hierarchy has mutated into a rhizomatic structure: from a central node a series of roots develop outwards in various directions. There is certainly a chain of command. However, commanders at every level now do not merely direct action below them, but co-ordinate horizontally with other assets. They represent a profound transformation of Europe's armed forces. At the tactical level of brigades, a transition which parallels changes at the operational level is evident. At the operational level, new highly capable rapid reaction corps are appearing in each country to form a crystallising transnational military network. At the tactical level, defence resources are being concentrated on favoured elite brigades in Europe to produce nodes of military capability in each country, connected to other military assets across the services. Interestingly, these nodes of military power are increasingly interacting with similarly empowered brigades in other countries to share expertise, training opportunities and to conduct increasingly difficult operations together. In comparison with the solidity of the NATO layer-cake, a quite different military geography is appearing in Europe; a more fluid, porous transnational network of smaller, more specialised centres of military excellence.

11 The future of Europe's armed forces

Overview

Reflecting the decline of state power, the armed forces of Europe diminished in size in the course of the late twentieth century. From their apogee during the Second World War, the armed forces have steadily shrunk until they are smaller now than they have been since before the Napoleonic Wars and the levée en masse. With the massive increase in Europe's population in the intervening two centuries, Europe's armed forces are minuscule in comparison with their historic forebears. It is possible that increased strategic pressure within Europe and Afghanistan may reverse this trend, but it is unlikely. Budgetary pressures do not suggest that any augmentation of military force will be possible; politically it is unlikely that European states will be willing or able to increase defence budgets. However, the armed forces of Europe today are not simply smaller, they are fundamentally different from their mass forebears of the twentieth century. Today's forces are smaller in number than the mass forces, but in many ways they are more potent. The fundamental dynamic of European military transformation today is not so much down-sizing as concentration.

The trajectory of European military transformation is becoming clear. Europe's militaries are much smaller than their twentieth-century predecessors, but in many ways they are more potent. By concentrating resources on elite forces, they are more mobile tactically and strategically than NATO's armoured divisions. They can deploy globally but, crucially, once deployed, they are able to manoeuvre around a dispersed and relatively empty battlefield. Traditional light forces are assuming a hybrid form where even paratroopers, traditionally designed for holding strategically important static points, are increasingly vehicle-borne. Light forces must be able to manoeuvre in order to reduce their vulnerability and to influence their operating areas, even when they are numerically few. In order to manoeuvre around this new environment and to co-ordinate a diversity of assets, digital communications have become essential to Europe's armed forces today. These communications have not only

271

allowed senior commanders to interact with tactical subordinates more easily but, crucially, digital communications have facilitated horizontal communications between forces. As a result of the concentration of resources on elite, light formations, a new 'empowered' brigade has begun to emerge in Europe. This formation has replaced the armoured division as Europe's centre of military gravity. The empowered brigade consists of expert professionals capable of mobile warfare across the spectrum of conflict and assumes the form of a hybrid joint structure, linked horizontally into other formations and forces in order to exploit available assets in any particular situation.

At the operational level of planning and command, a similar process of concentration is evident. In each European country, military command is being unified in joint operation commands, such as PJHQ, Einsatzfüh-rungskommando and Centre de planification et de conduite des opéra-tions, and alongside these national operational commands, new NATO rapid reaction corps have appeared. The rapid reaction corps have acted as, or provided, personnel for in-theatre NATO commands in the Balkans and Afghanistan, giving rise to a complex command relationship. The in-theatre NATO commands, often comprised of HRF nation framework HQs, try to co-ordinate a unified campaign, while the national operational headquarters such as PJHQ or Einsatzführungskommando ensure that national caveats and preferences are enacted in-theatre. At the operational level, the command structure of the operations in which European forces are engaged is complex; it is structured by an intricate transnational operational network in which national interests predominate. Neverthe-less, despite enduring nationalism, at this operational level it is possible to identify the rise of common professional expertise in Europe which is comparable to the new tactical proficiencies which are being developed at the level of the brigades. An operational complex is emerging.

Europe's armed forces are increasingly being concentrated into empowered centres of capability and competence. Resources are being focused on these favoured institutions in order to produce a radically reformed military structure within each country. National nodes of mili-tary power are appearing. At the same time, these nodes of expertise are interacting and operating more frequently and more closely with each other. At operational and tactical levels, Europe's armed forces are con-verging on common patterns of expertise. They are seeking to develop common forms of expertise so that they can co-operate with each other more effectively. In the light of the severe budgetary restrictions placed upon them and the operational pressures which new missions have cre-ated, this transnationalisation has been identified as the optimal solution by governments and the armed forces. Europe's armed forces are organising themselves into a transnational network at operational and tactical levels. The national sovereignty and culture of the armed forces remains important and, indeed, has been strengthened by current changes; nation-states exercise control over their deployed forces more strictly than in the twentieth century, enforcing caveats which limit the risks to which they are potentially exposed. The dense transnational co-operation which has been evident in places like Musa Qala does not undermine the primacy of national affiliations. National affiliation and the nation-state remain central to the dynamics of military reform, but a quite new transnational military complex is appearing.

Decisively, this transnational European military network is appearing under the aegis of NATO. The ESDP may play a subordinate role in European military development in the next decade, but the prime institution in which this development is likely to take place is NATO. Europe's armed forces will be influenced by their communal attachment to the United States. It is unclear what path Europe's armed forces will take after 2020, and it would be unwise to suggest one, but up to then it seems almost inconceivable that European military reform will not take place within NATO, heavily influenced by the United States.

European forces no longer organise themselves to fight on a lineal battlefield in which the conventional clash of armoured forces is decisive. Rather, Europe's wars in the first decades of twenty-first century will be contested on a dispersed area of operation. In the next decade, at least, and probably into the 2020s, Afghanistan, as a major counter-insurgency operation, is likely to be the decisive theatre for Europe, unless NATO is forced to withdraw more quickly. Thereafter, and depending on the outcome in Afghanistan, it is difficult to predict in what military missions Europe will engage. Colin Gray has identified a resurgent Russia, an increasingly aggressive China or rogue states as possible threats (Gray 2006: 177, 179–84). However, even if Europe becomes involved in a limited conflict against China, Russia or another state, these conflicts will not be characterised by a return to mass industrial warfare. The geographic context will demand that even in the case of these outbreaks of state warfare, small forces will be deployed. As Edward Luttwak (1995) has noted, the twenty-first century may mark a return to limited warfare. Small state forces, fighting in coalitions, augmented by mercenaries in pursuit of limited strategic goals may characterise the future.

European frictions

In the twenty-first century, Europe's armed forces, concentrated into expert headquarters and reaction brigades, are co-operating with each other ever more closely on new missions and, above all, in Afghanistan. A transnational military network, dependent upon and overlain by US influence, is evident in Europe today which contrasts markedly with the international order of the Cold War. Britain, France and Germany are at the heart of this nascent network. However, especially in assessing the prospects in Afghanistan, it is necessary to recognise the frictions which transnational interdependence has created and the considerable obstacles to genuine co-operation between Europe's armed forces.

There are evident strategic differences between Britain, France and Germany which impede European integration even under a US framework. Britain, the Netherlands, Denmark and the Central and Eastern European states, which are new EU and NATO members, are primarily transatlanticist in orientation; they prioritise NATO and, therefore, whatever the misgivings of their publics, Afghanistan. France has a quite different strategic position. Although it is re-integrating in NATO, they remain the most autonomous European military power, prioritising stabilisation missions in former colonies in Africa. Moreover, despite its forced rapprochement with the United States, France would still nominally like to pursue a European defence community in which its national voice would have an overwhelming say. Germany prioritises its NATO relations with the United States, but in order to sustain political relations with France it has also been central to the EU defence initiatives. Yet although apparently in a middle position between France and Britain, Germany's situation is quite distinctive. Appealing to the constitution and to the historic memories of the Second World War which inform public opinion of foreign and defence policy very strongly, Germany has been a reluctant military actor in the last decade. It has been forced into contributing to Afghanistan, but refuses to deploy troops, except for its special forces, into the south of the country.

The alternate strategic orientations of Britain, France and Germany are reflected in the intensely different military cultures of their forces; these are no less divergent. These cultures may have a significant bearing on the outcome in Afghanistan and for the possibilities of Europe's transnational military network. Britain's armed forces, for instance, maintain a quite different approach to other European forces. British defence doctrine highlighted a 'war fighting ethos' as one of its central military principles: 'A war fighting ethos, as distinct from a purely professional one, is absolutely fundamental to all those in the British Armed Forces' (JWP 01 2008: 5.7). This ethos distinguishes the armed forces from civilian organisations: 'Not only do they [service personnel] all accept the legal right and duty to apply lethal force, they also accept a potentially unlimited liability to lay down their lives in the performance of their duties' (JWP 01 2008:

5.7). *British Defence Doctrine* recognises that the armed forces are involved in many other operations and activities than combat, but this fact should not obscure their fundamental purpose: 'Notwithstanding the proportion of their career engaged in duties other than war fighting, it is essential that all Servicemen and Servicewomen develop and retain the physical and moral fortitude to fight' (JWP 01 2008: 5.7–8). Oriented to combat, Britain's armed forces recruit, train and, crucially, promote their personnel on the basis of their performance of this fundamental mission. As elite forces have become more important in the last decade – and proportionately more senior commanders have come from these forces (Macdonald 2004) – this predilection for high intensity combat may have actually increased. This distinctively martial orientation distinguishes Britain's armed forces from others in Europe and influences what kind of missions they are dispatched on and the way they conceive these missions.

The war fighting ethos of British military culture has structured the Helmand campaign in a manner which may militate against success there. From the outset, British commanders prioritised aggressive actions against the Taliban that they took to be a sign of success, rather than seeking the more modest and less spectacular route of securing the population. Thus, when 16 Air Assault Brigade deployed to Helmand in April 2006, they did not secure the Lashkar Gar triangle as they planned, but dispersed into platoon houses across the province. There, they were engaged in the most intense fighting in which many opponents (Taliban and otherwise) were killed. 16 Air Assault Brigade, actualising the collective memory of the Parachute Regiment, effectively re-created a series of minor 'Arnhems' across the province with paratroopers fighting against desperate odds. The institutional myth of the Parachute Regiment was re-vivified and the Regiment earned a Victoria Cross[1] for its efforts. Subsequent British forces have re-affirmed this pattern of high intensity, but under-resourced action. For instance, at the end of his tour in October 2008, Brigadier Mark Carleton-Smith, commander of the Helmand Task Force, announced to the dismay of senior generals: 'We're not going to win this war. It's about reducing it to a manageable level of insurgency that's not a strategic threat and can be managed by the Afghan army' (Lamb 2009). Despite the controversy which surrounded his comments, his judgement seemed to be broadly sustainable. Yet it did not prevent him from declaring in June 2008 that the new 'precise, surgical' tactics

---

[1] The Victoria Cross is the highest award for gallantry. Corporal Bryan Budd was awarded the VC posthumously for his actions against the Taliban just outside Sangin. Although an individual award, decorations are deeply political since they are employed as a metric of the operational effectiveness of a unit and have become the basis of investment or cuts.

had killed scores of insurgent leaders and made it extremely difficult for Pakistan-based Taliban leaders to prosecute the campaign. Indeed, Carleton-Smith claimed that very effective targeted 'decapitation operations' had removed 'several echelons of commanders', leading to 'a seminal moment in dislocating' their operations: '"I can therefore judge the Taliban insurgency a failure at the moment"' (Harding 2006).[2] Media reports can be distorting, but the dissonance between the two statements is striking and requires some interpretation. The obvious one is simply that Carleton-Smith's over-optimism in June was punctured by the end of a tour which had involved the death of over thirty soldiers.

There is another explanation. While in command of tactical forces, Carleton-Smith was encouraged to prioritise intense kinetic activity, including the tasking of special forces (the SBS) to kill key leaders such as Mullah Dadullah. This tactically successful activity in and of itself reassured him as a commander that he had seized the initiative and was prosecuting the campaign. Away from the theatre of operations, however, and away from the pressures of British military culture and command structures, he was able to take a more reflective view of the situation. Such an assessment in-theatre might have questioned the wisdom and purpose of 'decapitating' leaders who might be particularly influential in achieving a political settlement. The British approach may be problematic in itself. It also potentially dissuades European allies, especially Germany, from co-operating with the British and committing to Afghanistan fully. They fear that they may be dragged into an unwinnable war which the British have created.

The French also have a distinctive military culture. Like the British forces, French troops are willing to engage in intense military operations in which casualties are taken and inflicted. However, the planning and command of these operations is quite different from the British. The French retain a highly dirigiste command culture which impedes operational planning and initiative. This is demonstrated at the highest level with the operational authority wielded by the Chef d'état-major over the Centre de planification et de conduite des opérations. Partly as a result of this dirigisme and the lack of command authority invested lower down the chain, the French have adopted a distinctive approach to stabilisation operations. They emphasise the necessity of concentrating forces and having overwhelming numbers on a counter-insurgency mission:

---

[2] Interestingly, his predecessor made very similar arguments during and after 16 Air Assault Brigade's initial tour in 2006. He claimed that he had dealt the Taliban a decisive tactical blow. Yet three years later, they were still able to fight the British at any time of their choosing.

When you are deployed, whether you disperse or not depends on how your relations with the population are. If you are in Africa and the population has agreed to your presence, you can be dispersed with little insecurity. In Afghanistan, if it is not high intensity but a stabilisation operation, if you disperse it can be good. You stay in contact with population. But if the Taliban get into a village and you speak to them, the Taliban will kill them as revenge. If you want to prevent that you must be in all the villages. However, to be in each village, you need many more forces than you need when you are dispersed in Bosnia. There, with a relatively benign situation, you can disperse them. In a country against you: No, you cannot. When you are at high intensity, you can disperse as long as you are mobile. For instance, when you are fighting high intensity conventional conflict against an enemy you can identify, it is possible to disperse. Once in the second phase of an operation – looking for guerrillas – you cannot disperse, however. Dispersion of fire in remote situations is possible – but the opportunities for dispersal are not so frequent as people often assume on current operations.[3]

The point is certainly valid. One of the fundamental faults of British operations in Basra and in Helmand has been insufficient numbers of troops. However, the emphasis on numbers may also be a reflection of an unsubtlety in terms of planning and operational focus. Clearly, in Africa, where the French have extensive experience, this system has worked for them, but as their force numbers decline and as they commit more heavily to Afghanistan, it may be necessary for them to reconsider their current command culture and how they generate adequate force ratios.

The difficulty of European military integration is compounded by Germany. The Bundeswehr represents an interesting historical case. During the Cold War, the Bundeswehr provided two corps for the Central Front in Europe which were widely regarded as the best formations in NATO: 'In terms of the quality of its fighting forces, it is widely recognised among NATO military leaders that the German Army is the best in Europe, the Soviets included. Regarding equipment, the German and American Armies are the best equipped in NATO' (Mearsheimer 1982: 23). German officers are still among the best trained in Europe and their staff skills are highly regarded. Yet the Bundeswehr is now accused of becoming professionally disorientated, lacking military leadership and is viewed with dismay by many British officers. It is regarded as a hollow force, constrained willingly or unwillingly by domestic politics, history and a highly educated but timid officer corps:

Think of Germany. We used to admire them. They had great kit. Their senior officers in the Bundeswehr in early days were still from the German military caste, with experience or fathers with experience in the Wehrmacht and with

---

[3] Brigadier general, commander, 9 brigade légère blindée de marine, personal interview, 13 November 2003.

grandfathers who fought in World War I. But that has gone; they have become almost pacifist. They are flailing around.[4]

Although the reference to the Wehrmacht will be politically unpalatable to German officers, given its complicity with Nazism, the major general's perspective is not unusual. There is a common belief among British officers that as the post-War generation with Second World War experience retired from the Bundeswehr in the 1970s, the force has declined as a significant military entity:

It is the younger brigadiers and colonels who are more risk averse. Something happened in the Bundeswehr in the 70s and 80s in terms of ethical and legal training. General Ramms and the old guys are more active. For instance, you could imagine . . .[5] in a grey uniform. But the younger generation are risk averse.[6]

It is not only British officers who note this shift in military competence and confidence. General Py noted it during his time as ISAF commander: 'For instance, you ask a UK Company to break into a house; they will do it. A German company; they will not. Germany will not change. Some nations do not want non-national responsibility.'[7]

One of the most obvious examples here is the response of the German commander of KFOR, General Kammerhoff, to the Albanian riots in 2004. Reports recorded that he retreated into his office in the face of this pressure, and could not be called upon to direct operations even though rapid response was required. Uncorroborated reports suggest that SACEUR was close to removing him from post and, indeed, were it not for the political implications of removing an Alliance partner's commander, it seems likely that such an ignominy would have befallen General Holger Kammerhoff. David Binder described Kammerhoff and his staff as the 'cowards of Prizren':

From what I hear and read from the battleground that is Kosovo, the German contingent of KFOR 'peacekeepers' is led by men who plainly lack bravery. I don't extend that characterisation to the ordinary Landser; they are only following orders, as one would expect of German soldiers. I mean the officers. We are talking about the commanders of the 3,600 Bundeswehr soldiers stationed mostly in south-western Kosovo, with headquarters in the ancient city of Prizren. Specifically General Holger Kammerhoff, the KFOR commander, and his deputies. (Binder 2004)

[4] British major general, personal interview, March 2006.
[5] Name withheld: former German four-star general.
[6] British lieutenant general, personal interview, March 2007.
[7] General Py, commander ISAF IV, personal interview, 14 December 2005.

The example of Kammerhoff could be dismissed as an extreme case. He was under extreme pressure in an unfamiliar environment where political direction was lacking. Yet his inability to command decisively is reflected elsewhere among German senior officers. During the same riots in Kosovo on 17 March 2004, a Bundeswehr sergeant was tasked with protecting a Serbian monastery, the Monastery of Angels, near Prizren from Albanian rioters. Confronted by a large crowd, he ordered his platoon to escort the monks from the monastery to safety, allowing the Albanians to burn the UNESCO World Heritage site to the ground. While not perhaps ideal, the sergeant's decision might be interpreted as a reaction to a complex and stressful situation:

Here is what Father Sava Janjic, spokesman of the Decani Monastery, had to say this week: 'Germans definitely did not do anything to protect a single Orthodox church in Prizren. Demonstrations in Mitrovica began in the morning of March 17. They could have deployed their forces in Prizren to prevent escalation of violence but they remained in their base with very few soldiers outside. When the mob gathered in the streets of Prizren they say that they could not protect the Bishop's residence from Molotov cocktails and had to evacuate the priest. Afterwards the church was burned. The Seminary, the residence, Serbian homes were in flames. But they still had time to block the road which goes along the gorge of Bistrica river to the Holy Archangels Monastery ... The crowd ... headed several hours later after burning the Prizren holy sites towards the monastery which is 5 kilometres to the south. They did nothing ... When the crowd came to the monastery they only evacuated the monks and let Albanians burn the monastery ... The German flag over the monastery is still fluttering intact.' (Binder 2004)

However, in commenting on this action, Major General Dieter-Walter Löser affirmed the sergeant's decision not as a flawed but necessary act, but, rather, as the operationally and ethically correct course of action:

The sergeant major in the first instance had conducted himself bravely. At the same time, he showed, in an unavoidable situation, courage and a sense of responsibility not to follow his order to the letter, whatever the consequences. Not least he showed a special ability to make a moral judgement, determining appropriate duty given the situation, between two mutually competing duties. (Löser 2006: 11)

For Löser, the sergeant's decision was compatible with the Bundeswehr's concept of Innere Führung. The sergeant had fulfilled his duty of protecting the monks without escalating the level of violence. Yet, clearly, although not necessarily specifically part of their orders, the protection of the medieval monastery from criminal destruction was minimally an implied task. Löser's defence of the sergeant is instructive. It demonstrates the way in which senior German officers conveniently redefine their mission in order to justify the lowest level of engagement. More critically, this process of redefinition absolves commanders of the responsibility to act. Within the Bundeswehr, there is a recognition of the weakness of contemporary command culture. For instance, the disgraced Brigadier General Günzel, who has been critical of the concept of Innere Führung, noted that the incident at Prizren should be interpreted as a fundamental lack of command authority by German officers. It was unforgivable that a sergeant should have to make a decision of this significance. Günzel concludes simply: 'I don't blame the brave sergeant major. He made a difficult decision, for which he was unprepared, and which perhaps prevented something worse. But – where were his superiors?' (Günzel 2006: 78). British officers have noted this unwillingness of Bundeswehr officers to take command responsibility in a number of settings. Indeed, even on exercises they note that German officers will typically exaggerate the time it takes for their command to perform a function in order to ensure that they could never be embarrassed by failure.

The current weakness of the Bundeswehr's command culture does not seem to be the result of individual commanders, it is more general. Rather, institutional factors seem to be at work. There is such close political oversight of the Bundeswehr that it is very difficult for German officers to display the independence which is typical of British officer down to a very low level – or which they were able to demonstrate in the conventional context of the Cold War. The extent of this political oversight may itself be a product of more profound changes in German society. British officers claim that the current decline of command culture is a generational product, the result of the retirement of officers with memories of the Wehrmacht. The generational effect may be more complex. In the 1980s, sociologists noted a 'memory boom' especially in relation to the First and Second World Wars. These wars became a renewed focus of national commemoration and contemplation. The Holocaust, in particular, became the focus of intense investigation and, having been repressed by a generation of Jews who suffered it, the Shoah was used by Zionist activists and Israel more generally as a legitimating narrative after 1967. Germany seems to have been deeply affected by this memory boom around the Holocaust, especially after reunification. Reunification was greeted with euphoria, but it also problematically recalled the disasters of the mid-twentieth century when Germany had last been united. Accordingly, the re-interpretation of the Second World War has been critical to recent German culture as Germans today try to reconcile themselves with a barbarous past in order to establish themselves in a new Europe.[8] The Holocaust has been at the crux of this collective process

---

[8]   An interesting example of this is W. G. Sebald's contentious work (2004) on Allied bombing of German cities and the debates about whether this constituted a holocaust in itself.

of remembrance and reconciliation, and it might be possible to argue that the Holocaust has been institutionalised in Germany as the cultural vehicle of reunification. Reunification is possible so long as Germans unite around a memory of collective guilt and responsibility. The visit of President Kohl to Auschwitz on 15 November 1989 and the inauguration of the Holocaust memorial in May 2005 (sixty years after the defeat of Nazism) in Berlin, the new capital of Germany and the site of the Final Solution's ratification, have promoted the death camps as a unifying national memory for Germans today. Whereas Adenauer declared that Bonn was a convenient beginning for the Federal Republic because it was 'a city without a past', present-day Germans have had to reconcile themselves to the history of their new capital (Wise: 1998: 23). The Holocaust unites East and West Germany around a common traumatic experience for which they share collective guilt, enjoining a quite different contribution to European history.

The Bundeswehr may be situated within this complex culture settlement. In a reunified Germany, the horrors of Nazism and, therefore, the horrors of German military power are more emotive than they were throughout the Cold War. The basis of German unification may have actually undermined not only the status of the Bundeswehr, but the professional self-conception of its officer corps. The very prosecution of their profession is almost inevitably associated with atrocities – and their repudiation – which are now at the centre of national self-definitions. There are a number of examples in which German officers have displayed a sensitivity towards military action regarded as extraordinary by their peers. The cultural basis of German reunification seems to have played a role in transforming a force which was regarded by many as the best in Europe to one which seems unwilling and incapable of engaging in military activity. It fundamentally contravenes their national self-concept and sets them in opposition to their peers, who find their sensitivity hyperbolic and inappropriate.

The three major military powers in Europe demonstrate profoundly different professional cultures and strategic orientations which obstruct their co-operation. Of course, these differences are multiplied if other European forces are considered. Consequently, it is unclear precisely what kind of European military integration will emerge out of Afghanistan. Some co-operative transnational network may appear where European professionals are united around common practices. However, given the enduring national differences between just the three major European powers, that network will necessarily be riven with frictions and tensions. Nevertheless, despite the inherently problematic character of European military integration, the emergent transnational network demonstrates an important, perhaps, historical point. This network differs fundamentally from the international structure of NATO during the Cold War in which nations, unified strategically, operated mainly alone. There is evident convergence on common doctrine, concepts and practices and genuinely close co-operation in-theatre across national borders, inconceivable during the Cold War. It is perhaps precisely a function of working together ever more closely that the differences between Europe's armed forces become more obvious and operationally serious. The frictions within the transnational network may be evidence of its integration, rather than fission. In his analysis of NATO, this is precisely Thies' argument; intense argument can be a sign of close interdependence and, therefore, underlying unity. Governments and the armed forces may be increasingly arguing with each other because they are co-operating ever more deeply. As Europe's forces become more interdependent, the growing recognition of the evident differences between them may actually be a sign of integration. Differences which were irrelevant and unnoticed in the past have now become operationally significant. A necessary stage of convergence is an increasing sensitivity to difference.

Afghanistan: Europe's great game?

There have been a series of crises in relation to Kosovo, in March 2004 and, most recently, in February 2008, when Kosovar independence was announced. At this point, SACEUR designated Kosovo as NATO's main effort. Yet, Kosovo, while periodically problematic, carries none of the strategic seriousness of Afghanistan. No one has suggested that NATO might be defeated in Kosovo. Similarly, the EU will not be defeated in either Bosnia or Chad; the missions are not sufficiently big or demanding for that outcome. Yet strategic defeat is a realistic prospect in Afghanistan. NATO is involved in a militarily dangerous mission of great political difficulty. In July 2006, soon after having assumed command of ISAF, General Richards was confident about NATO's mission in Afghanistan. By November 2007, his interpretation of the situation had changed and his optimism publicly darkened. Strategic defeat in Afghanistan was eminently possible unless Europe could commit sufficient troops and resources to complement the contribution of the United States. Against all expectations, Afghanistan is likely to play a crucial role in the development of Europe's armed forces in the next decade at both the operational and tactical levels.

For most European forces, the ISAF mission is the first time they have deployed to Afghanistan; France and Germany played no historical role in that country. For the British, it represents a fourth adventure in this country, the first two of which were disastrous. In November 1841, Sir Alexander Burnes and his aides were killed in Kabul by a mob incited by Mohammed Akbar Khan. British forces under the ineffectual General Elphinstone failed to react, engaging instead in a series of negotiations with Akbar Khan (Hopkirk 2006: 239–56). Overly anxious about the threat he faced, General Elphinstone made a truce with Akbar. Bizarrely he agreed to relinquish his defensible position in Kabul and place himself at the mercy of Akbar's forces whom he believed would allow him to retreat unscathed to Jalalabad. In the event, almost immediately after the start of the retreat from Kabul on 6 January 1842, Elphinstone's force was subjected to attacks which became more severe as the march continued. Notoriously, of the 16,000 soldiers, women and children who began the journey, only one survivor, Dr Brydon, managed to reach Jalalabad on 13 January 1842. The fate of this force caused outrage in Britain, which found its expression in the famous oil painting of the last stand of the 44th Regiment of Foot on Gandamak Hill. Surrounded by their dead, the last members of the regiment stand nobly together in oblique reference to Waterloo, poised with bayonets fixed, as Afghan tribesmen, lurking in the background, gather for their final assault.

Although large losses are possible in Afghanistan today, especially if the Taliban destroy a NATO transport plane, a massacre of European forces like the annihilation of Britain's 44th Regiment is unlikely; another Gandamak Hill is improbable. European forces avoid the risks to which the incompetent Elphinstone exposed his garrison and have the benefits of US airpower to prevent a major rout of ground forces. Nevertheless, a comparable strategic defeat is possible. NATO could fail to stabilise Afghanistan in the short to medium term. The trajectory of such a defeat can be envisaged. The Taliban insurgency begins to inflict sufficient casualties on NATO that the political will for the campaign begins to erode. At the same time, as levels of violence increase against NATO and Karzai's government, development and governance reforms fail to materialise, alienating the population. At this point, warlords currently aligned to Karzai and the West, might reappraise their alliances and begin to support the Taliban overtly or covertly. The Karzai government would then falter and collapse. Such a collapse would shatter the Afghan National Police and the Afghan National Army, factions of which would become part of the insurgency. At this point, the security situation would deteriorate rapidly and NATO would begin to lose many more troops. It is uncertain what the United States would do in the face of this situation; they have become inured to taking casualties in Iraq and have identified Afghanistan as strategically critical. However, in the face of mounting casualties, European countries might be forced to withdraw, precipitating a collapse of at least the NATO mission in Afghanistan. As a result, NATO – and Europe – would have to endure its own retreat from Kabul. It would seem almost inevitable that such a defeat would have major, negative repercussions for NATO and European military integration.

Despite the frequent jeremiads, there is another future for Afghanistan and NATO and, therefore, European forces there. On 25 June 1950, North Korea invaded the Republic of Korea, routing the weak and surprised Korean and American forces, until they were surrounded in a small perimeter around Pusan. A UN mandate condemned the action and, under US leadership, an international UN force was assembled and deployed to Korea, including a significant European contribution from Britain, France, Belgium, Greece and Turkey. These European nations committed themselves to Korea not out of direct national interest, but in an attempt to sustain their alliance to the United States. Above all, they committed themselves to Korea in order to persuade the United States to maintain its military presence in Europe as part of NATO.[9] The strategic motivation is very similar in Afghanistan.

The Korean War was a limited conflict involving joint and combined operations across the spectrum of conflict. While the decisive operations were directed against the North Korean and Chinese armies, UN forces were engaged throughout in a bitter counter-insurgency campaign against North Korean guerrilla forces. Moreover, multinational forces were engaged in high intensity actions at the lowest level. The Belgian battalion fought alongside the British at the Battle of the Imjin in April 1951. Significantly, the French, despite their subsequent reluctance to commit themselves to NATO, distinguished themselves in the campaign. A French battalion was deployed under the command of pseudonymous, Ralph Monclar, who was, in fact, French Lieutenant General Magrin-Vernerey, the decorated First World War veteran (Appleman 1990: 210; Blair 1987: 664–8). The French battalion was integrated into an American brigade and was heavily engaged in numerous actions throughout the war. During the Thunderbolt Offensive, the French held Hill 453 under intense pressure, for which action Monclar was awarded the Presidential Unit Citation. Europe's armed forces during the Cold War were substantially forged from the Korean War, but the conflict usefully points to the potential future of European military operations. Europe's armed forces are once again committing themselves to a multinational

---

[9] Interestingly, the Korean War was directly responsible for the creation of the Bundeswehr and the incorporation of the German Federal Republic into NATO. The war convinced the United States that Europe could be defended effectively only with the contribution of West Germany.

expeditionary campaign. The Korean War offers other salutary lessons which may be relevant for European military development. The Armistice which ended the Korean War was signed on 27 July 1953. UN troops still patrol the 38th Parallel today. It would seem unwise to assume that Afghanistan represents a lesser commitment for European forces today. The Afghan campaign – if successful – may require the presence of European peacekeepers or trainers for over half a century, as it has in Korea. Yet it would seem certain that success in Afghanistan would require a commitment of at least a further ten years.

Strategic success in Afghanistan is possible, though difficult. This success would not in this case amount to the sometimes utopian rhetoric which occasionally punctuates US pronouncements on Afghanistan. Afghanistan will not be reformed into a Western industrial democracy even if long-term stability is possible. The best which NATO can hope for is a return to the kind of stability which existed in the mid-twentieth century. Afghanistan would be governed by a recognised central ruler with enduring alliances with locally dominant warlords in the regions and provinces. Minimising, but not completely eliminating tribal and ethnic conflict, this 'neo-feudal' order would create political conditions of sufficient stability that infrastructure could be rebuilt and developed. In this context, significant economic advance could occur, including the exploitation of tourism which was a significant and growing source of income until the present Afghan War began in 1979. If NATO successfully encouraged these conditions, forces could be gradually withdrawn possibly by 2020, allowing the Afghan government and its allies to maintain political order autonomously.

Such an outcome would depend upon the deployment of much higher troop numbers than are presently in-theatre. By December 2009, there were approximately 80,000 NATO troops in Afghanistan: nearly 40,000 were American, 3,000 Canadian and approximately 22,000 European troops, including 9,000 British, 4,000 German and 3,000 French. In 2010, the United States increased its troop numbers in Afghanistan by a further 30,000. European nations have agreed to contribute a further 7,000 troops, though the Dutch withdrew their 2,000 troops in August 2010. The increase in European forces was welcomed by General McChrystal, the then NATO ISAF commander but, ideally, Europe would deploy many more troops to the country and especially to the south. Indeed, given the relative size of Europe's armed forces in comparison with the United States, it is an indictment that Europe has so few troops in a theatre which European governments have themselves designated as strategically decisive. The Bundeswehr is particularly backward here, since it has deployed just under 7,000 (including 2,500 to Kosovo and 4,000 to Afghanistan) from a force of over 250,000.[10] More importantly, as a recent official Bundeswehr study has shown, 90 per cent of Bundeswehr personnel in Afghanistan do not leave their bases at all during their four-month deployments. Certainly, the failure of Europe to commit forces to Afghanistan increases the likelihood of a strategic defeat. European governments and voters have sometimes withheld from Afghanistan on the grounds that it was part of a neo-conservative war waged by George W. Bush. With the liberal and charismatic Obama in the White House, it may become increasingly difficult for European states to fail to deliver their commitments to Afghanistan, especially since Obama has explicitly called for European support.

It is unclear whether NATO will follow the USSR in being defeated in Afghanistan or not; it is not clear whether NATO will be compelled to leave this theatre in the next two years by an insurgent force or whether it will leave some time after 2020 of its own volition. These two outcomes will dramatically influence the long-term trajectory of European military transformation. If NATO achieves its aims in Afghanistan, it is likely that the current trajectory of European military reform will continue. The Afghan mission will require expert professional forces capable of bringing effects to bear on a dispersed operating area; they will need to be highly skilled, mobile and digitalised. They will, in short, need to co-ordinate not only with their own national forces but with other allies, above all the United States which will provide most of the air support. The current trend towards transnational military networks is likely to be affirmed and reinforced. Europe's forces will continue to concentrate investment and capability on their light, elite brigades which are capable of strategic and tactical mobility. Co-operative links between these organisations in terms of training and operations is likely to continue. In this context and especially in the light of France's historic ambivalence towards NATO and Afghanistan, Nicolas Sarkozy's decision to commit additional French troops to the theatre is deeply significant.

At the same time, the rapid reaction corps are likely to become more important as concentrations of command and planning competence. It is unlikely that one of these rapid reaction corps will take command of the whole ISAF mission as ARRC did in 2006. Political realities are likely to

---

[10] www.bundeswehr.de/portal/a/bwde/kcxml/04_Sj9SPykssy0xPLMnMz0vM0Y_QjzK Ld443DgoESYGZASH6kTCxoJRUfV-P_NxUfW_9AP2C3IhyR0dFRQD-G0VU /delta/base64xml/L2dJQSEvUUt3QS80SVVFLzZfQ180MkQ!?yw_contentURL=% 2FC1256EF4002AED30%2FW264VFT2439INFODE%2Fcontent.jsp.

prevent such an arrangement; the United States is likely to prefer a composite US-led headquarters in Kabul rather than a European corps headquarters. However, expert staff elements from the rapid reaction corps will deploy to Afghanistan. The German–Netherlands Corps deployed a significant proportion of its staff to ISAF HQ in 2009. It is also conceivable that the rapid reaction corps will provide planning and command staff for the two European-dominated regional commands in the north and west and, possibly, in the South-West. Indeed, at the end of 2010, the ARRC is providing a core of staff officers for NATO's new ISAF Joint Command in Kabul. A successful Afghan mission, possibly lasting for another decade, is likely to affirm the current trajectory of military transformation. The headquarters and tactical forces deployed recurrently on this operation will be increasingly favoured in terms of defence investment. They are likely to become increasingly dominant centres of military competence and capability and will converge on shared patterns of expertise with their European partners. A European transnational military network is likely to crystallise out of the Afghan deployment, if the campaign is successful.

Strategic defeat in Afghanistan in the next decade points to a different future for Europe's armed forces. With defeat in Afghanistan, US commitment to NATO is likely to wane. Rather than a primarily military organisation, the Alliance might become a forum of political discussion and co-ordination. Domestically, defeat in Afghanistan is likely to undermine the professional confidence and public legitimacy of Europe's armed forces and question the interventionist strategy of European states; transnational co-operation is, at this point, likely to become less desirable. European armed forces are likely to be retrenched to territorial defence roles on a national basis. Dense transnational collaboration is likely to diminish rather than increase in this context. Failure in Afghanistan is likely to undermine European military integration. In this context, Europe's armed forces are likely to return to some limited territorial and internal security mission. Although success in Afghanistan will be an ambiguous, problematic and perhaps distant event, it seems the more likely outcome at this point. As in Iraq, it seems probable that NATO, Europe and the international community will eventually define success in very generous terms in order to minimise the negative political implications of the campaign. Consequently, Afghanistan may, like the Korean War at the beginning of the Cold War, promote European military integration under and within NATO. If it does so, the most likely future for Europe's armed forces is as part of a transnational network consisting of concentrations of military power in each country which co-operate ever more closely with each other and converge on increasingly common professional concepts and practices.

Bibliography

Adam, Gordon and Ben-Ari, Guy 2006. *Transforming European Militaries: Coalition Operations and the Technology Gap.* London: Routledge.

Adshead, Robin 1987. 'Exercise "Certain Strike"', *Armed Forces* 6(12) December: 568–73.

Alexander, Michael and Garden, Timothy 2001. 'The Arithmetic of Defence Policy', *International Affairs* 77(3) July: 509–29.

Allied Joint Publications AJP-5 2006. *Allied Joint Doctrine for Operational Planning.* Washington, DC: NATO.

AJP-01 2002. *Allied Joint Doctrine.* Washington, DC: NATO.

Ambrose, Stephen 2001. *Band of Brothers.* Alresford: Pocket Books.

1997. *Citizen Soldiers.* New York: Touchstone.

Amin, Ash (ed.) 1995. *Post-Fordism: A Reader.* Oxford: Blackwell.

Appadurai, Arjan 1996. *Modernity at Large: Cultural Dimensions of Globalization.* London: University of Minnesota Press.

Appleman, Roy 1990. *Ridgway Duels for Korea.* College Station, TX: Texas A&M University Press.

Arkin, William 1978. 'Military Socialization and Masculinity', *Journal of Social Issues* 34(1): 151–66.

Arquilla, John and Ronfeldt, David 1997. *In Athena's Camp.* Santa Monica, CA: RAND Publishing.

Avant, Deborah 2005. *The Market for Force.* Cambridge University Press.

1994. *Political Institutions and Military Change.* Ithaca, NY: Cornell University Press.

Bagayoko, Niagale 2005. 'Les politiques européenes de prévention et de cestion des conflits en afrique subsaharienne', *Le Champs de Mars* 16(2): 93–111.

Bagnall, General Sir Nigel 1984. 'Concepts of Land/Air Operations in the Central Region: I', *RUSI Journal of the Royal United Services Institute for Defence Studies* 129(3): 59–62.

Bald, Detlef 2005. *Die Bundeswehr.* Munich: Beck, 2005.

Barbé, Esther and Johansson-Nogués, Elisabeth 2008. 'Victims of "Friendly Fire"? The NRF, the EU BG and Contested Identity Constructions within the Transatlantic Community', *European Security* 17(2): 295–314.

Barthes, Roland 1972. *Mythologies.* London: Cape.

Bartov, Omar 1992. *Hitler's Army: Soldiers, Nazis and War in the Third Reich.* Oxford University Press.

Baudrillard, Jean 1995. *The Gulf War Did Not Take Place*. Bloomington, IN: Indiana University Press.

Beattie, Doug 2008. *An Ordinary Soldier*. London: Simon & Schuster.

Bellamy, Christopher 1996. *Knights in White Armour: The New Art of War and Peace*. London: Hutchinson.

Ben-Ari, Eyal 2001. 'Tests of Soldiering, Trials of Manhood', in E. Ben-Ari and Z. Rosenheck (eds.), *War, Politics and Society in Israel*. New Brunswick, NJ: Transaction Publishers, 239–67.

Ben-Shalom, Uzi, Lehrer, Zeev and Ben-Ari, Eyal 2005. 'Cohesion During Military Operations: A Field Study on Combat Units in the Al-Aqsa Intifada', *Armed Forces and Society* 32(1): 63–79.

Berdal, Mats 2003. 'How "New" are "New Wars"? Global Economic Change and the Study of Civil War', *Global Governance* 9: 477–502.

Berdal Mats and Keen, David 1997. 'Violence and Economic Agendas in Civil Wars', *Millennium*, 26(3): 795–818.

Biddle, Steven 2005. 'Allies, Airpower and Modern Warfare: the Afghan Model in Afghanistan and Iraq', *International Security* 30(3): 161–76.

2004. *Military Power*. Princeton University Press.

2002. *Afghanistan and the Future of Warfare: Implications for Army and Defense Policy*. Carlisle Barracks, PA: Strategic Studies Institute.

Binder, David 2004. 'The Cowards of Prizren', 27 May 2004, available at: www.slobodan-milosevic.org/news/db052704.htm.

Binnendijk, Hans and Kugler, Richard 2002. 'Transforming European Forces', *Survival* 44(3): 117–32.

Biscop, Sven 2009. 'Change Against a Background of Continuity: The Emerging EU Strategic Culture', Paper presented to ISA Annual Convention.

2005. *The European Security Strategy*. Aldershot: Ashgate.

Biscop, Sven and Andersen, Jan Joel (eds.) 2008. *The EU and the European Security Strategy*. London: Routledge.

Bishop, Patrick 2007. *3 PARA*. London: Harper Press.

Bitzinger, Richard 2003. *Towards a Brave New Arms Industry*. Oxford University Press.

Blair, Charles 1987. *The Forgotten War: America in Korea 1950–53*. New York: Times Books.

Böene, Bernard 2003. 'The Military as a Tribe among Tribes', in G. Caforio (ed.), *Handbook of the Sociology of the Military*. London: Kluwer/Plenum, 167–85.

Bogaards, M. and Crepaz, M. 2002. 'Consociational Interpretation of the European Union', *European Union Politics* 3(3): 357–81.

Booth, B., Kestnbaum, M. and Segal, D. 2001. 'Are Post-Cold War Militaries Postmodern?', *Armed Forces and Society* 27(3): 319–42.

Bourdieu, Pierre 1977. *Outline of a Theory of Practice*. Cambridge University Press.

Bourke, Joanna 2000. *An Intimate History of Killing*. London: Granta.

Bowen, J. 1996. 'The Myth of Global Ethnic Conflict', *Journal of Democracy* 7(4) October: 3–14.

Bramley, Vincent 1991. *Excursion to Hell*. London: Pan Books.

Bratton, Patrick 2002. 'France and the Revolution in Military Affairs', *Contemporary Security Policy* 23(2): 87–112.

Bronfield, Saul 2008. 'Did Tradoc Outmanoeuvre the Manoeuvrists? A Comment', *War and Society* 27(2): 111–25.

Brummer, Klaus 2007. 'Superficial, not Substantial: The Ambiguity of Public Support for Europe's Security and Defence Policy', *European Security* 16(2): 183–201.

Bundesministerium der Verteidigung (Ministry of Defence) 2006. *White Paper 2006 on German Security Policy and the Future of the Bundeswehr*, available at: www. bmvg.de/fileserving/PortalFiles/C1256EF40036B05B/W26UWAMT995INFO EN/W_2006_eng_DS.pdf?yw_repository=youatweb.

2004. *Grundzüge der Konzeption der Bundeswehr*, retrieved 9 February 2005, available at: www.bundeswehr.de/misc/pdf/broschueren/broschuere_kdb.pdf.

Burk, James 2003a. 'Military Mobilization in Modern Western Societies', in G. Caforio (ed.), *Handbook of the Sociology of the Military*. London: Kluwer/ Plenum, 111–30.

(ed.) 2003b. *The Adaptive Military*. London: Transaction.

Buzan, Barry, Kelstrup, M., Lemaitre, P., Tromer, E. and Waever, Ole 1990. *The European Security Order Recast*. London: Pinter.

Byman, D. and Waxman, M. 2000. 'Kosovo and the Great Air Power Debate', *International Security* 24(4): 5–38.

Caforio, Giuseppe (ed.) 2003. *Handbook of the Sociology of the Military*. London: Kluwer/Plenum.

Cameron, Fraser 1999. *The Foreign and Security Policy of the European Union: Past, Present and Future*. Sheffield: Sheffield Academic Press.

Castells, Manuel 2000. 'Global Informational Capitalism', in D. Held and A. McGrew (eds.), *The Global Transformation Reader*. Cambridge: Polity, 311–34.

1998. *The Information Age: Economy, Society and Culture. Vol. 1: The Rise of Network Society*. Oxford: Blackwell.

1996. *The Informational City*. Oxford: Blackwell.

Centre de Doctrine d'Emploi des Forces 2005. *Doctrine General Review: Ongoing Reflections on the Future of Land Operations*. Paris: CDEF.

Chambliss, Daniel 1989. 'The Mundanity of Excellence: An Ethnographic Report on Stratification and Olympic Swimmers', *Sociological Theory* 7(1): 70–86.

Chief of the General Staff 1989. *Design for Military Operations – The British Military Doctrine*, Army Code No. 71451.

Chryssochoou, Dimitris 1998. *Democracy in the European Union*. London: Tauris.

Clark, Wesley 2001. *Waging Modern War*. New York: Public Affairs.

Clarke, Michael and Cornish, Paul 2002. 'The European Defence Project and the Prague Summit', *International Affairs* 87(4) October: 777–88.

Clausewitz, Carl von 1989. *On War*, ed. and trans. M. Howard and P. Paret. Princeton University Press.

Clement, Rolf and Jöris, Paul 2005. *50 Jahre Bundeswehr: 1955–2005*. Hamburg: Mittler und Sohn.

Cockerham, William 1978. 'Attitudes Towards Combat among US Army Paratroopers', *Journal of Political and Military Sociology* 6 (Spring): 1–15.

Coker, Christopher 2007. *Warrior Ethos: Military Culture and the War on Terror*. London: Routledge.

2002a. *Globalisation and Insecurity*. Oxford University Press.

2002b. *Waging War without Warriors*. London: Lynne Rienner.

2001. *Humane Warfare*. London: Routledge.

Collège interarmées de défense 2005. *Méthode de planification opérationnelle*, October.

Collins, Randall 2008. *Violence: A Microsociological Theory*. Princeton University Press.

2004. *Interaction Ritual Chains*. Princeton University Press.

Connaughton, Richard 2001a. *Military Intervention and Peace-Keeping: The Reality*. Aldershot: Ashgate.

2001b. Operation 'Barass', *Small Wars and Insurgencies* 12(2): 110–19.

2000. 'Organising British Joint Rapid Reaction Forces', *Joint Forces Quarterly* Autumn: 87–92.

Connor, Ken 1998. *Ghost Force: The Secret History of the SAS*. London: Cassell.

Cooper, Robert 2004. *The Breaking of Nations*. London: Atlantic.

Coram, Robert 2002. *Boyd: The Fighter Pilot Who Changed the Art of War*. New York: Bay Back Books/Little Brown.

Cordesman, Andrew 1987. *NATO's Central Region Forces*. London: Jane's.

Cornish, Paul and Dorman, Andrew 2009. 'Blair's Wars, Brown's Budgets', *International Affairs* 85(2): 247–61.

Cornish, Paul and Edwards, Geoffrey 2001. 'Beyond the EU/NATO Dichotomy: The Beginnings of a European Strategic Culture', *International Affairs* 77(3) (July): 587–603

Croft, Stuart 2006a. *Culture, Crisis and America's War on Terror*. Cambridge University Press

2006b. 'Images and Imaginings of Security', *International Relations* 20(4): 387–91.

Croft, Stuart, Dorman, Andrew, Rees, Wyn and Uttley, Matthew (eds.) 2001. *Britain and Defence 1945–2001*. Harlow: Longman.

Curtis, Mike 1998. *CQB: Close Quarter Battle*. London: Transworld Publishers.

Daalder Ivo and O'Hanlon, Michael 2000. *Winning Ugly*. Washington, DC: Brookings Institute Press.

Dandeker, Christopher 2003. 'Building Flexible Forces for the 21st Century: Key Challenges for the Contemporary Armed Forces', in G. Caforio (ed.), *Handbook of the Sociology of the Military*. London: Kluwer/Plenum, 405–16.

1998. 'A Farewell to Arms? The Military and the Nation-State in a Changing World', in J. Burk (ed.), *The Adaptive Military*. London: Transaction, 139–61.

1994. 'New Times for the Military', *British Journal of Sociology* 45(4): 637–54.

De la Billière, P. 1995. *Looking for Trouble*. London: HarperCollins.

Delbrück, Hans 1975. *History of the Art of War within a Political Framework: Vol. 1: Antiquity*. Westport, CT: Greenwood.

Demchak, Christine 2003. 'Creating the Enemy: Global Diffusion of the Information Technology-Based Military Model', in E. Goldman and L. Eliason (eds.), *The Diffusion of Military Technology and Ideas*. Stanford University Press, 307–47.

Dempsey, Judy 2007. 'NATO Retreats from Establishment of Rapid-reaction Force', *New York Times*, 20 September, available at: www.iht.com/articles/2007/09/20/europe/force.php.

Der Derian, James. 2001. *Virtuous War*. Oxford: Westview.

Development, Concepts and Doctrine Centre 2007. *Higher Level Operational Conceptual Framework*. Shrivenham: DCDC.

Dicken, Peter 1998. *Global Shift*. London: Chapman.

DiMaggio, Paul and Powell, William 1983. 'The Iron Cage Revisited: Institutional Isomorphism and Collective Rationality in Organisational Fields', *American Sociological Review* 48 April: 147–60.

Directorate of Defence Policy 1998a. *The Strategic Defence Review*, Cm 3999. London: HMSO.

Dorman, Andrew, Smith, Malcolm and Uttley, Matthew (eds.) 2002. *The Changing Face of Military Power*. London: Palgrave.

Du Picq, Ardant 2006. *Battle Studies*. Charleston, SC: Bibliobazaar.

Duffield, John 1995. *Power Rules: The Evolution of NATO's Conventional Force Posture*. Stanford University Press.

Duffield, Mark 2001. *Global Governance and the New Wars: The Merging of Development and Security*. London: Zed Books.

Dupuy, Trevor 1977. *A Genius For War*. London: Macdonald.

Durkheim, Emile 1976. *The Elementary Forms of the Religious Life*, trans. J. Ward Swain, London: George Allen & Unwin.

  1957. *Professional Ethics and Civic Morals*. London: Routledge & Kegan Paul.

  1952. *Suicide*, trans. J. Spalding and G. Simpson. London: Routledge & Kegan Paul.

Dyer, Jeffrey 2000. *Collaborative Advantage: Winning Through Extended Enterprise Supplier Networks*. Oxford University Press.

Echevarria II, Antulio 2007. *Clausewitz and Contemporary War*. Oxford University Press.

  2004. 'Centre of Gravity: Recommendations for Joint Doctrine', *Joint Forces Quarterly* 35: 10–17.

Edwards, Geoffrey 2000. 'Europe's Security and Defence Policy and Enlargement: The Ghost at the Feast?', Florence: EUI, RSC working paper 2000/69.

English, John 1996a. 'The Operational Art: Developments in the Theory of War', in B. McKercher and M. Hennessy (eds.), *The Operational Art*. Westport, CT: Praeger, 7–27.

  1996b. *Marching Together through Chaos*. Westport, CT: Praeger.

European Security Strategy 2003. 'A Secure Europe in a Better World', 12 December, Brussels.

Faringdon, Hugh 1986. *Confrontation. The Strategic Geography of NATO and the Warsaw Pact*. London: Routledge & Kegan Paul.

Farndale, General Sir Martin 1985. 'Counter Stroke: Future Requirements', *RUSI Journal of the Royal United Services Institute for Defence Studies* 130(4) December: 6–10.

Farrell, Theo 2008. 'The Dynamics of British Military Transformation', *International Affairs* 84(4): 777–807.

Farrell, Theo and Terriff, Terry (eds.) 2002. *The Sources of Military Change*. London: Lynne Rienner.

Favell, Adrian 2008. *Eurostars and Eurocities*. Oxford: Blackwell.

Fergusson, James 2008. *One Million Bullets*. London: Bantam.
Field Manual (FM) 100-5 1986. *Operations*. Washington, DC: Headquarters of the Army.
1982. *Operations*. Washington, DC: Headquarters of the Army.
1976. *Operations*. Washington, DC: Headquarters of the Army.
Fitschen, P. 2006. 'Network Operations Command as a Model of Transformation', in J. Krause and J. Irlen Kaeuser (eds.), *Bundeswehr – die nächste 50 Jahren*. Leverkusen: Barbara Budrich.
Fitz-Gibbon, Spencer 1995. *Not Mentioned in Dispatches*. Cambridge: Lutterworth.
Flanagan, Stephen 1988. *NATO's Conventional Defence*. London: Macmillan.
Forray, Gilbert 1988. 'French Ground Forces in Europe', *NATO's Sixteen Nations* October: 26–8.
Forster, Anthony 2006. *Armed Forces and Society in Europe*. London: Palgrave.
Forster, Anthony, Edmunds, Tim and Cottey, Andrew 1999. *The Challenge of Military Reform in Post-Communist Europe*. Basingstoke: Macmillan.
Freedman, Lawrence 1998. 'The Revolution in Strategic Affairs', *Adelphi Paper No. 318*. Oxford: Brasseys.
Gagnon, Victor 2006. *The Myth of Ethnic War: Serbia and Croatia in the 1990s*. Ithaca, NY: Cornell University Press.
Geraghty, Tony 1980. *Who Dares Wins*. London: Arms and Armour Press.
Gerlach, Michael 1992. *Alliance Capitalism*. Berkeley, CA: University of California Press.
Glantz, David 1996. 'The Intellectual Dimensions of Soviet (Russian) Operational Art', in B. McKercher and M. Hennessy (eds.), *The Operational Art*. Westport, CT: Praeger, 125–46.
Glasius, Michel and Kaldor, Mary 2006. *A Human Security Doctrine for Europe*. London: Routledge.
Glenn, Russell 2000. *Reading Athena's Dance Card: Men Against Fire in Vietnam*. Indianapolis, MD: Naval Institute Press.
Glenny, Misha 1992. *The Fall of Yugoslavia*. Harmondsworth: Penguin.
Gnesotto, Nicole (ed.) 2004. *EU Security and Defence Policy: The First Five Years (1999–2004)*. Paris: Institute for Security Studies.
Goffman, Erving 1961. *Encounters*. New York: Bobbs Merrill.
Goldman, E. and Eliason, L. (eds.) 2003. *The Diffusion of Military Technology and Ideas*. Stanford University Press.
Gomes-Casseres, B. 1996. *The Alliance Revolution*. Cambridge, MA: Harvard University Press.
Gompert, David, Kugler, Richard and Libicki, Martin 1999. *Mind the Gap: Promoting a Transatlantic Revolution in Military Affairs*. Washington, DC: National Defence University Press.
Goodson, Larry 2001. *Afghanistan's Endless War*. Seattle, WA: University of Washington Press.
Gowan, Richard 2009. 'Europe Retreats' *European Voice*, available at: www.euro peanvoice.com/article/2009/02/europe-retreats/63883.aspx.
Grant, Robert 1996. 'France's New Relationship with NATO', *Survival* 38(1): 58–80.
Grau, Lester 1998. *The Bear Went over the Mountain*. London: Routledge.

Gray, Colin 2006. *Another Bloody Century*. London: Phoenix.

2002. *Strategy for Chaos: Revolution in Military Affairs and the Evidence of History*. London: Frank Cass.

1997. *The American Revolution in Military Affairs: An Interim Assessment*. Shrivenham: Strategic and Combat Studies Institute.

Grossman, Dave 1995. *On Killing: The Psychological Cost of Learning to Kill and War and Society*. Boston, MA: Little, Brown.

Günzel, Reinhard 2006. *Und Plötzlich ist alles politisch*. Heidenheim: DTP & Druck Mattias Kopp.

Günzel, Reinhard, Walther, Wilhelm and Wegener, Ulrich 2006. *Geheime Krieger: Drei deutsche Kommandoverbände im Bild: KSK, Brandenburger, GSG 9*. Paris: Pour la Mérite.

Hall, Stuart and Jacques, Martin (eds.) 1990. *New Times*. London: Lawrence and Wishart.

Haltiner, Karl 1998. 'The Definite End of the Mass Army in Western Europe?', *Armed Forces and Society* 25(1): 7–36.

Harclerode, Peter 2000. *Secret Soldiers*. London: Cassell.

1993. *PARA!* London: Cassell.

Harding, Robert 2006. 'Afghan Insurgents on Brink of Defeat', *Daily Telegraph*, 1 June, available at: www.telegraph.co.uk/news/newstopics/onthefrontline/2062440/Afghanistan's-Taliban-insurgents-'on-brink-of-defeat'.html.

Harrison, B. 1994. *Lean and Mean: The Changing Landscape of Corporate Power in the Age of Flexibility*. New York: Basic Books.

Hayward, Jack and Page, E. (eds.) 1995. *Governing the New Europe*. Cambridge: Polity.

Held, David and McGrew, Anthony 2000. *The Global Transformation Reader*. Cambridge: Polity.

Henderson, Darryl 1985. *Cohesion: The Human Element*. Washington, DC: National Defence University Press.

Henriksen, Rune 2007. 'Warriors in Combat – What Makes People Actively Fight in Combat', *Journal of Strategic Studies* 30(2): 187–223.

Hirst, Paul 2001. *War and Power*. Cambridge: Polity.

H M Treasury, 2007. *Meeting the Aspirations of the British People: 2007 Pre-Budget Report and Comprehensive Spending Review*. London: The Stationery Office, October, available at: www.hm-treasury.gov.uk/d/pbr_csr07_completereport_1546.pdf.

Hobsbawm, Eric and Ranger, Terence (eds.) 1986. *The Invention of Tradition*. Cambridge University Press.

Hockey, John 1986. *Squaddies: Portrait of a Subculture*. Exeter: University of Exeter.

Hoffman, Oskar 2005. 'Das Mensch in der Transformation der Bundeswehr', in S. Collmer and G. Kümmel (eds.), *Ein Job wie Jeder Andere?* Baden-Baden: Nomos, 47–58.

Hopkirk, Peter 2006. *The Great Game*. London: John Murray.

Horsfall, Robin 2002. *Fighting Scared*. London: Cassell.

House, John 2001. *Combined Arms Warfare in the Twentieth Century*. Lawrence, KS: University of Kansas.

Howard, Michael 2000. *The Franco-Prussian War*. London: Routledge.

Howorth, Jolyon 2007. *Security and Defence Policy in the European Union.* Basingstoke: Palgrave Macmillan.

2001. 'European Defence and the Changing Politics of the EU', *Journal of Common Market Studies* 39(4): 65–89.

2000. 'Britain, France and the European Defence Initiative', *Survival* 42(2): 33–55.

1995. 'Towards a European Foreign and Security Policy', in J. Hayward and E. Page (eds.), *Governing the New Europe.* Cambridge: Polity.

Howorth, Jolyon and Menon, Antoine 1997. *The European Union and National Defence Policy.* London: Routledge.

Huntington, Samuel 1957. *The Soldier and State.* Cambridge, MA: Belknap Press.

Hutton, Will 1996. *The State We're In.* London: Vintage.

Ignatieff, Michael 2000. *Virtual War.* London: Chatto and Windus.

International Institute for Strategic Studies (IISS) 2010. *The Military Balance.* Oxford: Brasseys.

2007. *The Military Balance.* Oxford: Brasseys.

Jackson, Michael 2008. *Soldier.* London: Corgi.

Jacoby, Wade and Jones, Christopher 2008. 'The EU Battle Groups in Sweden and the Czech Republic: What National Defence Reforms Tell Us about European Rapid Reaction Capabilities', *European Security* 17(2): 315–38.

Janowitz, Morris [1960] 1981. *The Professional Soldier.* London: Free Press.

Janowitz, Morris and Shils, Edward 1975. 'Cohesion and Disintegration in the Wehrmacht in World War II', in M. Janowitz (ed.), *Military Conflict.* London: Sage, 177–220.

Jennings, Christopher and Weale, Adrian 1996. *Green-Eyed Boys.* London: HarperCollins.

Johnsen, W., Blank, S. and Young, T-D. 1999. 'Building a Better European Security Environment', *European Security* 8(3): 1–25.

Joint Warfare Publication (JWP) 01 2008. *British Defence Doctrine.* Shrivenham: Joint Doctrine and Concepts Centre.

Note 7/06 2006. *Incorporating and Extending the UK Military Effects-Based Approach.* September, Shrivenham: Joint Doctrine and Concepts Centre.

01 2004a. *Joint Operations.* Shrivenham: Joint Doctrine and Concepts Centre.

5.00 2004b. *Joint Operations Planning.* Shrivenham: Joint Doctrine and Concepts Centre.

0-01 2001. *British Defence Doctrine.* Shrivenham: Joint Doctrine and Concepts Centre.

Jones, Seth 2007. *The Rise of European Security Cooperation.* Cambridge University Press.

Jordan, Kelly 2002. 'Right for the Wrong Reasons: SLA Marshall and the Ratio of Fire in Korea', *Journal of Military History* 66: 135–62.

Jürgens, Ulrich 1989. 'The Transfer of Japanese Management Concepts in the International Automobile Industry', in S. Wood (ed.), *The Transformation of Work?* London: Unwin Hyman, 204–18.

Jürgens, Ulrich, Dohse, Knuth and Malsch, Thomas 1986. 'New Production Concepts in West German Plants', in S. Tolliday and J. Zeitlin (eds.), *The Automobile Industry and its Workers.* Cambridge: Polity, 258–81.

Kaldor, Mary 1999. *New and Old Wars: Organized Violence in the Global Era*. Cambridge: Polity.

1982. *The Baroque Arsenal*. London: Deutsch.

Kaldor, Mary, Albrecht, V. and Schméder, G. 1998. *The End of Military Fordism*. London: Pinter.

Kalyvas, Stathis 2006. *The Logic of Violence in Civil War*. Cambridge University Press.

2001. '"New" and "Old" Civil Wars: Is the Distinction Valid?', *World Politics* 54(1): 99–118.

Kaplan, Lawrence 2004. *NATO Divided, NATO United: The Evolution of an Alliance* Westport, CT: Praeger

Keen, David 2008. *Complex Emergencies*. Cambridge: Polity.

Kelleher, Christine 1978. 'Mass Armies in the 1970s: The Debate in Western Europe', *Armed Forces and Society* 5(1): 3–30.

King, Anthony 2006. 'The Word of Command: Communication and Cohesion in the Military', *Armed Forces and Society* 32(4): 493–512.

Kinzer Stewart, N. 1991. *Mates and Muchacos: Unit Cohesion in the Falklands/ Malvinas War*. New York, Brasseys.

Klein, Paul, Vom Hagen, Ulrich, Moelker, Rene and Soeters, Joseph (eds.) 2003. *True Love: A Study in Integrated Multinationality within 1 (GE/NL) Corps*. Brede and Strausberg: Sozialwissenschaftliches Institut der Bundeswehr.

Kupchan, Charles 2000. 'In Defence of European Defence: An American Perspective', *Survival* 42(2): 16–32.

Lamb, Christina 2009. 'War on Taliban Cannot be Won, says Army Chief', *The Sunday Times*, 5 October, available at: http://www.timesonline.co.uk/tol/news/uk/article4882597.ece.

Lane, Christel 1988. 'Industrial Change in Europe: The Pursuit of Flexible Specialization in Britain and West Germany', *Work, Employment and Society* 2(2): 141–68.

Latham, Andrew 2002. 'Warfare Transformed: a Braudelian Perspective on the "Revolution in Military Affairs"', *European Journal of International Relations* 8(2): 231–66.

Latour, Bruno 2005. *Reassembling the Social*. Oxford University Press.

Latour, Bruno and Woolgar, Steven 1987. *Laboratory Life*. Princeton University Press.

Leersch, Hans-Jürgen 2003. 'Bundeswehr-Verband begrüßt radikalen Umbau; Pläne des Generalinspekteurs umstritten', *Die Welt*, 19 December, available at: http://web.lexis-nexis.com/executive/form?_index=exec_en.html&_lang=en&ut=3283169693.

Lefebvre, Stephane, Fortmann, Michel and Gongora, Thierry 1996. 'The Revolution in Military Affairs: Its Implication for Doctrine and Force Development within the US Army', in B. McKercher and M. Hennessy (eds.), *The Operational Art*. Westport, CT: Praeger, 193.

Leinbaugh, Harold and Campbell, John. 1985. *The Men of Company K*. New York: William Morrow.

Leonard, Mark 2005. *Why Europe Will Run the 21st Century*. New York: Public Affairs.

Leonard, Robert 1991. *The Art of Maneuver*. New York: Ballantine Books.

Lewis, Damien 2006. *Bloody Heroes*. London: Chatto and Windus.

2005. *Operation Certain Death*. London: Arrow.

Liddell Hart, Basil 1987. *The Rommel Papers*. London: Arrow.

Lijphart, A. 1984. *Democracies: Patterns of Majoritarian and Consensus Government in Twenty-One Countries*. London: Yale University Press.

1979. 'Consociation and Federation: Conceptual and Empirical Links', *Canadian Journal of Political Science* 12(3): 499–515.

Lindley-French, Julian 2002. 'In the Shades of Locarno? Why European Defence is Failing', *International Affairs* 78(4): 789–811.

Livre Blanc 2008. *Défense et Sécurité Nationale: le livre blanc*. Paris: Odile Jacob, La Documentation Française.

Lock-Pullan, Richard 2006. *US Intervention Policy from Vietnam to Iraq*. London: Routledge.

2003. 'An Inward-Looking Time', *Journal of Military History* 67(2): 483–512.

Loisel, Sebastien 2004. 'Les leçons d'Artémis: vers une approche européenne de la gestion militaire des crises?', *Le Champs de Mars* 16(2): 69–92.

Longhurst, Kerry 2000. 'The Reform of the German Armed Forces: Coming of Age?', *European Security* 9(4): 31–44.

Löser, Walter-Diether 2006. 'Ethische Grundsätze der Bundeswehr – besondere Bedeutung vor dem Hintergrund des neuen Aufgabenspektrum', *Europäische Sicherheit* 6: 8–12.

Luttwak, Edward 1995. 'Toward Post-Heroic Warfare', *Foreign Affairs* 74(3): 109–22.

1981. 'The Operational Level in War', *International Security* 5(3): 61–79.

MacCoun, Robert, Kier, Elizabeth and Belkin, Aaron 2006. 'Does Social Cohesion Determine Motivation in Combat? An Old Question with an Old Answer', *Armed Forces and Society* 32(4) July: 646–54.

Macdonald, Keith 2004. 'Black Mafia, Loggies and Going for the Stars: The Military Elite Revisited', *Sociological Review* 52(1): 106–35.

Macgregor, Dan 1997. *Breaking the Phalanx*. London: Praeger.

Machiavelli, Niccolo [1520] 1965. *The Art of War*. Indianapolis, IN: Bobbs Merrill.

Manigart, Phillippe 2003. 'Restructuring of the Armed Forces', in G. Caforio (ed.), *Handbook of the Sociology of the Military*. London: Kluwer/Plenum, 323–43.

Marshall, S. L. A. 2000. *Men against Fire*. New York: William Morrow.

Martin, Michel 1977. 'Conscription and the Decline of the Mass Army in France, 1960–75', *Armed Forces and Society* 3(3): 355–406.

Matthews, G. 2003. *Operation Telic: 3 Commando Brigade's Desert War*. Portsmouth: RN Graphic Centre.

Maull, Hanns 2000. 'Germany and the Use of Force: Still a "Civilian Power"?', *Survival* 42(2).

McInnes, Colin 2002. *Spectator Sport Warfare*. London: Lynne Rienner.

1998. 'Labour's Strategic Defence Review', *International Affairs* 74(4): 823–45.

McKenna, Justin 1997. 'Towards the Army of the Future: Domestic Politics and the End of Conscription in France', *West European Politics* 20(4): 125–45.

McKercher, Brian and Hennessy, Matthew (eds.) 1996. *The Operational Art*. Westport, CT: Praeger.

Mearsheimer, John 1982. 'Why the Soviets Can't Win Quickly in Central Europe', *International Security* 7(1) Summer: 3–39.

1981. 'Maneuver, Mobile Defence and the NATO Central Front', *International Security* 6(3): 104–22.

Meiers, Franz-Josef 2005. 'Germany's Defence Choices', *Survival* 47(1): 153–66.

2001. 'The Reform of the Bundeswehr: Adaptation or Fundamental Renewal', *European Security* 10(2): 1–22.

Menon, Anand 2009. 'Empowering Paradise. The ESDP at Ten', *International Affairs* 85(2): 226–46.

2000. *France, NATO and the Limits of Independence*. London: Palgrave.

Metz, Stephen 1997. 'Racing Toward the Future: The Revolution in Military Affairs', *Current History* 96(609) April: 184–8.

Micheletti, Eric 1999. *French Special Forces*. Paris: Histoire and Collections.

Michta, Andrew 2006. *The Limits of Alliance: The United States, NATO, and the EU in North and Central Europe*. Lanham, MD: Rowman & Littlefield.

Milward, Andrew 1992. *The European Rescue of the Nation State*. London: Routledge.

Missiroli, A. 2003. 'ESDP – Post-Iraq. Building a European Security and Defence Policy: What are the Priorities?', The Cicero Foundation, available at: www.cicerofoundation.org/lectures/missiroli_jun03.html.

Moelker, Rene and Soeters, Joseph 2004. 'Das Deutsch-Niederlaendische Korps', in S. Gareis and P. Klein (eds.), *Handbuch Militär und Sozialwissenschaft*. Wiesbaden: VS Verlag, 366–78.

2003. 'Putting Collaboration to the Test, Munster and Kabul', in U. Vom Hagen, P. Klein, R. Moelker and J. Soeters (eds.), *True Love: A Study in Integrated Multinationality within 1 (GE/NL) Corps*. Brede and Strausberg: Sozialwissenschaftliches Institut der Bundeswehr, 126–46.

Moravcsik, Andrew 1998. *The Choice for Europe*. London: University College London Press.

Moravcsik, A. 2001. 'Federalism in the European Union: Rhetoric and Reality', in K. Nicolaidis and R. Howse (eds.), *The Federal Vision*. Oxford University Press.

Moskos, Charles 1989. *Soldiers and Sociology*. London: Macmillan.

1975. 'The American Combat Soldier in Vietnam', *Journal of Social Issues* 31(4): 25–37.

Moskos, Charles, Allen Williams, Jay and Segal, David 2000. *The Postmodern Military*. Oxford University Press.

Moustakis, Fotios and Violakis, Petros 2008. 'European Security and Defence Policy Deceleration: An Assessment of the ESDP Strategy', *European Security* 17(4): 421–33.

Münkler, Herfried 2005. *The New Wars*. Cambridge: Polity.

Murray, Robin 1990. 'Fordism and Post-Fordism', in S. Hall and M. Jacques (eds.), *New Times*. London: Lawrence and Wishart, 38–53.

NATO 2009. Summit Guide 2009, available at: www.nato.int/summit2009/summit-guide-, NATO.

2007. Military Structure: Briefing, April, available at: www.nato.int/docu/briefing/nms/nms-e.pdf.

1999. 'The Alliance's Strategic Concept', available at: http://www.nato.int/cps/en/natolive/official_texts_27433.htm.

1991. 'The Alliance's New Strategic Concept', available at: www.nato.int/cps/en/natolive/official_texts_23847.htm.

Naumann, Klaus 2000. 'Europa in NATO', in A. Volle and W. Weidenfeld (eds.), *Europäische Sicherheitspolitik in der Bewährung*. Bielefeld: Bertelsmann, 43–8.

Naveh, Shimon 1997. *In Pursuit of Military Excellence: The Evolution of Operational Theory*. London: Frank Cass

North, Richard 2009. *Ministry of Defeat*. London: Continuum.

O'Hanlon, Michael 1997. 'Transforming NATO: The Role of European Forces', *Survival* 39(3): 5–15.

O'Hara, Connor 2007. 'The Ivory Coast – An Exchange Officer On Tour', *Globe and Laurel* March–April: 118–20.

Overy, Richard 2006. *Why the Allies Won*. London: Pimlico.

Owens, William 2002. 'Creating a US Military Revolution', in T. Farrell and T. Terriff (eds.), *The Sources of Military Change*. London: Lynne Rienner, 205–20.

Palin, Roger 1995. 'Multinational Military Forces: Problems and Prospects', *Adelphi Paper No. 294*. New York: Oxford University Press.

Palmer, Diego Ruiz 1997. 'France's Military Command Structures in the 1990s', in T. D. Young (ed.), *Command in NATO after the Cold War*. United States Army War College, Carlisle Barracks, PA: Strategic Studies Institute, 93–134.

1987. 'Between the Rhine and the Elbe: France and the Conventional Defence of Central Europe', *Comparative Strategy* 6(4): 471–512.

Pape, Robert 1996. *Bombing to Win: Air Power and Coercion in War*. London: Cornell University Press.

Pflüger, Tobias 1998. *Die Neue Bundeswehr*. Koln: ISP.

Pinder, John 1995. *European Community: The Building of a Union*. Oxford University Press.

Piore, Michael and Sabel, Charles 1984. *The Second Industrial Divide*. New York: Basic Books.

Posen, Barry 1984. *The Sources of Military Doctrine*. Ithaca, NY: Cornell University Press.

Preece, Steven 2004. *Among the Marines*. Edinburgh: Mainstream.

Ratcliffe, Peter 2001. *Eye of the Storm*. London, Michael O'Mara.

Rayment, Sean 2008. *Into the Killing Zone*. London: Constable.

2004. 'Britain Forms New Special Forces Unit to Fight al-Qa'eda', *Daily Telegraph*, 25 July, retrieved from: http://dailytelegraph.com.

Richards, Lieutenant General David 2006. 'Commander's Intent', available at: www.afnorth.nato.int/ISAF/mission/mission_operations.htm.

Risse-Kappen, Thomas 1997. *Co-operation among Democracies: The European Influence on US Foreign Policy*. Princeton University Press.

Robertson, Roland 1992. *Globalization: Social Theory and Global Culture*. London: Sage.

Robinson, C. 2002. 'France: Preparing for New Types of Warfare in the New Century', available at: www.cdi.org/terrorism/french-reform.cfm.

Rogers, General Bernard 1984. 'Follow-On Forces Attack: Myth and Realities', *NATO Review* 6 December: 1–9.

Rose, General Sir Michael 1999. *Fighting for Peace*. London: Time Warner.

Rosen, Leora and Martin, L. 1997. 'Sexual Harassment, Cohesion and Combat Readiness in the US Army Support Units', *Armed Forces and Society* 24(2): 221–44.

Rosen, Leora, Knudson, Kathryn and Fancher, Peggy 2002. 'Cohesion and the Culture of Hypermasculinity in the US Army Units', *Armed Forces and Society* 29(3): 325–52.

Rosen, Leora, Durand, D., Bliese, P., Halverson R., Rothbert, J. and Harrison, N. 1996. 'Cohesion and Readiness in Gender-Integrated Combat Service Support Units: The Impact of Acceptance of Women and Gender Ratio', *Armed Forces and Society* 22(4): 537–54.

Rosen, Stephen 1991. *Winning the Next War: Innovation and the Modern Military*. London: Cornell University Press.

Rossiter, Mike 2008. *Target Basra*. London: Bantam.

Roy, Oliver 1986. *Islam and Resistance in Afghanistan*. Cambridge University Press.

Russell, James 2009. 'Innovation in the Crucible of War', unpublished PhD thesis, King's College London.

Ryan, Mike 2007. *Battlefield Afghanistan*. Stroud: Spellmount.

Sajer, Guy 1999. *The Forgotten Soldier*. London: Cassell.

Sarotte, Mary 2001. 'German Military Reform and European Security', *Adelphi Paper No. 340*. Oxford University Press.

Sassen, Saskia 1991. *The Global City*. Princeton University Press.

Sattler, Daniel 2006. 'Die Kosten der Bundeswehr und deren Finanzierung durch den Bundeshaushalt', in J. Krause and J. Irlen Kaeuser (eds.), *Bundeswehr – die nächste 50 Jahren*. Leverkusen: Barbara Budrich, 277–90.

Scales, Robert and Murray, Williamson 2003. *The Iraq War*. Cambridge, MA: Harvard University Press.

Scharping, Rudolph. 2000. *Der Bundesminister Der Vertidigung, Die Bundeswehr sicher in 21.Jahrhundert: Eckpfeiler fur eine Erneuerung von Grund auf*, retrieved 4 December 2004 from: www.friederle.de/krieg/scharpingeckpfeiler.pdf.

Schmitt, Burkard 2004. 'European Capabilities: How Many Divisions?', in N. Gnesotto (ed.), *EU Security and Defence Policy: The First Five Years (1999–2004)*. Paris: Institute for Security Studies, 98–110.

Scholzen, Reinhard 2009a. *KSK: Das Kommando Spezialkräfte der Bundeswehr*. Stuttgart: Motorbuch Verlag.

2009b. *Division Spezielle Operationen: Einsatzbereit, jederzeit, weltweit*. Stuttgart: Motorbuch Verlag.

Schreer, Benjamin 2006. 'Die Transformation des Heeres', in J. Krause and J. Irlen Kaeuser (eds.), *Bundeswehr – die nächste 50 Jahren*. Leverkusen: Barbara Budrich, 181–92.

Schulze, Carl von and Verhülsdonk, Torsten 1998. *Deutsche Fallschirmjäger heute: Von der 1. Luftlandedivision zum Kommando luftbewegliche Kräfte*. Herne: VS-Books.

Scott, Jake 2008. *Blood Clot*. Solihull: Helion.

Sebald, Winfried Georg 2004. *The Natural History of Destruction*. London: Penguin.

Shaw, Martin 2005. *The New Western Way of War*. Cambridge: Polity.

1991. *Post-military Society*. Philadelphia, PA: Temple University Press.

1988. *Dialectics of War*. London: Pluto.

Sheehan, James 2008. *Monopoly of Violence*. London: Faber & Faber.

Shepherd, Alistair 2003. 'The European Union's Security and Defence Policy: A Policy without Substance?'. *European Security* 12(1): 39–63.

2000. 'Top-Down or Bottom-Up: Is Security and Defence Policy in the EU a Question of Political Will or Military Capability', *European Security* 9(2): 13–30.

Siebold, Guy 2007. 'The Essence of Military Cohesion', *Armed Forces and Society* 33(2): 291.

Siedentop, Larry 2001. *Democracy in Europe*. Harmondsworth: Penguin.

Singer, Peter 2003. *Corporate Warriors: The Rise of the Privatized Military Industry*. Ithaca, NY: Cornell University Press.

Sinjen, Svenja and Varwick, Johannes 2006. 'Die Bundeswehr und die Afgaben der Nordatlantischen Allianz', in J. Krause and J. Irlen Kaeuser (eds.), *Bundeswehr – die nächste 50 Jahren*. Leverkusen: Barbara Budrich, 95–108.

Sloan, Stanley 2003. *NATO, the European Union and the Atlantic Community*. Lanham, MD: Rowman & Littlefield.

Smith, Martin 2004. *Europe's Foreign and Security Policy: The Institutionalisation of Co-operation*. Cambridge University Press.

Smith, Vicki 1997. 'New Forms of Work Organisation', *Annual Review of Sociology* 23: 315–39.

Smoler, Frederic 1989. 'The Secret of the Soldiers who Wouldn't Shoot', *American Heritage* 40 (March): 36–45.

Southby-Tailyour, Ewen 2008. *Helmand, Afghanistan: 3 Commando Brigade*. London: Ebury Press.

Speller, Ian 2006. 'The Seaborne/airborne Concept. Littoral Manoeuvre in the 1960s?', *The Journal of Strategic Studies* 29(1): 53–82.

Spence, Cameron 1998. *Sabre Squadron*. London: Penguin.

Sperling, J. (ed.) 1999. *Two Tiers or Two Speeds? The European Security Order and the Enlargement of the European Union and NATO*. Manchester University Press.

Spiller, Roger 1988. 'SLA Marshall and the Ratio of Fire', *Journal of the Royal United Services Institute* 133 (December): 63–71.

Stier, Norbert 2006. 'Die Gebirgsjager 23 als spezialister Grossverband des Heeres', *Europäische Sicherheit* 2: 52–5.

Stouffer, Samuel, Lumsdaine, Arthur A., Lumsdaine, Marion H., Williams, Robin M., Brewster-Smith, M., Janis, Irving L., Star, Shirley A. and Cotrell, Leonard S. 1949. *The American Soldier: Combat and Its Aftermath*. Princeton University Press.

Strachan, Hew 1999. *The British Army, Manpower and Society in the Twenty First Century*. London: Frank Cass.

Strange, Joe 1999. *Centers of Gravity and Critical Vulnerabilities*. Quantico, VA: United States Marine Corps Association.

Strange, Joe and Iron, Richard 2005. 'Center of Gravity: What Clausewitz Really Meant', *Joint Forces Quarterly* 35: 20–7.

Sünkler, Sören 2007. *Die Spezialverbände der Bundeswehr*. Stuttgart: Motorbuch, 2007.

Supreme Headquarters Allied Power Europe (SHAPE) 2005. *Guidelines for Operational Planning (GOP)*. Belgium: SHAPE.

Swain, R. 1996. 'Filling the Void: The Operational Art and the US Army', in B. McKercher and M. Hennessy (eds.), *The Operational Art*. Westport, CT: Praeger, 147–73.

Tarin, Florence 2005. 'Le Corps de Réaction Rapide – France', *Terre* 166 July–August: 24–40.

Terriff, Terry 2007. 'Of Romans and Dragons', *Contemporary Security Policy* 29(1): 143–62.

    2004a. 'The European Union Rapid Reaction Force: An Embryonic Cosmopolitan Military?', in L. Elliott and G. Cheeseman (eds.), *Forces for Good? Cosmopolitan Militaries in the 21st Century*. Manchester University Press, 150–67.

    2004b. 'Fear and Loathing in NATO: The Atlantic Alliance after the Crisis over Iraq', *Perspectives on European Politics and Society* 5(3): 419–46.

Teunissen, Paul 1999. 'Strengthening the Defence Dimension of the EU: An Evaluation of Concepts, Recent Initiatives and Development', *European Foreign Affairs Review* 4(3): 327–52.

Thies, Wallace 2007. 'Was the US Invasion of Iraq NATO's Worst Crisis Ever? How Would We Know? Why Should We Care', *European Security* 16(1): 29–50.

    2003. *Friendly Rivals: Bargaining and Burden-shifting in NATO*. London: M. E. Sharpe.

Thomas, James 2000. 'The Military Challenges of Transatlantic Coalitions', *Adelphi Paper No. 333*. Oxford University Press.

Toffler, Alvin and Toffler, Heidi 1995. *War and Anti-War*. London: Warner.

Tomforde, Maren 2005. '"Einmal muss man schon dabei gewesen sein …" Auslandseinzätze als Initiation in die "neue" Bundeswehr', in U. vom Hagen (ed.), *Armee in Demokratie*. Wiesbaden: Verlag für Sozialwissenschaft, 101–24

Tonra, Ben 2001. 'Constructing the CFSP: The Utility of a Cognitive Approach', *Journal of Common Market Studies* 41(4): 731–56.

Urban, Mark 2001. *Big Boys' Rules*. London: Faber & Faber.

Vallas, Steven 1999. 'Re-Thinking Post-Fordism: The Meaning of Workplace Flexibility', *Sociological Theory* 17(1): 68–101.

Van Creveld, Martin 2007. *Fighting Power*. Santa Barbara, CA: Greenwood Press.

    2006. *The Changing Face of War*. New York: Ballantine.

    1999. *The Rise and Decline of the State*. Cambridge University Press.

    1991. *The Transformation of War*. London: Free Press.

    1985. *Command in War*. Cambridge, MA: Harvard University Press.

Van Doorn, Jacques (ed.) 1968. 'Armed Forces and Society: Patterns and Trends', in *Armed Forces and Society*. The Hague: Mouton.

van Ham, Peter 1999. 'Europe's Precarious Centre: Franco-German Co-operation and the CFSP', *European Security* 8(4): 1–26.

Vaughan, David and Schum, William 2001. 'Motivation and US Narrative Accounts of the Ground War in Vietnam', *Armed Forces & Society* 28(1): 7–31.

Virilio, Paul and Lotzinger, Sylvie 1997. *Pure War*. Paris: Semiotexte.

Vom Hagen, Ulrich 2006. 'Communitae Valemus: The Relevance of Professional Trust, Collective Drills and Skills and Task Cohesion within Integrated Multinationality', unpublished paper.

Waddy, John 2003. 'The Air Assault Brigade – Why Did it Take so Long?', *British Army Review* 131 Spring: 10–17.

Webber, Mark, Terriff, Terry, Howorth Jolyon and Croft, Stuart 2002. 'The Common European Security and Defence Policy and the "Third Country Issue"', *European Security* 11(2): 75–100.

Webster, David Kenyon 2009. *Parachute Infantry*. New York, Dell.

Whiteclay Chambers III, John 2003. 'S.L.A. Marshall's *Men Against Fire*: New Evidence Regarding Fire Ratios', *Parameters* Autumn: 113–21.

Winslow, Donna 1997. *The Canadian Airborne Regiment: A Socio-cultural Inquiry*. Ottawa: Minister of Public Works and Government Services.

Wise, M. 1998. *Capital Dilemma*. Princeton University Press.

Wittgenstein, Ludwig 1976. *Philosophical Investigations*, trans. G. Anscombe. Oxford: Blackwell.

Wolski, Reinhard 2006. 'Die Luftbewegliche Brigade 1', *Strategie und Technik* August: 14–17.

Womack, James, Jones, Daniel and Roos, Daniel 1990. *The Machine that Changed the World*. New York: Macmillan.

Wong, Leonard 2003. *Why they Fight: Combat Motivation in the Iraq War*. Darby, PA: Diane Publishing.

Wood, Stephen (ed.) 1989. 'The Transformation of Work', in *The Transformation of Work?* London: Unwin Hyman, 1–43.

Woodward, Susan 1995. *Balkan Tragedy*. Washington, DC: Brookings Institute.

Y Magazine 2005. 'Elite: Schule der Unsehbar', 32–3.

Yost, David 2000a. *NATO Transformed: the Alliance's New Roles in International Security*. Washington, DC: United States Institute of Peace Press.

2000b. 'The NATO Capabilities Gap and the European Union', *Survival* 42(2): 97–128.

Index

1 Régiment Parachutiste d'Infanterie de
Marine (1 Para-Marine Regiment),
182, 185, 191, 226
3 Commando Brigade, 155, 173, 181,
217–18, 259–60
co-ordination of fires, 248–9, 250–1
co-ordination with other services, 244–5
information operations, 261–4
resourcing, 161–2
9 brigade légère blindée de marine, 156–8,
163–6, 173–4, 182, 257
co-ordination of fires, 252–3
co-ordination with other services, 245–6
cohesion, 184, 185, 189–91, 219,
220, 226
information operations, 266–7
9 Division d'infanterie coloniale, 190
16 Air Assault Brigade, 154, 173, 181,
251–2, 275
co-ordination with air force, 242–4, 245
co-ordination of fires, 248
in combined brigades, 257–8
information operations, 265
resourcing, 160–1
see also Parachute Regiment

active defence, 106–7
actor network theory (ANT), 14–15, 144
Afghan Development Zone (ADZ), 133–4,
137
Afghanistan
British military approach in, 275–6
co-ordination of fires in, 255
combined brigades in, 256, 257–9
Eurocorps in, 82–3
European involvement in, 4–5, 25–7, 27–8
French involvement in, 3–4
NATO in, 59
Brunssum headquarters, 73–4
ISAF IX see Allied Rapid Reaction
Corps

operational complex in, 100–1
role in European military transformation,
27–8, 39, 282–7
special forces in, 175, 176, 210
state collapse in, 21
transnational co-operation in, 43–4
air forces, 138–9, 149–50, 242–4, 245
Air Mobile Brigade 1 (Germany), 167
air strikes, co-ordination of, 246–55
AirLand Battle doctrine, 107, 108
Akbar Khan, Mohammed, 283
Alexander, Michael, 31
alliances
network alliances in industry, 97
political interdependencies and, 25–7,
73, 78
see also multinationalism; transnational
military networks; transnationalism
Allied Command Europe (ACE)
(later ACO), 66, 67, 68
Allied Command Operations (ACO)
(previously ACE), 68, 73
Allied Command Transformation (ACT),
57, 68, 70, 140
Allied Rapid Reaction Corps (ARRC),
78–82, 95–6, 99, 144–5
ISAF IX, 73–4, 78–9, 100, 126–7
Commander's Intent, 127–8
effects-based approach, 143–4
shared culture, 135–7
use of graphics, 129–35
amphibious operations, 164–5, 244–5
Apache helicopters, 160, 173, 248
armed forces
common models and co-operation,
176–7, 200–1
as dimension of European integration, 16–19
link with modern state, 16
relationship with civil society, 12, 37, 140
size of, 151–60
see also concentration

304